ASPHALT

ASPHALT

A HISTORY   Kenneth O'Reilly

University of Nebraska Press

LINCOLN

Publication of this volume was assisted by a grant
from the Friends of the University of Nebraska Press.

Library of Congress Cataloging-in-Publication Data
Names: O'Reilly, Kenneth, author.
Title: Asphalt: a history / Kenneth O'Reilly.
Description: Lincoln: University of Nebraska Press,
[2021] | Includes bibliographical references and index.
Identifiers: LCCN 2020030292
ISBN 9781496222077 (hardback)
ISBN 9781496226365 (epub)
ISBN 9781496226372 (mobi)
ISBN 9781496226389 (pdf)
Subjects: LCSH: Asphalt—History. | Asphalt—
Environmental aspects—History. |
Asphalt—Social aspects—History.
Classification: LCC TA455.A7 .O74 2021
DDC 620.1/9609—dc23
LC record available at https://lccn.loc.gov/2020030292

Set in Minion Pro by Laura Buis.
Designed by L. Auten.

Cover: Highway 63 Bitumen Slick, +57°1'9.82",
-111°34'47.97", Syncrude Mildred Lake, Alberta,
Canada. This image is part of Louis Helbig's *Beautiful
Destruction* project about the Alberta Oil/Tar Sands.
The project is presented as an exhibition, a book, and
at beautifuldstruction.ca. In the *Beautiful Destruction*
book, the image "Highway 63 Bitumen Slick" is
captioned with its geographical coordinates and in
the languages of the two First Nations within whose
territories the Oil/Tar Sands exist. In Dene Sulin the
name is Tulu k̃é 63 t'á tłes tué boret'ı, and in Cree it
is 63 mēskanaw ēkwa askiy-pimiy ē-pimicowahk.

For the latest arrivals:
Brigid, Ollie, James,
Bobby, and Theo

And mark what object did present itself.

SHAKESPEARE,
As You Like It, ca. 1599

CONTENTS

PREFACE

Asphalt, especially in its blacktop-pavement form, is present nearly everywhere we are present, so baked into the tale of our species that it rules even in absence. Too often for those who live where asphalt has not yet spread, there is only mud and poverty or dust and poverty. For virtually everyone else, the only true escape from asphalt is death.

What follows is less preface than epilogue as prologue because the chase to wring profit from this black goo has helped stoke the ever-present fear that our climate can also die. The asphalt on approximately 94 percent of paved roads in the United States has a chemical cousin in the oil sands (or tar sands) of Alberta, Canada, which began to form hundreds of millions of years ago, when organic life decomposed to create light oil. The formation of the Rocky Mountains pushed this deposit east, along with water and bacteria that fed off the lighter hydrocarbon molecules. This and other biodegradation processes left behind immense amounts of natural asphalt, a heavy complex hydrocarbon also known as natural bitumen.

For thousands of years the use of natural asphalt has shaped the course of human events in a myriad of ways. Road crews, however, did not use natural asphalt to pave until the late nineteenth century and soon abandoned it for the asphalt produced as a byproduct of oil refining. Regardless, nearly all asphalt products—from Nebuchadnezzar's bricks to pavement and hundreds of others—never burn. They capture carbon. They are carbon sinks. Now oil companies are converting natural asphalt into synthetic crude oil ("syncrude") or diluting it with chemicals ("dil-bit") so it can ship south. U.S. refineries are the principal destination and gasoline the principal product. In the unlikely event the Keystone XL pipeline comes online, syncrude and dilbit will pass under ice-jam prone rivers and floodplains, uncomfortably close to the Ogallala Aquifer, part of the High Plains Water Aquifer System, which provides water for one-fifth of the United States' agricultural harvest.[1]

Alberta reserves could guarantee that humanity would not run out of stock to create synthetic crude oil and thus not run out of gasoline for many additional decades. But the king's ransom—exploding atmospheric concentrations of carbon dioxide—might be more than our species can carry. While blacktop remains a carbon sink under the wheels of our personal vehicles, after the refineries have done their work, what was once natural asphalt will power internal-combustion engines and drive climate change in concert with our automobiles. If oil-sand product accounts for a mere 3 percent of total global oil production, it is the dirtiest oil or oil equivalent, and the industry expects production to increase in the coming decades (having recovered from the 2020 oil price collapse driven by COVID-19).

At worst, the additional carbon dioxide from the oil sands, as former NASA physicist James Hansen warned, will mean "game over for the climate."[2] At best, the incremental stress of the ever-escalating conversion of natural asphalt to syncrude and dilbit will make the time for taking efficacious action on anthropogenic climate change run out faster. Asphalt hacked or melted out of the ground for service as refinery feedstock already ranks among the Western Hemisphere's biggest carbon bombs and raises an image from John Milton's *Paradise Lost*: "Marching from *Eden* towards the West, shall finde / The Plain, wherein a black bituminous gurge / Boiles out from under ground, the mouth of Hell."[3]

Duality has characterized our use of asphalt for at least seven millennia. But this latest duality of carbon sink and carbon bomb has raised the stakes. Syncrude and dilbit underpin a primal nightmare captured by biblical imagery long before Milton wrote: our world destroyed by Armageddon's fires and floods. Global-warming imagery has the earth bleeding carbon dioxide and consumed by God knows what. Wild fire and rising sea? Drought and famine? Pandemic now and pandemic from now on? Asphalt helped shape our environment in so many ways. Now it might help destroy our environment in one simple way.

ASPHALT

Introduction   Power, Culture, Space

The United States began shipping asphalt into South Vietnam early on. It arrived in country before the military advisers and combat troops, before the fighter jets and napalm. The Dwight D. Eisenhower administration (1953–61) had asphalt shipped because the road system the French Empire had built in South Vietnam had deteriorated. Good roads, the president's men reasoned, would foster prosperity. Prosperity, in turn, would make the Vietnamese people in the south less susceptible to the machinations of the Vietnamese communists in the north.

Runways and airstrips required asphalt as well. During the Great Depression, the French found funds enough to pave Vietnam's first asphalt runway at Da Nang. During World War II the Japanese used that runway. After the war the French used it in their failed attempt, backed by U.S. aid, to defeat the communist resistance and reestablish Indochina *colonie*. To prepare for the next war after the French surrendered their garrison at Dien Bien Phu in 1954, the U.S. Americans extended the Da Nang runway from 7,800 feet to 11,483 feet. Then they built Da Nang East Airfield, complete with a second asphalt runway at 10,000 feet and asphalt overruns, taxiways, warm-up aprons, access roads, and strips of 1,000 feet and 5,000 feet. The strips accommodated helicopters and light planes. The longer runways accommodated some of the fast movers and bombers that would drop, over eight years (1964–72), nearly eight million tons of bombs smart and dumb on Vietnam (and Cambodia and Laos).[1] U.S. pilots even bombed, inadvertently, some of what other U.S. personnel had paved. Da Nang's runways, airstrips, and other blacktop surfaces suffered friendly-fire incidents. Friendly and unfriendly fire alike was such that John

McNaughton, an assistant secretary of defense, walked out of a White House meeting at the war's peak and said, "We seem to be proceeding on the assumption that the way to eradicate the Vietcong is to destroy all the village structures, defoliate all the jungles, and then cover the entire surface of South Vietnam with asphalt."[2] The defoliate reference was to Agent Orange, a dioxin-laced herbicide that arrived, like asphalt, in fifty-five-gallon drums.

Figuratively (and sometimes literally), the road to U.S. ground combat in Vietnam was also paved. By November 22, 1963, the day John F. Kennedy died, the United States had approximately seventeen thousand military advisers in South Vietnam, along with an unknown number of CIA agents, army helicopter pilots, and Navy Seabee construction workers. While waiting for combat forces to arrive, the Seabees built dozens of Army Special Forces camps and more generally poured concrete and laid asphalt at Da Nang and wherever else so ordered. On March 8, 1965, the first combat forces arrived. Over 3,500 U.S. Marines waded ashore at Nam O Beach, north of Da Nang. The second marine landing was by air at Da Nang. Regular army arrived soon thereafter. President Lyndon Johnson assigned marines and soldiers one primary mission: protect the runways and airstrips— protect Da Nang asphalt and the base's asphalt plants from the enemy's Soviet-manufactured 122 mm rockets that won the base a Rocket City nickname. The blacktop duty was as predictable as the asphalt plant fires that plagued Da Nang. It was predictable because asphalt is the environment of the United States at war and peace: bombs abroad, cars at home.

The enemy paved as well, though on a far lesser scale. Even the Ho Chi Minh Trail—the logistical system that supported communist guerrillas and the regular North Vietnamese Army—had a few blacktop stretches.[3] By 1968 the five hundred thousand U.S. military personnel in South Vietnam who faced the violence that came down the blood road had many missions beyond the protection of Da Nang asphalt. By the time the United States evacuated the last of its personnel in 1975, an estimated 2.7 million U.S. military personnel and civilians had served in Vietnam. Early on most of the soldiers and marines arrived by sea. After a few months the majority arrived at Da Nang by plane. Combat boot heels touched asphalt or concrete parking aprons before they touched anything else in Vietnam. Aircraft departing Da Nang's asphalt runways carried most of the U.S. warriors—whether on foot, on stretchers, or in body bags—"back to the world."[4]

Blacktop roads, parking lots, and runways constitute the central arteries of the United States' horizontally homogeneous environment, creating a distinct "political territory" and a "political economy of velocity" that changed the pace of life and gave people a new place to spend so much of their lives.[5] The pavement age began at the dawn of what economist Robert Gordon calls a special century (1870–1970), driven by successive and intertwined economic revolutions that moved the United States and much of the world from farm to city. Each revolution was labor intensive and driven by inventions and emerging technologies: the lightbulb, interchangeable parts, the internal-combustion engine, refrigeration, electric-power grids, indoor plumbing, telegraphs, telephones, radios, televisions, radiators, air conditioning, forced-air heating, and others.[6] Asphalt received scant attention because people too often take it for granted, even in the United States, where its impact has been most dramatic. But its impact has not been dramatic enough to rate as more than a dull-normal commodity confined, the cultural historian Jeffrey Schnapp states, within "the domain of the necessary but presupposed," lurking "beneath the perceived surface of the modern landscape like a hidden god."[7]

Common usage in the United States treats the words *asphalt* and *blacktop* as synonyms. Technically, blacktop is "asphalt-concrete pavement," composed of aggregate—gravel, sand, and other coarse particulate material—and hot liquefied asphalt. Aggregate typically makes up 95 percent of blacktop. Liquid asphalt, which constitutes the remainder, fixes aggregate. The engineers call it "asphalt cement." One key difference between asphalt-concrete pavement and concrete pavement is the binder. Portland cement is the usual binder for concrete.

Many nonengineers use the words *cement* and *concrete* interchangeably, just as they use the words *blacktop* and *asphalt* interchangeably. Regardless, blacktop is just one synonym for asphalt. There are over two hundred more synonyms. Usage can be confusing. There is no standard definition for asphalt, the U.S. Geological Survey notes: "Terms generally have been adapted to suit particular requirements of geologists, engineers, refiners, or lawyers."[8] What U.S. Americans call *blacktop*, the British call *tarmac*. Then again, U.S. Americans often refer to airport pavement, whether asphalt or concrete, as tarmac. They also use the word in dozens of contexts as an adjective (for example, asphalt emulsions) and dozens more as a noun (for example, oxidized asphalt). Much of the world, however, prefers the word *bitumen* rather than *asphalt* (or *tarmac*).

Under each and every name, asphalt is a complex material composed primarily of high molecular-weight hydrocarbons containing saturated and unsaturated aliphatic and aromatic compounds. For asphalt found in nature, the chemical composition varies depending on the source of the deposit. For asphalt produced in oil refineries, the chemical composition varies depending on the source of crude oil, refinery processes, and any additives necessary to meet product specifications. Most asphalts regardless of source contain 79–88 percent carbon, 7–13 percent hydrogen, trace–8 percent sulfur, trace–8 percent oxygen, trace–3 percent nitrogen, and minerals (most commonly, nickel and vanadium) at hundreds of parts per million. Asphalt is thermoplastic, meaning it softens when heated and hardens upon cooling; at certain temperatures it is viscoelastic, meaning it exhibits viscous flow and elastic deformation (like a memory-foam mattress). At room temperature asphalt appears to be a solid. In fact, it is a slow-moving liquid. In 1944 Trinity College physicists poured hot asphalt into a funnel, allowed it to cool, and cut a hole in the funnel's stem. They counted nine drops of asphalt through the funnel in sixty-nine years.[9]

In the twenty-first century, the oil industry uses natural asphalt to create synthetic crude oil, while the paving industry continues to rely on the asphalt produced in refineries. Refinery asphalt eclipsed natural asphalt for road paving duty primarily because (1) it is a residuum and thus has no real production cost; (2) chemists and engineers can more easily manipulate it according to the demands of asphalt plant owners and other customers; and (3) there is no need to remove rocks, sand, and other physical objects found in natural asphalt. Refinery asphalt, in effect, hides in each barrel of crude oil that arrives at the refinery. Modern refining began with atmospheric distillation in 1862 and then vacuum distillation after 1870. Refinery workers and their equipment produce asphalt from crude oil by removing lighter fractions based on initial boiling and vaporization points. A light fraction like butane can vaporize at ninety degrees Fahrenheit. Asphalt and other residuum might not even begin to boil until temperatures reach or surpass one thousand degrees Fahrenheit.

Asphalt as a material put to use by humanity has two basic characteristics. First, it is ubiquitous because it is useful and profitable, durable and malleable. Blacktop pavement is so widespread that the road to self-sufficiency in the United States might place more value on having a driver's license than a high-school diploma. The CIA *World Factbook*, partially updated weekly, tracks both poverty and asphalt's creep across the planet by tallying paved and unpaved road mileage in every nation (and in nearly every nation, over 90 percent of paved roads are paved with asphalt). Others measure poverty by counting the evicted in inner cities, people whose property sits on asphalt streets or concrete sidewalks. Mental health professionals track the homeless by pondering such things as "asylums, asphalt, and ethics." In 2017 the Department of Housing and Urban Development counted 115,000 homeless U.S. children on a given night. That is a modest number compared to the tens of millions of children, according to the United Nations Children's Fund (UNICEF), who live on the planet's streets. For many homeless of whatever age in whatever nation, asphalt in its blacktop pavement form is their de facto home.[10]

Blacktop in the United States is so visible and so widespread that it sprouted a depaving movement and inspired such questions as this one: Would the suburbs have grown so quickly without asphalt? According to John Stilgoe, a landscape historian, before the blacktop age suburbs existed primarily in the imagination of developers. Now things are quite different. "Once a property is subdivided," environmental consultant Robert Lenzner emphasizes, "asphalt is the last crop."[11] Beyond covering roads and parking lots in horizontal sheets and lines, over 85 percent of airports that have paved runways feature asphalt. (International airport runways are an exception; they are often concrete, but there are many exceptions beyond Da Nang International Airport.) And asphalt's horizontal sheets and lines are present in such other places as driveways and alleys, playgrounds and golf-cart paths, tennis and basketball courts, automobile racetracks and four-hundred-meter running tracks, the expanse of county and state fairgrounds, and so on.

Asphalt's sloped sheets and lines are most often present on residential roofs in the form of asphalt shingles (especially in North America, where asphalt shingles dominate). In hundreds of other nooks of daily life, asphalt is present if largely invisible. How many people know that asphalt lines many reservoirs, landfills, sea walls, dikes, groins, and funerary caskets; that farmers and others brush it on wooden fence posts to inhibit rot; that automobile manufacturers coat an odd part here and there with asphalt to inhibit noise and vibrations; that shotgunners scatter asphalt when hitting clay pigeons; that railroad workers use asphalt to stabilize or replace traditional track-bed ballast; or that a German company pioneered the use of asphalt as the central core material for embankment dams? And new uses are always on the horizon. For example, a type of porous carbon derived from asphalt has shown promise in enabling high-capacity lithium batteries to charge faster.

Asphalt Americana is nearly as ubiquitous as blacktop and shingles. It includes, among many other examples, the Asphalt Yacht Club (a clothier for those who move on such blacktop-dependent products as skateboards); *Asphalt Jesus* (a book); *Asphalt Xtreme* (a videogame series); Asphalt Orchestra (a marching band); Asphalt

Green (a fitness-center complex anchored on the site of New York City's former Municipal Asphalt Plant); *Asphalt One* (the George H. W. Bush family's campaign bus); a plastic model kit for the U.S. Army workhorse truck during World War II, complete with an asphalt tank in the bed; the asphalt spreaders' boots on the monster in the classic film *Frankenstein* (1931); a Marilyn Monroe poster for *The Asphalt Jungle* (1950); and the album cover for the Beatles' *Abbey Road* (1969). Whether romanticizing blacktop's encompassing presence or despising it, these cultural sightings are nothing new. William Dean Howells chronicled his New York City walks a century ago with a reference: "These pretty, wilding growths which I had been finding all the season long among the streets of asphalt." Nor are cultural nods confined to the United States. The flâneur and other bourgeoisie loungers on *derives* in Berlin, wrote Walter Benjamin, a Jewish Marxist who fled Germany in 1932, "botanized the asphalt." Naturalists of the unnatural environment, they were ever observing, collecting, identifying, and preserving specimens.[12]

Asphalt's second basic characteristic as a material put to use by humanity is its duality. Because asphalt is nearly everywhere we are, it is as contradictory as we are . . . a substance where incongruities fester. It symbolizes both hope and despair. "If the whole world were to be covered with asphalt," Russian writer Ilya Ehrenburg mused in defense of fellow dissident Boris Pasternak, "one day a crack would appear in the asphalt; and in that crack grass would grow."[13] Harvard once offered a course that explored the dichotomy between asphalt's omnipresence and its status as a hated material. One recent reason for that hate, given the mining and melting of natural asphalt in Alberta, is the threat of environmental horror. Yet the blacktop that covers so much of the earth's surface not only traps hydrocarbons. It is recyclable nearly in its entirety.

For 1990–2009 the Environmental Protection Agency compiled lists of petroleum products in the category of "nonfuel uses of energy fuels." These uses "for purposes other than their energy value," EPA explained, "create carbon dioxide emissions and . . . sequester carbon in nonfuel products." The list for U.S. carbon dioxide emissions did not include asphalt pavement because it has no emissions beyond trace. Rather, asphalt pavement sequesters carbon because the carbon in blacktop, barring catastrophic accidents and such other horrors as wartime bombing, will never burn and thus will never enter the atmosphere. In fact, the amount of carbon sequestered in blacktop is immense. The annual calculation of asphalt and road oil on the EPA's carbon sequestration list ranges up to one hundred million metric tons carbon dioxide equivalent. A single gallon of gasoline weighing slightly over six pounds, in contrast to however many miles of blacktop pavement, releases over nineteen pounds of carbon dioxide via evaporation and tailpipe emissions. (Gasoline mixes with oxygen from the air to account for the weight difference.) Then again vehicles driving on blacktop produce roughly 70 percent of global tailpipe emissions.[14]

Asphalt's duality can be symbolic as well. An example: the state of Illinois broke one "interstate asphalt ceiling" in 2007 by naming a stretch of I-90 north and west of Chicago after a woman. Having founded Hull House in 1889 on Chicago's Near West Side, Jane Addams was the matriarch of the settlement-house movement on behalf of the urban poor, especially immigrants newly arrived in the land of child labor.[15] She never owned a car. She walked or peddled a bicycle. She stood with those who would never resent tolls because they would never own cars either. Now her name—the Jane Addams Memorial Tollway—is attached to a pay-to-drive interstate. The duality here is clear. Chicago's mix of black (asphalt) and white (concrete) lanes expands business, recreation, and consumer opportunity while drawing lines that segregate by ethnicity, race, and class with an astonishing precision.

The cast that inhabits asphalt world is a sprawling mix representing interests sometimes at odds and sometimes in harmony. This list of players is long but hardly exclusive: plant owners and workers; public and private research institutions; manufacturers and operators of tankers and road-building machinery; shingle distributors and roofers; Big Oil executives and hard-hat refinery workers; realtors and highway engineers; billboard-industry magnates and parking-lot developers; pipeline-company owners and their dig crews; armies and their construction battalions; government policy makers and bureaucrats; and motorists and their ever-escalating demand for the convenience of smooth speed and ample parking day or night. All deserve coverage, especially the men and women who planned or worked on state-sponsored economic development. These public-works projects (broadly defined) range from Nebuchadnezzar's gates, walls, roads, and palaces in ancient Babylon to those of Robert Moses in twentieth-century New York City and from the New Deal's Works Progress Administration to Boston's Big Dig (the Central Artery/ Tunnel Project).

A focus on public-works projects will help structure asphalt's sprawling story—so will a focus on power and culture. From emperors and dictators centuries ago to contractors and elected officials in the twenty-first century, human beings have used asphalt to acquire and project power and to prevent others from doing likewise. Asphalt, plainly put, is a material that has helped humanity do the right thing and the most abhorrent things. In recent times and for good or evil, those who used asphalt were catalysts for profound cultural changes. The most significant of these changes paralleled the spread of asphalt pavement. "We live in a motorized civilization," Robert Moses wrote in 1974, as if no one else understood that plain fact.[16] Neither asphalt as a material nor the technology underpinning asphalt paving are as important as the car and the internal-combustion engine as catalysts for change. Yet asphalt was not a bit player either. If one can use the words *car culture*, than one can certainly use the words *asphalt culture*. Asphalt and its ecosystem are more important, in effect, as a subculture of the larger car culture. Both function as social constructs and both largely share the same complex ecosystem dominated by regulatory laws and policies on one hand and interest-group politics and technological innovation on the other.

Asphalt, landscape architect Pierre Bélanger emphasizes, was at "center stage for a theater of explosive invention"—"vulcanized rubber, refined petroleum, the air tube, the pneumatic tire, the ball bearing, cold pressed steel, die-cast metal, hydraulics, and lubricants"—that profoundly changed the North American landscape. That landscape is a bionic blacktop web with a "scale and form practically render[ing] impossible the conception of it as a single bounded system. Yet its function depends precisely upon the singular continuity of a horizontal surface . . . reaching deep across the sea, the air, and the ground, effectively interlocking global commercial activities, regional transportation infrastructures, and contemporary land uses. Seen from space, the consolidated surface of North America looks less like a landlocked continent and much more like a borderless construction site."[17]

Robert Moses and others with sufficient authority used asphalt as a core material in remaking the urban United States and in the process creating a car culture that spread beyond the cities. To state the obvious, cars are useless without roads. It is equally obvious that not all roads are paved and that not all paved roads are blacktop. But nearly 94 percent of the United States' 2.7 million miles of paved roads are blacktop. By any measure, paved roads are the default environment of the automobile, and asphalt is the default environment of paved roads. "Americans drive because in most places the built environment all but requires them to do so. Landscapes in the United States that are easily navigable without personal vehicles have become rare—small islands in the vast sea of Car Country," writes Christopher W. Wells in his environmental history of the automobile.[18] We cannot have a car country without cars. We cannot have the built environment that exists and that makes cars necessary without asphalt. We could have paved over 90 percent of paved roads with concrete. We did not. We paved them with asphalt.

Asphalt culture is a subculture of martial culture as well. The U.S. military has taken paving equipment abroad for every war since the Spanish-American War of 1898. But it was during World War II that asphalt truly emerged as a core material for the U.S. Armed Forces. Army engineers and navy construction battalions labored from Normandy's beaches to Germany's Autobahn in one theater, and in the other from Guadalcanal to the Tinian Island blacktop that carried the weight of the planes that turned to Hiroshima and Nagasaki. One simple number demonstrates asphalt's status as a subculture of the larger martial culture. On June 6, 1944, nearly sixteen thousand long tons of liquid asphalt in fifty-five-gallon drums landed with U.S. troops.[19] As with the Vietnam War that lay in the near distance, the United States needed asphalt to repair and build roads, runways, and airstrips across France to facilitate the movement of troops and gear and to provide safe haven for fighters, bombers, and other aircraft. However mind-boggling that D-Day number (again, blacktop pavement generally requires only 5 percent liquid asphalt and 95 percent aggregate), it is modest compared to the amount of asphalt U.S. forces used in the Pacific theater to pave runways for the bombing campaigns against Japan. Over seven decades after World War II and over four decades after U.S. withdrawal from Vietnam, the cover of the U.S. Department of Defense's *Base Structure Report* for 2017, which summarizes real property inventory at hundreds of U.S. bases at home and abroad, features a color photograph of a double-barrel asphalt roller sitting on fresh blacktop.

A focus on place also helps to structure asphalt's sprawling story. Asphalt in contemporary times is a cultural force not only for its seepage into popular culture and subculture status beneath car and martial cultures or for its relentless ubiquity that is, arguably, the dominant spatial feature of our built environment. A focus on place demonstrates the folly of ignoring or minimizing the degree to which so many of our culture's key events, so much of our lives, and so many of our deaths play out on blacktop.

Finally, the asphalt story has a distinct chronology marked by two points in time. The dawn of the pavement age marks the first: the world before blacktop and the world after blacktop. The pavement age also pushed the United States into the asphalt story's starring role. The more recent mining and melting of natural asphalt marks the second point: the world before synthetic crude oil and the world after synthetic crude oil. In this brave new world, the United States and its refineries share the starring role with Canada and its 2.2 trillion barrels of natural asphalt in the oil sands of Alberta.

Part 1 BEFORE BLACKTOP

1 Nature

Tar Pits and
Asphalt Volcanoes

The crew of the *Alvin*, a deep-ocean research submersible operated by the Woods Hole Oceanographic Institution in Massachusetts, has had many adventures over the past half century. They include these three: In 1966, after a midair crash between a B-52 strategic bomber and a refueling aircraft tumbled an H-bomb into the Mediterranean, the *Alvin*'s crew found it. In 1987 another crew dove to the wreck of the RMS *Titanic*. In 2007 yet another crew discovered a field of asphalt volcanoes on the Santa Barbara Basin seafloor off the Southern California coast.[1] That last was not a total surprise. While exploring the southern Gulf of Mexico in 2003, scientists on RV *Sonne*, a German geoscientific research ship, discovered the first asphalt volcanoes at depths up to ten thousand feet near the Bay of Campeche. Other researchers on other vessels located additional asphalt volcanoes in the Campeche Knolls, a field of ductile salt bodies intruding among rocks on the seafloor and known for oil and gas seepages. Beyond the *Sonne* and *Alvin* discoveries, research teams on surface-ship and deep-ocean vessels charted additional asphalt volcano fields in the southwest Atlantic off Brazil's coast and along the Angolan margin off Africa's southwest coast.

In the Campeche Knolls the initial focus was on a specific asphalt volcano, dubbed Chapapote Knoll from the Aztec word for tar. One team hypothesized that fractures in the rock and sediment cover allowed asphalt to "migrate upward, ultimately leading to the discharge of tar-like fluids onto the seafloor." Over centuries and millennia the vertical spreads can collect immense amounts of asphalt that gradually form mounds, like Chapapote Knoll, resembling volcanoes. This particular asphalt volcano "likely erupts during phases of intensified activity separated by periods of reduced activity . . . creating distinct flow units and . . . varied morphologies of asphalt." It appears that there were three separate eruption events for Chapapote Knoll, with each consisting of "a single large eruption or of several small eruptions closely spaced in time." Another research team offered a slightly different hypothesis after studying a wider range of asphalt volcanoes in the Campeche Knolls: "The outflow of heavy oil either created whips or sheets floating in the water that subsequently descend and pile-up . . . or spread at the seafloor forming flows ranging from meters to tens of meters in diameter." Asphalt on or near the seafloor presents not only as mounds but lumps, linear bands, and even "petrified tar whips" filled with compressed gas (often methane and other trace gases).[2]

The asphalt that spread horizontally around many of the volcanoes resembled pavement under the sea. In other cases seafloor asphalt might be "ropy with little signs for degradation" or "degraded to blocks without visible flow structures." For the vertical spread some of the asphalt volcanoes resembled "tar lilies" because "the thick petroleum 'lava' had built elegant flower-like forms." By whatever name or shape, there were thousands of these asphalt structures ranging in size from less than a yard high and less than a yard across to the Santa Barbara Basin's Il Duomo at twenty yards high and six hundred yards across. They have one thing in common: they are habitats for life. Chris Reddy, a Woods Hole marine chemist, said, "There were all types of life forms living on [Il Duomo] . . . almost like an artificial reef, except it was an asphalt reef. . . . Some of the samples we brought back to the surface also had these perfectly cylindrical holes. . . . We were sitting there, measuring the holes, taking pictures, and the next thing you know, we see a worm [a chemosynthetic tubeworm] crawling right out of a hole." Sponges, sea cucumbers, octopi, and many other creatures are among the benthic (or seafloor-dwelling) animals living on or near the asphalt.[3]

Il Duomo was at a modest depth, for *Alvin*, of seven hundred feet. But Chapapote Knoll was nearly ten thousand feet down. A seafloor mud environment at those depths is not particularly habitable. Regard-less, even the deepest asphalt volcanoes are colonized by bacteria and epifauna (that is, benthic animals that live on the substrate—sediment—covering rocks, sand, gravel, clay, or other material). In simple terms asphalt volcanoes and other asphalt seepage support a broad spectrum of marine life by providing a hard surface on the seafloor. The asphalt volcanoes today are gentle seeps. But one the-ory holds that major tectonic activity thirty-five thousand years ago created fissures—open cracks—on the Santa Barbara Basin seafloor, spewing massive amounts of oil that spread enormous slicks on the surface. That oil created hypoxic dead zones. Massive destruction of life, in other words, may have preceded the creation of the asphalt volcanoes and an entire asphalt ecology on the seafloor.[4]

There is no scientific consensus on the question of how much asphalt—or oil, for that matter—lies under seafloors. And there is no consensus on the question of when asphalt first emerged. Asphalt traces found in rocks millions of years old inspired incorrect specula-tion that asphalt is a primordial material (that is, a material present at the earth's creation). Others erred in thinking asphalt was present in carbonaceous meteorites because they look like asphalt chunks.[5] Two thousand years ago, Pliny the Elder (23–79 CE), the Roman naturalist, philosopher, and military commander, divided the natural asphalt that he saw on the earth's surface into two categories: "muddie *slime*" and "verie earth or mineral."[6] Pliny's observations hold up in a general sense. There are approximately one hundred billion tons of natural asphalt in eighty-nine of the planet's sedimentary basins in the form of lake asphalt, smaller seeps ("muddie *slime*"), carbonaceous rock asphalt, and, as in Alberta, sand asphalt ("verie earth or mineral"). One layperson's difference between rock asphalt and sand asphalt is that the former can be brittle.[7]

So-called asphaltite minerals also exist in nature. Chemists clas-sify them as asphaltites because they are, like the various types of asphalt, a black or brown bituminous material. The three asphaltite classifications are Gilsonite, found in the Uinta Basin of northeastern Utah; glance pitch (manjak), found in Barbados and Colombia; and grahamite, found in Cuba, Mexico, and the United States (in Oklahoma and West Virginia). Wurtzilite, found in the Uinta Basin, and albertite, found in Alberta County, New Brunswick, are two of the so-called asphaltoids. Chemists differentiate asphaltoids from asphaltites based on their density, solubility, and other factors. Regardless, the differences are minor. "It is doubtful," as the preeminent asphalt chemist James G. Speight put it, "that the asphaltoid group can ever be clearly distinguished from the asphaltites."[8]

The Western Hemisphere is home to at least 85 percent of all asphalt that lies on or under the earth's surface. Deposits in the present-day United States are in the Arctic coastal plain and six basins beyond Uinta (Gulf Coast, Black Warrior, Cherokee, Illinois, Paradox, and Santa Maria). Utah's oil sands are the largest of these reserves, with an estimated 4 billion barrels embedded in sandstone at Asphalt Ridge and over twenty other named locations. Regardless, Utah's reserves are minuscule compared to the Canadian reserves in Alberta's Athabasca, Peace River, and Cold Lake basins: an estimated 2.2 trillion barrels, including reserves of a related resource, bitumen carbonates, trapped in the Grosmont Formation's limestone and dolomite. The Athabasca River, part of the Mackenzie River system, is the dominant geographic feature of the general area. The McMurray Formation is the dominant geologic feature. Bits and pieces of the formation's natural asphalt have been present in the entire area's aquatic ecosystem, including the Athabasca riverbed, long before the ancestors of today's First Nations people arrived in the area.[9] Venezuela is the only nation with natural asphalt reserves that rival, and perhaps even surpass, Canadian reserves. This natural asphalt has also been present in the aquatic ecosystems of the Orinoco Basin, one of the largest river basins in South America, long before human beings arrived.

The earth, almost literally, bleeds hydrocarbons through thousands of land and seafloor seepages. Earthquakes and other tectonic activity, as noted, can fracture the layers of rock that cover oil deposits deep underground and creature fissures on the seafloor or land. Buoyancy and pressure can push gas, oil, and degraded oil (asphalt) through the fissures. On land, asphalt seeps are visible and self-contained. In the absence of major tectonic activity, asphalt seeps on the seafloor rarely cause significant environmental damage. In the Gulf of Mexico, scientists have identified scores of seep locations beyond the asphalt volcano locations, most at depths greater than three thousand feet and with estimated seepage rates ranging from four barrels a day to seventy barrels a day. Asphalt flowing at such rates poses almost no environmental hazard. Even oil at such modest flow rates does not pose an acute danger because these seeps are part of nature, and the biota in the vicinity has adapted to the presence of hydrocarbon molecules over many thousands of years.

Whether on seafloor or land, hydrocarbon seeps can be active or inactive. (An active seep has oil and/or asphalt continuously migrating from a subterranean source.) Surface seeps form in a manner similar to seafloor seeps, with heavy molten oil migrating up. If cap rock—impermeable rock—prevents upward migration, the oil is contained, and it will accumulate until oil companies arrive with their drilling rigs or tectonic activity creates fissures that allow some of the trapped oil to escape. On the way to the surface, migrating oil (as opposed to pumped oil) picks up water and clay (among other things) while gradually cooling and undergoing chemical changes. These changes are often dramatic enough that, when the hydrocarbons arrive at the surface, the petroleum engineers and chemists no longer classify them as oil. Rather, the engineers and chemists classify these hydrocarbons as surface asphalts. Generally, asphalt seeps represent less than 20 percent of the original oils with microbial oxidation and other bio-degradation processes driving oil-mass loss.

The Abu Jir fault zone in Iraq's Hit-Kubaisa region is home to one of the planet's larger surface asphalt seeps. Scientists and hobbyists alike call the big ones "asphalt lakes" or "tar pits," even though they contain no tar (which is not a natural material; it is created by the destructive distillation of coal or a variety of other organic material).

Abu Jir's asphalt seeps form shallow crater lakes more than a mile wide, along with much smaller "beds . . . interbedded with the marls and carbonates of the Fatha (L. Fars) Formation."[10] Other than these seeps and the Binagadi tar pits in Azerbaijan, all remaining major asphalt seeps are in the Western Hemisphere. Three are in Southern California.[11] The others are in South America.[12] Venezuela's Lake Bermudez sprawls across 1,100 acres and contains an estimated thirty-five million barrels of asphalt. In 1879 MIT professor William O. Crosby likened Trinidad's Pitch Lake—containing an estimated forty million barrels below 115 surface acres—to a volcano crater filled to the brim. Nineteen years later, in 1898, a U.S. Geological Survey researcher compared Pitch Lake "to a vast asphalt pavement with many holes filled with inky water in which swim ugly fish and black beetles." Apparently, life exists below the inky water as well. Recent research has shown that minuscule water droplets under two hundred feet of Pitch Lake asphalt are microhabitats for microbial, metabolically active life that consumes hydrocarbons.[13]

Oil, natural asphalt, and life forms are inseparable, from the greatest of the oil fields and asphalt volcanoes to the tiniest of the oil and asphalt seeps. "Typically," James Speight summarized in his handbook on asphalt materials science and technology, "these naturally occurring bitumen deposits are formed from the remains of ancient, microscopic algae (diatoms) and other once-living things. These remains were deposited in the mud on the bottom of the ocean or lake where the organisms lived. Under the heat and pressure of burial deep in the Earth, the remains were transformed into materials such as petroleum and bitumen." Many of the natural asphalt deposits, in turn, captured and killed living things and hold a fossilized record of the carnage. If conditions were right, a few inches of asphalt could trap even the largest species. For more than a century, scientists have hunted mammal and other fossils in these so-called tar pits (what scientists call asphaltic paleontological localities). Though skin, muscles, fur, and feathers decay quickly, asphalt aids preservation by soaking into bone and teeth.[14]

Venezuela has hundreds of asphalt seeps (referred to as *menes* across much of South America) and several sizeable tar pits that are notable sources for fossils. Researchers believe these tar pits may in time yield the planet's oldest and most diverse fossil record because they captured land and freshwater fauna migrations between North America and South America via Central America (the Great America Biotic Exchange).[15] Other notable *menes* include Peru's Talara Tar Pits, which have produced extinct fossilized megafauna and nearly thirty thousand bones from a variety of birds, amphibians, and carnivores. Recent research in Ecuador, however, suggests that some tar pits are more accurately characterized as bone beds because death preceded asphalt infiltration. Cuba also has tar pits with fossils preserved secondarily by asphalt.[16]

The La Brea Tar Pits in Los Angeles, occupying an area that was once forest and savannah, are thus far the planet's most productive tar pit source for fossils. No one recognized the animal remains in the pits as fossils until 1875. La Brea gained national exposure 33 years later, when *Sunset* magazine published an article titled "Death Trap of the Ages."[17] In 1909 a high school biology teacher launched the first significant excavation. In 1912 University of California–Berkeley professors arrived. In 1914 archaeologists discovered the only human remains ever found in the pits: La Brea Woman. (Native Americans began using Southern California's tar-pit asphalt as caulk and adhesive at least 10,000 years ago; they even used it to makes casts for broken bones.) Excavation of the latest major find, Project 23, began in 2006, after workers constructing a new underground parking garage for La Brea Tar Pits and Museum uncovered signs of what proved to be sixteen separate fossil beds. A nearly complete Columbian mammoth skeleton ranked as the most spectacular find. For the pits as a whole, carbon 14 radiometric testing has dated the oldest mammal fossil, a coyote, to 46,800 years. The oldest fossil overall, a wood specimen, dates to 55,000 years.

Excavation has been most consistent in La Brea's Pit 91, first excavated nearly a century before the Project 23 discovery and home to over 40 percent of the 3.5 million fossils unearthed thus far. This was the ninety-first pit dug because it was underground, hidden by a thick cover of dirt and sand. Today Pit 91's emphasis is on microfossils: "tiny remains of plants and animals like seeds, twigs, snake bones, bird beaks, insect exoskeletons, and fish teeth."[18] The carnivore category of fossils in Pit 91 and the other pits includes, in addition to coyotes, saber-toothed tigers (and saber-toothed tiger kittens), scimitar-toothed cats, giant jaguars, giant short-faced bears, ring-tailed cats, a domestic dog, gray wolves, bobcats, and many others. Herbivores stuck in the goo might take days to die, and their cries and then the stink of their slowly sinking carcasses attracted carnivores. That is why there are so many fossils of the prehistoric and extinct dire wolf in the pits. Dire wolves, like today's wolves, moved in packs. (The George C. Page Museum at La Brea has four hundred skulls on its dire wolf wall.) Beyond paleoecology La Brea researchers use the fossils to investigate questions related to evolution and climate change during the Pleistocene (colloquially referred to as the Ice Age), the geologic epoch that began well over two million years ago and ended approximately twelve thousand years ago.

The West Coast's major earthquake fault, the San Andreas Fault, lies fifty miles east of La Brea Tar Pits. But Los Angeles has dozens of lesser earthquake faults and fissures within its borders, including the so-called Sixth Street Fault, which runs through the Salt Lake oil field. This fault is the apparent conduit for oil migration to La Brea. Oil-mass loss continues along the way from Salt Lake to La Brea until what was once oil emerges on the surface as tar-pit asphalt. La Brea is on the Salt Lake oil field's southern boundary, near Wilshire Boulevard in the city's Hancock Park neighborhood. For three decades after its discovery in 1902, Salt Lake was California's most productive oil field. Its wells—approximately 450 of them—produced fifty million barrels of oil before giving way in the 1930s and 1940s to residential and commercial construction. What lies below the homes and businesses—abandoned wells, sump basins, and buried oil from spills—has complicated the natural upward hydrocarbon migration along the Sixth Street Fault. Further complications arose in 1961, when drilling resumed, with the drilling island concealed behind walls and screens and covering a single acre on La Cienega Boulevard, bordering what is now the Beverly Center mall. Per industry standards the operators disposed of methane and saltwater by injecting these substances back into the well.[19]

Complications aside, nature is relentless. Nothing beyond a monumental engineering project can stop the flow of oil from the Salt Lake field to La Brea Tar Pits, and nothing can stop the transformation of that oil to asphalt as its lighter fractions bleed off. Occasionally, oil and asphalt outside the park and museum grounds seep onto Wilshire Boulevard across from the tar pits. When that happens StreetsLA (formerly the Los Angeles Bureau of Street Services) pumps, shovels, and otherwise removes the oil and asphalt and gets the underground containment system of seepage pits back to normal. Removing hydrocarbons that spill onto concrete sidewalks and blacktop streets is a small part of StreetsLA's responsibilities. The agency also operates two asphalt plants, using product produced at oil refineries and not the seepage pumped up or scraped up. That refinery asphalt patches potholes and resurfaces streets as refinery asphalt does in every other U.S. city. Thousands of years before such modern uses, of course, humanity found more localized uses for natural asphalt at La Brea or wherever else it spread on the earth's surface.

All tar pits and surface seeps have this in common with the asphalt volcanoes that lie on the seafloor in both the Atlantic and the Pacific: they capture asphalt's duality, asphalt's basic nature, whether it lies undisturbed or not. Like all hydrocarbons, asphalt's origins lie in decomposing organic matter, decomposing life. While asphalt volcanoes, once dormant or semidormant, support life, their creation created oil slicks that destroyed life. Obviously, the tar pits often ended life. This life-and-death duality was present before our species emerged. It was present when humanity first put asphalt to use in prehistoric times. And it is present in our era of the automobile, the internal-combustion engine, and the blacktop road, the era of fossil fuels, oil sands, and global warming.

2 Use

Fired Bricks and
Mummy Wars

Hitler allowed Arierdämmerung (Aryan twilight), cultural historian Suzanne Marchand noted, as a concession to the Nazi Party's *völkisch* (folkish) troupe.[1] Arierdämmerung enlisted archaeologists in a campaign to claim the ancestors of Germany's "master race" were responsible for classical antiquity's achievements. After the invasion of Poland in 1939 interrupted the work, there was a sense of déjà vu because the prior war had also interrupted archaeological digs. "It is most desirable . . . that the excavation of Babylon should be completed," German archaeologist Robert Koldewey wrote in the months before World War I began in 1914.[2] After Koldewey died in 1925, his admirers formed the Koldewey Society. Many society members honored his work by opposing Arierdämmerung and other Nazi attempts to corrupt archaeologists and their discipline.

Koldewey's team dug in Babylon year round from 1899 to 1914. The Ishtar Gate was the principal find.[3] The world's first glimpse of the legendary city, however, came early in the dig, with excavation of the Procession Street of Marduk, the patron god of Babylon. The discovery came in 1902. That was early in the pavement age. Across every continent save Antarctica (which had none), most streets and roads remained dirt or gravel at the turn of the twentieth century (especially so beyond urban areas). They were graded rather than paved. Yet not only did Nebuchadnezzar II (ca. 634–562 BCE), the Babylonian king, build the Procession Street 2,500 years before Koldewey's diggers arrived. He paved it with burned bricks and asphalt.

The story of how asphalt marked the United States and the world began long before the Federal Aid Highway Act of 1956 and the coming of the interstates, long before almost any burg could pave roads little and big. Neanderthals may have used asphalt as a glue over seventy thousand years ago.[4] Archaeologists and scientists of various stripes do not know when *Homo sapiens* first used asphalt. But they have certainly shown that our cradle-of-civilization ancestors in Mesopotamia and environs, much like Paleo Indians and their descendants in the Western Hemisphere (let alone the long-gone Neanderthals), used asphalt as a hafting material to affix handles to flint tools. In the Indus Valley, located in present-day Pakistan, builders used asphalt to make a mortar for waterproofing rock-filled reservoirs seven thousand years ago. Asphalt began shaping the human environment at an accelerated pace with the rise of local trading and then trading networks. The artisans and artists of Ur in ancient Mesopotamia did not give away such treasures as a lyre sound box with asphalt fastening inlay panels of gold. They calculated costs and profits. So did Lukulla, a merchant who inscribed the first-known list of prices for grades of asphalt on a stone tablet four thousand years ago.[5] By that time asphalt had emerged as a basic commodity—because it was useful and readily available—in the fertile crescent of the Tigris and the Euphrates Rivers, in the land of Mesopotamia's ancient city-states. Three of the most notable asphalt seeps across what is now Jordan, Syria, and Iraq are at Nineveh, Ur, and Hit.

The Dead Sea supply of asphalt dwarfed all known asphalt sources in antiquity. With a surface area of over 400 square miles in ancient times, this landlocked body of water is nowadays much smaller (230 square miles and rapidly receding) and asphalt-locked by two ribbons, Highway 90 on the Israeli side and Highway 65 on the Jordanian side. With a shoreline 1,300 feet below sea level, the Dead Sea's waters are too saline for life, although pockets of bacteria and fungi exist on seafloor areas fed by freshwater springs. Asphalt splinters and chunks drift up from these and other seafloor areas to bob on the surface. Giant chunks—some as big as football fields—were once common. The last giants surfaced in 1837 with the last of the area's major earthquakes.[6]

Aristotle (384–322 BCE), the Greek philosopher, said the Dead Sea emitted "stinking, choking and sometimes deadly fumes." "The odour [the rotten-egg stink of hydrogen sulfide gas], borne on the wind," added the Greek historian Diodorus Siculus two centuries later (90–30 BCE), "renders the bodies of the inhabitants susceptible to disease and makes the people very short-lived."[7] On the other hand, many believed asphalt had medicinal value. Its use in dentistry might date to 11,000 BCE, as two incisors found in Tuscany suggest a practitioner hollowed them out with sharpened rocks and filled them with hair, vegetable fibers, and asphalt. Harder documentation exists for asphalt's medicinal use by the Greek physician Hippocrates (ca. 460 BCE–375 BCE) and other physicians across the Dead Sea basin. Pliny the Elder (23–79 CE) listed ailments treated with asphalt in his native Rome and beyond: boils, cataracts, bleeding, toothaches, skin diseases, lumbago, rheumatism, and gynecological disorders.[8]

Ancient Egypt used asphalt to make such tools as a wooden sickle with flint teeth set in asphalt, circa 3500 BCE, found in a granary. Other uses included waterproofing boats constructed from wood or marsh reeds; killing "worms and things that creep" in homes and fields; and caulking palace baths. The Egyptians may have borrowed here and there from the Akkadian Empire (Mesopotamia's first empire ca. 2330–2150 BCE), as a few of that empire's baths featured asphalt flooring, bricks, and seats.[9] In 1987 Egyptologists made a remarkable discovery of asphalt's use to preserve objects in the funerary chamber of Aper-el, a civil officer under two Eighteenth dynasty pharaohs (ca. 1386–1334 BCE). Because asphalt had melted in a fire and resolidified into a mass, a painstaking excavation was required to reveal the well preserved jewelry and gold.[10]

Asphalt helped keep out moisture and otherwise preserve mummified bodies along with objects. A chemical analysis of a random sampling of thirty-nine Egyptian mummies and their wrappings suggests asphalt's use after 1000 BCE rose from 50 percent of New Kingdom mummies to 87 percent of Ptolemaic and Roman period mummies. (The belief that the guilds treated all so-called black mummies with asphalt persisted for centuries even though many other substances could turn black over time.) Another study documented biomarker distributions similar to those of Dead Sea asphalt chunks from the twenty-first century.[11] "The Aegyptians and their followers had two sorts of Embalming, the one curious, and costly for great and rich Men; the other cheap," the Scottish surgeon Alexander Read wrote in *Chirurgorum Comes, or The Whole Practice of Chirurgery* (1687). One cheap process stuffed every body cavity of a corpse with asphalt. On the other hand, even the costly process for the rich might be compromised, according to the Greek historian Herodotus (ca. 484–430 BCE), for such reasons as necrophilia. The authorities might order a three- or four-day delay before embalming a famous or exceptionally beautiful woman on the assumption that decomposing flesh might dissuade the embalmers from violating the corpse. Regardless, the spread of mummification of whatever quality might explain why the guilds embraced asphalt only after 1000 BCE. Resin was the first choice to keep out moisture. Depletion of resin-producing trees was a plain fact for those who prepped and wrapped the dead. Asphalt supplemented increasingly scarce resins and in some cases—what Read called the cheaper cases—replaced resins altogether.[12]

Israeli geochemist Arie Nissenbaum and others have suggested ancient-world use of asphalt for military purposes. Most notably, asphalt appears in several of the incendiary weapon recipes sometimes lumped under the generic header "Greek Fire." The Athenian historian Thucydides (ca. 460–400 BCE) was among the first to note the terror of an asphalt-sulfur mix. Hannibal (ca. 247–182 BCE), the Carthaginian (or Punic) general, may have used a concoction of oil, lime, sulfur, and asphalt. When the Romans burned Carthage after the Third Punic War in 146 BCE, the flammable asphalt mixture used to waterproof rooftops may have fueled a blaze started by flaming arrows that may have included a pinch of asphalt. Pliny noted an even more fearsome battle concoction: inflammable mud, brewed from asphalt seepages, that "sticks to any solid body" and thus "pursue[s] those who seek to flee from it."[13]

Ancient builders used asphalt from the Dead Sea and elsewhere as mortar and mastic for constructing walls, waterproofing roofs and flooring, and strengthening timber in areas where natural stone was scarce. Strengthening was necessary because the most common wood source, date palm, was not nearly as strong as cedar, oak, or fir. The practice of coating palm pillars with asphalt, dating to 3000 BCE, also allowed decorative inlay, given asphalt's adhesive properties.[14] Herodotus focused on the asphalt used as mastic mortar to build Babylon's baked-brick walls. Because poor-quality fuel limited kiln temperatures, the bricks were far more porous than modern bricks. They gained what today's engineers call compressive strength through absorption of the asphalt mastic mortar (which Herodotus called cement).[15]

Dating to 3500 BCE, if not earlier, asphalt was a common tool of imperial construction. The Assyrians built an irrigation canal to bring water from Bavian to Nineveh that included a stone aqueduct with a concrete-asphalt mix protecting the canal bed.[16] In the wake of the Assyrian Empire, Nebuchadnezzar used asphalt extensively for his ambitious sixth century BCE construction projects. Use of asphalt in Nebuchadnezzar's lands began long before his reign or that of his father's. It probably dated to Hammurabi, the sixth king (ruled ca. 1792–1750 BCE) of the first Babylonian dynasty. But no king used asphalt for construction purposes more extensively than Nebuchadnezzar. He even used asphalt, according to Diodorus, when building the Hanging Gardens of Babylon. Although many contemporary scholars doubt the gardens ever existed, Diodorus believed they were real. He noted that asphalt lined plant beds and the pipes that carried water to the beds. Overall, he described the gardens as a great theater, with galleries rising "one above the other" and supported by beams of stone and a "layer of reeds laid in great quantities of bitumen." The words "great quantities of bitumen" referred to a mastic composed of asphalt, sand, fillers, and fibrous material. Mastic compositions, however, were not standardized. They might also include loam, limestone, and quarry dust. Or they might not.[17]

Because burned bricks and asphalt were expensive, given fuel costs (the neo-Babylonian Empire was asphalt rich and fuel poor), many dwellings had walls made from sun-dried bricks laid in mud. Builders were most likely to use burned bricks and asphalt for palaces and temples. "I made a nabalu and laid its foundations against the bosom of the underworld, on the surface of the (ground) water in bitumen and brick," one of Nebuchadnezzar's many inscriptions reads. "I raised its summit and connected it with the palace, with brick and bitumen I made it high as a mountain."[18] For elite residencies, asphalt protected doors, floors, roofs, gutters, drains, grain bins, basins, and sewers. Asphalt also fortified a bridge across the Euphrates and the most important defensive walls. The Greek historian Xenophon (ca. 431–354 BCE) recalled passing one such wall and other constructions in Mesopotamia that were built of baked bricks laid in asphalt mortar.[19]

The Hanging Gardens of Babylon were one of the two constructions attributed to Nebuchadnezzar that counted among the Seven Wonders of the World. The king's dedication plaque for the other—the Babylon wall's Ishtar Gate—emphasized asphalt: "I pulled down these gates and laid their foundations at the water table with asphalt and bricks and had them made of bricks with blue stone on which wonderful bulls and dragons were depicted. . . . I let the temple of Esiskursiskur (the highest festival house of Marduk, the Lord of the Gods a place of joy and celebration for the major and minor gods) be built firm like a mountain . . . of asphalt and fired bricks."[20]

Nebuchadnezzar did not mention the slaves who built such monuments as a wall supposedly fifty-six miles long and wide enough atop for chariot races. He also failed to mention his demolition projects. (The Bible portrays him both as "the arch-villain who destroyed Jerusalem . . . and the repentant sinner.")[21] He had slaves build roads too, though he was certainly not the first to build roads. The first "roads" were animal trails that humans used as game paths. Formal road construction began thousands of years ago, as far apart as Ur, with its stone-paved roads in today's Iraq, and Glastonbury, with its timber roads in today's England. The Egyptians also built roads to help with pyramid construction. And they occasionally paved processional roads using limestone and marl gravel with alluvial clay as a binder. Around 2000 BCE, the Minoans on Crete used a clay-gypsum mortar as a binder. A hundred years before Nebuchadnezzar, an Assyrian king issued this decree: "Royal Road—let no man decrease it." This was an ancient example of a parking regulation, as it prohibited decreasing (that is, blocking) a road by whatever means (an abandoned chariot, for example). The Persians who toppled the neo-Babylonian Empire built a 1,500-mile track from the Persian Gulf nearly to the Mediterranean. Herodotus marveled at a three-month journey now cut to nine days: "Many are the men and horses that stand along the road . . . and these are stayed neither by snow nor rain nor heat nor darkness."[22]

Prior to the Roman invasions, Europe had a primitive road system, constructed piecemeal to facilitate trade. Logs provided most of the surfacing. The Romans, who borrowed engineering techniques from a dozen other cultures, were the ancient world's only great road builders. Their soldiers and slaves built fifty thousand miles of road in straight lines (sight point to sight point), including the Appian Way, with construction beginning in 312 BCE; and twenty-nine *viae militares* (military roads) radiating from the city.

Unlike the Romans who came later, Nebuchadnezzar used asphalt as a binder, and that use was a small step toward blacktop pavement. The tablet dedicating what Robert Koldewey would later excavate reveals the king's road-building pride: "The Procession Street of Nabu and Marduk my lords, which Nabopolassar, King of Babylon, the father who begot me, had made a road glistening with asphalt and burnt bricks; I, the wise suppliant who fears their lordships, placed above the bitumen and burnt bricks, a mighty superstructure of shining dust, made them strong within with bitumen and burnt bricks as a high-lying road."[23]

For Nebuchadnezzar, roads were strictly ceremonial, as the chemist and historian of science Robert J. Forbes noted. They supported the rituals of kings and priests by connecting temples and royal palaces. They did not support the main roads, which "remained in their primitive state, needing no paved surface, for they carried only pedestrians and beasts of burden, for which the pounded or rolled clay soil was quite sufficient."[24] Nonetheless, not only did Nebuchadnezzar and his asphalt-plastering slaves earn their ranking among history's greatest builders for the spectacle of the temples and palaces and the Ishtar Gate and Procession Street. They earned their ranking by building Babylon's functional gates, outer walls, moats, levies, canals, and sewers, constructions driven by a problem-solving impetus as much as a king's desire to honor himself and his gods. "From Tigris bank to Euphrates bank," Nebuchadnezzar's dedication of one hydraulic project reads, "I heaped up a mostly earth-wall and surrounded the city for 20 beru [nearly seventy miles, supposedly] like the fullness of the sea. That the pressure of the water should not harm the dyke, I plastered the slope with asphalt and bricks." "Bitumen scattered about," said the nineteenth-century digger who documented the king's Habl-es-Sakhar wall near Sippar on the east bank of the Euphrates. Archaeologists north of Sippar uncovered a levee once lined on both sides with bricks, each one bearing a "skin of bitumen" and a "stamp of Nebuchadnezzar."[25]

Over two centuries after Nebuchadnezzar's death and nearly immediately after Alexander the Great's death in 323 BCE, asphalt had sufficient heft as an imperial prize to ignite the Middle East's first fossil-fuel war. It was largely instigated by Antigonus the One-Eyed, one of Alexander's generals. During the Third War of the Diadochi (the Wars of Alexander's Successors), Antigonus hoped to conquer the Nabataean Arabs, who controlled the Dead Sea asphalt trade and much of the frankincense, myrrh, and balsam trades, thereby enriching his empire and damaging that of Ptolemy, ruler of Egypt and another of Alexander's former generals. The Nabataeans raised sheep and camels and controlled a string of oases and secret underground cisterns constructed with a type of concrete similar to stucco (and possibly further waterproofed with asphalt). That was their advantage in the desert. They knew where the water lay. Their culture provided another advantage. "It is their *nomos* to plant neither trees nor grain, nor to drink wine, nor to construct any house; and the penalty for infringement of this law is death," wrote the classicist Jane Hornblower. "They believe that those who live a settled life pay for the good things they possess by the sacrifice of their freedom to the powerful."[26]

The Nabataeans built caravan routes from Arabia to Palestine and extending west to Puteoli, an Italian port first colonized by the Greeks. Gradually, they moved away from raiding to charging tariffs and providing services—shelter, food, and water—for the region's traders and trade network. That network gave them a stranglehold on the Dead Sea's rough asphalt trade. Whenever the sea filled with bobbing asphalt, Nabataeans and their rivals had the same goal: sell their harvest on the Egyptian market. "Both sides," Diodorus wrote, worked "to carry it off like plunder of war. . . . When they have come near the asphalt they jump upon it with axes and . . . cut out pieces and load them on [their reed] rafts."[27]

Antigonus reasoned that Ptolemy's riches and support among the priesthood might erode without the Dead Sea asphalt the priests needed for mummification. So he invaded to control the asphalt trade (and desert trade generally from what is today Gaza to Sinai). But he miscalculated when sending over four thousand infantry and six hundred cavalry under Athenaeus to attack while Nabataean men of fighting age were away at their annual festival and market in the vicinity of Petra (or Selah) in the mountains of today's Jordan. According to Diodorus's history, Athenaeus seized the Nabataean rock fortress in the dead of night, murdering many old men, women, and children and seizing others as prisoners. He also took approximately seven hundred camels and all the silver, myrrh, and frankincense his men could find and haul. Athenaeus fled near dawn. But he made camp in late afternoon, and that was his mistake. Some eight thousand Nabataeans arrived in the dead of night and attacked their sleeping enemy, killing everyone save fifty or so cavalry who escaped.[28]

Demetrius the Besieger, the One Eyed King's son, launched a second invasion, sending four thousand infantry and four thousand cavalry against the Nabataean rock fortress. The steep slopes—and the fact that men of fighting age were not away this time—gave the Nabataeans an advantage that brought this would-be conqueror to grief. When the assaults failed, Demetrius made peace after hearing Nabataean terms (a gift of silver and other "presents," including an escort of old men as hostages to guarantee the safety of the retreat). On the way home Demetrius stopped at the Dead Sea for a hollow pronouncement about the asphalt that lay at the root of things. He proclaimed himself "lord of all the oil fisheries."[29]

Antigonus would not give up just yet. He criticized his son on the one hand, saying the treaty terms had merely emboldened the Nabataeans (whom he dismissed as barbarians). On the other hand, he praised his son for surveying the Dead Sea and its prize. So Antigonus ordered a third invasion with a specific order to his generals to "collect all the asphalt." Neither the invasion nor that asphalt task ended well. On the Dead Sea six thousand Nabataeans sailed up on their reed rafts and killed nearly all of the alien asphalt harvesters with their arrows.[30] Three strikes were enough. Antigonus finally gave up, leaving the Nabataeans in command of the asphalt trade. But other challengers emerged, beginning with Egypt's pharaohs deciding to bypass these "barbarian traders." The Nabataeans managed to retain a degree of autonomy because their struggle, and for that matter the failed plotting of Antigonus, lay within the larger conflict between Egypt's Ptolemies and Syria's Seleucids. Seleucus, yet another of Alexander's generals, defeated Antigonus at the Battle of Ipsus in 301 BCE.[31]

The Nabataeans would not survive the Romans once that empire's epic civil wars ensnared them. This pushed all the way down to the Antony and Cleopatra drama after he awarded her control of the asphalt trade—the Dead Sea "oil fisheries"—and a strip of Nabataean territory along the Red Sea. Cleopatra leased the asphalt rights back to the Nabataean king, Malchus I, and succeeded, at least temporarily, where Antigonus had failed. The Nabataeans and their king, however, would never forget that she had ended their asphalt monopoly. Herod the Great served as her "rent collector" (the guarantor) until the day that Malchus stopped lease payments. With Antony's backing, Cleopatra coerced Herod into the difficult task of subduing the Nabataeans and their deadbeat king. Though Cleopatra had Herod invade to bring the Nabataeans to heel, she prevented him from crushing Malchus as part of a larger game. "She had laid a plot against the kings [of Judaea and Arabia]," wrote the Jewish historian Flavius Josephus (37–100 CE). "She prevailed with Antonius [Antony] to commit the war against the Arabians to Herodes [Herod]; that so, if he got the better, she might become mistress of Arabia, or, if he were worsted, of Judaea; and that she might destroy one of those kings by the other." Antigonus instigated the Middle East's first fossil-fuel war. Cleopatra instigated the second.[32]

When the Nile queen's world collapsed, she used some of the asphalt fees extracted from the Nabataeans to finance what she hoped would be a great escape to India or other points east. She had the larger portion of her fleet, with their hulls perhaps coated with asphalt, hauled across the desert sand to the Red Sea. The ships might have taken queen, lover, riches, and slaves to a new life. But the Nabataeans burned every one of her ships as they arrived. Malchus had his revenge. Now trapped in Egypt, Cleopatra could do little more than ponder how best to kill herself. Had asphalt played no role in the Roman civil wars (and what Josephus called the *War of the Jews*), Cleopatra might have died an old woman in India. We might have no Shakespeare lines of an asp on a breast: "With thy sharp teeth this knot intrinsicate / Of life at once untie: poor venomous fool / Be angry, and dispatch."[33]

After Octavian defeated Antony in 31 BCE at the Battle of Actium (and first Antony and then Cleopatra committed suicide), the Romans largely left the Nabataeans to their own affairs. With Egypt (slowly) ending mummification, the asphalt trade collapsed. The Romans used asphalt for various things, but not in large quantities. Modest households coated goods with asphalt to ward off decay. For wealthier Romans, one scholar wrote, "even on the toilet tables of the Roman ladies it was always to be met with, and it was used by them to colour and to beautify their eyebrows." Overall, the Romans were more likely to note use of asphalt by others than to use it themselves. Trajan (ruled 98–117 CE), for one, admired neo-Babylonian brickwork still solid after half a millennium. "[He] saw the asphalt with which the walls of Babylon had been built," noted the Greco-Roman historian Cassius Dio (185–235 CE), and concluded that it made the bricks "stronger than rock and any kind of iron."[34]

With no major markets for their Dead Sea asphalt, the Nabataeans became more settled and less likely to seek vengeance. They were no longer nomads but a mix of village dwellers and—because of their hydraulic-engineering skills—farmers. While Nabataean culture flourished for a time (however much it had changed), the Romans gradually imposed a more comprehensive rule on Arabia from the Red Sea to the Dead Sea and beyond. Under Trajan the empire finished the process of annexing what remained of a once-glorious Nabataean trade network. With their kingdom gone forever and now merely Arabia Petraea, the Nabataeans abandoned their beast-in-the-field ways and their asphalt hacking on the Dead Sea. They accepted the Pax Romana. And a pernicious stereotype sunk roots. "The Arabians," as the Greek geographer Strabo (63 BCE–23 CE) called them, "are not very good warriors on land, rather being hucksters and merchants."[35]

By the time Strabo wrote those words, the asphalt trade had declined nearly in its entirety . . . though it did find niches here and there, including one in the wine trade. Strabo described an asphalt mine on Crete and a concoction of asphalt and olive oil used to kill grapevine-eating insects "before they can mount the sprouts of the roots." The Greeks learned what the Egyptians knew. Asphalt could kill "things that creep."[36]

However unfamiliar the details of the asphalt story in the ancient world, the overarching outline of its rise and fall is quite familiar. Asphalt as a commodity rose and fell just as the Nabataeans rose and fell, let alone the empires of Sumerians, Akkadians, Assyrians, Baby-lonians, Persians, Greeks, Egyptians, and Romans. All had differences. Asphalt was among the things they had in common. They all found uses for it—especially hydraulic, funerary, and adhesive. Nebuchad-nezzar's use of asphalt for his ceremonial and practical constructions foreshadowed asphalt's rise as a major construction material. The wait, however, would be a long one. A millennium after the king's death, Late Antiquity gave way to the Middle Ages, often called the Dark Ages, and for asphalt they were certainly dark. Another millennium down, the Middle Ages gave way to the Modern Age. But we would be half a millennium into the Modern Age and another half a cen-tury after Robert Koldewey uncovered Babylon's Procession Street before the words *pavement* and *asphalt* became synonyms, accord-ing to nearly every English-language thesaurus. In all, it would be 2,600 years after Nebuchadnezzar boasted of his roads glistening with asphalt and burned bricks.

3 Faith

Asphalt's Dark Ages

Exodus, the second book of the Bible, has Jochebed using asphalt to save Moses after Pharaoh ordered the murder of "every Hebrew boy that is born": "When she could no longer hide him, she took a papyrus basket, daubed it with bitumen and pitch, and putting the child in it, placed it among the reeds on the bank of the Nile." Genesis, the Bible's first book, has a larger vessel in need of waterproofing. God commanded Noah to build a wooden ark coated "with pitch inside and out." The *Epic of Gilgamesh*, an earlier flood story with vessel waterproofing lines, has Utnapishtim responding to God's command ("build a boat") and chronicling his labors on all fronts, including the melting of asphalt: "Three times 3,600 (units) of raw bitumen I poured into the / bitumen kiln."[1]

Babylonian epics aside, the belief that Bible stories are literally true has led to such asphalt-centric debates as this: Did Noah waterproof the ark with asphalt or wood pitch? Creationists side with wood pitch, arguing that fossil fuels did not develop from decaying organisms over millions of years. Rather, pressure from the flood's mass die-off of organic matter created fossil fuels over a few thousand years. Noah used wood pitch because there was no asphalt until the flood's aftermath created it in short order. In 2007 the organization Answers in Genesis sided with wood pitch when opening a Creation Museum in Boone County, Kentucky, complete with an animatronic Noah.[2] Nine years later this apologetics ministry opened an Ark Encounter theme park in nearby Grant County, with the state contributing $3.5 million to upgrade Kentucky Route 36 blacktop from I-75 to the park's blacktop parking lot. The park's ark, which includes dinosaur quarters, boasts Genesis specs (though starboard consists of masonry towers for modern conveniences): 51 feet high, 85 feet wide, and 510 feet long. That makes it 1,000 feet less in length than the biggest oil tanker ever built, but only 90 feet less than the big asphalt tankers.

Assuming both the Bible's literal truth and that the argument is worth having in the first place: to coat the ark's 1.54 million cubic feet with wood pitch, Noah would have to tap an enormous number of trees and slowly drain resin. Ancient builders certainly waterproofed boats with wood pitch. But they just as certainly waterproofed boats with asphalt in the regions where trees were scarce and asphalt was so plentiful that they could scoop it by the bucket (as opposed to the drop-in-the-bucket patience wood pitch required).[3] Besides, as one old-earther noted, "The Hebrew word for the waterproofing material is kopher. Bible translations, commentaries, dictionaries, and lexicons all consistently define kopher as some type of bitumen . . . the Latin Vulgate uses the word bitumine, the Greek Septuagint uses asphal-tos . . . and the New Living Translation uses the word tar."[4] The point is not to question anyone's faith. The point is that humanity has been in conflict about asphalt since we came up off our knuckles—or since "God formed man of the dust of the ground."[5]

Asphalt's dark ages began with the decline of Egyptian mummifica-tion. They lasted through 1859, the year Darwin published *On the Origin of Species*. What the Nabataeans and their enemies fought and died over on land and Dead Sea had collapsed in value and esteem, resting at the interface of utilitarian and symbolic values. While its material worth contracted, its symbolic value expanded, by building on a polytheistic foundation constructed in the ancient world. For the Egyptians and their decision to include asphalt in funerary practices, asphalt's color might have been as important as its preservative virtues. "Black was associated with the colour of the rich, fertile silt deposited by the annual Nile flood, a symbol of regeneration, rebirth and res-urrection, and a colour, together with green, attached to Osiris, god of the dead, lord of the afterlife, and master of resurrection," recent researchers reasoned. "By darkening the deceased's body during the final phases of mummification so that it became black, he or she was literally transformed into Osiris, living eternally." Asphalt, in other words, "democratized death."[6]

The Sumerians, in contrast, considered asphalt both a symbol and form of underworld evil. So did the Assyrians, who associated asphalt with arbitrary and hateful gods. King Tukulti-Ninurta II (reigned 890–884 BCE) described the Hit Tar Pits as if it were a motel with deities on the cable TV: "By the bitumen spring, the place of the Usmeta stones, in which the gods speak, I spent the night." "The noises, caused by the passage of gases through fissures in the earth's surface, were associated with the voices of the gods in the underworld," explained science historian Robert J. Forbes. "It is only natural that bitumen, oozing with water and gas from the seepages, should have been thought of as a typical product of the underworld . . . [a] symbol of the powerful evil spirits when it came, rising to harm mankind."[7] Though the neo-Babylonian empire shared many of the same gods as the Assyrians, they were more likely, like the Egyptians, to see asphalt as a force for good. "Mystical characters," Forbes continued, "were painted in gypsum and bitumen on the doorpost of a sick person's room. Bitumen was supposed to afford protection from the terrible female demon Labartu, who was believed to drink the blood of children and animals." Neo-Babylonians also believed that an enemy could be bewitched by "the burning of a bitumen image of the person" while reciting incantations, and that armor could be strengthened by soaking it in a mix of asphalt and the blood of a child.[8]

Pliny the Elder (23–79 CE) believed Dead Sea asphalt had magical and medicinal properties. He used menstrual blood rather than a child's blood to make the point. Though certainly aware that menstruation was necessary for life, he despaired that "this maladie, so venomous and hurtfull as it is, followeth a woman still every thirtie daies" with such "monstrous" effect that it could "wither any standing corne in the field," sour any "vessel of wine," or "runne made" any dog. Menstrual blood's one virtue, Pliny believed, lay in its magical power over asphalt: "Nay the very clammie slime Bitumen . . . cannot be parted and divided asunder, (for by reason of the viscositie, it cleaveth and sticketh like glew, and hangeth all together, plucke as a man will at it) but onely by a thred that is stained with this venomous bloud."[9]

Judaism and Christianity emphasized asphalt's duality, with the Old Testament mentioning Dead Sea asphalt as a symbol of both wealth and damnation. If the third Abrahamic religion had little to say about asphalt there is anecdotal evidence that Islam recognized no duality. "The Moors," as a seventeenth-century English traveler visiting the Hit Tar Pits said, "call it 'the Mouth of Hell.'"[10] Asphalt was not much of an Islamic symbol. And it certainly was not a major Christian symbol (like the cross) or Jewish symbol (like the Star of David). But asphalt did continue, during its dark ages, as a symbol of devils and other dark creatures, a symbol of damnation and hell itself.[11]

Biblical references to asphalt, beyond the ones to Noah's ark and Moses's basket, mix practical application with myth and magic. Whether it tumbled or not, asphalt likely fortified the Wall of Jericho referred to in Joshua. "The vale of Siddim" in Genesis, the valley where the kings of Sodom and Gomorrah fled and fell, was "full of slime pits" (a near-certain reference to asphalt). A Tower of Babel line in Genesis reads as if written by Herodotus: "And they had brick for stone, and slime had they for morter."[12] Jubilees, which is considered part of the canon in the Roman Catholic and Greek Orthodox churches but not in the Protestant churches, has a similar Babel line about bricks: "And the clay with which they cemented them together was asphalt which comes out of the [Dead] sea, and out of the fountains of water in the land of Shinar." The Testament of Solomon, which is not part of the Jewish or Christian canon, describes how the king built the First Temple of Jerusalem with the help of Archangel Michael, who gave him a precious ring that allowed him to imprison the demon Kunopegos in a vessel sealed with asphalt.[13]

The Bible and other canonical writings have additional references that might or might not refer to asphalt. Herbert Hoover, among others, had his doubts. Hoover and his wife, Lou Henry, had studied geology at Stanford University, an academic path that led them to tackle a translation of Renaissance scholar Georgius Agricola's *De re metallica* (1556). An explanatory footnote includes this caution: "Attempts to connect Biblical references to petroleum and bitumen . . . require an unnecessary strain on the imagination."[14]

Nonetheless, those references, along with the ancient world's polytheistic and magical ones, inspired literary giants and their imaginings of hell and various defilements. Dante (1265–1321) mentioned "pitch" in his *Inferno* (ca. 1314), the first of three cantica that make up the *Divine Comedy*. He meant wood pitch at times. But he almost certainly meant asphalt with canto 21's portrayal of hell with winged demons policing the damned trapped in a tar pit: "They stretched their hooks towards the pitch-ensnared, / Who were already baked within the crust . . . / boiling down below there a dense pitch / Which upon every side the bank belimed. / I saw it, but I did not see within it / Aught but the bubbles that the boiling raised." Canto 22 has demons falling prey themselves: "He turned his talons upon his companion . . . and both of them / Fell in the middle of the boiling pond." Obviously, "wood pitch pits" do not exist in nature. Asphalt pits (again, commonly referred to as tar pits) do exist in nature, and methane gas escaping from those pits forms bubbles on the surface that make the asphalt appear to boil. Dante imagined damned souls and demons, rather than flora and fauna fossils, hidden forever below the crust.

Milton (1608–74), in *Paradise Lost*'s book 11, used the word "pitch" in reference to Noah: "Then from the Mountain hewing Timber tall, / Began to build a Vessel of huge bulk, / . . . Smeard round with Pitch." He might have meant wood pitch. More likely, he meant asphalt. He certainly meant asphalt when writing these book 1 lines about the Dead Sea and Canaan: "And Eleale to th' Asphaltick Pool . . . when he entic'd / Israel in Sittim on thir march from Nile." In another book 1 reference, Milton uses the word "asphaltic" to characterize hell: "Now they lye / Groveling and prostrate on yon Lake of Fire." Later in book 1 Milton begins with an image of hell ("veins of liquid fire / Sluc'd from the Lake") and ends with the abrupt duality of "level pavement" and the "suttle Magic . . . Of Starry Lamps and blazing Cressets fed / With

Naphtha and Asphaltus." From those contradictory images (asphalt feeding both hellfire and starry lamps), Milton returns in books 10 and 12 to asphalt and damnation. He has Satan and his fallen crew fleeing Eden across "The Plain, wherein a black bituminous gurge / Boiles out from under ground, the mouth of Hell." Closer, they see no subtle magic of starry lamps but the blazing fate that awaits beyond the gate, beyond the "foaming deep high Archt" of a bridge: "Asphaltic slime" running "Smooth, easie, inoffensive down to Hell."[15]

For Dante and Milton asphalt had little utilitarian purpose beyond that of a material that could help torture the damned and construct hell's gate, bridge, and road. For others asphalt rested at the interface of utilitarian and symbolic values in an entirely different way that nonetheless rivaled any of the ancient world's myths and superstitions. A thirteenth-century Holy Land pilgrim echoed Pliny on asphalt's supposed magic: "Bitumen. . . . can only be dissolved with menstrual blood, and is called Jew's glue." Unfortunately, that reference was apt. Asphalt as a commodity would remain entwined with antisemitism for hundreds of years. Voltaire, in his *Philosophical Dictionary* (1764) entry for "Asphaltus," commented on contemporary economic use ("sold for balm of Mecca") before returning to the Bible's "ridiculous fables" that might contain at most a grain of truth. "It would, however, be very natural for some Jews to amuse themselves," he wrote of Sodom and those pillars of salt, "with cutting a heap of asphaltus into a rude figure, and calling it Lot's wife." Asphalt's antisemitic taint came courtesy of a black market in black mummies that rose up in the Middle Ages and continued into the Enlightenment. Much of the Christian world assumed Jews controlled the trade—"Bitumen Judaicum"—with Europeans seeking good health through asphalt, alchemy, and a pinch of cannibalism.[16]

The Arabic word *mūmiyah* may have originally translated as a type of black rock asphalt. This new product translated in German as "'pharmacopoeia of filth' (*Dreckapotheke*)." The trade took Egyptian mummies, including those preserved in asphalt, and ground them into powder and peddled the powder as just another common drug. Even Francis Bacon and Robert Boyle, two late Renaissance–early Enlightenment pioneers of the experimental scientific method, thought ground mummy—or mummy tincture, elixir, treacle, and balsam—had medicinal value. But not everyone bought in. "This wicked kinde of drugge," one critic wrote, "doth nothing helpe the diseased," producing only "stomacke." Thomas Browne, the English physician and polymath, mocked the practice as "dismal vampirism. . . . Mummy is become merchandise, Mizraim cures wounds, and Pharaoh is sold for balsams." In 1671 Browne's contempt did not stop him from kneeling for his knighthood before an abider. When ill, Charles II ordered "The King's Drops," a libation of crushed mummy skull in alcohol.[17]

The mummy craze went on and on. In 1203, nearly half a millennium before Browne took his knighthood, Abdel Latif, a Baghdad physician practicing in Cairo, said the market was as saturated with mummies as asphalt supposedly saturated those mummies: "It is sold for a trifle. For half a dirhem I purchased three heads filled with the substance." Two centuries later, in 1424 a traveler noted fruitless efforts to suppress the trade: "People who had made large piles of corpses were discovered in Cairo. They were brought before the provost, who had them tortured until they confessed that they were removing the corpses from tombs and were boiling the dead bodies in water over a very hot fire until the flesh fell off; that they then collected the oil which rose to the surface of the liquid to sell it to the Franks [Europeans]." In 1586 Turkey Company agent John Sanderson descended into a mummy hole filled with "bodies of all sorts and sizes . . . and some [fetuses] embalmed in little earthen Pots, which never had forme." Having broken off "all the parts of the bodies to see how the flesh was turned to drugge . . . onely altered blacke," Sanderson then "bribed his way out of Egypt" with six hundred pounds of contraband, including "one little hand," which he gave to his brother. Three centuries later *Madame Bovary* (1857) author Gustave Flaubert crawled into another mummy hole, where "everything oozes bitumen." He "broke up some of the mummies, seeking scarabs in their bitumen-filled bellies." Sanderson gave away his souvenir. Flaubert kept his in his study: a little foot "shined up with shoe polish."[18]

Demand for medicinal mummy had largely collapsed when Flaubert had his mummy-hole adventure. At its peak demand created "medical corpse" and "counterfeit mummy" markets. In 1564 Guy de la Fontaine, a physician to the kingdom of Navarre in the north of Spain, helped expose those abuses—with Jews continuing to receive the blame because many Christians continued to assume that Jews dominated the black mummy trade along with all other aspects of the asphalt trade. Whatever the intent, antisemitic implications followed a question posed to Fontaine by a mummy broker in Alexandria, Egypt's second-largest city. Who would believe "that the Christians, so daintily mouthed, could eat the bodies of the dead"? The antisemitism was palatable. Its spread had more to do with the Black Death than black mummies, and Jews in the Spanish kingdoms had long suffered pogroms (notably, the Massacre of 1391). The enduring antisemitism, moreover, was not confined to the European continent and the Middle East. In 1858 a *Harper's* magazine editor in New York called that Alexandria mummy broker "one candid Hebrew" while commenting on the trade: "The Jews . . . lived magnificently on the dried bones of Egypt. The supply failing to satisfy the demand, they bought up in secret corpses which had died of leprosy, small-pox, or the plague, executed criminals, etc., filled the heads and trunks with asphaltum . . . [and] made incisions into the muscular parts of the limbs, and filled those also with asphaltum." A pauper's body cut from the gallows might fetch the lowest price. Genuine Egyptian mummies with hard asphalt coats were expensive, though not as expensive as embalmed virgins—what the trade called, after processing, *fille vierge, reduire en poudre* (ground virgin girl).[19]

Other than its role in the mummy craze and literary and biblical imagery, medieval and early modern Europe had little use for asphalt and little knowledge of its historical uses. Agricola gave an asphalt-processing method a few lines that ended with this: "The mixtures containing bitumen are also [boiled] . . . in pots having a hole in the bottom, and it is rare that such bitumen is not highly esteemed."[20] When Sir Walter Raleigh (1552–1618) arrived in Trinidad in 1595, he found no El Dorado gold but did claim "discovery" of Pitch Lake asphalt.[21] "There is that abundance of stone pitch that all the ships of the world may be therewith laden from thence," he wrote a year later. "And we made trial of it in trimming our ships to be most excellent good, and melteth not with the sun as the [wood] pitch of Norway." Raleigh returned in 1617 and took back asphalt samples to England. Atop a sad end (James I had him beheaded), Raleigh's claim to have discovered asphalt for the Crown has not held. The assumption that the black organic material found at a seventh-century ship burial at Sutton Hoo was pine tar turned out to be incorrect. The material is actually geochemically similar to Dead Sea asphalt.[22]

That Sutton Hoo ship seems to have been an aberration. European shipbuilders continued to use wood pitch in almost every case for waterproofing, largely ignoring Raleigh and such others as Denis Diderot, whose "Pentateuch" entry in the *Encyclopédie* mentions Noah's Ark and the "bitumen of Babylon." Asphalt made no serious inroads into the English caulking industry until the seventeenth century's end, when an enterprise called Eele, Portlock, and Hancock received a patent to produce pitch, tar, and oil "out of a sort of stone." The owners built a factory at Pitchford-on-Severn, Shropshire, to extract asphalt from sandstone.[23] Nearly a century later, in 1787, canal diggers in England's Ironbridge Gorge discovered a natural asphalt bonanza. However, nearly another century passed before production at this so-called Tar Tunnel of Coalport began in earnest, peaking at 4,500 gallons a week, mined at a depth of 360 feet.

In 1798, during the United Irishmen Rebellion, a North Cork militiaman known as "Tom the Devil" found a use for asphalt dating to the Assyrian habit of pouring molten asphalt onto the heads of those who broke their moral code. This torturer "pitch capped" Irish rebels—especially Catholic priests—by shearing off hair (and often an ear) and then pouring hot pitch or asphalt, or both, into a jerry-rigged cap. He put the cap on a head, allowed it to harden, and then ripped it off. Or he added gunpowder and set the pitch cap on fire. Those few who survived were scalped and blinded. "Universal rape and robbery" and "every kind of atrocity," wrote Lord Cornwallis, who had surrendered to George Washington at Yorktown and was now viceroy of Ireland: "The yeomanry are in the style of the loyalists in America, only much more numerous and powerful, and a thousand times more ferocious."[24]

European empire found use for asphalt in the Americas as well. The Spanish and their Franciscan priests established twenty-one missions in California from Mission San Diego de Alcalá, founded in 1760, to Mission San Francisco Solano, founded in 1823. They used asphalt from the black and bulging Carpinteria Tar Pits and other tar pits to waterproof several of the roofs of their adobe structures. To connect the missions, the Spanish built El Camino Real (the Royal Road), which began as a simple trail but now lays claim as the oldest road in the United States. Nebuchadnezzar had used asphalt's hydraulic properties for roads as well as roofs. Now, finally, that neo-Babylonian practice was creeping back into the imaginations of builders and the first of those we would eventually call highway engineers. By the time the Spanish built their last mission in California, the idea that asphalt might help conquer dust and mud had begun pulling asphalt out of its dark ages and into the dawn of the pavement age. Though asphalt would remain at the interface of utilitarian and symbolic values, hereafter the symbolism would not evolve from the ancient world's polytheism and magic; nor would it evolve from a close reading of the Bible or the myths that gave rise to antisemitism and medicinal mummy. The new symbolism would arise from our embrace of the secular culture that lay on the horizon, a culture of the automobile, gasoline, and the paved road.

Part 2 COMING TO AMERICA

4 Triumph

The Blacktop Dawn

The run up to the asphalt story of the Gilded Age industrialist and engineer George Pullman began late in his life. It began when the Panic of 1893 sent his Palace Car Company reeling. Pullman responded to this economic crisis by slashing wages but not rents in his company town of Pullman, Illinois. When he fired the delegation of workers who complained, their co-workers went on strike. The dispute grew into a national railroad strike after American Railway Union workers began unhooking Pullman cars in support of the Palace Car Company strikers. Deeming the injunction secured against the union's founder, Eugene V. Debs, insufficient, the Grover Cleveland administration sent in marshals and troops to crush the strike in the name of protecting the mail (which often traveled by train). Over thirty strikers died. After Pullman died of natural causes in 1897, his family worried that bitter Palace Car Company employees or retirees might steal the corpse and demand ransom.

These fears struck close. In 1876 grave robbers tried to steal Abraham Lincoln's body, and Lincoln's son, Robert Todd Lincoln, had served as Pullman Company counsel during the strike and succeeded Pullman as company president. Pullman had endeared himself to the Lincolns after the assassination when an exhausted Mary Todd Lincoln left her Pullman car in the funeral train and returned to the family home in Springfield aboard another Pullman car. Having escaped the draft for "Mr. Lincoln's war" by hiring a replacement, Pullman went on to hire former house slaves as porters, always searching for "the blackest man with the whitest teeth" who wanted to move up from "tamping asphalt or cleaning spittoons." Each one was a "George," as palace-car passengers used the tycoon's first name when calling for, say, a doily.[1]

George Pullman's lead-lined mahogany coffin went into a pit at Chicago's Graceland Cemetery that nonunion labor reinforced with timbers and concrete slabs up to eighteen inches thick. Another course of concrete went on top of the coffin, then eight railroad track rails bolted together to create a steel cage, and finally another course of concrete. To this day Pullman's remains remain safe even from all that concrete. Before workers fixed the last courses, they draped the coffin with tar paper and coated it with asphalt an inch thick.

The year of George Pullman's death was early in the era of asphalt's transition from its primary historical purpose as a general water-proofing and binding material to the more focused waterproofing and binding purpose of making road surfaces relatively impermeable. Asphalt conquered dust and mud by first conquering water. Asphalt pavement did not need to be perfectly impermeable, just impermeable enough. A perfectly waterproof surface of mastic asphalt would be too slippery for horses, not to mention the motor vehicles that were arriving just as Pullman was leaving.

Graded roads preceded paved roads. The Inca had their unpaved road network and the Chinese had their Silk Road trade routes. Roads in Europe, however, declined when Rome fell. In 1607 an Englishman, Thomas Procter, wrote one of the first important books on roads: *A Profitable Work to This Whole Kingdom concerning the Mending of Highways*. The French took the lead later in the seventeenth century with the military engineer Sébastien Le Prestre de Vauban (1633–1707) organizing a Corps of Bridges and Roads. In 1747 a National School of Bridges and Roads opened in Paris. In the 1770s Pierre-Marie-Jérôme Trésaguet (1716–96) used a base layer of larger stones and a second layer of smaller stones that compressed under traffic load into a relatively resistant surface. His system influenced a Scot, Thomas Telford (1757–1834), who rose from stone-mason apprentice to president of the United Kingdom's Institution of Civil Engineers.

Both men influenced another Scot, John Loudon McAdam (1756–1836), whose opus, *Remarks on the Present System of Road Making* (1823), explained his basic observations: "It is the native soil which really supports the weight of traffic; and that while it is preserved in a dry state, it will carry any weight without sinking. . . . Poor roads stem from the use of rounded stones lacking angular points of contact by which broken stones unite."[2] McAdam prescribed small stones, perhaps his key innovation, no more than six ounces in weight and no more than two inches across. Eli Whitney Black, nephew of the cotton-gin inventor, helped the broken-stone cause in 1832 with his invention of a steam-driven mechanical stone crusher.

No matter the angles of McAdam's broken stones, voids remained, and the binder—stone dust and dirt—used to fill the voids proved only minimally effective (though effective enough that the road-building community continues to use McAdam's name in the centuries after his death as both adjective and noun). If macadam roads stood up remarkably well to horse and wagon traffic compared to previous road innovations, sooner or later water would penetrate. A coal-tar coating helped. But coal tar was smelly, easily rutted, and widely available only if there were municipal gas works nearby. Pre-blacktop road builders, of course, did not rely solely on McAdam's innovations. Cobblestones, granite setts, and fired bricks were more impervious than macadam surfaces, but they amplified the clap of horse hooves and were slippery when wet. Wood blocks were quieter but slipperier and less durable even if coated with creosote. Roads built to McAdam's specifications simply had fewer disadvantages than other surfaces.[3]

In a rough parallel with McAdam's work, the French began mining rock asphalt at Seyssel in the Rhone Valley and at nearby Val-de-Travers, Switzerland. Rudimentary paving of sidewalks, bridge decks, and floors of commercial buildings may have begun as early as 1802. Real progress came in the 1850s, when Léon Malo developed an efficient system for brushing or rolling powdered Seyssel asphalt on a macadamized road or a concrete foundation. Civil engineers invented a new term, *sheet asphalt*, to characterize Malo's method of using three-ton rollers to compress asphalt after workers sprinkled it from handheld cans or tanks. Obviously, this method had limitations. Even sprinkling via a pressured steel tank would only coat the surface stone, producing a binder that could not keep water out for long. Limitations aside, asphalt was now unleashed. Under the direction of Georges-Eugène Haussmann, prefect of the Seine department of France, street crews began removing paving stones and replacing them with crushed stone and sheet asphalt. The quest for a better surface, however, was only one motivator. The French Revolution of 1848 was another. "This ingenious Napoleon," Mark Twain said of Haussmann, "paves the streets of his great cities with . . . asphaltum and sand. No more barricades of flagstones—no more assaulting his Majesty's troops with cobbles."[4]

In the Western Hemisphere, Pitch Lake asphalt—the first of two lake asphalt empires—was emerging as a major resource in the British colony of Trinidad. (The other asphalt empire, Lake Bermudez, was eighty miles away, in Venezuela.) Pitch Lake's story began early in the nineteenth century, with British Royal Navy officer (later Adm.) Thomas Cochrane (1775–1860), a veteran of the Napoleonic Wars (Napoleon himself called him "the Sea Wolf"). Eight years after securing election to the House of Commons, Cochrane was among those caught up in the London Stock Exchange fraud of 1814. The Crown expelled him from Parliament and the Royal Navy and briefly imprisoned him. Cochrane's constituents sent him back to Commons, where he served until 1818, when he became, at his father's death, the Tenth Earl of Dundonald, in the peerage of Scotland. No longer eligible to sit in Commons, he fought as a privateer in various colonial wars of independence in the Western Hemisphere, received a pardon from the Crown, and rejoined the Royal Navy, where his adventures brought asphalt to his attention. In 1847 or thereabouts Trinidad's governor, seeing little value in the black goo, granted him a lease in perpetuity for Pitch Lake asphalt.[5]

Lord Cochrane secured numerous patents for asphalt mixtures that might power steamships or solve hydraulic-engineering problems. He had some success with the latter, none with the former. Cochrane also befriended fellow inventor Abraham Gesner, the Canadian physician who invented kerosene by distilling it from albertite, the asphaltite found in New Brunswick's Albert County mines. In 1853 Gesner moved to New York City and formed the Asphalt Mining and Kerosene Gas Company.[6] Cochrane failed to match his friend's success and there is no record of any serious attempt on his part to use asphalt to pave roads. Regardless, he noted what nature had placed under his carriage wheels on the road to Pitch Lake: a hardened stream of asphalt.[7]

In 1864, four years after the master and commander's death, one of Cochrane's sons negotiated production and distribution agreements with British investors. Within a year Trinidad was exporting five thousand tons of asphalt annually, almost all of it to France, Belgium, and the United Kingdom. But the trade produced almost no profit for the Cochrane family. According to the company's official history, "There was considerable litigation between lease-holders on the Lake and those digging the so-called 'land asphalt' on the margins of the Lake and in the La Brea region." The U.S. consul said the Cochranes lost their Pitch Lake lease by failing, as required, to ship a bit of asphalt to London each year for research. They retained rights to a few less valuable land asphalt pits that they described as "Asphaltic Sandstone and Shaly Sand with Asphaltic Oil oozing out."[8]

"Pitch farmers," who held lake-asphalt leaseholds, did most of the chopping and hauling for the new British investors, leaving scars on the lake surface that would congeal overnight. The farmers and their helpers carried asphalt chunks on their heads and dumped them into the holds of ships for transport abroad. Because the chunks would soon congeal into a solid mass, others repeated the hacking and hauling upon arrival in European ports and the occasional U.S. port.

The use of asphalt for pavement duty remained little more than a curiosity in the United States. Cornelius Vanderbilt may have been the first U.S. American to build an asphalt road, broadly defined. Before selling his interest in the Accessory Transit Company in 1853, the commodore made millions off the forty-niner gold rush by carrying passengers by boat from New York to Central America, by carriage across Nicaragua, and then by boat again to California. For a few miles of the overland stretch in Nicaragua, the mules pulling carriages enjoyed a thin asphalt surface.[9] Asphalt remained a novelty in 1870, when Edward J. de Smedt, a Belgian immigrant, supervised the paving of William Street in Newark. The United States had less sheet asphalt at that time than France or England and scarcely more than Russia, which had little beyond the terrace of the Romanovs' Winter Palace in Saint Petersburg. Sheet asphalt broke through in the United States in 1876 with the decision to pave Pennsylvania Avenue in Washington DC (after the city's Board of Health recommended replacement of the rotting woodblock pavement). Three days before Christmas, Congress approved President Ulysses S. Grant's request to fund fifty-four thousand square yards of sheet asphalt, with the project managed by the Army Corps of Engineers. In the spring workers wielding brooms and other hand tools spread Trinidad lake asphalt on one section of Pennsylvania Avenue and Val-de-Travers rock asphalt on another section.[10]

Asphalt's gradual spread in the United States led to a modest asphalt rush in California, Utah, and a handful of other states. Santa Barbara County hosted the Alcatraz Asphalt Company's mines at the Carpinteria Tar Pits. Tunnels ranged up to 550 feet deep. In the 1890s production peaked at sixty tons of asphalt per day, with no concerns for the environment. The company dumped mine tailings in a lagoon. Although mine-tunnel depths were more modest at the McKittrick Tar Pits in another California county (Kern), environmental negligence was nearly identical until 1896, when mining gave way to oil drilling in the Midway-Sunset field. Farther east in Utah, Uinta Basin rocks yielded an asphaltite named after Samuel H. Gilson, a former Pony Express rider and deputy U.S. marshal. (From the latter post, he presided over the firing-squad execution of John Doyle Lee in 1877 for his role in the long-ago Mountain Meadows massacre of 1857, where Mormon militia and Paiute allies murdered approximately 120 Arkansas emigrants on their way to California.) Gilson and his crews hacked with pickaxes and drove ox carts filled with their black gold across the Uintah and Ouray Reservation. In 1888 the U.S. Congress obliged Gilson by removing seven thousand acres of reservation land containing Gilsonite claims. The Utes received about twenty dollars per acre. Meanwhile, Anheuser-Busch saw a use for the product beyond coating pilings and varnishing buggies: lining their vats and barrels. The beer barons bought out Gilson in 1889.[11]

Neither the United States' asphalt and asphaltites nor Europe's rock asphalt from Val-de-Travers and Seyssel could compete with lake asphalt from Trinidad for the road-paving duty that lay on the horizon. The British investors who moved out the Cochrane family moved on to an alliance with Amzi Lorenzo Barber, a U.S. American seeking product for his sheet-asphalt–paving enterprise. Shortly after the British declared Trinidad and Tobago a single colony in 1888, Barber received exclusive rights to Pitch Lake asphalt for twenty-one years in return for a $48,000 annual payment. He would turn that modest investment into an empire.

Born in Vermont in 1843, Amzi Barber grew up in Ohio as the son of an abolitionist. He briefly took up the antislavery cause but, like George Pullman, did not serve in Lincoln's army. Instead, he studied at Oberlin and in 1867 moved to Washington DC, having accepted the invitation of Gen. Oliver Otis Howard, the head of the Freedmen's Bureau, to teach at Howard University. In 1873 Barber earned a law degree and entered the coal and real-estate businesses.[12] After buying forty acres from Howard University for $50,000, Barber and his brother-in-law built the segregated residential community of LeDroit Park (named after his father-in-law, J. LeDroict Langdon, sans the *c*). Because armed guards patrolling the surrounding fence upset Howard students and residents of the segregated African American neighborhood of Howard Town, lawsuits and countersuits ensued until 1891, when a judge ordered the fence removed. The first Black family to move in suffered gunshots through a window. Soon white families fled and the community became a haven for Black families. James and Daisy Ellington, among many others, bought a house. Their son "Duke" grew up there.[13]

The LeDroit Park fence foreshadowed an ugly legacy of the pavement age. Douglas Massey and Nancy Denton, in *American Apartheid*, described "residential segregation" as "the principal organizational feature of American society" and largely "responsible for the creation of the [African American] urban underclass." Residential segregation did not dominate the physical environment of pre-asphalt cities. Black people were as likely to share a neighborhood with whites as with other Blacks: "People got around by walking, so there was little geographic differentiation between places of work and residence. . . . Such an urban spatial structure is not conducive to high levels of segregation."[14] Obviously, asphalt pavement did not cause segregation. Responsibility for that lies with lawmakers, urban planners, developers, and other elites who, when not directly animated by racism, placed convenience over conscience. But Barber's (and others') use of asphalt in its pavement form helped give segregation what it required: spatial boundaries more impenetrable than that LeDroit Park fence. Asphalt's duality here is plain. The spread of blacktop on streets and roads increased mobility and opportunity for some, while restricting mobility and opportunity for others.

When Amzi Barber entered the asphalt business in 1878, he quickly established Washington as the nation's leading asphalt city. H. L. Mencken, the Baltimore journalist, humorist, and cultural critic of those he called the "booboisie," remembered visiting as a boy and "wallowing delightedly in its marvels. The greatest of them, in that era, was not the Capitol at the end of Pennsylvania Avenue, nor even the Washington Monument, but the asphalt streets. Asphalt was then a novelty in the United States, and Washington was the only city that could show any considerable spread of it."[15] By 1885 Washington had seventy miles of asphalt streets, with Barber's company doing nearly all the paving. From there Barber dreamed of paving every U.S. city. He moved his business to New York, traveled an average of one thousand miles per week aboard Pullman cars, and dominated the nation's asphalt trade, given his control of Pitch Lake asphalt. Hazen Pingree, the progressive mayor of Detroit (1889–97) and then governor of Michigan (1897–1901), visited Venezuela and Cuba in an unsuccessful search for unclaimed asphalt beds that might be developed and compete against Barber's Trinidad product.[16]

Urban mayors and ward bosses, as a *Harper's* editor noted at the Progressive Era's zenith, "decide how much it shall cost to live in a city, and to be furnished with asphalt" and such other pillars of civilization as "policemen, and firemen, and parks, and electric light."[17] The United States' first true asphalt king could charm (some said con) investors along with pols easier to fool than Hazen Pingree. More modest asphalt barons like Brig. Gen. (Ret.) William Woods Averell, owner of the Trinidad Asphalt Company, were not easily fooled either. In 1876, a dozen years before Barber secured his Pitch Lake rights, Averell's company laid some of that Pennsylvania Avenue asphalt based on Edward de Smedt's formula. Although de Smedt was Averell's employee, Barber found a job for him with the City of Washington and sweetened that with a $10,000 real-estate deed to his wife. Averell sued for tampering and hired Pinkerton detectives to investigate Barber. They found nothing useful.[18]

This first wave of Averell-Barber lawsuits ended with an out-of-court settlement to form the American Asphalt Pavement Company, with Barber chairing the executive committee and Averell chairing the board of directors. But Barber had all the power. When he left to form a new Barber Asphalt Paving Company in 1883, Averell sued him for patent infringement and won a $700,000 judgment. Barber could afford to pay, as he had incorporated various asphalt companies under his London-registered enterprise, the New Trinidad Lake Asphalt Company. He merged that company with the General Asphalt Company of America, raised capital, issued stock, and otherwise went about building exactly what the Sherman Antitrust Act of 1890 outlawed (in theory, at least). Averell scarcely enjoyed his victory. He died less than two years after winning in court.

Amzi Barber indulged in what the economist and sociologist Thorstein Veblen called "conspicuous consumption."[19] His offices on the sixteenth floor at 11 Broadway had a spectacular view of the Statue of

Liberty. His favorite mansion (of many), Ardsley Towers upstate on the Hudson River, included the Ardsley Casino, a country club that he helped establish. It had a dock for members to park their yachts; stables for stagecoach horses; and a membership that included Cornelius Vanderbilt and J. P. Morgan.[20] While Barber was no Vanderbilt or Morgan, he had heft enough to serve as a corporate director for half a dozen banks and own three real-estate companies and such other concerns as a creosote plant that sold product to the railroads for coating ties. He found time to join all the right clubs (Metropolitan, University, Engineers, Riding, Lawyers) and societies (New England, Ohio, American Geographical). He joined all the right yacht clubs as well (New York, Atlantic, American, Larchmont, Royal Thames). And he was an American Society of Civil Engineers fellow, a Metropolitan Museum of Art patron, and an Oberlin College trustee.

Barber bet on the future even before 1899, when he formed what the newspapers called the Asphalt Trust. Sheet asphalt arrived west of the Mississippi River in the early 1880s, when Barber's workers paved Douglas Street in Omaha, Nebraska. Nonetheless, it remained a novelty a decade later. Laura Ingalls Wilder, author of *Little House on the Prairie* (1935), had a childhood memory of the asphalt—which she called "dark stuff"—under her family's wagon in Topeka. At first, she thought it was rubber. Sheet asphalt was so rare and (briefly) controversial that Milwaukee's Charles Pfister had the entire block in front of his Jefferson Street hotel paved at his own expense. The reluctance of others to follow Pfister reflects the plain fact that streets were public places. Efforts to stop paving were common, as pavement would increase traffic volume and speed and thus destroy a street's dual function of carrying traffic and serving as playgrounds for children and gathering places for all ages. Without asphalt, public transportation might have dug deeper roots and city streets might have remained public places for a few more years.[21]

By 1898 Amzi Barber claimed to have paved 1,500 miles of streets in more than one hundred cities. Those cities still included relatively few west of the Appalachians, though there were notable exceptions beyond Milwaukee, Omaha, and Topeka. New Orleans, for one, got its first sheet-asphalt street in 1880. Asphalt would not move west or into small towns on a significant scale until portable asphalt plants came online. Barber was a pioneer here too. After his Buffalo-based Iroquois Iron Works began manufacturing portable plants in 1898, he began buying the flatbed railcars needed to haul them. Loading product was efficient because Barber had an asphalt-processing plant in Buffalo, one that emitted odors foul enough to cause local residents to sue. He appeased the plaintiffs by taking a technological leap, investing "in a blower to recycle stack fumes back through the ovens, which consumed them." On the other hand, loading product into tank cars was not environmentally friendly, as Barber and other shippers stoked fires under the cars to keep the product warm and soft. Not surprisingly, the railroad owners objected. They did not object to the next innovation, internal steam lines and insulation through quilted blankets.[22]

Amzi Barber recognized three things that allowed him to stay ahead of the competition for the entirety of the nineteenth century's last decades. First, he recognized that asphalts other than the stone mastic type provided better traction for horses than concrete pavement (which Barber realized would eventually pose a major threat to his profits). Second, Barber recognized that asphalt's future lay in chemistry. So he hired Clifford Richardson, a Harvard-educated chemist who had succeeded de Smedt as the District of Columbia's engineer inspector of asphalts and cements. Richardson worked at Barber's research laboratory in New York City, where he learned enough to write the first decent technical book on asphalt paving.[23] Third, Barber recognized that asphalt had both a public-health lobby and a bicycle lobby at its back.

New York and other large cities had ungodly pollution in thoroughfares, inflamed by horse droppings and urine and dropped-dead horses staying where they lay. Had he accepted New York mayor William Lafayette Strong's offer to serve as street-cleaning czar, Theodore Roosevelt would have starred in this part of the asphalt story.

(Roosevelt served as president of the board of police commissioners instead, where he launched a clean-up campaign targeting vice.) The street-cleaning post went to George E. Waring Jr., a Civil War veteran who touted sheet asphalt as a weapon against disease, as it scarcely soaked up horse urine and had no gaps for horse manure to collect. He formed a Street Cleaning Department in 1895, complete with white uniforms and pith helmets for the crews. Waring resigned in 1898 and went to Cuba to help the Department of War clean up after the Spanish-American War ended. Sanitation contracts went to Amzi Barber and others, who paid Cuban workers to lay sheet asphalt and asphalt-paving blocks. (Most of those other contractors were small-scale; for example, one billed $127.84 for seven barrels of Trinidad asphalt.) Waring's sanitation legacy in Cuba was limited, as his own fate suggested (yellow fever killed him on October 29, 1898). His sanitation legacy in New York is easier to document. Paved streets meant less disease, and this had an impact on life expectancy. By 1910 the work of Waring and his immediate successors helped increase Manhattanite life expectancy by nearly five years.[24]

Nonetheless, asphalt's duality is such that it helped those promoting nativist rot even as it helped keep streets clean. Barber's marketing strategy of hooking asphalt to sanitation briefly ruled at Ellis Island, given concerns about immigrant "filth." An 1892 remodel, newspaper reporters noted, emphasized Ellis Island's "hygienic apparatus. . . . It may be found necessary in furtherance of this idea to cover the entire island with a coat of asphalt, as the sail has given evidence at times of being malarial." Another remodel in 1900 emphasized asphalt flooring "with raised edges around the walls, so that they can be thoroughly cleansed" (that is, hosed down).[25]

Amzi Barber and other pavers benefited even more from a bicycle lobby on both sides of the Atlantic. By the 1880s urban cyclists were pouring out of the cities to ride on unpaved country roads that might be impassable, from mud one week and rock-hard ruts the next week. Urban congestion on granite setts and sheet asphalt provided another incentive for rural touring. In London the Duke of

Teck complained to the Duke of Cambridge "about 2,000 to 3,000 Bicycles, through the roads of the [Richmond] Park, not as if guided by sensible People, but by Maniacs, Persons in a state of madness. They went about in a pace like Lightening, looking neither right nor left."[26] The high wheelers (penny-farthings) compounded problems of mud, ruts, and maniacs. With their tiny rear wheels and front wheels up to sixty inches in diameter and saddles of equal height, they were fast—men and women raced them professionally on wooden-board and sheet-asphalt tracks—but dangerous. The next jump in veloci-pede evolution came in the late 1880s, with the "safety," used for both recreation and transportation and with a design similar to modern bicycles. Women, especially, embraced the safety. "It has done more to emancipate women," the suffragist Susan B. Anthony said, "than anything else."[27]

The Good Roads movement, the main bicycle lobby in the United States, was a vast and varied amalgamation. Its champions included individuals like Columbia bicycle manufacturer Albert Pope and orga-nizations like the National League for Good Roads and the League of American Wheelmen. The Wheelmen, publisher of *Good Roads* magazine, counted John Jacob Astor and other Gilded Age notables among its one hundred thousand peak membership. On October 3, 1893, Congress responded to the bicycle lobby by creating, within the Department of Agriculture, an Office of Road Inquiry. The nation had its first asphalt bike path within a year, a "wheel way" in Brooklyn. And good-roads advocates like Detroit's Horatio Earle, chief counsel for the League of American Wheelmen, were promising victory over mud and dust. Dust clouds had "been around since the beginning of time," Jeffrey Schnapp observed. "But the coaching revolution . . . transformed them into signifiers of accelerated movement . . . differen-tiat[ing] driver passengers from pedestrians, the enfranchised from the disenfranchised. . . . Dust was the pollutant of the nineteenth century. Asphalt came to the rescue. It cleaned up speed." Horatio Earle helped secure what the League of American Wheelmen demanded: not only victory over mud and dust but "equal privileges" for the bicycle with horses and wagons. When beginning his tenure as Michigan's highway commissioner in 1903, however, Earle realized that the bicycle would never have equal privileges with the automobile.[28]

Pope, Earle, and the bicycle lobby in its entirety were delighted that Congress had created an Office of Road Inquiry with a good-roads booster at the helm: Gen. (Ret.) Roy Stone, a Civil War veteran who fought at Gettysburg.[29] Unfortunately, delight dimmed, as the new office had scant resources. Stone's impressive job title—special agent and engineer for road inquiry—contrasted with a meager annual appropriation ($10,000) and space (two rooms in the Department of Agriculture's attic). Stone could do little besides publish technical and promotional bulletins. Rather than sulk, Pope and comrades continued their petition drive, calling for Congress to establish a properly funded federal department of roads. They submitted 150,000 names on December 20, 1893, and moved on to organize demonstrations and parades complicated by racial segregation. The League of American Wheelmen denied membership to the Colored Cycle Club of Oakland but allowed the group to participate in the decade's biggest protest calling for good roads. It was held in San Francisco in 1896, the year the Supreme Court institutionalized the separate-but-equal doctrine in *Plessy v. Ferguson*.[30]

Amzi Barber leveraged the public-health and bicycle lobbies and then a third lobby—the emerging automobile lobby. (In 1902 the League of American Wheelmen closed its door while the American Automobile Association—AAA, or Triple A—opened its door.) Had those lobbies been enough, Barber would not have launched his own lobbying campaign focused on the bidding process for municipal paving contracts. In New York he was remarkably successful, as Tammany Hall often awarded contracts specifying specific asphalt mixes that only Barber could produce, as he held patents for those mixes. That Barber formed an asphalt trust was no great surprise either. Since John D. Rockefeller formed the first modern trust in 1863, the drive to monopolize whatever industry spread like a plague. Barber had no need to form a trust at first, given his control of Trinidad's lake asphalt and his competitors' failure to produce a product of equal quality. He organized a trust in the late 1890s because competition for quality asphalt pavement had finally emerged, and his Trinidad monopoly faced threats.

The asphalt trust, in the words of Henry George, author of *Progress and Poverty* (1879), was "monstrously inflated."[31] Barber reeled in investors by promising a monopoly both on the supply end and the back end of municipal paving contracts. The money poured in because the trust overpaid when swallowing thirteen smaller asphalt-paving companies. The public offer of watered stock allowed Barber and such select partners as Francis V. Greene to clear $2.6 million on four of those small companies alone. After finishing his service for the asphalt trust, Greene served one year as New York City police commissioner, where he promised to attack corruption of the sort he and Barber had fostered. Meanwhile, the inflated capitalization caused the asphalt trust to default. It could not pay interest on its $30 million worth of bonds.

Even before the asphalt trust went into receivership, Barber could never quite monopolize the industry's paving side. Not that he was the only one trying. The Warren family of Newton, Massachusetts, built an asphalt empire that would outlast Barber's empire. It pre-dated Barber as well. Herbert M. Warren and his five brothers began importing Trinidad asphalt in the 1840s, experimenting with a coal tar and asphalt mix for roofing material. Herbert Warren had seven sons, and six of them worked for or with Barber, a not surprising development, given Barber's control of raw material in Trinidad. By 1900, however, the Warrens had split with Barber, with the exception of an uncle, who helped the trust swallow the Warren-Scharf Asphalt Paving Company. The family's new company, Warren Brothers, began battling Barber through patent-infringement lawsuits, including one for their bitulithic pavement, which debuted in 1901 on Harvey Street in Pawtucket, Rhode Island. The Warrens' principal contribution to the asphalt industry was simply this: aggregates and fines required quality standards no less than liquid asphalt. Bitulithic, arguably the first major step toward full-depth, hot asphalt-mix pavement, used twice as much rock as Barber's sheet asphalt, which emphasized sand. Bitulithic also required less asphalt in the mix. At first, the Warren family used coal tar, as Barber had cut off their Trinidad asphalt supply (which prompted another lawsuit). They soon found another source of asphalt: refinery residue, which Rockefeller's Standard Oil was only too happy to sell.

With a main office in Boston and a production facility—the nation's first modern asphalt plant—in Cambridge, the Warrens secured contracts across the United States and Canada. They even did paving work in Spain, Poland, and Japan. At their peak Barber's companies produced one of the planet's best asphalt pavements (if not the very best). Warren Brothers, however, had an even better product that they could sell because they won nearly all the patent-infringement lawsuits. Those victories, however, were short lived. In 1910 a Kansas court ruled that asphalt mixes with aggregate sizes of less than one-half inch did not violate the bitulithic patents.[32]

The smaller asphalt companies that did not fall to Barber's asphalt trust included the Sicilian Asphalt Company, which survived because it held a New York City subway contract, signed in 1900, to lay nearly eight hundred thousand square yards of asphalt waterproofing. The first design for a New York "steam subway" dated to 1864 and an engineer's recommendation for asphalt. The engineers who followed in the 1880s and 1890s, in the face of resistance from street-railway lobbies, emphasized asphalt as well. They took "extra precautions" to provide "waterproofing under the floor, up the sides and over the roof of the tunnel[s]." Final plans for the first round of construction mandated all "fabric" and "brick or hollow tile" waterproofing material to be "laid in hot pitch or asphalt, and in from three to six thicknesses or plies." Asphalt mastics, moreover, required "one third pure bitumen." Because so much asphalt created a steam-bath effect, the engineers mandated less asphalt thereafter except in tunnels below sea level.[33]

Asphalt trust stockholders were not as fortunate as Warren Brothers or Sicilian Asphalt. With the General Asphalt Company and the

National Asphalt Company in receivership, Amzi Barber walked away. A second asphalt trust rose and fell in a blink. In 1903 a third asphalt trust swallowed forty-four of the nation's estimated sixty-nine asphalt companies. In addition to New Trinidad Lake Asphalt and New York and Bermudez (NY&B), the other prominent companies were the reorganized General Asphalt, which functioned as the trust's lead vehicle, and the Barber Asphalt Paving Company. The third trust kept the Barber name while blackballing the man. Regardless, the insiders envied his asphalt bubble and decision to cash out before the bubble burst and sheet-asphalt prices in New York dropped from $2.65 to $0.93 per square yard.[34]

During his asphalt hiatus, Amzi Barber briefly entered the automobile business through the Locomobile Company, an enterprise manufacturing a steam-engine rival to the Stanley Steamer. When that failed, he turned to an equally unsuccessful internal-combustion rival to Henry Ford's letter cars. (The asphalt industry, if not Barber himself, found a customer in Ford; the paint on millions of Model Ts produced from 1908 to 1927 was often a Japan black lacquer made from Gilsonite.)[35] The latest asphalt trust provided an opportunity for Barber to flee the automobile business and reenter the paving business, when the New York and Bermudez asphalt company, among other corporate interests, fomented civil war in Venezuela. The press called it an "asphalt war."

The first imperial acquisition of Lake Bermudez asphalt came in 1882, when one Horatio R. Hamilton of the baked-goods industry arrived in Caracas and married a woman whose family was close to Antonio Guzmán Blanco, who served three nonconsecutive terms as Venezuela's president between 1870 and 1887. Guzmán Blanco granted Hamilton asphalt-mining rights. In 1885 NY&B bought out the cookie man. For the next twenty years, the political situation in Venezuela was explosive, mixing nationalism, European colonialism, and U.S. attempts to implement a less formal economic hegemony.

The roots of the asphalt and civil war that gave Amzi Barber his opportunity to reenter the business dated to 1899, when Cipriano Castro, the "Lion of the Andes," marshaled his forces in Colombian sanctuaries and then marched them to Caracas. After Castro seized power, his enemies mobilized "Down with the Reds" forces in Colombia and raided border towns. Castro invaded in retaliation, but Colombian soldiers, backed up by French warships, routed his troops. In search of a conquerable foe, Castro settled on NY&B and the means of a lawsuit. Even before that decision the asphalt trust saw Castro, whose family made its fortune not from asphalt but coffee, as an enemy. The trust wanted to keep Bermudez asphalt off the market. By artificially limiting supply, prices would rise. Castro objected to this business model because it meant Venezuela would receive practically nothing from its asphalt resource (in contrast to Trinidad's Pitch Lake profits). NY&B, in turn, suspected that Castro would expropriate their asphalt holdings whether he prevailed in litigation or not.[36]

To keep the United States on the sidelines, Castro framed the asphalt war as a conflict between rival U.S. entrepreneurs, even as he inflamed that conflict by inviting Warner-Quinlan Asphalt to develop properties that NY&B had left dormant. When Warner-Quinlan bought those properties for $40,000, NY&B executives pleaded with the Roosevelt administration to send warships. Likewise, Warner-Quinlan urged intervention on their behalf. Meanwhile, NY&B's attempt to bribe two judges clouded the litigation in the Venezuelan courts. So did Venezuela's attorney general, who proposed a $50,000 commission for himself. Having little confidence in the courts, the facts, or the efficacy of the various bribes, NY&B again asked the Roosevelt administration to help. Secretary of State John Hay, who thought the company "shady," nonetheless sent three gunboats with orders not to intervene.[37] The firepower was for show only.

NY&B executives decided to act unilaterally. They sparked revolution by mobilizing their private army, originally organized to intimidate other asphalt companies, and supporting the so-called Matos revolt. Manuel Antonio Matos, a banker who ranked as Venezuela's richest man, met with asphalt-trust representatives in New York and Paris for help in searching for a ship that he could convert to a gunboat. Matos bought an iron-screw steamer, the *Ban-Righ* (King's wife), renamed it *Libertador*, outfitted it with cannons, and loaded it with weapons for gun-running duty. The civil war opened in December 1901, continued for eighteen months, and left fifteen thousand dead. Beyond *Libertador* deliveries NY&B supplied the rebels with $145,000 in supplies and weapons shipped in British-flagged vessels. With his government facing damage claims, Castro countered by refusing to honor foreign debt (not that he could, given the collapse of the coffee market). Britain, and to a lesser extent Germany and Italy, responded by seizing ships, blockading the coast, and bombarding Puerto Cabello. Britain also allowed anti-Castro rebels to stage on a nearby island. Castro survived the civil war only because Britain, Germany, and Italy, under Roosevelt administration pressure, agreed to arbitrate their claims.

Requests for military intervention were common in the Progressive Era. Less than a year earlier, Roosevelt sent the USS *Nashville* and other warships with marines aboard to Colombia on behalf of Panamanian independence and U.S. rights to dig a canal (a construction project that required asphalt).[38] In Venezuela, however, the problem as Roosevelt defined it—bringing "those Dagos" to heel—required finesse. Anti-imperial fallout from the Spanish-American War of 1898 and suppression of the Philippine Revolution constrained the president. So did his "trust buster" image. "Even the Big Stick," a magazine editorial read, "would not look pretty all dripping with asphalt." Roosevelt's solution—his corollary to the Monroe Doctrine—was simple: to keep European creditor nations from sending troops, the United States would exercise an international police power to ensure that Caribbean countries honored their debts.[39]

The Roosevelt administration wanted international law and arbitration to decide things in Venezuela. NY&B wanted U.S. gunboats to decide. Cipriano Castro wanted to dictate a solution. Even though NY&B won its lawsuit against Warner-Quinlan based on the original Hamilton concession (however dubious its constitutionality), Castro knew that the company's involvement in the Matos revolt tainted that win. He had an ally here in Amzi Barber. After the Venezuelan courts ruled for NY&B in 1904, Barber's agents began releasing documents to the newspapers regarding the company's role in fomenting the Matos revolt. For his part Castro ordered his soldiers to seize the NY&B property that the courts had ordered sequestered. Castro also sued the company. Back in Washington, and as if a Greek chorus, the asphalt trust again asked Roosevelt to send gunboats. Hoping for additional intervention from England, the trust transferred some NY&B assets to New Trinidad Lake Asphalt, chartered in London, because British citizens held nearly all of that company's debt.

Barber's cause received a boost in 1905, when the U.S. press pursued NY&B's role in a U.S. Department of State bribery scandal in Venezuela. After Herbert W. Bowen, the minister in Caracas, accused the assistant secretary of state, Francis B. Loomis, of taking a $10,000 NY&B bribe, Secretary of War William Howard Taft investigated the charge. President Theodore Roosevelt, for his part, reminded all parties of his earlier executive order cracking down on whistleblowers: "No officer of the diplomatic or consular service of the United States shall . . . publicly criticize any other officer in either service, except in a communication to the Department of State." After reading Taft's report, Roosevelt concluded "that Caracas is seething with scandal, and that . . . Mr. Bowen's conduct is especially reprehensible." He fired the whistleblower. It made no difference that Loomis admitted that there was a $10,000 check and two more for $5,000 and $1,244. (The $244 was for the sale of "wines and supplies" to the asphalt trust's man in Caracas.) But Loomis said he simply solicited NY&B's help to move personal funds out of Venezuela without taking a loss when later converting bolivares to dollars. Asphaltic slime, Milton had said. Though Bowen agreed with the poet, Taft and Roosevelt agreed with Loomis, and that was that.[40]

There is no evidence that Amzi Barber played a role in fomenting the Bowen-Loomis affair. But he did play a role in helping arrange this outcome: the receiver appointed to oversee NY&B property in Venezuela was Barber's number-one man in Venezuela. Barber had leaped at the chance (arranged by himself) to get back in the game and deal a blow to the asphalt trust. He organized the A. L. Barber Asphalt Company, signed up many of NY&B's customers, and escalated his public relations and lobbying by hiring former secretary of state John W. Foster and Foster's son-in-law, future secretary of state Robert Lansing. Barber next hinted at a fourth asphalt trust under his control, with the formation of the Independent Asphalt Association, even extending a membership invitation to the third trust's paving companies. The Roosevelt administration upended Barber's plans, relying less on gunboats and marines and more on international law and, as ever, racism and racialism. One president, Roosevelt, considered the other president, Castro, an "unspeakably villainous little monkey."[41]

The Venezuela courts, relying on Barber's documents, fined NY&B $5 million for its role in fomenting the Matos revolt. But Venezuela never collected. In 1908 President Roosevelt severed diplomatic relations at the recommendation of Secretary of State Elihu Root, Hay's successor. Then, when Cipriano Castro went to Europe for a medical procedure, the head of the Venezuelan military, Juan Vicente Gómez, seized power. At Gómez's request the Roosevelt administration sent warships and an emissary, who negotiated a settlement that restored NY&B's right to mine asphalt. The company, in turn, agreed to pay a $60,000 fine and award Venezuela a 25 percent discount on asphalt purchases. Elihu Root had U.S. warships prevent Castro—whom he dubbed a "crazy brute," as if in a pejorative-slinging contest with TR—from returning to Venezuela. He then congratulated himself for standing "up against the pressure to bulldoze Venezuela." Actually, as one scholar of the affair noted, a bulldozer came for both Castro and U.S. direct investors, who received less than 1 percent on their claims compared to foreign investors, who received just over 21 percent.[42]

Theodore Roosevelt intervened in the asphalt war because he shared the asphalt trust's concerns about Castro—with one difference. The trust wanted to monopolize Lake Bermudez asphalt. Roosevelt wanted access to oil and rightly judged that Juan Vicente Gómez might be more hospitable to that industry's foreign entities. Gómez had a brief reign as president (1908–13) but a long reign as de facto dictator (1913–

35), and big oil pretty much got what it wanted, from the discovery of the first oil field in 1913 until Venezuela nationalized its oil on January 1, 1976. The government, as noted, did not nationalize the Orinoco Belt until 2007. Those reserves contained enormous amounts of what they called, in Barber's day, "land asphalt" to distinguish it from the lake asphalt that had once seemed so important.[43]

While the asphalt war played out in Venezuela, the asphalt industry was experiencing two seismic changes. Barber and his chemist, Clifford Richardson, had helped pioneer the first: an explosion in asphalt chemistry and civil-engineering research. Barber had failed to stop the second: the rise of refinery asphalt for road-paving duty and the attendant fall of lake asphalt, whether from Trinidad or Venezuela. However unlikely it seemed at first, the Office of Road Inquiry and its $10,000 annual appropriation led the research charge. By 1903 the annual appropriation had risen to $35,000, an amount sufficient to establish a road-material laboratory housed in the Department of Agriculture's Bureau of Chemistry. The lab offered free testing services to "any person residing in the United States" and free technical services to any community willing "to furnish all necessary material and common labor" for the construction of "object lesson roads." Technical services, Road Inquiry director Martin Dodge promised, included everything from "didactic literature" to construction machinery. The literature, to use a contemporary term, was a deliverable. The construction machinery was not.[44]

The need for scientific research and technological innovation was paramount, given urban United States' accelerating demand for quality product. Before asphalt could triumph on a grand scale, chemists and lab technicians would have to become commonplace. The dominant testing method of asphalt properties at the turn of the century—scooping a bit from a melting kettle and chewing it—would have to give way to thermometers and eventually more sophisticated penetration-test equipment. The problem was that municipal asphalt paving expanded so quickly in the United States and attracted so many start-up paving companies that asphalt quality, overall, regressed. With the collapse of the various asphalt trusts, entrepreneurs with little or no experience or understanding of asphalt's physical properties were increasingly bidding on and winning municipal paving contracts. Many failed to grasp the basic facts that not all asphalts are alike and that paving methods that worked well with one asphalt might utterly fail with another asphalt. The proliferation of paving companies coincided with the rise of municipal warranties to create more problems. Amzi Barber introduced the first warranties on materials and workmanship to help keep competition at bay. By 1896 New York City moved beyond Barber's ten-year warranties by requiring fifteen-year warranties. Errors and corruptions could cause premature pavement failure, but so could other factors beyond a contractor's control. Warranty obligations drove most paving start-ups into bankruptcy.

By 1905 the Office of Public Roads (OPR; the Office of Road Inquiry's successor) had a $50,000 budget and ten employees.[45] Logan Waller Page, appointed director that same year, focused on four areas: road construction; testing of road materials; dissemination of information about the need for more roads and how to pay for them; and instruction in the road-building arts. Congress required the OPR director to be a scientist, and Page fit that bill. He studied geology at Harvard and trained at the School of Bridges and Roads in Paris. Today's Federal Highway Administration credits Page with introducing a "scientific movement in road building," a movement that included "methods of asphalt analysis." He had plenty of help. The American Society for Testing Materials, founded in 1898, worked with Page and his staff to develop standards for asphalt tests. Universities already training civil engineers in road-building techniques expanded their curriculum and began cooperating with Page's agenda. Other universities added road-building techniques to their civil-engineering programs. In turn OPR began offering internships for civil-engineering majors and recent graduates. For common labor the office offered modest training programs but no support whatsoever for unionization.[46]

While research laboratories were ushering in profound changes, the asphalt industry experienced a second seismic shift. In 1900 work crews used natural asphalt on nearly all U.S. streets and roads that had sheet-asphalt pavement. California refiners, however, began shipping asphalt that year to Atlantic coast markets in barrels by railcar or freighter around Cape Horn. In 1902 the Gulf Refining Company began producing asphalt in Port Arthur, Texas. That marked the beginning of the end for natural asphalt, because refineries were simply producing a higher quality and more profitable product.[47] Not surprisingly, those with stakes in natural asphalt resisted this gradual but inexorable shift. It is even less surprising that the resisters included Amzi Barber. In 1909 he boarded a Pullman car and traveled to the West Coast to investigate product from Southern California's various tar pits. On his return trip to New York, he developed pneumonia. His fight against refinery asphalt ended with his death on April 17.

Office of Public Roads officials hoped to avoid conflict by refusing to recommend refinery asphalt over natural asphalt or vice versa. Nor did the office take a side in the looming competition between asphalt pavement and concrete pavement. The competition between natural asphalt and refinery asphalt had a clear-cut winner. The competition between asphalt and concrete did not. OPR developed standards for each material while deferring to federalist principles and otherwise encouraging state and local road builders to choose their own materials. Asphalt producers and pavers already had a questionable reputation on the corruption front, given the adventures of the various asphalt trusts and Barber's manipulation of municipal paving contracts. The office's decision to defer to state and local officials would be one of the factors that helped the road construction industry maintain its dubious reputation for corruption for the remainder of the century and into the twenty-first century.

Those with an interest in selling natural asphalt to the nation's road pavers made their last stand through outfits like Kentucky Rock Asphalt and its trademarked Kyrock.[48] The Choctaw Asphalt Company of Jumbo, Indian Territory (the state of Oklahoma after 1907), owned not by the tribe but by Saint Louis investors, operated a typical rock-asphalt mine complete with a tram line to a railroad depot. The mine had an elephant-shaped vein so the investors named the town after P. T. Barnum's renowned circus elephant. Population never rose past two hundred in Jumbo, but that was enough to support a pool hall. The mine closed in 1914 shortly after an explosion blew body parts out the mine entrance and killed fourteen miners. Prospectors mined for asphalt elsewhere in Indian Territory, but the profits were scarcely better than they were at Jumbo. In 1906 the four companies that held leases and worked their holdings on Choctaw and Chickasaw land paid royalties of ten cents a ton to the tribes. The next year these companies shut down their asphalt mines. When the Department of the Interior offered asphalt leases for public sale in 1918 and again in 1921, there were few bidders.[49]

Rock asphalt's collapse played out against oil's rise. The statehood year for Oklahoma, 1907, also marked the year that oil refineries began rendering natural asphalt largely irrelevant for road paving, even if asphalt prospectors did not yet realize that fact. Whether mined or refined, asphalt lost on other fronts too, even as refinery asphalt advanced for road-paving duty. By July 30, 1916, when German sabo-teurs blew up two million pounds of munitions at Black Tom pier in New York Harbor, causing damage on nearby Ellis Island, the product had lost some of its hygienic allure. Red Ludowici tile replaced the original asphalt floor in the Registry Room (or Great Hall) of Ellis Island's main building. Filthy people, the xenophobes said, had worn out the asphalt. The asphalt industry responded with its own floor-tile entry, widely used after the war in residential kitchens and bathrooms and the hallways of the nation's schools and other public buildings.[50]

Over 90 percent of U.S. roads remained unpaved on October 12, 1916, two years deep into the world war that the United States would soon join. On that day in Indianapolis, Woodrow Wilson gave what the Good Roads movement called the first "good roads" speech by a chief executive since George Washington. In his first message to Con-gress, the first president called for "due attention to the Post-Office and Post-Roads." Wilson simply said, "You have got to have an intricate and perfect network of roads throughout . . . this great continent."

Five months later, on March 4, 1917, a Sunday, Wilson took the oath of office at his desk. The next day horseshoes scuffed Pennsylvania Avenue blacktop as the president rode in his carriage to the Capitol's East Portico to view the Inaugural Parade. The avenue receives a fresh coat of asphalt before every presidential inauguration, but Wilson's second inaugural parade was the first and apparently the only time the asphalt was painted white.[51]

World War I sparked a road-building boom in the United States for three reasons: (1) the preparedness movement; (2) the Federal Aid Road Act of 1916 (which continued an emphasis on rural post roads with the states and the federal government each paying half the construction costs); and (3) intensified lobbying by the auto, tire, concrete, and asphalt industries.[52] Even "the owners of mules" piled on. Regardless, the paving boom was not without difficulties. Whether carrying war materials or common freight, trucks usually rode on steel or solid rubber tires that destroyed asphalt and concrete pavement alike. (Pneumatic tires did not dominate until manufacturers solved the problem of frequent blowouts in the mid-1920s.) Asphalt's role "over there," in contrast to the home front, was modest. Warren Brothers and Buffalo-Springfield Roller Company machines accompanied the American Expeditionary Forces. And army engineers operated a rock quarry in France that produced crushed stone for asphalt duty. Nonetheless, paving was rare. The army primarily used logs to build roads and sandbags to repair them.[53]

Six months after the combatants signed the armistice on November 11, 1918, asphalt producers and pavers responded to the specter of future competition from the concrete industry and the ever-present need to further material research by forming the Asphalt Association (renamed the Asphalt Institute on January 1, 1930, and hereafter referred to by that name). The institute primarily functioned as a research and testing hub that cooperated with the Bureau of Public Roads (BPR; formerly OPR). The ten charter members were Warner-Quinlan, Freeport Mexican Fuel, Atlantic Refining, Prudential Oil, Imperial Oil, Sun Oil, Island Oil and Transport, Standard Oil of New

York, Standard Oil of New Jersey, and Standard Oil of Louisiana. The Asphalt Institute fostered cooperation between private-sector engineers and chemists and federal, state, and municipal engineers and chemists, a strategy that quickly rendered moot the once common practice of securing patents for particular asphalt mixes.

Thomas "Chief" MacDonald, who served as BPR commissioner from 1919 until 1953, served as the spokesperson for applying scientific principles. His experience dated to 1904 in his native Iowa, where he traveled to road construction sites by horseback and concluded that corruption, incompetence, and inefficiency were rampant. Too often, he said, road builders delivered "about a dime's worth of road for every dollar they spent." In 1910 Logan Page hired him to collect road data in Iowa at a salary of one dollar per year. Two years into his tenure as Page's successor, the Federal Aid Highway Act of 1921 kept the federal aid cap at 50 percent of road-construction costs but broke new ground in encouraging a "connected system of highways, interstate in character." For the workers who actually built the roads, the model was not scientific. In the 1920s road construction's manual labor became synonymous with chain-gang labor in the South. MacDonald's BPR took no position on chain gangs. The bureau also remained agnostic on the competition between asphalt pavers and concrete pavers. Still, asphalt held its advantage. A mid-1920s Asphalt Institute survey of paving materials in the twelve largest U.S. cities had asphalt at 54.6 percent and concrete at a mere 2.7 percent (though a concrete base often underlay an asphalt surface).[54]

Along with chain-gang guards and prison wardens and BPR chemists and engineers, the asphalt industry's friends in the 1920s included Commerce Secretary Herbert Hoover. He tracked asphalt use for road building all the way down to such miniscule burgs as Green Camp, Ohio, and presided over Bureau of Standards regulations for "sheet asphalt, asphaltic concrete, and asphalt macadam." With different municipalities demanding different grades, the nation's fourteen liquid-asphalt manufacturers were producing at least eighty-eight varieties. The asphalt-industry representative who sat on the bureau's advisory committee recommended cutting down to nine varieties.[55] Beyond efficiencies Hoover saw asphalt and concrete road paving as a job-creating juggernaut. Road labor, California hotel mogul Sam S. Porter told Hoover, might also help maintain livable wages for all. To the surprise of nearly everyone, the conservative (and often reactionary) William Randolph Hearst and his newspaper empire signed on to the good-roads cause as well. The campaign opened with Hoover's call for the construction of a highway system that would bring economic benefits to every state.[56] Unfortunately, the crown jewel of that proposed system stalled until 1937, when construction finally began to extend U.S. Route 6—the Grand Army of the Republic Highway—from Brewster, New York, to Long Beach, California.

Herbert Hoover demonstrated more sympathy for public works and worker wages than the other argument the good-roads lobby advanced. In 1922 the army gave the Bureau of Public Roads a list of roads considered of "prime importance in the event of war." The bureau used that list to compile the thirty-two-foot long "Pershing Map," featuring U.S. Geological Survey drawings of existing and proposed roads. Planning commissions across the country responded by referencing the Pershing map in their push for federal highway-plan funds. In a typical pitch Los Angeles planners emphasized that attention to military transportation requirements was a patriotic obligation. Hoover's tepid response was predictable, the road boosters said, given an upbringing steeped in Quaker pacifism.[57]

Herbert Hoover's failure to understand the paving business, in contrast, was shocking because he was a Stanford University–educated geologist whose work on four continents won him a Quaker-plain moniker: the Great Engineer. Hoover's road-building crusade had the singular strategy of convincing state and county road commissions to award a healthy number of construction contracts in the fall and thus guarantee year-round employment for road workers rather than seasonal employment. Across much of the United States, however, workers simply could not pave roads over winter's frozen ground and expect the road surfaces to hold up beyond a few weeks. And the road commissions, as Maryland's state chair put it, realized that road-crew wages always dropped from fall (the end of paving season) to spring (the beginning of paving season), and workers would not accept low pay unless the only alternative was unemployment.[58]

While Hoover hoped to increase employment for all, the Ku Klux Klan complained that immigrants were taking jobs from "real Americans." In 1925 and again in 1926, the year that work commenced on U.S. Route 6 to honor Union Army veterans, the Klan organized nativist parades on Pennsylvania Avenue. Texas dentist and future asphalt hustler Hiram W. Evans was at the Klan helm, gracing *Time* magazine's cover on June 23, 1924, halfway through year three of his seventeen-year tenure as Imperial Wizard of the Knights of the Ku Klux Klan. He recruited from the "'hicks' and 'rubes' and 'drivers of secondhand Fords'" who worried about "aliens," especially Irish and Mexican Catholics. "Many of them Communist," Evans said of the latter, "waiting to cross the Rio Grande." When the Klan declined in the 1930s, Evans incorporated the Cooperative Asphalt Association and worked as an "asphalt dealer" for American Bitumuls, Emulsified Asphalt Refining, and Shell Union Oil. He parlayed friendship with fellow Klansman and Georgia governor Eurith D. Rivers into a virtual "emulsified asphalt monopoly" over Georgia highway-department projects. In 1940 a federal investigation of Rivers administration corruption caught Evans, once the United States' whitest man and now just another blacktop crook. He pleaded nolo contendere and paid a $15,000 fine by transferring the money, according to a later U.S. tax-court finding, from a company account "to [his] personal account" and never "repaid or reported [the amount] as income."[59]

The Great Mississippi Flood of 1927 was another horror that played out along the color line, complete with a backstory involving asphalt. Levees were relatively rare until 1879, when Congress created the Mississippi River Commission. In 1885 the commission adopted the Army Corps of Engineers proposal for "levees only" on the assumption that levee containment would increase the river's force sufficiently to scour out the river floor and send floodwater safely out to the Gulf of Mexico. Instead, the levees restricted the Mississippi's natural floodplain. That raised the stakes if the levees were to break. The 1927 flood did exactly that, with water pouring through 226 breaches, submerging twenty-seven thousand square miles, killing hundreds, and displacing nearly one million. At Mounds Landing, Mississippi, the floodwater dead included more than one hundred African Americans who had been piling sandbags under the discipline of armed national guards.[60]

"To control the Mississippi is not a difficult engineering job," the Great Engineer said. "It's merely a matter of financing."[61] The Army Corps of Engineers took up the task not only by raising the levees but by strengthening them with asphalt-coated revetments and "asphalt mattresses." The mattress project was especially ambitious. The corps built dozens of asphalt terminals and an "experimental plant . . . to manufacture and sink asphalt mattresses" along 1,600 miles of the Mississippi and 600 miles along the south banks of the Arkansas River and the Red River. By mid-1934 a "full-sized plant" was up and running, complete with an "asphalt revetment unit." "In the fiscal year ending June 30, 1936," the plant shipped, in addition to asphalt mattresses, over five hundred thousand "square feet of asphalt revetment" and "experimental asphalt wave-wash protection . . . placed below New Orleans on old and new levees," plus construction and installation over several years of 4.9 million square feet of asphalt revetment below Cairo, Illinois. This included, for Mississippi tributaries, "revetments of asphalt or stone over willow or lumber mattresses." The corps prioritized concave banks where the rivers exerted the greatest force. Unfortunately, asphalt could not conquer chuckholes and seepage that eroded soil and revetments alike.[62]

With twelve major tributaries beyond the Red and Arkansas (the Wisconsin, Missouri, Rock, Saint Croix, Illinois, Kaskaskia, Ohio, Minnesota, Des Moines, and White), the Mississippi drains nearly two-thirds of the continental United States. One distributary, the Atchafalaya River, feeds the Atchafalaya Basin, the largest wetland in the United States. Herbert Hoover was right, in a sense. The engineers tamed the Mississippi to a degree, though they did so at a steep price.

Nearly every engineering triumph accelerated subsidence. Simply put, the more pumping, the faster New Orleans sinks. While asphalt certainly strengthened the revetments and levees, as the decades rolled on other engineers further shrunk the natural floodplain by draining wetland and then crisscrossing and checkering the land with blacktop roads, parking lots, driveways, tennis courts, and dozens of other impermeable surfaces.

The 1920s ended with the Great Depression, a calamity that scarcely slowed the Army Corps of Engineers or the Bureau of Public Roads. At the end of the Depression's first full year, the bureau's annual appropriation had risen only to $75,000. Federal-aid roads built over a decade earlier compounded funding constraints, as those roads were beginning to require significant maintenance. For the Depression's second full year, 1931, Congress increased BPR funding to $125,000, with an additional $80,000 apportioned among the states. President Hoover, in the manner of his policy as commerce secretary, hoped to use road work as a tool to fight unemployment. The bureau highlighted this fact by including, for the first time, a section in its annual reports titled "Employment of Labor." By June 1931 over 365,000 people were working on road maintenance and construction projects. While battling unemployment as best they could and within the limits of the administration's budgetary strictures, BPR engineers and chemists continued their asphalt-materials research, conducting much of it in Virginia, at the Department of Agriculture's Arlington Experimental Farm. Among other things they tested, on a circular track, how various pavement surfaces would hold up to traffic loads.[63]

The Herbert Hoover administration, for its part, ended with yet another Pennsylvania Avenue disgrace, with asphalt playing a symbolic role in the key event that demonstrated both the Depression's depth and what many considered the callousness of the White House response. The World War Adjusted Compensation Act of 1924 awarded veterans certificates that they could redeem for cash in 1945. With need of that money in 1932, over twenty thousand veterans and their families—the Bonus Expeditionary Forces (BEF)—came to Washington in boxcars over rails and in cars and trucks over asphalt and gravel, camping on the Washington and Maryland sides of the Anacostia River. Given orders by President Hoover to remove the BEF from their Washington camps, Gen. Douglas MacArthur placed Maj. George S. Patton in charge of six tanks, accompanied by cavalry and infantry. He placed Maj. Dwight D. Eisenhower in charge of public relations. After accomplishing the BEF eviction task, MacArthur disobeyed Hoover's order not to cross the river into Maryland and burn the BEF camp. When the veterans regrouped in 1933, the new president , Franklin D. Roosevelt, did not send MacArthur, Patton, and Eisenhower charging down Pennsylvania Avenue blacktop. "Hoover sent the army," one veteran said. "Roosevelt sent his wife."[64]

From the early road pioneers to the engineers and chemists at the Bureau of Public Roads and elsewhere, false starts littered the scratching and clawing of those determined to ring pavement and profit out of asphalt. A Sea Wolf from the Napoleonic Wars roamed the oceans only to die an old man, his anchor stuck in a pitch-black lake. Anheuser-Busch turned Gilsonite into nickels and dimes and coatings for their beer barrels. A father stood against slavery, while his son found the road to his asphalt throne paved with segregation. Nativist barkers promoted asphalt as an Ellis Island "hygienic apparatus" to protect against the huddled masses and their "malarial sail." An endless stream of asphalt trusts in New York dreamed of gunboats in the Caribbean. Woodrow Wilson had Pennsylvania Avenue blacktop painted white for his inauguration. Ku Klux Klan minions had their wives wash white sheets and hoods for their marches on that same glory road. The lyrics for George M. Cohan's patriotic song of 1917 did not tell us that our Yanks took asphalt with them "over there, over there." No one needed telling that those Yanks who did not die at the Argonne were "on the run, on the run" back home—run off Pennsylvania Avenue blacktop by Mac and Ike and Patton's tanks. They turned Cohan's lines on their Yankee Doodled heads: "Send the word, send the word to beware. . . . Hoist the flag and let her fly."

Under Franklin Roosevelt asphalt would move off capitalism's periphery and locate at its beating heart, sometimes for better and sometimes for worse. For the better, asphalt would prove essential to the New Deal assault on the Great Depression, the New Deal crusade to save capitalism from itself. It would prove just as essential to the Allied assault on the Reich and its Axis partners. In the middle ground after Roosevelt's death, the product would prove essential to the United States' prosecution of the Cold War. For the worse, asphalt with or without the free market would facilitate Hitler's crimes in Germany and Stalin's purges, liquidations, and gulags in the Union of Soviet Socialist Republics. Asphalt as a material thing would prove to be a useful tool not only for capitalists pursuing profits but for anyone pursuing power for themselves or determined to deny it to others.

5 Duty

Conquering Poverty and Mud, Reich and Rising Sun

Though his parents named him after the hero of a children's book, *A Dog of Flanders* (1872), Nello Leguy Teer (1888–1963) cared little for books and reckoned grade three was enough. In 1897, at age nine, he fled the Durham Public Schools to haunt his father's brickyard until landing on the payroll. At eighteen a clay-grinding machine took a hand. At twenty-one he rented mules and hauled limestone for the University of North Carolina and graded the site for the Benjamin N. Duke mansion. (Duke gave him his first artificial hand, a split-hook prosthetic.) By 1924 he owned over four hundred mules and had sufficient heft to host the Pan-American Highway Commission at a Yanceyville barbeque attended by seven thousand road enthusiasts from a dozen nations. A few years later he helped drag his state and much of the South into the machine age. "People went from trucks and mules and drag pans and old wagons," his son Dillard recalled, "and all of a sudden . . . the whole equipment industry was revolutionized."[1]

Batista's Cuba was one of the few places Nello Teer refused to do business, though not for lack of trying (he offloaded a road contract, given the constant threats of revolution and government demands for bribes). His company's sole-source and joint-venture projects spanning six decades included the construction of Israel's Ramon Air Base and its two asphalt runways (a redeployment after Israel surrendered Sinai bases per the Camp David Accords); Tanzania's Great North Road; Nicaragua's Rama Road; and the Guatemala section of the Pan-American Highway (which extends from Deadhorse, Alaska, to Ushuaia, Argentina, thirty thousand mostly asphalt miles interrupted only by the hundred-mile Darién Gap in Panama). The grading and paving of the Blue Ridge Parkway in Virginia and North Carolina, however, sits at the heart of company lore.[2]

"Mr. Roosevelt didn't build that road to keep the Japs from comin'," Dillard Teer said of the Blue Ridge project and the tiny dent it made in unemployment, the nation's number-one enemy during the 1930s. Of the hundreds of road-building projects launched under the New Deal's Works Progress Administration (WPA), few could match the vistas the Blue Ridge provided for those U.S. Americans fortunate enough to have an automobile and vacation time during the Great Depression. The Blue Ridge required the construction of 27 tunnels, 168 bridges, 6 viaducts, and 469 miles of pavement between Shenandoah National Park and Great Smoky Mountains National Park. "Aside from a handful of skilled workers and superintendents," the Teer family boasted, "[we] drew [our] entire labor force from the Appalachian population. Most . . . walked to work every day." To maximize employment, workers divided into two six-hour shifts at a quarter per hour, and the WPA awarded contracts in six- or seven-mile sections (with the Teer Company completing seventeen sections). State and local government provided raw materials. The WPA provided paychecks. This was a "ballot-box tradeoff," as the recipients voted Democratic. On the materials end a reporter for Robert "Colonel" McCormick's *Chicago Tribune* noted in disgust, "gravel and asphalt don't vote."[3]

Blue Ride Parkway planning began in 1933, when President Franklin D. Roosevelt, Interior Secretary Harold Ickes, and Senator Harry F. Byrd (D-VA) secured a $16 million congressional appropriation. Construction commenced two years later. Where it was too far to walk, the labor force was housed near job sites in WPA and CCC (Civilian Conservation Corps) camps. A polio epidemic interrupted the construction schedule—so did the Japanese. Teer Company employees and machines paved the Blue Ridge's first section in 1935 and its last section in 1987. A personal tragedy accompanied the early crush-stone work and asphalt spraying. Teer's son Marion, fourteen, frequently visited job sites where the superintendent, his uncle (Nello Teer's brother), allowed him to drive a "pick-up, up and down the roads." The uncle had no children of his own. He treated the young man as his own son. One day while driving the truck, Marion lost control and went over an embankment. The ten-foot drop broke his neck.[4]

Nello Teer had lost his hand and then a son, who died on a graded section of the Blue Ridge Parkway as a work crew was setting up to spray asphalt. Three decades later, in 1963, Teer lost his life on an asphalt road. He died, at seventy-five, from injuries sustained in an automobile accident, leaving behind his company's legacy of over ten thousand miles of paved roads in the United States and abroad.

Asphalt pavement came into its own during the Great Depression. Still, the paving machines that helped transform the nation's environment would have sat idle had it not been for the New Deal. During its brief run (1933–34), the Civil Works Administration created shovel-ready construction jobs for four million workers who, in round numbers, laid 12 million feet of sewer pipe; built 250,000 outhouses, 40,000 schools, 3,700 playgrounds, and over 900 airports; and built or improved approximately 250,000 miles of dirt, gravel, concrete, and asphalt roads. During its longer run (1935–43), the WPA put 8.5 million people to work building "more than 650,000 miles . . . of roads; 125,000 public buildings; 75,000 bridges; 8,000 parks; and 800 airports and 700 miles of airport runways." Private contractors usually did the paving. They continued to do so when World War II began and the WPA earned a nickname, the War Preparation Agency. For contractors that meant paving work "on 1,800 command installations and 2,200 industrial facilities." All priority projects—airfields and runways and all roads deemed necessary for military transport—used enormous amounts of asphalt.[5]

For New Dealers in Washington's Georgetown neighborhood, the march of asphalt was not always welcome. John Ihlder, who battled segregated housing as director of the Alley Dwelling Authority, ran point here. He recruited Dean Acheson, an attorney and later secretary of state, and other P Street neighbors to counter Q Street residents who demanded the widening and paving of P Street "in the hope that it would reduce the traffic before their houses." Ihlder's gang hoped to keep the cobblestones in place and prevent their street from becoming a blacktop artery.[6] That asphalt helped the nation recover from the Depression and prepare for war scarcely slowed the odd New Dealer concerned with property values . . . let alone critics of New Deal infrastructure spending. A typical *Chicago Tribune* complaint had seven wPA workers on a road project, with four doing nothing more than holding flags.[7]

The New Deal's conservative foes could not stop the blacktop march any more than P Street liberals could. Nor could radical conservationists stop paving in the Blue Ridge or the national parks. By 1919 seven tourists drove to Yosemite for every tourist who arrived by train. By 1925 park visitors numbered over two million annually and boosters were calling for a "park-to-park highway." In the 1930s ccc work in the parks and beyond included 125,000 miles of new roads, improvements on 600,000 miles of existing roads, and eight million square yards of parking lots.[8] Today the National Park Service has over 5,000 miles of blacktop roads, and contractors continue to maintain Blue Ridge asphalt and the road surfaces of the other national parkways (George Washington Memorial, Natchez Trace, Colonial, Foothills, and Baltimore-Washington). The blacktop march, however, has slowed recently. Several national parks are removing pavement in pursuit of revegetation. Paving in the national forests has also slowed with President Bill Clinton's Roadless Area Final Rule of January 12, 2001, a rule that has survived legal challenges and other threats (most recently, the Donald Trump administration's removal of the roadless rule for Alaska's Tongass National Forest).[9]

Robert Moses, the New York City parks commissioner from 1934 to 1960, would have scoffed at any roadless rule. He secured scores of New Deal–funded projects, ranging from swimming pools and Jones Beach State Park to the Lincoln Tunnel and the Triborough Bridge (now the Robert F. Kennedy Bridge). When Moses died on July 29, 1981, at age ninety-two, the word *asphalt* appeared only once in his

New York Times obituary. It could have appeared in every paragraph. Although the things Moses built are more important than asphalt or any other construction material, his use of asphalt was so all encompassing that it affirmed the cultural change he envisioned. Nearly all of the 658 playgrounds he championed were blacktop. So were most of the ramps, toll plazas, and decks for thirteen bridges. Above all, the Cross-Bronx Expressway and other "superhighways" built straight through the city and out to the budding suburbs best captures Moses's linear legacy of wielding "power to lay down asphalt." The roads had a color-line legacy too. They required relocation, the parks commissioner said, of "ghetto folks."[10]

From Moses's blacktop rivers to the Blue Ridge and beyond, asphalt was inseparable from hundreds of the nation's iconic landmarks and millions of common structures. The Empire State Building's steel frame received rust-inhibiting coats of linseed oil and asphalt. The five years (1931–36) of Hoover Dam construction featured 4,360,000 cubic yards of concrete that could not arrive until completion of a blacktop road from Boulder City, Colorado, to the dam site. (The road the tourists drive across the dam top remains asphalt today.) For the Grand Coulee Dam, Standard Asphalt's "powdermonkeys" moved 25,000 cubic yards of rock with a single dynamite blast. They crushed that rock and used it as gravel for the roads the project demanded. Gravel was on rooftops too, as it was a key material in asphalt shingles. Frank Lloyd Wright, when designing "sensible houses," preached the virtues of a "good asphalt roof." Asphalt shingle and roofing manufacturing, in fact, was big enough by the New Deal's first year that the National Recovery Administration recommended minimum wages for workers in these industries: forty-five cents, forty cents, and thirty-seven and a half cents an hour on the Pacific Coast, Northeast, and South, respectively, and thirty-five cents an hour for women all over. Asphalt appeared below the roof too. From the 1930s to the 1950s (and to a much lesser degree thereafter), builders used asphalt-infused kraft paper as a vapor barrier and asphalt-shingle siding as a maintenance-free cover for weathered paint or rotted clapboard in rundown neighborhoods.[11]

Asphalt played a surprising role in Depression-era crime and a predictable role in the monotonies of everyday life. "The great vector change of the 1920's into the 1930's was the confluence of the automobile and asphalt," FBI director James B. Comey noted in 2015. John Dillinger could now travel "unimaginable distances" and rob banks in Illinois, Indiana, and Michigan all in one day.[12] Asphalt allowed law-abiding U.S. Americans to move as well, and no path was more iconic than Route 66 from Chicago to Los Angeles. John Steinbeck called it the "mother road, the road of flight," for Dust Bowl refugees. Commissioned in 1927, it was not fully paved—a mix of blacktop, concrete, and other surfaces—until 1938. Contractors did the paving, but the CCC and WPA provided most of the manual laborers. A Route 66 job site in Missouri was the first to be paved with the Barber-Greene paving-machine company's key invention: the floating screed, which allowed a level surface as it placed more asphalt in a roadbed's low spots and less in the high spots. During the war years the mother road transitioned into a military highway of sorts, with contractors building airfields for training fighter pilots "up and down 66." Gen. George Patton drilled his troops and their tanks in the Mojave Desert near 66 blacktop.[13]

John Steinbeck also romanticized asphalt in California's Central Valley after concrete pavements failed: "The county maintenance crews poured tar in the [concrete] cracks to keep the water out and that didn't work, and finally they capped the roads with an asphalt and gravel mixture. That did survive, because it . . . gave a little and came back a little." Concrete had its charms for Californians as well, and by the Depression's last gasps highway construction included the Arroyo Seco Parkway (now the Pasadena Freeway) and its mix of concrete and asphalt. Lanes of a different color, the engineers hoped, would keep drivers focused and alive. (An accident involving "three carloads of dignitaries" marred the parkway's opening in 1940.) Urban planners also hoped those black-and-white lanes would "lure shoppers to the center of Los Angeles." Instead, they lured city residents to the budding suburbs.[14]

Germany, not the United States, led the world in freeway construction first under the Weimar Republic and then the Reich. The Cologne to Bonn highway, completed in 1932, was the first limited-access, high-speed highway. In 1933 work began on the Autobahn, what Joseph Goebbels, the Reich minister of propaganda, called "der Führer's roads."[15] Hitler turned over a spade of dirt at the ceremonial inauguration of construction, and the National Socialist Party promoted it as a job-creating juggernaut that would advance the Reich's industrial and martial might. A year later, in 1934, Franklin Roosevelt's antennae were up when the Permanent International Association of Road Congresses chose Munich to host its annual meeting. When the U.S. delegation's request for funding and a message of support crossed his desk, FDR asked his budget director: "Is this OK?" The delegates got their funding, but no message of support from the White House. Roosevelt was right to worry. Rudolph Hess, the deputy führer, spoke at the event, and the program committee listed Hitler, Goebbels, and Hermann Göering (soon to be named supreme commander of the Luftwaffe). When construction ended in 1943, the Autobahn's concrete pavement (only about 10 percent was asphalt) stretched four thousand miles. After D-Day "der Führer's roads" would prove less useful to the Wehrmacht than to the advancing U.S. Army.[16]

Fritz Todt, a flight officer during World War I and a Nazi since 1922, supervised Autobahn construction. His proposals for employing manual labor on infrastructure projects brought him into Hitler's orbit by 1930, and he was soon serving on the staff of Heinrich Himmler, Reichsführer of the SS. A few years later he formed Organisation Todt. This construction conglomerate built the West Wall's nearly four hundred miles of bunkers, tank traps, and the like, and the Wolf's Lair complex, including the runway and access roads (some of which were asphalt), which served as Hitler's initial headquarters for the war on the Russian front. (Todt died in a plane crash near the Wolf's Lair airfield in 1942.) The decision to pave the Autobahn with concrete was predictable, given Todt's long-standing preference for concrete (a preference that Hitler shared). Regardless, Organisation Todt paved thousands of miles of non-Autobahn roads with asphalt (especially in German-occupied Europe). And today's Autobahn is almost entirely blacktop.[17]

Nazi Germany's brief ally and then great enemy, the Soviet Union under Stalin, launched its own ambitious road-building program. In contrast to Hitler, Stalin was an asphalt devotee—a fact that his great rival noted. "The real program of the coming Soviet five-year plan," Leon Trotsky wrote, "is to 'catch up with Europe and America'" by building "a network of autoroads and asphalt highways in the measure-less spaces of the Soviet Union. . . . In barbarian society the rider and the pedestrian constituted two classes. The automobile differentiates society no less than the saddle horse."[18] Stalin's beasts of burden were human beings before, during, and after the war. A captured Luft-waffe fighter pilot remembered asphalt arriving in Studebaker trucks near Moscow. "Stalin asphalt," Panzer tank crews called it, because it did not hold up, hardly surprising as the Red Czar used bricks from demolished churches to make aggregate.[19]

That Luftwaffe pilot was relatively fortunate. He could have been assigned asphalt work in Siberia. Stalin's decision to make road con-struction in the deep forests a priority produced what one prisoner called "a peculiar paradox . . . the Gulag was slowly bringing 'civili-zation'—if that is what it can be called—to the remote wilderness. Roads were being built where there had been only forest. . . . Native peoples were being pushed aside to make way for cities, factories, and railways." In 1932 gulag labor began work on the notorious R504 Kolyma Highway in eastern Siberia. They called it the "road of bones" because frozen ground made digging graves impractical for those who died on site. Construction ended in 1953 (the year Stalin died). Even today the highway is mostly compacted gravel and clay. But asphalt pavement has covered the first few hundred miles out of Magadan since the 1930s.[20]

As the world moved out of the Great Depression and into World War II, asphalt proved useful to construction projects beyond roads. This was especially so in the United States. Nearly all of the approximately seven hundred home-front POW camps holding over four hundred thousand German soldiers had asphalt flooring and asphalt shingles or other asphalt-based products on rooftops. While Pentagon construction (1941–43) required an immense amount of reinforced concrete for its seventeen miles of corridors, asphalt ruled the parking lots and access roads. Unfortunately, rumors of war profiteering were rampant. Arlington Asphalt Company principals, columnist Drew Pearson howled, "quick-chang[ed] Uncle Sam out of $500,000" through various scams. He said Senator Harry Byrd intervened to prevent the indictment of these alleged "blacktop crooks."[21]

Construction of a U.S. merchant fleet to meet wartime demand was another area in which asphalt played a role tainted by the occasional scandal. The Merchant Marine Act of 1936 created a Maritime Commission with power to award subsidies for companies that built ships in U.S. yards. In extraordinary circumstances the law allowed the Maritime Commission to place its own orders for ship construction.[22] Those circumstances arrived with France's surrender to Germany on June 22, 1940, and the Japanese attack on Pearl Harbor on December 7, 1941 . . . a day of infamy that included asphalt stories. The freighter USS *Jupiter*, bound for Pearl on that day, carried asphalt in its hold, and Japan's bombers targeted Pearl's asphalt runways and airstrips. Within hours of the last bomb falling, U.S. sailors began using asphalt to repair the runway and airstrip damage.

Asphalt's role during the United States' own years of infamy began with President Roosevelt's Executive Order 9066 of February 19, 1942, resulting in the internment of nearly 120,000 persons of Japanese descent in inland camps. Internment housing, like POW camp housing, usually had asphalt flooring below and asphalt shingles above. At the Tule Lake War Relocation Center in California, for example, the army assigned some internees housing far enough from the other buildings to be nicknamed "Alaska." But it could get so hot in that building that metal cot legs sank into the asphalt floor. Before departing for the camps, the army held internees at assembly centers, including one at Santa Anita Park in Arcadia, California, home to a racetrack. Even decades later survivors remembered trying to sleep on barn floors, lying on blacktop surfaces thin enough to provide almost no protection from the horse manure below.[23]

While Japanese Americans poured into internment camps, Maritime Commission orders flooded shipyards. The war years saw the construction of the USS *Asphalt* (IX-153) and other concrete barges constructed with wire-mesh ferrocement (a construction material consisting of wire meshes and cement mortar). (In 1945 the navy abandoned the *Asphalt* after it ran aground in the Caroline Islands.) More conventional cargo vessels included 531 Victory ships and 2,710 of the larger and faster Liberty ships.[24] Henry J. Kaiser, the son of German immigrants and the most prodigious Liberty shipbuilder, started out as an asphalt and concrete man. In 1914 he signed his first contract, a modest assignment to pave Victoria Avenue in Vancouver, British Columbia, and then moved his business to Oakland, California, because he thought his German name was less upsetting to U.S. Americans than to Canadians. The Federal Aid Road Act of 1916 confirmed the wisdom of the move, as he secured paving contracts across the Pacific Northwest. One county engineer in Washington State said the commissioners who awarded road contracts "needed only 'a thermometer and a beautiful faith in Mr. Kaiser and the asphalt industry.'" In 1927 Kaiser accepted an invitation from his frequent partner and source of capital, Warren Brothers, to work the two contracts that made him a major player.[25]

The first, Mississippi levee reconstruction after the Great Flood of 1927, was a nightmare. Kaiser's company paid workers in cash. With the exception of Warren Brothers, however, the other contractors did not. It was peonage, a Kaiser superintendent said: "We were glad to get out in 1929." Kaiser's company, Warren Brothers, and a Cuban company also began work in 1927 on Cuba's east-west Carretera Central, a twenty-five-foot-wide strip topped with two inches of asphalt and running nearly the island's length. From there Kaiser and his crews helped build the San Francisco–Oakland Bay Bridge, and the Hoover, Bonneville, and Grand Coulee Dams. For a few of the Great Depression's worst years, he added partners to form the Bechtel-Kaiser-Warren Company (one of over a hundred companies he founded from the obscure Nanaimo Paving to Kaiser Aluminum, Kaiser Steel, and Kaiser Permanente). The Maritime Commission kept his shipyards especially busy. His workers built 1,490 Liberty and Victory ships and, after FDR overruled the navy's objection, fifty Casablanca-class escort carriers. (The fleet admirals thought the escort carriers were too small to be of much use; they were wrong.) "That's another home run I'm chalking up for you," the financier and presidential adviser Bernard Baruch told Roosevelt. "Whatever faults [Kaiser] may have—imagination and lack of courage are not among them."[26]

While still undecided about whether to run for a fourth term, Franklin Roosevelt asked Margaret Suckley, cousin and confidant, what she thought of Kaiser as a possible presidential candidate. "[She] asked *how* he would get on with the Churchills, Stalins, etc." FDR replied, "He's more like them than I am."[27] Upon deciding to run, the president considered Kaiser for the vice-presidential spot and asked the FBI to see if he "belonged to any cults." The vetting centered on Kaiser's connection to Fritz J. Hansgirg, an Austrian chemist with a stepson characterized by military intelligence as "the Chief Psychologist of the German Army." Kaiser had sponsored Hansgirg when he immigrated to the United States during the early 1930s because he had developed the carbothermic magnesium–reduction process for mass producing magnesium. Kaiser built a plant, with the help of a Reconstruction Finance Corporation loan, and produced an "extraordinarily flammable" mix of magnesium and asphalt that he sold to the Army Chemical Weapons Service. Unfortunately for Kaiser's newfound chemist, the FBI arrested him ten days after Pearl Harbor and sent him to an enemy alien internment camp. Though FDR passed on Kaiser for the vice-presidential slot, there were no hard feelings. "Eisenhower would like to have Henry Kaiser come [to the front]," Bureau of Labor Statistics director Isador Lubin told the president. "Our troops . . . would like to see the guy who made so many ships."[28]

Asphalt played a role in the production of those ships. With steel for armor plate in short supply, Kaiser and other manufacturers substituted quarter-inch steel plating buttressed by thick slabs of Trinidad asphalt and crushed stone. This "plastic armor" protected Liberty ship bridges, chart rooms, captain's quarters, radio rooms, and 20 mm gun tubs. On the backend, beyond bombs, bullets, beans, and bodies (each ship could carry six thousand caskets), Liberty ships like the ss *Michael J. Stone* carried asphalt. Named after a Maryland Congress representative and slave owner whose brother had signed the Declaration of Independence, this steamer survived a U-boat torpedo off Gibraltar without the loss of life or a single drop of asphalt. Merchant steamers carried asphalt and road and runway-building machinery too, and they were not always as fortunate as the *Michael J. Stone*. An example: On June 15, 1942, near Trinidad, a U-boat sank the *Kahuku*, killing seventeen and destroying "7,480 long tons of excavating, transportation, gravel, rock plant, and asphalt equipment."[29]

Asphalt proved its value as a war material again when the U.S. Army contracted, in 1941, with Morrison-Knudsen, a Boise, Idaho, company, to build a blacktop runway and staging area at Northway, Alaska. This was in support of Lend-Lease Act aid to the Soviet Union; in round numbers, 1.75 million tons of food, 400,000 jeeps and trucks, 12,000 tanks and other armored vehicles, and 11,000 aircraft. Most went to the Soviets by naval convoy and then overland. To get supplies to the Red Army, the Army Corps of Engineers built and upgraded roads across Iran using "cut-back asphalt and . . . soil asphalt."[30] A full 80 percent of the aircraft, however, went through Northway. To accommodate the traffic Morrison-Knudsen and other contractors, working with army and navy engineers, built runways, aircraft hangers, barracks, warehouses, movie theaters, garages, powerhouses, sawmills, and machine shops. To connect everything they laid down snowplow-friendly blacktop using what the industry now calls a primitive cold mix of cutback asphalt (that is, solvent-diluted asphalt cement, a mix rarely used nowadays given the environmental hazards posed by the solvents).

Though the Northway base did not appear on maps until after the war, it was hard to keep secret the bulldozers and scrapers that arrived by ship at Valdez, the largest port on Prince William Sound, which were driven under their own power across three hundred miles of Alaska's primitive roads. The five thousand tons of liquid asphalt that arrived by air in twenty-eight thousand drums helped win the war, but at a price. Spillage and burial of surplus product polluted soil and ground water. Sixty-three years after V-E Day and V-J Day, the state of Alaska announced, Northway pollutants "no longer pose an unacceptable threat to human health."[31]

Northway's blacktop was part of the Alaska-Siberia Air Road. The ALSIB's two points of origin, Minneapolis and Great Falls Army Air Base in Montana, both converged on Edmonton, Alberta. North of Edmonton, the Canadians built nearly two dozen airfields, auxiliary bases, and emergency-landing strips. The ALSIB's Alaska portion began at Northway and included Tanacross Air Base, Big Delta Army Airfield, Ladd Army Airfield, Galena Airport, Marks Army Airfield, and Gambell Army Airfield on Saint Lawrence Island in the Bering Sea. Most had asphalt runways. U.S. pilots turned over aircraft to Soviet pilots at Ladd Army Airfield because Stalin would not allow U.S. pilots into Russian airspace. Those who made the first stop in Siberia (188 died in crashes) landed at Uelkal's wooden-plank runway. (Asphalt was rare on the seventeen runways and airstrips dotting the ALSIB's Siberian portion.) Beyond Uelkal the Soviet pilots flew over gulag camps or landed to refuel at those camps where prisoners built runways. (Lend-Lease food shipments helped feed that enslaved work-force.) The thousands of aircraft "ferried through" included fighters, bombers, transports, and trainers. Nearly all arrived in Alaska with Soviet Air Forces markings.[32]

The Alaska-Canada Military Highway (Alcan) functioned largely as an ALSIB supply route. Construction began on March 8, 1942, and finished nine months later, a dirt and gravel road running 1,700 miles from Dawson Creek, British Columbia, to Delta Junction, Alaska. The Army Corps of Engineers supervised an eleven-thousand-person crew, with segregated African American engineer regiments constituting over a third of that number. Because white engineer regiments had all the heavy equipment, Black troops used only hand tools to build the Alcan's first bridge, the Sikanni Chief Bridge, across three hundred feet of fast-moving river. Asphalt paving began after the war, finishing in 1964 for the Alaska portion and 1992 for the Canadian portion. Global warming has exacerbated Alcan maintenance, given melting permafrost. In some areas crews have paved over deformities so often that the asphalt is ten-feet thick.[33]

Both Alcan and ALSIB escaped combat. The Aleutian archipelago, an island chain extending over one thousand miles west to Attu Island, hosted what combat Alaska experienced. Neither the indigenous Aleut people nor U.S. military personnel found the climate hospitable. Pilots joked about island wind socks: log chains, which could weigh over three hundred pounds per hundred feet, hanging from poles. Brig. Gen. William "Billy" Mitchell, the most persistent proponent of air power during the New Deal years, emphasized the Aleutians and Alaska proper six years before Pearl Harbor, telling Congress, "He who holds Alaska will hold the world."[34] Given the belief that the war against Japan would center in the Pacific Rim's northern reaches, the army removed and interned, under abysmal conditions, nearly nine hundred Aleuts from not only the Aleutians but the Pribilof Islands, where Russian fur traders had relocated them in the late eighteenth century. (Many Pribilof Aleuts lived in frame houses with green asphalt siding.)

War arrived in the Aleutians on June 3, 1942, the day before the Battle of Midway opened, and ended just two months later, on August 15, with a navy task force bombarding Kiska Island in preparation for a landing. Problems of weather and distance were such that U.S. and Canadian troops discovered, only when charging ashore, that the Japanese had abandoned Kiska. That was the end of combat on U.S. soil.[35] Nonetheless, cleanup in the Aleutians was even more difficult than at Northway. For seventy-five years and counting, Attu Island remained dotted with tiny asphalt lakes that trapped seabirds and marine mammals "almost like the La Brea tar pits." (Attu lies within the Alaska Maritime National Wildlife Refuge, protected land since 1909, when Theodore Roosevelt designated two Aleutian islands, Bogoslof and New Bogoslof, a bird sanctuary.) The Army Corps of Engineers and their cleanup equipment arrived in 2016, by sea and by air at Attu's blacktop runway. Funding of $10 million from the Formerly Used Defense Site program was not enough to remediate even the two designated sites. The corps found more abandoned and often leaky asphalt drums than anticipated.[36]

At Fort Randall on Cold Bay, cleanup of World War II contaminants remained minimal to nonexistent through the 1980s. As the twentieth century drew to a close, the state of Alaska and the Army Corps of Engineers "identified two [asphalt] seeps and . . . two burial trenches suspected of containing [nearly 3,000] 55-gallon drums . . . [the] result of disposal of excess drums of asphalt following runway paving." Fortunately, recovered asphalt could often be recycled. At Port Clarence Army Base, operational for eight years (1942–50) on a narrow peninsula jutting from Alaska's northwest coast, the Army Corps of Engineers recovered 1,400 asphalt drums suitable for salvage. Cleanup and recycling, however, are not the norm. Army engineers are most likely to manage the World War II–era "asphalt disposal areas" scattered around the globe as landfills.[37]

The army operated nearly all of the World War II–era roads and airfields in Alaska from the Aleutians to Nome, part of a building boom totaling more than three hundred military installations. Beyond the Alcan and the ALSIB's runways and airstrips, the corps supervised road construction in and around Anchorage, Fairbanks, Yakutat, Kodiak, and Unalaska; and port and pier construction across the Aleutians and south-central Alaska. Every month the Adak pier alone handled up to 130,000 tons of cargo, including asphalt, arriving via Liberty ships. The corps had help from Morrison-Knudsen, other contractors, and CCC labor. The Department of the Interior also prioritized employment "consideration" for indigenous peoples.[38]

Navy construction battalions (CBS or Seabees) provided another labor force for military projects in Alaska. Seabee roots date to the creation of the Bureau of Navy Yards and Docks in 1842. During World War I Yards and Docks organized a modest construction regiment based at the Great Lakes Naval Training Station, north of Chicago. By the late 1930s Yards and Docks was supervising base and airfield construction across the continental United States and U.S. territories. Navy construction expanded dramatically in 1940, when the Roosevelt administration traded fifty destroyers for a string of British naval bases across the Caribbean, including bases on the Galápagos Islands and at Trinidad where the asphalt trust once roamed. (Besides paving three parallel runways and dozens of roads on Trinidad, the navy built a blimp hanger.) In nearly every instance the navy relied on civilian labor to do the work, a reliance that proved problematic after Pearl Harbor, as civilian labor had few protections under the laws of war. (The Martens Clause in the Hague Convention II of 1899 was open to interpretation even on the question of whether captured civilians who had worked on military projects could be summarily executed.) The navy responded by creating the Seabees. They could build and fight (*Construimus, Batuimus*) and, if captured, they had rights.[39]

Seasoned construction workers with an average age of thirty-seven populated the first Seabee battalions. When voluntary enlistments gave way to Selective Service, younger men populated the battalions. In the Atlantic theater Seabees operated from the Caribbean to the Snowball Route in the North Atlantic. At Keflavík, Iceland, a refueling point for flights to Europe (and later a NATO airfield paved by Nello Teer), they built four 6,500-foot blacktop runways, using pulverized lava as aggregate. They built additional bases and runways in New-foundland and Greenland for the ferrying of aircraft to England. When the weather was good, over a hundred planes a day moved through each base. Seabee combat demolition units, moreover, were among the first to arrive in North Africa in 1942 and at Normandy in 1944.[40]

Army air forces construction personnel served in the Atlantic the-ater too, and their numbers were massive enough to include seven "Colored Battalions" assigned to build airfields as far south as Kenya. While training, these segregated forces faced all the problems their white counterparts faced plus such "additional difficulties," according to today's U.S. Air Force, as "substandard living and recreational facilities, and suspicion or outright hostility from the white units and the local civilian population living near the training bases." Whenever possible for heavy-bomber runways, the work crews, Black or white, followed the British Class A Airfield design: six to nine inches of concrete slab covered with a layer of asphalt. (Whether for their own runway construction or U.S. construction, the British often sent rubble—collected from London buildings destroyed in Luftwaffe raids—to job sites for use as aggregate.) U.S. Army senior staff limited "the long-term presence of blacks in England," today's U.S. Air Force reiterated, to avoid conflict "between black and white troops and with the English people" on or near many of the approximately 850 airfields England supported during the war.[41]

In the Pacific, Navy Seabees and Army Engineer Aviation Battalions (EABS) did the lion's share of construction. Of the army's 157 EABS, each made up of over eight hundred personnel, 70 served in the Pacific. Nearly a third were designated "colored." The all-white EABS, like the Alcan's all-white work crews, were more likely to have a full complement of construction machinery: tractors, bulldozers, scrapers, graders, shovels, rollers, mixers, compressors, rock crushers, and concrete and asphalt pavers. Of the 325,000 Seabees who served in World War II, 80 percent did so in the Pacific, with "southern officers exclusively" commanding the segregated battalions, including fifteen special all-Black battalions primarily but not exclusively assigned stevedore duty. Seabees, white and Black, built "111 major airstrips, 441 piers, 2,558 ammunition magazines, 700 square blocks of warehouses, hospitals to serve 70,000 patients, tanks for the storage of 100,000,000 gallons of gasoline, and housing for 1,500,000 men." After the navy reversed its Jim Crow policy in January 1944, several Seabee units were among the navy's first fully integrated units.[42]

The Seabees used blacktop whenever possible, dismissing nonasphalt roads and runways as "fair-weather strips." In the Aleutians they operated rock quarries, crushing plants, and portable asphalt plants.

The magnitude and impact of Seabee labor along asphalt's black line in the South Pacific, however, dwarfed their work in the North Pacific. Japan lost the paving war long before Hiroshima and Nagasaki, though not for lack of effort. The Japanese paved island airstrips and roads, projects that attracted the attention of the U.S. Office of Strategic Services. (The oss *Simple Sabotage Field Manual* provided tips for wrecking pavement.) The Japanese also used pow labor for paving projects. One officer in the Philippines tortured prisoners by dumping truckloads of fruit on sunbaked asphalt and forcing starving prisoners, all civilians and nearly all U.S. Americans, to stare at the pile but not eat anything until the fruit was fit only for flies. After V-J Day, a U.S. Army military commission hanged the man for war crimes.[43]

The United States won the asphalt war in the Pacific theater on a quantitative front. A single requisition from U.S. Armed Forces in Australia included 3.25 million gallons of liquid asphalt. Australian construction companies helped by producing coal tar, which the engineers added to asphalt mixes. Back home many refiners specializing in downstream petroleum products made fortunes. Nonetheless, producing more asphalt than Japan was not enough to alleviate chronic asphalt shortages. One reason for shortages: not all refiners bothered with barrel bottoms. On the Caribbean island of Curaçao, a Dutch colony forty miles off the Venezuelan coast, Royal Dutch Shell's Isla Refinery produced light oil products for military use but began dumping what would grow to 1.5 million tons of asphalt and other residuals into Busca Bay's mangrove-covered swamps. Curaçao residents called the dump site Asphalt Lake.[44] A second reason for demand outpacing supply: home-front shortages of aluminum, steel, copper, zinc, and lead exacerbated asphalt shortages abroad, as "asphalt had to replace sheet metal and copper exterior materials. . . . Metal use in the average dwelling went from 8,300 lbs. to 3,200 lbs." A third reason for shortages: home-front demand for asphalt to construct military airfields and roads. Overall shortages were so great that the United States imported twelve thousand tons of liquid asphalt a month from Mexico.[45]

Henry Byroade, who served with the Army Corps of Engineers and then as a career diplomat, explained how asphalt shortages hampered runway construction in Chengdu, China:

> We quite secretly designed and laid out four or five . . . of the big fields, for the B-29s, and seven fighter fields for protection. I say secretly, because when we moved into an area in China and started construction, the prices of everything went sky high. . . . The Generalissimo [Chiang Kai-Shek], of course, drafted the work force, coolies. They would arrive there in groups, walking from as far as a hundred miles. . . . We had 496,000 laborers on that job. We located the big fields along rivers, as a source of rock, and they would carry the rock on their shoulders and heads up to seven miles in each direction; break the rock by hand. We had no concrete . . . no asphalt. . . . Ninety days after we started that project, the first B-29 came in. . . . General Curt LeMay . . . had been running hundred-bomber missions over Europe, and . . . wanted to run that kind of mission over Tokyo. But the dust was so bad that they couldn't take off that fast. . . . He said, "Well, we've got to pave them." I said, "Well, there's nothing here to pave them with."[46]

Asphalt shortages slowed but never stopped the Army Corps of Engineers or Navy Seabees. They improvised. Army engineers built nearly a hundred airfields in France using "prefabricated Hessian surfacing" infused with asphalt-impregnated jute, a cordage commodity from India, laid out in rolls three feet wide and three hundred feet long. For airstrips suitable for planes up to fighter-bomber weight, the Seabees used "stamp lickers" to lay down enormous strips of "rolled asphalt" sprinkled with ground mica to prevent adhesion.[47] When concrete and asphalt was available for heavy-bomber runways, the Seabees battled Britain's Corps of Royal Engineers, who favored concrete over "soggy" asphalt. The Seabees countered by reminding the Sappers that the volcanic and coral subsurfaces that led to those problems could cause concrete runways to crack.[48]

Seabee use of asphalt in the Pacific was especially relentless. Construction on Espiritu Santo in the South Pacific's New Hebrides provides an example. With such "helpers" as a "company of colored infantrymen," the Seabees cut through enough jungle and coral in twenty days to complete a 6,000-foot runway that allowed B-17s to launch bombing runs against Japanese positions on Guadalcanal. The Seabees followed with a 4,500-foot runway, a 5,000-foot runway, a 6,800-foot runway, 27,000 feet of taxiway, and seventy-five hardstands. Crushed coral provided the surfacing, often topped off with steel matting and an emulsified asphalt binder to counter the incessant rains. The Seabees next built or upgraded thirty-four miles of roads. By the war's end Espiritu Santo was supporting heavy bombers, fighters, two carrier groups, an armory, and the Pacific theater's largest repair and maintenance facility.[49]

On Okinawa over 50,000 Seabees worked with "21 Army engineer aviation battalions, 14 Army combat engineer battalions, and 7 Army engineer construction battalions." They built roads and airfields to accommodate four thousand planes, using asphalt not only for paving runways, airstrips, and roads but also for waterproofing drainage canals and tidal gates.[50] After marines suffered 1,200 deaths taking the Tarawa Atoll in the Gilbert Islands, Seabees built Mullinix Field and paved a 6,598-foot runway. Mullinix hosted VII Bomber Command Headquarters for a few months and then served as an emergency airfield. The remains of many of the marines who died at Tarawa are still there. Some lie under a blacktop parking lot that the Seabees paved in 1944.

The first Seabee battalion ashore on Iwo Jima suffered more casualties than any other Seabee battalion in any war before or since. The Seabees regrouped and launched projects complicated by "sulphur-laden steams" drifting out of crevices. They built an unpaved 9,400-foot runway and built and paved a 9,800-foot runway, a 6,000-foot fueling strip, and two fighter strips of 6,000 feet and 5,000 feet. One Seabee officer, however, took too much pride in his work. Jack Cornwell, a Caterpillar equipment operator, remembered the lieutenant who commanded the asphalt crews threatening another operator who "gouged a stretch of asphalt." "The Cat skinner pulled his Ka-Bar knife and slit [the lieutenant's] shirt bottom to top." After Cornwell's backhoe scraped the edge of an airstrip, causing a fire because a crew "had laid asphalt right over an ammunition dump," the same officer accused Cornwell of "wrecking my blacktop" and "pulled his .45." "I swung my bucket so it was hanging over his head," Cornwell said, "and told him if he shot me my foot would go off the brake and the bucket would chop him in two."[51]

In the Northern Mariana Islands, the Seabees paved two 10,500-foot runways on Guam. Chief of Army Engineers Eugene Reybold summarized Seabee and engineer work completed in five months on Saipan: "two coral mountains had vanished, superhighways and pipe lines had appeared, asphalt lay where mud had been too deep for an Iowa hog, and B-29s were taking off from an airstrip longer than the longest one at New York City's LaGuardia Field."[52]

After dislodging the Japanese on Tinian, Navy Seabees and army engineers turned that Northern Mariana island into the largest and busiest air base of them all. The Japanese had occupied Tinian for both economic reasons (sugar-plantation profits) and military reasons (the island's "extensive plateau [made it] ideally suited for a large airdrome"). They finished one airstrip and began constructing two more prior to July 1944, when the Battle of Tinian opened. Seabees saw combat even after the enemy abandoned Tinian. Some of the Japanese soldiers who refused to flee or surrender hid in a cave, prompting the Seabees to drill through the cave's roof, pour diesel fuel into the borehole, then tamp and ignite dynamite. The explosion and fire killed dozens.[53]

The Seabees faced other dangers on Tinian, everything from construction accidents to nighttime bombing runs and strafing from Japanese fighters. They also faced such nonlethal frustrations as asphalt shortages (as ever) and round-the-clock traffic jams. Regardless, nothing stopped them from implementing plans drawn up in Hawaii by the Army Corps of Engineers. Initial phases included the construction of access roads from the beaches to the existing Japanese road network (thirty-five miles in all) and repair of the damaged Japanese airstrip using shrapnel fragments to fill bomb and shell craters. (ADR—airfield damage repair—has always been one of the Seabees' core competencies.) Next they extended the airstrip to 6,000 feet and constructed new 8,500-foot runways to accommodate b-29s. The blacktop scale is suggested by the additional construction that accompanied four of the 500-foot wide runways (all located at Tinian's North Field and all parallel at 1,600 feet apart): 8 taxiways, 265 hardstands, 2 service aprons, 173 Quonset huts, 92 buildings, and a fuel system requiring a submarine pipeline connecting 86,000 feet of land pipeline.

Coral and earth excavation and fill at North Field totaled 2,109,800 cubic yards and 4,789,400 cubic yards, respectively. Because the Seabees used coral as a runway base material, dust was a problem (though these runways were not as dusty as the ones in China that bothered General LeMay). To keep the dust down, the Seabees sprayed the coral with saltwater, often mixed with molasses, to improve the "cementing action of the coral particles." Grading and rolling followed, with the entire process repeated three or four times, creating a usable runway while waiting for asphalt to arrive (and hoping the salt would not inflict much damage on the bombers in the interim). Once the Seabees got asphalt plants up and running, they topped the coral runways with 2.5 inches of blacktop. By V-J Day they had rolled enough asphalt on Tinian to pave a two-lane highway from New York to Cleveland. Gen. Henry "Hap" Arnold, a Billy Mitchell protégé who took his first flight instruction from the Wright brothers and worked his way up to commander of army air forces, called the island "just one large airport."[54]

The Seabees used power shovels to scoop Tinian coral, dump trucks to haul it, and rock crushers to turn it into aggregate. Though the Barber-Greene company delivered over two hundred asphalt travel plants and five hundred asphalt finishers during the war years in both the Atlantic and Pacific theaters, it was not enough. Whenever the Seabees had asphalt on hand but not enough machinery to process it, they built asphalt plants out of scrap, rolling fifty-five-gallon drums of asphalt on ramps constructed with Japanese narrow-gauge rails; welding together empty drums for use as smokestacks and conducting coils; melting the asphalt with steam; and mixing it with crushed coral.

Between the Barber-Greene travel plants and the improvised plants, the Seabees produced over five hundred thousand tons of asphalt on Tinian and could scarcely keep up. Paving machines would be crawling down one not-yet-completed runway, while B-29s were lifting off or touching down a few hundred yards away.[55]

Much of the war's most destructive bombing in either theater began on Tinian's blacktop. Tokyo was 1,500 miles away, within a B-29's range, and the March 9–10, 1945, firebombing of Tokyo, arguably the most destructive single bombing raid in history, began and ended on North Field. Up to one hundred thousand people died. Tokyo asphalt melted and boiled because nearly three hundred B-29s had dropped over sixteen thousand tons of bombs loaded with thermite, napalm, and other incendiaries. Napalm was a relatively new weapon. While the British were borrowing from the ancient world's Greek fire and experimenting with asphalt as an ingredient in their liquid bomb formulas, a Harvard University chemist and Standard Oil chemists developed a more gruesome product. Napalm, which the army began using in 1941 not only in bombs but backpack and tank flamethrowers, featured polystyrene rather than asphalt as an adhesive. Still, as noted, asphalt played a role in both incendiary and conventional explosives. Henry Kaiser's Permanente Metals Corporation manufactured M74 and M76 bombs containing, respectively, ten pounds and five hundred pounds of "goop," a mix of liquid asphalt, magnesium, white phosphorous, and gasoline that was used to mark targets. Its nickname— "block burner"—was apt, as it targeted blocks where Japanese workers lived in their wood-and-paper houses. In all, the Allies dropped over seventeen thousand tons of M74 and M76 goop during the war years.[56]

Back home Gen. Leslie Groves directed the Manhattan Project. At the project's 586-square-mile site in Hanford, Washington, where scientists worked to process plutonium for the first atomic bombs, Groves offered a job to Buena Maris, dean of women at Oregon State College (now Oregon State University). The great majority of Hanford's female employees were in their late teens or early twenties, and Maris's mission as supervisor of women's activities was to reduce the high turnover rate. Barracks life in a construction camp took its toll. The women wanted those men who were drunk and abusive to stay away when the working day was done. And they wanted the walkways paved, as high heels sank in the mud when it rained and broke off in the ruts when things dried out. The day after Maris brought up the issue, Groves had asphalt pavement rolled out.[57]

General Groves sent another Manhattan Project employee, physicist Philip Morrison, to Tinian in early August 1945. "A miracle," Morrison said at first sight of a facility that could handle eight heavy-bomber takeoffs and landings per minute: "A great coral ridge was half-leveled to fill a rough plain, and to build six runways, each an excellent 10-lane highway, each almost two miles long. Beside these runways stood in long rows the great silvery airplanes . . . by the hundred. From the air this island . . . looked like a giant aircraft carrier, its deck loaded with bombers." (To service 268 B-29s, Tinian needed eleven miles of asphalt taxiways in addition to the four runways at North Field and the two runways at West Field.) Morrison's presence on Tinian was no coincidence. J. Robert Oppenheimer, director of the Manhattan Project's scientific work, had directed his doctoral dissertation at the University of California–Berkeley. Just a few weeks earlier in New Mexico, Morrison helped pack the core of the Trinity test device ("the Gadget") into his Dodge and drove it to the test site. The planet's first nuclear bomb exploded at 5:30 a.m. on July 16, 1945, "vaporizing the [test] tower and turning the asphalt around the base of the tower to green sand." The son of Dana P. Mitchell, a Los Alamos National Laboratory manager, recalled the aftermath: "So we drove in, and I immediately asked my father, 'How come the road didn't get blown up?' He said, 'Oh, it got melted and somewhat vaporized, but it is asphalt and it just solidified again.'"[58]

Philip Morrison waited on Tinian for the USS *Indianapolis* en route from the Hunters Point Naval Shipyard at San Francisco. The heavy cruiser carried two Trinity gadgets to a dock that the Seabees had secured with steel planks driven into ocean floor (and with asphalt filling the narrow gaps between the planks). Seabees unloaded the gadgets and their components, stored them in a special air-conditioned shed they constructed, guarded the shed, and served as both muscle and skilled labor for Morrison's pit crew of scientists who assembled the gadgets. Finally, Seabees helped place the gadgets aboard two B-29s, *Enola Gay* and *Bockscar* (or *Bock's Car*). On August 14, eight days after Little Boy detonated over Hiroshima and five days after Fat Man detonated over Nagasaki, several hundred B-29s took off from North Field and other asphalt airstrips on Guam and Saipan for a final raid. The Japanese surrendered a few hours later (a decision also influenced by the Soviet declaration of war on August 8). A few weeks later as Lieutenant General Reybold observed, jungle began reclaiming North Field blacktop and many of the other "great carpets for airmen" that Navy Seabees and army engineers had scratched out "on every continent and in every sea."[59]

Forty years later, in 1985, the Department of the Interior designated Tinian's North Field a National Historic Landmark. "Just to the north of the northernmost runway," according to a National Park Service guide, lay the two pits where "'Enola Gay' and 'Bock's Car' were loaded." The pits were necessary "because the bombs were too large to be placed under the B-29s for normal loading procedures. The pits are now filled with earth and landscaped and in front of each is a bronze historic plaque mounted on a concrete pedestal." "A special asphalt service apron," the Park Service added, served as a run-up to those plaques and pits. The Park Service did not note that liquid asphalt sealant had coated Fat Man's casing seams.[60]

Asphalt played a more modest role for the Allies in World War II's Atlantic theater. In Italy the Army Corps of Engineers used civilian road workers (the Cantonieri) for asphalt work. At Normandy 116 million maps and "15,800 long tons of asphalt" in fifty-five-gallon drums landed with the troops. U.S. and British engineers built seventy-four airstrips in the ninety days after D-Day. Most were no more than graded dirt covered by wire-mesh track. British factories shipped one million square yards of the stuff per month to France. (Generally, only bomber strips more than one hundred miles behind ground forces received asphalt or concrete pavement.) The maps pointed the Army Corps of Engineers toward such obvious tasks as the need to reconstruct the roads that would allow troops to move. The work involved filling bomb and artillery-shell craters with debris and then crushed rock and asphalt. Army engineers often built makeshift asphalt plants. They also salvaged German stockpiles of asphalt and aggregate, repaired damaged German equipment (especially rock crushers and paving machines), and put undamaged equipment to immediate use. Retreating German soldiers were under orders to plant antitank Teller mines and cover "them with hot asphalt to resemble patches." As often as not, they simply fled, abandoning both mission and asphalt machinery.[61]

Allied bombers heated blacktop in their own way, as they had in the Pacific. Rumors of boiling asphalt were rampant in Germany. On occasion rumor was fact. "The asphalt road had melted," a survivor of the Hamburg bombing recalled. "There were people on the roadway, some already dead, some still lying alive but stuck in the asphalt. They must have rushed onto the roadway without thinking. Their feet got stuck and then they had put out their hands to try to get out again. They were on their hands and knees screaming."[62] The Dresden bombing melted even more asphalt, as it created surface temperatures well over one thousand degrees Fahrenheit. Kurt Vonnegut, an army private captured at the Battle of the Bulge and sent to a work camp in Dresden, survived by retreating to a slaughterhouse meat locker. Still later he wrote about it in his novel, *Slaughterhouse Five* (1969).

The real asphalt story in the Atlantic theater was not how the product helped the Allies but rather how asphalt helped Germany's Nazis commit their crimes against humanity. On January 20, 1942, Reinhard Heydrich, a principal Holocaust architect, convened the Wannsee Conference in Berlin to consider how best to exterminate Europe's Jews. Slave labor was paramount. So was asphalt, by implication: "In the course of the final solution the Jews are to be allocated for appropriate labor . . . on roads [and runways]." That meant able-bodied men and women. At the Lublin airstrip in Poland, for example, Jewish women from the Majdanek camp "engaged in heavy physical labor such as laying asphalt."[63] The Reich would win both ways. Jews who crushed rock and laid asphalt before perishing from road-gang exhaustion or starvation were just as dead as those shot or gassed. Asphalt was there as well, in the gas chambers and crematoriums. It helped the Reich kill Jews the way the Wannsee Conference's odd mix of bureaucrats, functionaries, and cultists wanted Jews killed—efficiently. On a symbolic plane asphalt was so widely used in the labor and death camps that it routinely emerged in survivors' accounts. This was true to the end. When the war turned, the Reich paved over evidence of war crimes at many of the labor and death camps.

"We were sent to Dachau," Arthur Haulot, a journalist and member of the Belgian resistance recalled. "And when we arrived and saw the smooth asphalt parade-ground and camp roads some of us knelt down to kiss the ground."[64] Rarely have first impressions been so wrong. Seventy years later the Dachau Concentration Camp Memorial includes remnants of the original asphalt paving leading from the railway station to the camp. The Appellplatz, an asphalt expanse where upward of twenty thousand prisoners assembled for roll calls, was the camp's central feature. Many died during those assemblies. Cecylia Ziobro, a Polish Christian sent to a slave-labor farm in Germany as a child, had an equally mistaken first impression: "A quiet farm community nestled in a dense forest. . . . Geese and ducks swam and flew. . . . Brooks and streams meandered across some of the fields." But that image gave way to this one: French and Russian POWs marching off each morning to "disassemble a mountain," hammering at stones to make aggregate and then laying "asphalt to turn the dirt paths of our small community into a paved road." That farm, she continued, "included an asphalt and cement factory. What we didn't know at that time was that we were part of the notorious Buchenwald network of camps."[65]

When it came to killing Jews, few camps could compete with Auschwitz-Birkenau (or Auschwitz II) in Poland. The United States Holocaust Museum called it the "largest killing center in the entire

Nazi universe." In 1942, as one Holocaust scholar noted, eleven contractors worked on the Birkenau crematoria. J. A. Topf and Sons built the furnaces and installed the ventilation systems. Huta Civil Engineering built the shells for crematoriums II, III, IV, and V. Vedag, a Huta subcontractor, handled the asphalt waterproofing for the underground morgues of crematoriums II and III. But Vedag did not have enough asphalt in stock to finish the job. Karl Bischoff, chief of the Waffen-ss construction office that designed and built the Auschwitz-Birkenau camp, secured an exemption to the Reich's strict asphalt quota and rationing system. He secured the release of the asphalt needed to seal the morgues. Other contractors "asphalted" the ground around all five crematoriums. For his part Bischoff received a War Merit Cross for burning up to five thousand bodies a day. On October 7, 1944, inmates forced to help dispose of gas-chamber victims revolted. Before the ss slaughtered nearly all of them, these Birkenau *Sonderkommandos* tried to destroy the watertight crematoriums and managed to damage one.[66]

Nonetheless, the word *asphalt* was widely used as a pejorative in Nazi Germany, even as the Reich deemed it vital enough to ration it. "The word used over and over again to express aversion is '*Asphalt*,'" wrote Victor Klemperer, a Jew who survived and chronicled Nazi Germany. Goebbels used the word to symbolize urban decadence with Jews and their "asphalt press" having turned Berlin into a "great asphalt wasteland" boasting a single redeeming virtue: it was a good place for blood to flow, especially the blood of Jews and their "asphalt culture."[67] Even some Waffen-ss units denigrated the ss unit that served as the führer's personal bodyguard (the Leibstandarte) as "asphalt soldiers" deemed fit only for such duties as goose-stepping. Today few remember the asphalt-soldier pejorative. Few remember ss Reichsführer Himmler as a chicken farmer (which he was). The Nuremberg tribunal found the Waffen-ss and all other ss units and branches to be criminal organizations, and we remember them for that. We remember their crimes up and down the Eastern Front and at such other places as asphalted crematoriums and morgues.[68]

Five miles west of Hanover, Germany, at the Ahlem camp, one of at least sixty-five satellite camps that made up the Neuengamme concentration camp system, the ss Main Economic and Administrative Office had slave labor enlarge a quarry and dig out an asphalt mine's tunnels. Underground space, the ss reasoned, would allow the production of aircraft and Panzer parts—halted by Allied bombing—to resume. About 40 prisoners died each week in the asphalt mine. When the ss abandoned Ahlem on April 6, 1945, approximately 600 prisoners endured a march to Bergen-Belsen.[69] Four days later Henry Kissinger was among the U.S. Army soldiers who discovered 250 prisoners still in Ahlem, as the ss had deemed them too weak to march. Kissinger was a recent recipient of a Bronze Star and only twenty-one years old, a number nearly equal to the number of his family members murdered by the Reich. He remembered Ahlem's "skeletons in striped suits," the asphalt road, the tunnel into the asphalt mine, and the mine itself. Forty-nine years later, when the Ahlem memorial opened, it included 750 asphalt panels to commemorate the suffering and death in that mine.[70]

At Schandelah, another Neuengamme subcamp, the ss blinked on the matter of winter clothing. The contractors did not. Deutsche Asphalt and Civil Engineering's use of slave labor to mine asphalt and oil shale as part of the company's effort to produce synthetic fuels was so ruthless that the Neuengamme commandant launched a search to acquire sufficient winter clothing for the prisoners. The ss agreed to cover the costs. Deutsche Asphalt agreed to pay for nothing. Rather, the company complained that prisoners stole empty cement bags and stuffed them under what clothing they had to ward off the cold. Deutsche Asphalt considered that a problem because the company paid bag deposits to Lime and Cement Works, and that contractor was refusing to refund the deposits. A Deutsche Asphalt executive demanded that the camp commandant "remedy this situation." The ss rarely enforced the twenty-lash penalty for using a cement bag for insulation. But Deutsche Asphalt hirelings "kept an eye on the prisoners and reported all thefts to the Kapos, who would . . . beat them with truncheons."[71]

Farther east, at the Maly Trostinec death camp in the Blagovshchina Forest near Minsk, Jews and other prisoners worked at an asphalt plant run by a contractor. They also built the so-called Path of Death, connecting the camp to the Minsk-Mogilev highway. The Germans sent any prisoner who wore out to a shooting squad or mobile gas chamber. When the war turned, the ss had bodies dug up and burned in an attempt to destroy evidence. Later the Red Army discovered over thirty mass graves. At least sixty thousand Minsk Jews died at Maly Trostinec.

Granitwerke Mauthausen dabbled in the aggregate side of the asphalt business. This ss company owned one of the world's largest stone crushers near the Gusen camp, part of the Mauthausen-Gusen complex and its stone quarries. The crusher straddled a rail line, enabling efficient shipment to any Reich construction site that needed aggregate for blacktop or concrete. ss investors branched out in the war's third year by "lending" Gusen prisoners to contractors like Asphalt and Roofing, as that company held antiaircraft defense and air-raid–shelter construction contracts in nearby Linz (home to three subcamps).[72] ss officers also serviced Messerschmitt and other arms manufacturers by shifting much of the slave-labor force from the quarries. For the Gusen II camp and Hecht (or Hecht/Stein), a Buchenwald subcamp at Holzen near Eschershausen, prisoners hollowed out additional asphalt mines that dated to the 1860s.[73] After a U.S. bombing raid on the nearby Volkswagen factory, Ferdinand Porsche, founder of the car company bearing his name and a designer of the Volkswagen Beetle and the Tiger tank, inspected the abandoned Holzen asphalt mines in hope of moving his factory machinery underground.

Other German industrialists did the same. Italian pows with picks and shovels working alongside Jewish and Catholic Poles, a Buchenwald concentration camp historian wrote, expanded five asphalt mines in a mountainside on behalf of Organisation Todt, the Volkswagen Company, several armaments companies, and the German Asphalt Corporation. Intensely interested in protecting their machinery as well as their creature comforts (such as they were), these outfits fought over everything . . . even office space that slave labor chiseled out of asphalt mine walls.[74] Beyond office space, historian Hans Mommsen documented, Volkswagen and other contractors believed the underground asphalt mines could accommodate the machinery required to mass produce a manned version of the v-1 buzz bomb and parts for high-altitude fighter interceptors. In all they hoped the slave-labor force could create 240,000 square yards of factory floor space by hollowing out the asphalt mines. The first 250 prisoners assigned to hack and haul asphalt lived in tents until "they had constructed their own huts" at the expense of their own sleep. Over 1,100 prisoners labored in the mines, with the ss sending anyone unable to work back to Buchenwald and to near-certain death. The 240,000-square-yard underground asphalt-cavern goals were absurd. Even the scaled-back goals of 24,000-square-yard caverns were absurd.[75]

Not to be dismayed, the Germans kept inventing novel ways to use asphalt. The U.S. Army Quartermaster Corps used asphalt-infused paper bags for the conventional purpose of protecting dry goods—for example, an asphalt-laminated paper and cloth bag (using kraft paper and coarse Osnaburg cloth, material once used to make slave garments in the U.S. South and cover wagons driven across the prairie). Germans soldiers, in contrast, used their asphalt-infused bags when ordered to disinter the bodies of deceased POWs, especially Soviet POWs, for reburial elsewhere—stuffing and pouring disinterred corpses into those bags. The Supreme Army Command dictated "wrapping paper" procurement policy: "In view of the scarcity of the above kinds of paper"—oil paper, tar paper, and asphalt paper—"they may be used only for wrapping corpses."[76]

Norway found similar disinterment-and-reburial duty for asphalt-infused paper bags. Germany had operated nearly five hundred prison camps in Norway, holding (again, in round numbers) over forty thousand Norwegians, five thousand eastern Europeans, and one hundred thousand Soviets. When the occupation ended, the Norwegian government imprisoned several thousand Nazi collaborators and executed nearly two dozen. With the coming of the Cold War, the

government launched Operation Asfalt to counter possible espio-
nage by Soviet citizens visiting the grave sites of relatives who had
died in the camps. Dig crews disinterred "the remains of dead Soviet
POWs in the northern counties Nordland, Troms and Finnmark,"
the historian Jon Reitan wrote, and placed those remains in "large
sacks of asphalt" for transport and reburial. Because families of the
dead considered Operation Asfalt grave desecration, the dig crews
needed armed bodyguards. The first eight thousand corpses stuffed
and poured into asphalt-infused paper bags headed south by ship
for reburial at the Russian war cemetery on Norway's Tjøtta Island.[77]

Asphalt played a role in the aftermath of another atrocity, Operation
Reinhard, which claimed the lives of an estimated 1.4 million Polish
Jews at Treblinka, Sobibór, and Belzec. Even the slave-labor force that
built these ss camps in the first place suffered "experimental gassing"
upon completion of their labors. Subsequent arrivals escaped slave
labor only because the ss sent them directly from the freight trains
to the "reception area," where they were stripped naked and marched
to the gas chambers. "Unlike Auschwitz," *Der Spiegel* emphasized,
"no barracks or mountains of glasses, shoes and human hair or visible remains of extermination facilities were left behind in Operation
Reinhardt."[78] This was so because the Nazis spent thirteen months,
beginning in November 1942, exhuming bodies, killing nearly all the
remaining prisoners, burning human remains, stripping camp buildings down to their foundations, hauling rubble away, planting trees
on the grounds, and establishing farms. They even paved a portion
of the area.

The Sobibór site was mostly farmland until construction in 1965 of
a museum and symbolic mausoleum. The extensive paving of the area
that accompanied these monuments unintentionally added an extra
layer of protection for the ss secrets buried below. The Sobibór cov-
er-up ended in the twenty-first century, when archaeologists, having
located the Himmelfahrsstrasse (Road to Heaven) that led to the gas
chambers, had a good idea where to dig. They broke through the thick
asphalt that covered what they believed to be the camp's gas-chamber

building (where death had often arrived in the form of exhaust produced by Russian tank and tractor motors). One scholar ranked the discoveries among the most important Holocaust findings. "From under the asphalt," he said, "come voices of Jews who are speaking to us." With no security for several years, however, the Sobibór site became "the new 'Disneyland' of Nazi death camps," with tourists and dog walkers botanizing the killing fields, hunting white bone fragments among tire tracks and litter, footprints and dog shit. The Disney designation rose from a specific artifact: the image of Mickey Mouse on a child's ceramic cup.[79]

After V-E Day asphalt continued to be present on a number of surprising fronts—including the mystery of what happened to Hitler's corpse. This is the most likely answer to that mystery: In Berlin on May 4, 1945, the Red Army discovered the burned bodies of Hitler, Eva Braun, and their dogs in a bomb crater near the Führerbunker. (What remains of that air-raid shelter's underground portion and much of the site as a whole now sits below a blacktop parking lot; it is popular with tourists even though there are no plaques and no accessibility.) With the exception of Hitler's jawbone, teeth, and a section of skull with a bullet hole (which were packed in ammunition crates and eventually sent to Moscow), Soviet counterintelligence had what remained of the bodies buried "under an asphalt courtyard at a Soviet counterintelligence base in Magdeburg." The bodies remained there until 1970, when the KGB tore up that East German asphalt, retrieved the remains, incinerated them on a bonfire at a garbage dump outside the town of Shoenebeck, and disposed of the ashes in the Biederitz River.[80]

Neither the führer's person nor his ambitions could escape blacktop, in life or death. If asphalt mines hollowed out by slave labor wielding pickaxes was a Reich pipe dream to hide armament production from Allied bombers, Jews and others died in the mines and thus advanced the final solution. Death-camp machinery could not work properly without waterproofing provided by asphalt, a hydraulic-engineering solution thousands of years older than the Thousand-Year Reich that

Hitler had predicted at a Nuremberg rally. In simple terms asphalt deep in the earth and asphalt on the roads and crematoriums' walls helped Waffen-ss and contractors alike enslave Jews more profitably and murder Jews and dispose of their corpses more efficiently. At the same time asphalt's contradictions were equally stark. Blacktop runways helped the United States and its Allies win the war. Though winning that war was a good thing by any definition, no one could deny that asphalt did its job by enabling bombs, whether atomic or merely incendiary, like Henry Kaiser's magnesium-asphalt mixes, to kill people more relentlessly and efficiently in the Atlantic and Pacific theaters. No one could say that was a good thing.

Before bombs melted asphalt and people from Dresden and Hamburg to Hiroshima and Nagasaki, blacktop roads helped the New Deal drag the United States out of the mud and Great Depression poverty. Its virtues aside, that spasm of road building across the Western world and even deep into Stalin's gulag created a brave new world of a different kind. The combination of blacktop roads and the internal combustion engine represented a giant step forward in our species' unthinking drive to exterminate itself more relentlessly and efficiently—even as those roads at home made it easier to experience the wonder of treasures like the Blue Ridge. Whether the planet's automobile age pushed near or past the point of no return in the 1930s and 1940s, it would bring us to the brink in the 1950s. Every nation that had the wherewithal embraced one German model: the Autobahn. For the United States that meant construction of the Interstate Highway System. It meant a bonanza for the asphalt and concrete pavers. Abroad it meant an opportunity for the pavers to demonstrate that their products could help win more wars—in Korea, Vietnam, Afghanistan, Iraq, and elsewhere—under the strictures of the Cold War and other doctrines of convenience waiting their cue.

6 Crusades   Asphalt in the Cold War

Under color of the Federal Housing Act of 1949, the Los Angeles Housing Authority sent eminent domain letters to Palo Verde homeowners and renters telling them to vacate their barrio. Palo Verde and two other predominantly Mexican American neighborhoods, Bishop and La Loma, made up the habitable parts of Chávez Ravine, where four hundred families lived in an urban wilderness, growing their own food, letting chickens roam, playing *norteño* on the radio, sending their children to the public schools or the Catholic schools if they could pay the tuition. But the City of Los Angeles chose Palo Verde and much of Chávez Ravine as the site for Elysian Park Heights—a massive public-housing project projected to include two hundred buildings. (Part of Chávez Ravine lies within Elysian Park, and the park surrounds the ravine on three sides.) Government officials promised the families facing removal first crack at the new housing, promoted as the first integrated public-housing project west of the Mississippi River. Few homeowners sold and moved out at first. Then a trickle became a stream. The last of the holdouts (and their children) faced hands-on removal by police officers and fires that destroyed their homes. The Los Angeles Fire Department set most of the fires, the fire chief said, for training purposes.

The Elysian Park project died because Los Angeles police and the California Senate Fact-Finding Subcommittee on Un-American Activities launched investigations underwritten by the FBI and the U.S. Congress, via the House Committee on Un-American Activities (HUAC). The principal target, Los Angeles Housing Authority assistant director Frank Wilkinson, received a subpoena in 1952 from the subcommittee, known as the Tenney Committee after its Red-hunting chairperson. (Jack B. Tenney, in another life ca. 1923, wrote the music for "Mexicali Rose.") When Wilkinson refused to answer questions about his political affiliations, the housing authority fired him. In the aftermath the housing project died, as it was associated with the so-called Communist Party line. For his part Frank Wilkinson came to regret his presumption that public housing was best for Palo Verde, Bishop, and La Loma: "I was responsible for uprooting I don't know how many hundreds of people."[1] That wisdom came after he launched a new career crusading against HUAC. The committee responded by subpoenaing him in Los Angeles in 1956 and Atlanta in 1958. Again he refused to discuss his political views.

The full House cited Frank Wilkinson and Carl Braden, another activist who defied HUAC, for contempt of Congress. Following their prosecution and conviction, the Supreme Court denied Wilkinson's appeal (which rendered Braden's appeal moot). They spent their last night of freedom at a Morehouse College reception in Atlanta. "These men are going to jail for us," one of the speakers said.[2] That evening Wilkinson and Braden had a private dinner with that speaker, Martin Luther King Jr., and his wife, Coretta Scott King. The next day, May 1, 1961, they reported to the federal prison in Lewisburg, Pennsylvania.

Walter O'Malley, owner of the Brooklyn Dodgers major-league baseball team, proved the ultimate victor in the Battle of Chávez Ravine. After his negotiations with Robert Moses for land to build a new stadium in Brooklyn fell through, O'Malley decided to move his team to the West Coast. The City of Los Angeles offered a stadium site not dedicated for public purposes. But O'Malley held out for Chávez Ravine, a site dedicated for public purposes. He received 352 acres for a pittance, a total that included 30 acres of Elysian Park. Baseball needed a hard sell for the final hurdle, a stadium referendum, as not everyone thought a for-profit venture met the definition of public-purpose use. Ronald Reagan and other celebrities took up the cause, dismissing opponents as "baseball haters."[3] In 1958, while Wilkinson and HUAC battled in Atlanta, the referendum passed by 3 percent. What else was there to do? Move eight million cubic yards of earth.

Build the thing. Truck in eighty thousand tons of asphalt. Connect six lanes of Stadium Way with I-5. Pave the roads. Pave the lots. Play ball.

For over half a century, Dodger Stadium and its asphalt parking lots have covered much of what was once Palo Verde. "Whenever you are in . . . Dodgertown," the ball club's CEO said in 2009, when the stadium received a postal-service zip code, "you know where home is." The original construction plans for the stadium and lots noted the "2½ acre site of abandoned Palo Verde School." It is still there, now at 90090. But no children walk to that school. "[It] was simply buried beneath the blacktop northwest of third base."[4]

In March 1947, two years before Palo Verde families tried to stare down the bulldozers, Harry Truman announced a global policy to contain communism. It would begin with $400 million in aid for Greece and Turkey, aid that included asphalt. A year later Greece and Turkey received additional aid under the $12 billion Marshall Plan. That program stretched across western Europe, with the infrastructure task in the most populous nations a straightforward one. "To fix," as one historian put it, "the (many and large) potholes caused by war and occupation. That Paris might prefer asphalt, and Washington concrete, was never going to make the difference between ultimate recovery and stagnation." In Greece and Turkey, in contrast, the Truman Doctrine and Marshall Plan aid launched road revolutions. The Army Corps of Engineers supervised road construction in Greece carried out in the midst of civil war that saw communists destroy one asphalt plant and attempt to destroy all nine asphalt plants operated by joint-venture contractors. In all Greece received 29,512 tons of liquid asphalt under the Truman Doctrine and Marshall Plan.[5] Infrastructure aid was even more generous in Turkey. The George C. Marshall Foundation concluded that "20% of all dollar aid went into . . . roads." When World War II ended, Turkey had less than four hundred miles of blacktop. When the Marshall Plan aid ended, Turkey had "Marshall Boulevards, London Asphalt, and NATO Roads." An Istanbul newspaper editor said the "road program made [Turkey] a country."[6]

In 1948, the Marshall Plan's year one, President Truman urged Congress to approve $500 million for roads at home to facilitate commerce and "meet the needs of our national security." That was the same amount authorized by the Federal Aid Highway Act of 1944 (the D-Day year). Robinson Newcomb, an economist with the President's Council of Economic Advisers, explained this reluctance to push for major infrastructure spending at home beyond wartime levels. He did so by reference to corruption in the road-building industry: "Truman was involved in roads and their construction back in Missouri. He understood this up and down." Among other examples, Newcomb cited the president's response to Senator Robert Kerr (D-OK), who threatened to gut the Bureau of Public Roads budget because its director, Thomas "Chief" MacDonald, refused on the eve of an election to support blacktop paving in every Oklahoma county. "A complete waste of money," the chief said. Truman backed MacDonald after receiving an affirmative answer to a single question: "Is this a courthouse operation?"[7]

Truman Doctrine and Marshall Plan aid demonstrated that asphalt could advance the Cold War cause abroad (if not in Oklahoma). Asphalt helped as well after North Korean forces crossed the thirty-eighth parallel in 1950. Construction of runways in South Korea and any other relatively friendly nation relatively nearby was a priority for U.S. military engineers. Those runways also advanced desegregation, another weapon in the Cold War arsenal, as policy makers hoped to counter global Soviet messaging that emphasized how white U.S. Americans treated non-white U.S. Americans. That messaging was one factor that helped convince Truman to issue an executive order desegregating the military. Army sergeant Henry W. Mack, among the first soldiers to integrate all-white units, paved airstrips in Korea with the 808th Engineer Aviation Battalion. Another African American paver with the 808th, John Conyers, went on to a fifty-two-year career in Congress.[8]

An Engineer Aviation officer described one of the projects Mack and Conyers worked on, the K-47 Airfield in Chuncheon, South Korea: "I had an asphalt augmentation . . . with 16 D-8 dozers . . . [and] about 24 five-ton dump trucks, rollers, scrapers, and compactors. We could do just about anything." "We had a problem with the asphalt," another officer said of another project. "All the asphalt came in 55-gallon drums, and we had no easy way of getting it out of there into the production machinery. . . . It was so cold there—we could cut these drums open with axes and the stuff would handle just in chunks. We'd throw them into the mixing machine, which had plenty of heat, so they would melt quickly. We paved on frozen ground, which is something you just don't do." Enemy fire presented yet another problem: "Light planes—Bedcheck-Charlie type of aircraft—flew over and threw out mortar shells or small bombs. They could see us because we were working at night and we had lights."[9]

The U.S. Air Force, created as a separate branch of the military in 1947, did most of the Korean War blacktop work. Typically, that meant filling in bomb craters, laying down temporary surfaces, erecting temporary housing, waiting on heavy machinery to arrive, and then hiring "local labor to help construct asphalt runways." Nonetheless, Navy Seabees often handled the Korean War era's biggest jobs, including the Cubi Point project in the Philippines, after contractors declined. Commissioned on July 25, 1956, three years after the war ended, Naval Air Station Cubi Point had a 9,003-foot runway and 15.3 miles of roads. In all the Seabees moved 23 million cubic yards of earth and laid 36,000 tons of blacktop.[10]

Asphalt played a more enduring role in the chest-thumping Cold War mission of the Strategic Air Command (1946–92), with over one hundred bases in the United States and nearly fifty abroad.[11] SAC runways were concrete or asphalt, up to thirteen thousand feet long, and capable of withstanding the weights of the biggest tankers and bombers. In 1951 the Kiewit Corporation, based in Omaha, Nebraska, built the most remote SAC base, in Thule, Greenland, 947 miles from the North Pole. The Army Corps of Engineers tried to mitigate damage from thawing permafrost by having four million square feet of blacktop runway and other surfaces painted white. The engineers abandoned the costly project because the paint caused aircraft-braking problems. The northernmost military bases on U.S. soil are in Alaska—notably, Joint Base Elmendorf-Richardson, which has two blacktop runways; and Eielson Air Force Base, which has a concrete runway. Because strategists concluded that stopping communism required paving Alaska's roads, the ports of Valdez and Anchorage featured "two large asphalt storage plants . . . permitting bulk delivery of asphalt in ocean tankers."[12]

Whether for SAC or other military runways, competition between asphalt and concrete remained hot. White House aide Robert B. Landry said asphalt and Portland cement suppliers hounded President Truman in pursuit of "a ruling . . . that their material be designated for . . . all airports where government funds are involved." Though concerned with cement lobby "skullduggery," Truman said "comparative cost" would inform his decisions.[13] Under Dwight Eisenhower in 1955, however, the air force mandated concrete. Asphalt-industry lobbing resulted in House Committee on Armed Services hearings that convinced (forced?) the air force to test aircraft takeoffs and landings on asphalt runways (as if there were not thousands of takeoffs and landings on asphalt runways during World War II and the Korean War). Because blacktop held up even under the B-52 bomber's maximum takeoff weight of 488,000 pounds, the air force lifted the concrete-only directive begrudgingly and belatedly in 1959.[14]

Whether contractors paved runways with asphalt or concrete did not concern President Eisenhower. But he was troubled by the enormous consumption of those materials and other resources by the military-industrial complex. On January 17, 1961, four months before Martin Luther King offered his tribute to Frank Wilkinson and Carl Braden, the president's farewell address emphasized the "economic, political, even spiritual" dangers excessive military spending posed to the "very structure of our society." He had issued a similar warning in a speech delivered in his first term's third month (and only five weeks after Stalin's death). The collapse of the World War II alliance with the Soviet Union had created a militarized world heading down "two distinct roads," wasting "the sweat of its laborers, the genius of its scientists, the hopes of its children." After laying out the "cost of one heavy bomber" (thirty schools, two power plants, two hospitals, fifty miles of pavement), he said Cold War nostrums had left "humanity hanging from a cross of iron."[15]

Dwight Eisenhower's critique of military-industrial complexes here and elsewhere—what Nikita Khrushchev, Stalin's successor, called "steel eaters" in the Soviet Union—does not square with one of his greatest achievements as president. The Eisenhower administration, wrote Daniel Patrick Moynihan when serving as President Richard Nixon's urban adviser, ushered in one lone domestic program of "transcendent, continental consequence": the Interstate Highway System.[16] Eisenhower's complaints about our own steel eaters aside, the logic of Cold War militarism drove the decision to build the interstates (rechristened in 1990 as the Dwight D. Eisenhower System of Interstate and Defense Highways).

Even the Interstate Highway System's roots lie in martial soil. Eisenhower himself was there at the beginning, in 1919, when he participated in a Transcontinental Motor Convoy, a sixty-two-day road trip for 39 army officers and 258 enlisted men aboard eighty-one vehicles. His interest in good roads continued into the 1930s, when he mapped French and German roads. During World War II's last months, he used the Autobahn to move Allied troops and equipment. "The old convoy had started me thinking about good, two-lane highways," he said, "but Germany had made me see the wisdom of broader ribbons across the land."[17] President Eisenhower selected Gen. (Ret.) Lucius Clay to chair his highway-advisory committee. Clay, who left the army in 1949 for the Continental Can Company, certainly had the credentials. He supervised construction of some five hundred airports in the United States and abroad during the early 1940s. As military governor of the U.S. occupation zone in Germany, he administered the Berlin Airlift (Operation Vittles) to counter the Soviet blockade. The immediate problem was the lack of concrete and asphalt runways capable of handling cargo planes carrying 4,500 tons of food and coal per day. So the Truman administration airlifted not only food and coal but road-building equipment and asphalt (550,000 gallons of liquid asphalt for Tegel Airfield in West Berlin alone).[18]

For interstate-highway planning, General Clay relied on advice from investment bankers and lobbyists from the oil, real-estate, automotive, service-station, concrete, and asphalt industries.[19] Clay also signed Robert Moses as a consultant, service that would bring to twelve the number of unelected titles the New York City parks commissioner held simultaneously. The advisory committee had no room for mayors and other state and local government officials who were directly involved in approving and financing road-construction projects. The Eisenhower administration dismissed them as "special interests" at odds with the notion that only the advisory committee's members represented the national interest. Clay briefed the president on the lone exception to the road lobby's cardinal rule: "While the Teamsters Union does have a special interest in highways, it is still more desirable for labor to have a representative on the committee."[20] So Teamster president Dave Beck, a union member since first driving a laundry truck in 1914, joined Stephen D. Bechtel, the construction tycoon; William A. Roberts, president of Allis-Chalmers Manufacturing; and S. Sloan Colt, president of Bankers Trust.[21]

Maj. Gen. (Ret.) John S. Bragdon, special assistant to the president, was the White House advocate for asphalt pavement on the interstates. He had no dog in the asphalt versus concrete saga per se. He simply wanted to avoid a road-surface monopoly. Many in the engineering community still questioned whether asphalt could bear the weight of a "superhighway" on its own. That view began to change in 1947, with completion of the Maine Turnpike ("the first superhighway in the world to be paved entirely with asphalt—not concrete"). Doubts about asphalt disappeared with the opening of the New Jersey Turnpike in 1951, billed as a Cold War imperative for "evacuating civilians" and transporting soldiers "and materials to and from the important embarkation and debarkation points on the Atlantic seaboard." Construction of the turnpike's 118 miles required "14 million gallons of asphalt binder for the penetration macadam base, 11.3 million gallons of asphalt for the hot-mix, 870,000 tons of aggregate and 15 large asphalt plants to do the mixing." To ensure quality, inspectors set up field laboratories in tents by each of those plants.[22]

John Bragdon agreed with the asphalt industry that the Interstate Highway System's ninety-ten funding formula discriminated against asphalt because it provided an incentive for state and local governments to insist on concrete. Because the federal government would pay 90 percent of construction costs, J. E. "Jess" Buchanan, president of the Asphalt Institute, called ninety-ten "the 'Santa' clause in the Federal Highway Act." World War II had pushed asphalt into the lead, Buchanan told Bragdon. Now the cement industry was claiming extraordinarily low maintenance costs for concrete pavements, telling state governors they could "afford the costlier concrete pavement because you are paying *only ten percent* of the construction cost—but you pay *all* the maintenance costs." Bragdon agreed with Buchanan on this point too: because concrete pavement was often repaired with an asphalt overlay, "for statistical purposes, such pavements cease to be concrete . . . and all further maintenance is usually charged against the asphalt surface." In other words, maintenance liabilities for concrete disappeared.[23]

Buchanan next referenced President Eisenhower's military career, emphasizing how asphalt replaced concrete at the World War II tank test tracks because the concrete "slabs crumbled beneath the pounding of the metal lugs." Next Buchanan emphasized asphalt pavement's "exclusive features that are invaluable in military planning. It can be constructed swiftly, repaired and strengthened easily and rapidly. Under emergency conditions an asphalt pavement need never be out of service. Traffic may be slowed or briefly interrupted, but never denied the use of the road." "West Germany," Buchanan added, "is engaged also in a massive highway program which includes the reconstruction of her old autobahns"—"in various stages of galloping disintegration"—"and the constructions of hundreds of miles of new ones. . . . Germany's engineers are pulverizing the cracked old concrete pavements and resurfacing them with asphalt; they are building virtually all their new autobahns with asphalt."[24]

Bragdon also agreed with Buchanan on the importance of a seemingly unrelated problem exacerbated by the ninety-ten formula: lobbying by big-city mayors determined to use interstate highway construction to clear slums and solve congestion problems caused by commuter traffic. Most roads, as noted, are not under the jurisdiction of the federal government or even state governments. They are under the jurisdiction of counties, cities, and towns. Many mayors of large cities did not grasp how interstate construction could damage their cities. Both Bragdon and Eisenhower favored a "policy of routing interstate highways close by but not through central cities, using ingress and egress routes to congested portions." Congress, however, sided with the mayors, in most cases providing funds for running the interstates straight through the central cities. Staff notes of a White House meeting recorded the president's surprise "that the program . . . turn[ed] out this way"; and his lament that it was simply too late to do anything about it.[25]

The results were predictable. In language that differed from the Eisenhower-Bragdon view only because hindsight allows more details, one critic noted that city planners "were recommending highways as a cure all for traffic congestion and its accompanying environmental issues." And highways put an "immense and practically no-cost public works programs at their fingertips; all they had to do was funnel interstate highway construction through the central city and out to the suburbs." This accelerated a trend that sociologists (and realtors) call white flight, a reality that left urban U.S. America less diverse and with a shrinking tax base. A case study of the I-81 route through the heart of Syracuse, New York, showed how "it decimated a close-knit African American community. And when the displaced residents . . . moved to other city neighborhoods, the white residents fled. It was easy to move. There was a beautiful new highway that helped their escape." Urban renewal meant Mexican American removal in Chávez Ravine. It meant African American removal in most other locales.[26]

The local, state, and federal government response to the dislocation crisis was tepid. The Federal Aid Highway Act of 1962 provided a maximum payout of $200 to families displaced by interstate construction in central cities. Although the law called for continuing, cooperative, and comprehensive urban transportation planning (the 3C process), participation was voluntary. Policy makers were more aggressive with the Highway Beautification Act of 1965, designed to regulate billboards, junkyards, dumps, and the like along the interstates. But that law did nothing to slow urban dislocation in dozens of cities beyond Syracuse, as urban historian Raymond A. Mohl noted. I-94 planners "found and displaced" the small Black population in Saint Paul, Minnesota. In Chicago the twelve miles of the Dan Ryan Expressway (over half of which is designated as both I-94 and I-90) "effectively separated the Robert Taylor Homes, a massive black public housing project, from white ethnic neighborhoods to the west." In Camden, New Jersey, I-95 displaced "1,093 minority families out of a total of 1,289 families." Nearly 1,200 miles south, I-95 obliterated Overton, "the commercial and cultural heart of black Miami." The "relocation of blacks from central-city areas triggered a massive spatial reorganization," producing the "larger, more spatially isolated, and more intensely segregated second ghettos characteristic of the late twentieth century."[27]

The Bureau of Public Roads, responsible for administering interstate construction, facilitated the process by deferring to state partners, rarely challenging their motives for route selection. These motives, including demand for routes with low right-of-way costs and high revitalization demand, formed a perfect storm along the color line—even if the planners and city officials were usually more discreet, according to Alfred Johnson (a particularly candid road lobbyist), than the dozen or so who saw proposed interstate routes through their cities as "a good opportunity to get rid of the local n——town."[28]

The decision to build the Interstate Highway System was, at bottom, a decision to pave. Without pavement, whether asphalt or concrete, the interstates are not even imaginable. Interstate pavement changed urban areas by accelerating two ongoing trends: the decline of central cities and the rise of suburbs. The irony is that the level of federal (and to some extent state and local) spending was unprecedented, even as those dollars contributed to the hollowing out of neighborhoods and schools, public transportation, and employment opportunities. To make way for pavement through cities, interstate construction destroyed over three hundred thousand homes between 1957 and 1968, dislocating over thirty-two thousand families each year. Reginald H. Booker, a Washington DC–based activist, framed the mantra for the displacement resistance: "White Men's Roads thru Black Men's Homes."[29]

Nonetheless, a cold-hearted use of Interstate Highway System construction as a slum-clearance tool did not threaten funding. Rather, congressional opposition to gasoline taxes and rumors of construction-industry corruption threatened to strangle the interstates in their infancy. "Almost hair-raising," President Eisenhower said when briefed on media accounts of briberies and kickbacks. A *Cincinnati Enquirer* exposé from July 3, 1960, called interstate construction a "rat hole" of criminality. President John F. Kennedy sent a special message to Congress just weeks after his inauguration: "Our Federal pay-as-you-go highway program is in peril." Rex Whitton, who served as the federal highway administrator, tackled the twin problems of opposition to gasoline taxes and corruption with help from the road lobby. They lobbied successfully for the Federal Aid Highway Act of 1961, which included a four-cents-a-gallon gasoline tax. And they damped the corruption issue with a public-relations campaign arguing that actual law breaking was minimal and the benefits of the interstates immense.[30]

On February 4, 1962, the corruption issue reignited with Jack Anderson's story in *Parade*: "The Great Highway Robbery." A dozen Congress representatives piled on with "wild speeches," Whitton said, about "waste, graft and so forth." Media interest peaked on October 1, when NBC broadcast "The Great Highway Robbery" on an hour-long episode of *David Brinkley's Journal*. The House Committee on

Public Works responded by creating a Special Subcommittee on the Federal-Aid Highway Program, chaired by John A. Blatnik (D-MN). The Bureau of Public Roads responded by hiring former FBI special agent Joseph M. O'Connor to direct a new Office of Audit and Investigations. Understanding that their true mission was containment, Blatnik and O'Connor followed Whitton's lead, arguing that corruption was present but minute and usually measureable in hundreds or just a few thousands of dollars. One Florida highway official, for example, "received 8 to 10 turkeys, 6 to 15 hams, 4 to 5 cartons of cigarettes, 18 to 20 quarts of whiskey, and 2 or 3 fruitcakes from highway contractors during the 1961 Christmas season."[31]

The Blatnik subcommittee's most dramatic findings focused on bureaucratic inertia rather than corruption. In 1956, for example, the Department of Commerce mandated bridge-clearance minimums of fourteen feet for all interstate bridges, even though the Department of Defense needed sixteen feet of clearance for road transport of missiles. By the time the Department of Commerce raised the clearance requirement in 1960, contractors had built over two thousand bridges with a fourteen-foot clearance. Blatnik called the delay in raising the minimum bridge clearance "unconscionable, incredible, inexcusable and indefensible," a "classic example of bureaucratic indecision." His subcommittee noted that there was enough blame to go around: "The Defense Department was not consulted when the 14-foot clearance was set, but neither did the Department make any effort to alert the Bureau of Public Roads or the American Assn. of State Highway Officials that its ability to transport weapons was impaired."[32]

Until tax resisters gained the upper hand in more recent times, neither corruption nor anything else seemed capable of slowing construction of an ever-expanding Interstate Highway System. "So we head inexorably toward the 44-lane highway," Russell Baker wrote, "cheered on by the incantation of real-estate developers and asphalt tycoons."[33] As of 2019, the system's length was approximately 48,000 miles, with seventy primary highways; three major coast-to-coast highways (I-10, I-80, and I-90); seven major border-to-border highways (I-5, I-15, I-35, I-55, I-65, I-75, and I-95); and an auxiliary system of three-digit bypasses, beltways, and spurs. I-375 in Detroit needed a mere 1.062 miles to connect I-75 with downtown, but that was enough to obliterate the historic Black Bottom district and its Paradise Valley entertainment strip.[34]

Aversion to raising gasoline tax rates—the federal excise tax on gasoline was last raised in 1993—has led to a plethora of other taxes, user fees, borrowing, and tolling to carry the cost of building, expanding, and maintaining the Interstate Highway System over the decades. If the need for road maintenance is the one great constant, nowadays there is nothing certain about how to pay for interstate maintenance or even whether to pay for interstate maintenance (or maintenance of any other U.S. road for that matter). Budget concerns have presented asphalt entrepreneurs with advantages over their concrete rivals because blacktop is less expensive in the short term. Although asphalt pavement covers less than half of the Interstate Highway System, its percentage is growing. The U.S. Geological Survey estimates that interstate pavement includes fifty-five million tons of cement and forty-four million tons of liquid asphalt. That last number was four times the amount of asphalt produced in all U.S. oil refineries when President Eisenhower signed the Federal Aid Highway Act of 1956.[35]

The Eisenhower administration sold the Interstate Highway System by defining it as a Cold War imperative. No one needed to contort logic to define nuclear testing as a Cold War imperative. Fear of global thermonuclear war sparked a fallout-shelter boom (with the exteriors of many shelters mopped with hot asphalt). Fear also cost asphalt-shingle manufacturers a sliver of market share because competitors claimed that asphalt shingles would hold radioactive fallout indefinitely. Fallout fears arose from the sheer scale of nuclear testing. From 1946 to 1992 the Soviet Union conducted over seven hundred atmospheric and underground tests. The United States conduced over nine hundred tests at the Nevada Proving Grounds alone. The test site's 680 square miles kept asphalt contractors busy, with 400 miles of sidewalks and paved roads within blast radiuses because the Department of Defense wanted to test how pavement would respond to plutonium contamination. The United States conducted another sixty-seven tests in the Pacific Proving Grounds on two Marshall Island atolls, Enewetak and Bikini. "What was once a productive atoll," a Senate committee said of Enewetak, became a wasteland. Post-test work included removal of radioactive topsoil and then "laying of asphalt on the land."[36] That basic task—laying asphalt—was relentless. Kwajalein Atoll, the command center for the early Bikini and Enewetak tests, had its own U.S. Army asphalt plant.[37]

Other nations tried to keep up with the Soviets and the U.S. Americans. To help with nuclear and thermonuclear tests in the Pacific, the British operated an asphalt plant on Christmas Island. When departing in 1964, they left in place, until 2005, "drums of unused asphalt and other toxic wastes."[38] The French used asphalt to contain radioactive material in Algeria until 1962, when Algeria won its independence. They moved testing to Polynesia thereafter, conducting at least 175 tests on two Tuamotu Archipelago atolls. On Morurora they dropped a nuclear bomb from a plane, hoping to determine whether one would detonate in a crash. The test bomb did not detonate. It did fracture, scattering plutonium-239 that the French tried to fix in place by paving over the area. Unfortunately, storms have since washed away some of that "plutonium-impregnated asphalt."[39]

Beyond such Cold War mainstays as nuclear testing, asphalt emerged as part of the United States' pursuit of sports and recreation. By 1960 blacktop had covered the Indianapolis Motor Speedway track (except for the Yard of Bricks at the finish line). (Nearly all NASCAR tracks and most IndyCar tracks are asphalt.) Asphalt even arrived under ball fields. Chemists at a Monsanto subsidiary developed a product, Chemgrass, first installed at the Moses Brown School in Providence, Rhode Island.[40] Management rechristened their product AstroTurf two years later, when it was installed in the Houston Astrodome atop a drainable asphalt base rolled out by S. T. Bunn Construction (formerly S. T. Bunn Asphalt) of Tuscaloosa, Alabama. Because AstroTurf was little more than "green carpet glued to asphalt," injury rates skyrocketed (especially for football players). Synthetic turf manufacturers make safer products today, but they still rely on asphalt as a base in most cases. Koch Industries, for example, supplied "roughly 375 liquid tons of polymer-modified asphalt" for Minnesota's U.S. Bank Stadium, home to the NFL Vikings.[41]

No aerobic sport has been more closely associated with asphalt than basketball, whether on suburban driveways or urban playgrounds (like New York's famous Rucker Park court). But the asphalt game is fading. With the rise of Amateur Athletic Union tournaments for young players, the best summer games are now indoors. Midnight Basketball, proposed by George H. W. Bush and funded as part of Bill Clinton's anticrime initiatives, did not cater to elite players but still meant indoor ball (often on asphalt tile).[42] Vandals have also limited opportunities by destroying playground rims. In some circles rim-removal criminology is seen as a crime-fighting tool, given the assumption that outdoor courts attract street gangs.[43] In yet another example of the duality inherent in how we use asphalt, other cities erect hoops on blacktop playgrounds as a crime-fighting tool, reasoning that the game provides an outlet for teenage energy. Where rims remain, hoop dreams still drive city kids to sweep puddles or shovel snow off asphalt courts so they can play. When suburban kids do the same in their driveways, they unmask asphalt yet again as a socioeconomic marker. Some families can afford their own private asphalt patch—the driveway—and some cannot. This had a multiplier during the COVID-19 pandemic, as many cities pulled down playground rims in the cause of social distancing. Homeowners did not pull down driveway rims for that cause.[44]

Aerobic or not, virtually every sport has an asphalt story. Lee Elder, the first Black professional golfer to play in the Masters Tournament at Augusta National Golf Club in Georgia, remembered being denied clubhouse privileges when he first joined the PGA Tour in 1968. He had to change clothes on parking-lot asphalt. In 1971, four years before he integrated the Masters, Elder toured South Africa, where asphalt helped enforce apartheid. (To travel the N2 blacktop highway even today, a

Cape Town scholar wrote, "is a tour through the remnants of apartheid.") The government denied Elder's request to visit Nelson Mandela at Robben Island Prison, where Mandela's work included breaking rocks into aggregate for pavement duty. In 1990 Mandela walked out of another prison (he served twenty-seven years at three different prisons), finally a free man. That same year the Augusta National chair announced that the club had admitted its first "black gentleman."[45]

Both before and after the 1960s, as Lee Elder's story suggests, the struggle for racial justice played out on blacktop parking lots as well as blacktop streets and playgrounds. "We had to park in a certain area north of the gate back to what we called the river," recalled a worker at the Firestone plant in Memphis. Blacktop was for whites only. Blacks parked on gravel. For an African American who drove a new car to the plant, even the gravel was no guarantee that those obsessed with the "uppity" other would not slash a tire or key the paint. Lot segregation, moreover, spread to the home. Suburbs often required two or even "2.5 parking spaces per dwelling unit in multifamily rental housing." These requirements, according to a U.S. District Court ruling about Parma, a Cleveland suburb, restricted low-income housing and thus had the purpose of preserving "the all-white character of the City."[46]

Asphalt was present at those small moments in Memphis and Parma. It was present as well at the seminal events of the modern civil rights movement. The Children's March in Birmingham and Bloody Sunday on Selma's Edmund Pettus Bridge played out on asphalt. When the struggle for racial justice exploded in Watts, Newark, Detroit, Washington DC, and hundreds of other cities, the urban rioting and rebellions played out on asphalt. Obviously, asphalt does not cause uprisings. But it has been part of the environment of urban rioting and all too often a tool to enforce de jure segregation in Jim Crow days and de facto segregation in any day. This is so in rural as well as urban areas. In the heartland asphalt remains a black thing too often for whites only. In Steve Earle's antilynching song, "Taneytown," the doom that awaits in the white world begins with a walk away from rural poverty, a walk to where the dirt road gives way to blacktop.

The struggle for racial justice was the first of two dominant issues in the United States during the 1960s and early 1970s. For the other, a failed colonial war in Vietnam, asphalt played a symbolic role in anti-war demonstrations on blacktop streets and a practical role on the battlefield. Southeast Asia's blacktop story spilled into Laos, with the CIA supervising the construction of a dirt runway and road at Long Tieng. Eventually, a crew extended that runway, topped it with asphalt, and paved a "city block–sized asphalt tarmac at the [runway's] west end." (CIA blacktop work was common elsewhere as well; for example, to facilitate the training of Cuban pilots in preparation for the Bay of Pigs invasion, the agency paved a sod airstrip at Retalhuleu, Guatemala.) The CIA had chosen Long Tieng as the focal point for its Secret War in Laos (1964–73) with Air America, the agency's proprietary airline, and the Laotian Air Force sending aircraft stuffed with humanitarian and military aid to the Hmong tribes recruited to fight Pathet Lao communists backed by North Vietnam. The forty-six million pounds of aid was supposedly secret. The 2.5 million tons of bombs dropped on Laos over nine years was supposed to be secret too—and so was the drug trade organized by several of the CIA's highest-ranking Hmong mercenaries. At best the agency turned a blind eye to the poppy growing, heroin processing, and heroin shipping to the market target of U.S. soldiers in Saigon. Long Tieng blacktop facilitated it all—humanitarian and military aid, bombs and narcotics.[47]

The enemy depended on asphalt as well. "The Pathet Lao and the North Vietnamese swept away all paramilitary forces west of Route 46," one secret war historian wrote, "so that in early 1970, the entire Nam Beng valley down to the Mekong was under Communist control; in March, Pathet Lao troops even reached the Thai border. By April 1971, Route 46 had been expanded into an all-weather, two-lane asphalt strip, guarded by some 400 antiaircraft guns." Defeat at the hands of the Pathet Lao sent some fifty thousand Hmong fighters and their families and others to Long Tieng blacktop, hoping for evacuation aboard C-130 and C-46 transports to U.S. airbases in Thailand. The CIA helped evacuate no more than three thousand.[48]

The asphalt story in Laos centered on a single runway. The asphalt story in South Vietnam enveloped the entire country. During their occupation the French paved roads along with the Da Nang runway. By the time the French surrendered in 1954, the war had damaged over two-thirds of Vietnam's twelve-thousand-mile road system. Monsoons, lack of maintenance, and encroaching bush extracted an additional toll. The Eisenhower administration responded by shipping asphalt pavers, quarrying machinery, and other specialized equipment into South Vietnam to reconstruct and upgrade roads. In contrast to World War II, where blacktop work focused on runway construction for heavy bombers, in Vietnam it focused on roads and heliports. The Da Nang runway and a few dozen other blacktop projects aside, most runways and airstrips constructed by the United States in Vietnam were concrete.

After the Gulf of Tonkin incident in 1964, asphalt paving of roads and heliports was immense. In just one year ending in June 1966, the army sent 325,000 tons of supplies, including portable asphalt plants and liquid asphalt in fifty-five-gallon drums. The Army Corps of Engineers supervised the construction of all-weather supply routes that, they hoped, would be "difficult for the enemy to mine." The Viet Cong did not find it difficult. They hoped the mines would kill Transportation Corps truckers. These soldiers were "out on the blacktop," the U.S. military newspaper *Stars and Stripes* reported at the war's height, "rolling in endless dirty brown caravans north and west," billowing "red dust . . . as the asphalt withers and dies, leaving only dirt and mud in its trace. All day, every day, they grind on."[49]

At An Khe the Army Cops of Engineers designed a twelve-million-square-foot heliport. At Port Lane they designed a heliport with sixty-four minipads, each resting on "pierced steel planking placed directly over sand treated with peneprime, a dust-control material with an asphalt base." Metal-plank matting for heliports and airstrips came in all shapes, and asphalt nearly always found a niche. MX19 product, for example, consisted of "four-foot square aluminum sheets encasing an aluminum honeycomb" laid out on a surface base covered by an "asphalt-treated vinyl cloth" (a North Korean product).[50]

At Chu Lai asphalt met its match. Marines and Seabees "turned the coastal area into a major military installation" complete with a temporary SATS (Short Airfield for Tactical Support). To do so they used AM-2 aluminum slab matting to form a runway featuring a "catapult system, arresting gear, carrier lighting system, expeditionary control tower, and a fuel dispensing system to allow Douglas A-4 Skyhawks to land and perform catapult or jet-assisted takeoffs." An aircraft carrier deck moved ashore, as it were. To stabilize the sand underneath the matting, the engineers mixed it with asphalt. That failed. In the end they used laterite, a soil rich in iron and aluminum that bonds, when losing moisture, with other particles to form a "concretionary laterite" that has been used to make bricks for thousands of years.[51]

Regardless of asphalt's many uses in Vietnam, its primary duty remained road duty. Senior staff monitored the blacktop march closely, a fact emphasized by an officer with the army's Fifty-First Asphalt Platoon:

> The men and equipment arrived in Qui Nhon by LST locked, loaded, scared to death and ready to fight. . . . Our new Barber-Greene Asphalt Plant . . . was set up next to the A Company Quarry operation outside the perimeter of the An Khe compound. . . . We were on the General's tour. . . . Every 7–14 days we would have visitors fly in by helicopter to look at the crushing operation, asphalt plant production, and the road trip to that day's paving site. I didn't know there were that many Generals until I visited the Pentagon many years later.[52]

To combat aggregate shortages army engineers and contractors formed the Delta Rock Agency to move aggregate from thirteen quarries by barge to off-loading sites and then trucking it to construction sites. The Eighteenth and Twentieth Army Engineer Brigades ran eighteen rock crushers and eleven asphalt plants from 1969 to 1973, producing 27 million tons of rock and 2.5 million tons of liquid asphalt.[53]

Road construction during that four-year period came under the Lines of Communication (LOC) program. "The largest single engineer project ever undertaken by the United States military in a foreign country": over 2,500 miles "of modern high-speed highways," said Maj. Gen. Robert R. Ploger, a D-Day veteran and command engineer (and father of a son who would die on 9/11). "A network of asphaltic concrete roads," a Seabee historian added, "24 feet wide with eight-foot shoulders. In the areas with heaviest traffic, the roads grew to 40 feet in width, with the same shoulder—so important in Vietnam for scooter, scooter-bus and scooter-truck traffic." LOC work was dangerous. The enemy not only mined roads. They destroyed paving machines and attacked the men who operated the machines. A single firefight at Kham Duc left thirty-one army engineers wounded and bulldozers, dump trucks, and 360 drums of asphalt abandoned. For military engineers and contractors alike, however, the principal foe was not Viet Cong but monsoon mud. They attacked that enemy by scraping clay from rice paddies, backfilling, and then constructing roadbeds raised for drainage and topped off with a "double course of asphaltic concrete."[54]

The army, navy, air force, and marines all did asphalt work in Vietnam. And military engineers trained South Vietnamese soldiers and civilians to operate asphalt plants and paving machinery. RMK-BRJ, however, functioned as the sole contractor for construction projects, with the contracts administered by the Navy Bureau of Yards and Docks (Naval Facilities Engineering Command after 1966). Raymond International and Morrison-Knudsen were the RMK half of this contractor consortium. Brown and Root and J. A. Jones Construction were the BRJ half. Things began in 1962, when an RMK team landed on Da Nang blacktop with a mission to build a radar station and blacktop road on Monkey Mountain. By the time the war ended, RMK-BRJ had worked on 1,100 projects in South Vietnam, utilizing eight thousand pieces of heavy equipment and a labor force of 51,700. It seemed, as one war chronicler noted, as if they were trying to prove the literal truth of Ronald Reagan's quip: "We could pave the whole country and put parking stripes on it and still home by Christmas."[55]

For security the army often deployed infantry platoons to guard RMK-BRJ's personnel, quarries, asphalt plants, and eighty-nine-thousand-square-foot Saigon headquarters, located in a former car dealership. Morrison-Knudsen's Bertram L. Perkins was the principal manager.[56] Brown and Root, however, was in the spotlight because the company, besmirched as "Burn and Loot" by antiwar activists, had a campaign-cash history with Lyndon Johnson. Herman Brown entered the construction business in 1911 as a laborer in Belton, Texas. With his brother George and brother-in-law Dan Root, he founded a road-paving company four years later. Eighteen mules received "in lieu of back wages" provided the startup capital. Herman Brown, as Robert Caro documented, was usually paid not in mules or cash but "'paving notes' secured by municipal real estate and due to mature in five or ten years—by which time various tiny Texas towns and sparsely inhabited communities hoped to have sufficient cash to redeem them." Handsome profits came in the 1940s, as Brown secured navy contracts with then Congress representative Johnson's help. When Brown died in 1962, LBJ delivered the eulogy. That same year, the RMK-BRJ consortium formed, and the oil-fields service company Halliburton purchased Brown and Root.[57]

Beyond road construction the five largest RMK-BRJ projects in South Vietnam were the "massive bases, airfields, and ports" at Da Nang, Long Binh, Newport, Tan Son Nhut, and Cam Ranh Bay. "The kind of infrastructure being put in place was explicitly military and did not aid in the development of an independent southern state," historian James M. Carter noted. Rather, "[it] created considerable chaos in social, political, and economic terms. . . . The great paradox was that these latest physical transformations of the southern Vietnamese landscape further undermined the larger objectives, while they made possible a wider and more efficient war." At home the Johnson administration's partisan adversaries joined antiwar activists on the attack. In the House, Donald Rumsfeld (R-IL) condemned the RMK-BRJ contracts as corrupt and illegal.[58]

In South Vietnam, Brown and Root and other contractors faced rocket and rifle fire, but to a lesser degree than Navy Seabees who worked in the Mekong Delta and along the Cambodian and North

Vietnamese borders. By 1969 over twenty-six thousand Seabees were serving worldwide, with well over half that number assigned to Vietnam. In addition to building access roads and tactical airstrips, Seabees fortified camps in advance areas to better withstand attacks; trained South Vietnamese civilians in basic construction skills; provided medical assistance; and completed various other civic action projects. When forced to fight, they acquitted themselves well. When presenting the Congressional Medal of Honor posthumously to Seabee Marvin G. Shields, who died at Don Xoa, President Johnson said the Seabees "are building schools and hospitals . . . bridges and dams . . . dikes and roads. . . . [They] are fighting with one hand—and they are building with the other."[59] LBJ borrowed those words from a biblical construction project, rebuilding the wall surrounding Jerusalem, described in Nehemiah 4:16.

With asphalt plants closing and paving machinery redeploying as the United States withdrew from Vietnam, the most politically charged asphalt and concrete road scandal in U.S. history was emerging at home. In April 1972, two months before the arrest of burglars in Democratic National Committee offices at the Watergate office building, Vice President Spiro Agnew addressed the American Road Builders Association in New Orleans. With one gaggle of federal prosecutors in Washington following the Watergate money trail by midsummer, another was pursuing Agnew in Maryland. In January 1973 one Lester Matz received a subpoena for his engineering consulting company's financial records. He promptly alerted Agnew, who had served as Baltimore County executive prior to his 1966 election as Maryland's governor. Agnew, in turn, asked White House chief of staff H. R. "Bob" Haldeman for help in "turning off" the investigation into Matz's company and other companies suspected of paying kickbacks on Maryland highway construction projects. Haldeman took the request to John Ehrlichman, assistant to the president for domestic affairs, and that led to an Oval Office meeting between President Nixon and Vice President Agnew. They hoped to enlist Republican senator J. Glenn Beall Jr., brother of the U.S. attorney for Maryland, in their obstruction of justice scheme. "Is he a good boy?" the president asked his vice president.[60]

Agnew told Nixon that he was especially worried about Jerome B. Wolff, formerly on the vice president's staff and, before that, the chair of the Maryland State Roads Commission. When told that Wolff had agreed to cooperate with prosecutors, the president had another question: "Well, can we destroy him?" Matz and a developer also agreed to testify against Agnew for taking kickbacks from at least seven engineering consulting firms (kickbacks that continued during Agnew's vice-presidential tenure). Denying everything, Agnew contacted Alexander M. Haig Jr., a four-star general and the new White House chief of staff. But Haig refused to help. "Bad stuff," he told Nixon. "Kickbacks." Agnew also asked former White House counsel Charles Colson to represent him. On his way to prison (like fellow Watergate casualties Haldeman and Ehrlichman), Colson declined. No other notable helped either, though Frank Sinatra stepped up with over $200,000 in loans. Agnew gave up. He pleaded nolo contendere on a felony charge of tax evasion and received a sentence of three years' probation and a $10,000 fine. "Morally obtuse," said those who disbarred him. In 1976 Maryland taxpayers sued to recover the bribe money. In 1981 the courts ordered Agnew to repay $268,482. He paid a year later when living in Rancho Mirage and deducted half the amount from his California state income tax return. The state denied the deduction and Agnew lost his appeal in 1989, twenty years after taking his first oath of office as vice president of the United States and eleven years after he paid back the Sinatra loans.[61]

While the Agnew scandal was wrapping up, others were brewing. In the late 1970s a New York State Assembly subcommittee chaired by Charles "Chuck" Schumer uncovered several of these. In the 1980s asphalt played the role of little brother to concrete in the findings of an organized-crime task-force investigation of the construction industry in New York City. Nonetheless, blacktop corruptions were common. A typical example: In 1987 Jet Asphalt and Mount Hope Asphalt lost contracts, given ties to a company recently convicted of bid rigging on state contracts. The two companies next in line to receive these paving contracts withdrew, given ties to defendants in other bid-rigging cases. Further details aside, departure and endpoint were the same. After a round of emergency bidding, the city awarded the final contracts to a company that subcontracted the work to Jet Asphalt and Mount Hope Asphalt.[62]

Asphalt was part of the backstory for what became known as the Iran-Contra affair, a 1980s scandal with roots dating to 1953, when the CIA helped organize a coup in Iran that installed a new prime minister who promised, in a radio address, that his economic program would include "extensive asphalt road-building." (He made that promise from the Radio Tehran building, with soldiers inside yelling in celebration of the coup, and soldiers outside firing guns in the air.)[63] Three decades later the Ronald Reagan administration noticed, among many other things, that the Soviet Union was helping Nicaragua's Sandinista government build asphalt plants. The president's concern with Soviet influence played out in aid to the Contras, guerrilla forces determined to overthrow the Sandinistas. After Congress terminated the aid (because the Contras terrorized villagers), the administration sold U.S. Army missiles to Iran and used the profits to fund the Contras. These missile sales were inconceivable, given the Iranian hostage crisis. On November 4, 1979, after an Islamic revolution toppled the Iranian monarch (a U.S. ally), Iranians stormed the U.S. embassy in Tehran. They held fifty-two U.S. Americans for 444 days before releasing them on the day Reagan took his oath of office. The administration continued to sell missiles to Iran thereafter on the assumption that Iran could facilitate the release of additional U.S. American hostages held in Lebanon. The missile sales ended on October 5, 1986, after a Sandinista soldier's Soviet-made shoulder-fired missile knocked down a cargo plane carrying supplies for the Contras.

Saudi Arabia's Adnan Khashoggi, an asphalt baron and self-described "merchant statesman," had a cameo in Iran-Contra. He was a character colorful enough to inspire Harold Robbins when writing his best-selling novel, *The Pirate* (1974), and the authors of the U.S. Foreign

Corrupt Practices Act of 1977. A conspiracy buff's dream, Khashoggi had links, however vague in some cases, to a plethora of scandal. His nephew, moreover, dated and died with Princess Diana. He sold heavy trucks manufactured by Kenworth Truck Company, based in a Seattle suburb, to the bin Laden family's construction business. And he was a conduit between the Saudis and British, French, and U.S. American weapons manufacturers. That resumé earned him an Iran-Contra role. In 1985 Iran-Contra independent counsel Lawrence Walsh said that Khashoggi helped arrange "bridge financing," using Israel as a cut out, for the sale of over five hundred U.S. Army missiles to Iran. Bridge financing was necessary "because the Iranians would not pay for the weapons until they were delivered, and Israel would not ship the weapons before Iran paid for them."[64]

Khashoggi's asphalt entry came through Triad America, his Salt Lake City investment firm, and its purchase of Edgington Oil, founded six days before Pearl Harbor to meet World War II demand for asphalt to pave airfields in the Pacific theater. He used Edgington, based in Long Beach, California, and generating up to $500 million per year in heavy oil and asphalt sales, as a "cash cow" to pay for such things as *Nabila*, his $70 million yacht. When Iran-Contra broke, Khashoggi sold his asphalt business for $52.5 million to pay off creditors. He sold the yacht to the sultan of Brunei, who later sold it to Donald Trump for $29 million. (It had been named after Khashoggi's daughter; Trump renamed it the *Trump Princess*.) With debt issues of his own, Trump sold the yacht at a loss. A Saudi prince bought it for $20 million.[65]

Iran-Contra's investigations, prosecutions, and pardons—President George H. W. Bush pardoned six of the scandal's principals—nearly exactly paralleled the Cold War's end. Asphalt played a bit part in the era's spy games with the CIA hiding dead-drop secrets in asphalt chunks in the case of agency asset and Soviet diplomat Alexandr Ogorodnik. Martha Peterson, an agency operative, carried the asphalt chunk in her purse. The asphalt had a hidden compartment, sealed with four threaded screws, containing messages, a miniature camera, rubles, and other items. Peterson left the asphalt in a stone tower on a Moscow bridge for Ogorodnik. Minutes after making the drop, the KGB detained Peterson and confronted her with the asphalt. The KGB released her within hours. Three days later Peterson was in the Oval Office for a twenty-minute meeting with President Jimmy Carter to tell her story about asphalt and spies. She brought along a replica of the asphalt chunk. Ogorodnik was not as fortunate. Earlier and at his request, the CIA had given him a cyanide capsule hidden inside a fountain pen. After the KGB arrest Ogorodnik bit down on that pen and died.[66]

Asphalt chunks as spy paraphernalia was surprising enough. Even more surprising was the blacktop bicycle path rising as a symbol of the Cold War's end and the Soviet Union's collapse. The symbolism played out on the Iron Curtain Trail and the Berlin Wall Trail. The former is 4,750 miles of blacktop from the Baltic Coast to the Black Sea. Planning for the latter began nearly to the day in November 1989 when the Berlin Wall began to fall. The trail is one hundred mostly blacktop miles that tracks several routes once patrolled by East Germany's heavily armed border guards.

Russian novelist and historian Alexandr Solzhenitsyn used Iron Curtain and blood-on-the-asphalt imagery in his 1970 Nobel Prize lecture: "And if the tanks of his fatherland have flooded the asphalt of a foreign capital with blood, then the brown spots have slapped against the face of the writer forever." When communism collapsed, dissidents and state actors alike in several of the former Soviet republics used asphalt to cover up the memory of crimes ordered by party bosses and functionaries. They tore down monuments, hauled them away, and paved over the sites (ironically) with Stalin's favorite downstream hydrocarbon. (Stalin even used asphalt for his personal security; he had his Kuntsevo District dacha "surrounded by a vast expanse of asphalt to facilitate detection of intruders.") The monument purge peaked over eighteen months, beginning in December 2013 with Ukrainians alone knocking down approximately five hundred Lenin statues.[67]

The United States has a black-and-bronze version of "Lenin fall" (an idiomatic expression in the former Soviet republics to indicate the toppling of communist monuments). Remnants of the Jefferson Davis Highway in Virginia and across other states all the way to California still stand complete with hundreds of markers. Some signage has come down. But until all signage comes down, those stretches of blacktop will remain, as one historian noted, "the largest monument to the Confederacy." On the bronze front activists have forced the removal of dozens of statues honoring Confederate generals and such other characters as a "racist gynecologist." The purge of Confederate monuments accelerated after the May 25, 2020, killing of George Floyd by Minneapolis police. Demonstrators under the Black Lives Matter banner toppled dozens of statues. Elected officials ordered others removed. Monument Avenue in Richmond, Virginia, lost its J. E. B. Stuart and Stonewall Jackson equestrian statues and Jefferson Davis memorial. But the Robert E. Lee equestrian statue remained, pending the outcome of a lawsuit. Artwork and signage more modest than the Lee statue—sixty feet high, including the base—grace the site of Richmond's former city gallows, where Gabriel Prosser hanged in 1800 for leading a slave revolt; and the Burial Ground for Negroes, which closed in the early nineteenth century. A portion of that burial ground may have extended under a parking lot and a nearby stretch of I-95. It is likely that Gabriel's remains are under blacktop.[68]

Shortly after Soviet walls and monuments began giving way to blacktop, the First Gulf War opened. Asphalt had played a role in every twentieth-century U.S. war, and this latest war, fought with our Cold War military, would be no exception. The enemy, for their part, had their own asphalt stories; for example, Saddam Hussein remembered his father administering childhood beatings with an asphalt-covered stick. Iraq's president, of course, ordered the invasion of Kuwait in 1990 with oil in mind and not asphalt (though the latter played a combat role as Iraqi engineers built supply roads in country). The George H. W. Bush administration responded to the invasion by organizing a coalition of thirty-nine nations that contributed soldiers and funding for a military incursion. Troops grouped in Saudi, invaded Kuwait on January 17, 1991, and declared Operation Desert Storm a victory on

February 28, a victory marred by Iraqi troops, in their scorched-earth retreat, setting at least six hundred oil wells on fire. The fires scattered tarcrete, an asphalt-like substance that left a hardened layer of soot and oil mixed with sand and gravel, on 5 percent of Kuwait's total area.[69]

Operation Desert Storm was hard on U.S. troops and their equipment alike. While Abrams main battle tanks chewed up blacktop, Kuwait's talc-like sand chewed up the tanks. It clogged air filters, prevented hatch closure, damaged engines, and interfered with weapons systems. Helicopter engines and blades were another casualty. Military engineers and contractors tried to keep sand from damaging equipment by paving or spraying asphalt emulsions or other dust palliatives at helipads, airfields, hardstands, warehouses, wash racks, large tents, and so on. It was a losing battle. Army Corps of Engineers historian Janet McDonnell explained, "No service brought into the theater adequate resources to produce asphalt, concrete, or crushed rock." (The army's solution for "future" wars was to "establish strategic stockpiles" of asphalt.) Even when asphalt was available, shipments often "did not arrive on schedule," or they "contained oversized aggregate and were delivered cold." At times deliveries stopped altogether. At other times "contractors had difficulty finding [truck] drivers." Rollers and paving machines, moreover, were scarce. And the hard desert soil quickly wore out road-grader blades. Given these difficulties, ingenuity was in order. Military engineers routinely brought decrepit asphalt plants back to life, including one in King Khalid Military City in Saudi Arabia. Unfortunately, that rehabilitated plant could produce only 150 tons per hour, more than enough to keep the Military City's twelve-thousand-foot runways in good shape but scarcely enough to keep even a single asphalt platoon busy.[70]

With or without an adequate asphalt supply, the U.S. Army Engineer School conceded that the dust and sand problem could not be solved. At times army regulations frustrated mitigation efforts. When a chemical spray failed as a dust palliative at King Fahd International Airport, engineers on-site requested approval of an indefinite delivery contract of $3.5 million to create a temporary heliport by laying two inches of asphalt over 1.3 million square yards. The Middle East and Africa Projects Office rejected the proposal, given a $200,000 limit on dust palliative contracts. This meant that $12 million helicopters remained at risk because the engineers had to use cheaper and less effective methods of dust and sand control at King Fahd and elsewhere. These methods ranged from spreading or spraying crude oil, waste oil, and diesel fuel to resins, brine solutions, cement, lime, and asphalt emulsions. The two products used most often, oil and diesel fuel, were among the most harmful to the environment. Unfortunately, heavy traffic broke down all dust palliatives. Worse still, as McDonnell noted, "vehicle operators tended to drive on any black surface even if it was designated as a non-traffic area."[71]

Better prepared for asphalt duty than the army, the navy sent three thousand Seabees and 1,375 pieces of construction equipment into Kuwait, allowing them to pave and build whatever needed paving and building in both Kuwait and Saudi Arabia (provided they could scrounge enough asphalt). Odd jobs included paving 1,500-foot runways for drones and such out-of-theater work as construction of "two mosques on Guam to support the religious needs of approximately 2,100 Kurdish evacuees." The primary Seabee missions were to build and maintain (1) supply roads and (2) the road network that Gen. Norman Schwarzkopf planned to use for his attack strategy. The latter "required more than 200 miles of roads" in Saudi and hundreds more in Kuwait. The six lanes of asphalt on one east-west corridor alone supported daily traffic of over "500 heavy haulers and thousands of tactical vehicles."[72]

During the Second Gulf War build-up a decade later, U.S. Marines massed at an asphalt expanse dubbed the Kuwait Arrival and Assembly Operations Element. From there they headed out on Highway 80 blacktop to Iraq. "Kind of ironic," one of them said. "The Iraqis are going to wish that little part of the desert was never paved." There was a déjà vu element here, given Highway 80's history in the First Gulf War. On February 26, 1991, U.S. aircraft bombed the front and rear of a two-thousand-vehicle convoy—a mix of civilian and military vehicles—fleeing Kuwait City. The cratered asphalt and burning vehicles created a bottleneck, allowing a blacktop slaughter that some pilots embraced. Others saw no glory in attacking a traffic jam. This so-called Highway of Death remained dangerous in the aftermath, given the volume of unexploded ordinance. A less dramatic but equally problematic fact further complicated bomb-crater repair: contractors had to keep asphalt hot during the two-hundred-mile drive from Saudi Arabia.[73]

On June 8, 1991, a military parade celebrated Operation Desert Storm victory with seventy-ton Abrams tanks rolling down Pennsylvania Avenue blacktop designed to carry no more than thirty-ton vehicles.[74] Eighteen months later, on December 4, 1992, the Bush administration launched Operation Restore Hope in Somalia with an emphasis on protecting humanitarian-aid workers and stabilizing things so a political reconciliation was at least imaginable. When Navy Seabees arrived, they supported the mission by removing three hundred thousand square feet of blacktop at the Baidoa Airport (originally paved by the Soviets in the 1970s) that had not held up under the stress of relief flights. After pulverizing the asphalt, the Seabees mixed it with Portland cement and then graded and compacted the mixture. The first major group of marine reinforcements in Somalia camped on a "big asphalt mess" at the Port of Mogadishu. Whether the goal was sanitation or sinking eighty-one-millimeter mortar pads, marines and Seabees alike kept "chopping at the asphalt."[75] Seabee support of Operation Restore Hope ended in March 1993, seven months before Somali militia downed two Black Hawk helicopters and dragged the bodies of two U.S. soldiers through the city's dirt, gravel, and asphalt streets.

Asphalt also played a role when Navy Seabees arrived for the decade's Balkan wars. The Bosnian War (1992–95) and the Kosovo War (1998–99) began with four of Yugoslavia's six republics declaring their independence. The violence in Bosnia was worse than in Kosovo, with Serb forces attacking Muslims and Croatian civilians (who also targeted Muslims before joining forces with them against Serbian nationalists). The war-crime carnage led to intervention by the United Nations and North Atlantic Treaty Organization against Serb forces, with twenty thousand U.S. armed forces personnel participating. The Seabees contributed in both Bosnia and Kosovo by building "camps for Army personnel," maintaining roads, and building new asphalt roads, container laydown areas, and ammunition handling areas. Contractors also helped on the blacktop front. In Kosovo, for example, DynCorp International and its partners won the contract to manage "operations and maintenance for the entire NATO infrastructure, including . . . asphalt roads" and "parking structures."[76] Peace in the Balkans did not come easily. It required three enforcement operations (Joint Endeavor, Joint Guard, and Joint Forge) and close air support. (During the Clinton era's decompression from the Cold War, peace still required bombs.) Ethnic cleansing in Bosnia displaced over one million and claimed approximately one hundred thousand lives. Up to 80 percent of the casualties were Muslims. No estimate exists of the number of people killed or "maimed . . . from the thousands of land mines that saturated the country." All sides in this Balkan war buried mines under asphalt roads.[77]

On April 19, 1995, eight months before the Dayton Peace Accords ended the violence in Bosnia, Timothy McVeigh, a right-wing extremist, detonated a rental truck packed with four thousand pounds of explosives in front of the Alfred P. Murrah Federal Building in Oklahoma City. The blast killed 168 people, including 11 Federal Highway Administration employees and 19 children under the age of six enrolled in the building day care. A ninety-year-old American elm tree in the blacktop parking lot across the street survived the asphalt chunks and other missile-like debris from the explosion. Investigators nearly had this Survivor Tree removed so they could more easily recover physical evidence that hung from branches or embedded in branches and the trunk. Families of those killed insisted that the tree remain. This was no easy task. Work crews had to use jackhammers to remove thick asphalt sheets that had bowed up. Like the missile-like debris, these asphalt sheets also embedded in the trunk.

The road to justice began ninety minutes after the bombing on I-35 blacktop, when a state trooper stopped McVeigh's 1977 Mercury Grand Marquis outside Perry, Oklahoma, because the car was missing a license plate. "The door of the Mercury was already open," the trooper testified at the trial of McVeigh's accomplice. "The driver's feet came out, placed down on the asphalt."[78] McVeigh's last steps lead to a gurney at the federal penitentiary in Terre Haute, Indiana. The lethal injection on June 11, 2001, was exactly three months before a terror attack that was not homegrown.

Asphalt held steady through the Cold War years and on into the twenty-first century. The air force once ruled for concrete runways exclusively. In practice the commanders could not rid themselves of asphalt any more than they could rid themselves of Iraq's sand. Asphalt had gathered a momentum that no directive could stop. The Department of Defense's annual *Base Structure Report* for 2017 included this boast: "DoD is still the Federal government's largest holder of real estate managing a global real property portfolio that consists of over 568,000 facilities (buildings, structures, and linear structures), located on 4,794 sites worldwide and covering approximately 27.2 million acres." The count for linear structures was 112,931, valued at nearly $180 billion. Over 90 percent of the roads and parking lots in the linear structure category are blacktop. The cover of the 2017 *Base Structure* report, as noted earlier, features a photograph of an asphalt roller on fresh blacktop.[79]

Asphalt is once and always a ubiquitous and contradictory material, and its contradictions might be conspiratorial on occasion. Mena Intermountain Municipal Airport and its two asphalt runways in western Arkansas emerged in fertile imaginations as a haven for gun and drug running by everyone from the Medellín cartel to the CIA, the Reagan administration and the Contras, and even Bill and Hillary Clinton. The contradictions might be personal on other occasions. A child on the way to Dodger Stadium in Chávez Ravine might walk across blacktop covering the Palo Verde Elementary School buried below. Asphalt remained a symbolic material as well for the Cold

War's duration, with bike trails symbolizing something positive (the Cold War's end) and roads and parking lots too often symbolizing and helping to enforce something negative (segregation). Asphalt was present for the United States at play and the United States at war. Paving machines and barrels of asphalt always accompanied the troops. But asphalt met its match in Iraq.

Asphalt (and concrete) incited a sixty-year war of a different kind, with the rise of the Interstate Highway System. Its wonders aside, that system waged war on a multitude of fronts. One was against the romance of the road, whether the mother road (Route 66) or other back roads of Jack Kerouac's counterculture epic, *On the Road* (1957), written just as the interstates were beginning to destroy the allure of the road. Literary critic Harold Bloom's characterization of that allure did not apply to the interstates: "The road, stretching across the breadth of this nation, becomes the symbol of America's true wealth and potential. Kerouac's road is literal; it is the highway to the West, the old Oregon Trail by which the dispossessed and the hopeless could travel in search of a new life . . . the dharma path made manifest in asphalt."[80] The interstates opened a more direct war front on that dharma path and even more so on the nation's cities. And they opened yet another war front both direct and indirect on the planet's atmosphere. Asphalt would help carry that last to an extreme in the new century, the oil-sand century.

7 Angles

Terrorists, Tricksters, Tea Partiers

Asphalt roofing, a distant second to asphalt paving, was big enough to help a shingle peddler rank as this nation's richest self-made woman in 2016 and again from 2018 to 2019. In an Election Day 2010 plea in *USA Today*, the owner of ABC Supply of Beloit, Wisconsin, channeled Ronald Reagan: "Government, get out of the way of business. . . . Taxing job creators is a sure way to stop the engine of economic growth." Scott Walker won Wisconsin's gubernatorial election that day with the help of shingle money from Diane Hendricks in Rock County. Those campaign contributions would continue. "Any chance we'll ever . . . become a right to work [state]?" Hendricks asked Walker. "The first step is we're going to deal with collective bargaining for all public-employee unions," the governor replied, "because you use divide and conquer."[1] The Wisconsin Budget Repair Bill of 2011 gutted collective bargaining for public employees with the exception of police and firefighters. Less than four years later, the governor signed a bill banning labor contracts requiring private-sector workers to pay union dues or fees. Hoping her man could ride the right-to-work express to the White House, Hendricks donated $5 million to a pro-Walker super PAC. When he dropped out of the 2016 GOP presidential primaries, she gave $5.5 million to a super PAC that ran ads attacking Hillary Clinton, joined the Donald Trump presidential campaign as an economic adviser, and, after the election, sat on the Trump inaugural committee.

Asphalt and taxes were very, very good to Diane Hendricks during the run that opened with that Election Day 2010 yelp. Worth an estimated $7.9 billion in 2020, she had a modest property tax bill well into 2017. Town of Rock assessment rolls showed a 1,663 square-foot house where her 8,500 square-foot mansion stood. And she paid nothing in state-income taxes for 2010, the year of the complaint, and then, for 2012–14, three more years of zeroes.[2]

Asphalt-based businesses are generally more modest than ABC Supply. Until the past few decades, hedge funds and multinational corporations with major interests in the asphalt-paving business have been relatively rare. CRH is an exception. Its Atlanta-based subsidiary, CRH Americas Materials, is this nation's largest asphalt paver and producer (and a major cement and aggregate producer as well). The *New York Times* characterized the Dublin-based parent company, with over 3,600 facilities in thirty-two countries and eighty-five thousand employees, as a throwback to the Amzi Barber era: "an immense roll-up, built by acquiring dozens of small companies, generally family owned." "We try to keep the crusty entrepreneurs on board," CEO Liam O'Mahony explained in 2000. That model has not shielded CRH from the shadow of scandal. O'Mahony said he was "upset to have our name in any way linked to the Ansbacher controversy," through a former CEO who had managed an "illegal banking operation from our registered office." CRH suffered more unwanted attention after purchasing an interest in a company that produced asphalt and cement used for the construction of Israeli infrastructure in the West Bank.[3]

Ben-Gurion International Airport near Tel Aviv has three asphalt runways. The Yasser Arafat International Airport in Rafah, owned and operated by the Palestinian National Authority, had an asphalt runway for only two years. After the Oslo II Agreement of 1995 authorized the airport, Bill and Hillary Clinton attended the opening ceremonies. In 2001–2 Israel responded to the al-Aqsa Intifada by bombing the radar station and control tower and sending in CAT D9 bulldozers, nicknamed "Zionist Monsters" by Navy Seabees, to destroy the runway. D9s often received, at the Israel Military Industries Plant, a modular protection suite of hybrid ballistic-armor plating. However, U.S. workers built them in such places as Peoria, Illinois, with an optional Single Shank ripper for tearing up asphalt in hard-to-reach places. It is a testament to how easily asphalt can be recycled and how poverty was so endemic that Palestinians carted away much of the Arafat Airport's busted blacktop.

An airport named after Yasser Arafat, the Palestine Liberation Organization icon who died in 2004, was a minor issue compared to Israel's commitment to a West Bank barrier to contain what some Israelis considered an Arab demographic threat. Barrier construction began in 2002, and when completed, this mix of fences, concrete walls, and accessories will be 330 feet wide in spots and 450 miles long, with each mile commanding 12,000 square yards of asphalt pavement. Israel's position is that the barrier is a temporary deterrent to prevent suicide bombers and not a manifestation of the "world's largest open-air prison." Others disagree. "You have to be almost insane to think that somebody uprooted mountains, leveled hills and poured billions here in order to build some temporary security barrier 'until the permanent borders are decided,'" an Israeli journalist concluded. "The hill was cut in the middle, and the route of the fence is paved beneath it," he continued, zeroing in on one section. "On the eastern side, the Palestinian side, there is barbed wire, then a deep ditch, then a dirt road, then the fence itself, eight meters high, and then another dirt road, then an asphalt road ('wide enough for a tank,' the Defense Ministry explains to me later)." The Israelis, Donald Trump said six days after his inauguration as the United States' forty-fifth president, "were having a total disaster coming across and they had a wall. It's 99.9 percent stoppage." Nonetheless, at any given time upward of fifty thousand Palestinians are in Israel in contradiction to Israeli law. Blacktop pavers, among others, do not hesitate to hire them.[4]

It was perfectly legal to profit from the Israeli occupation, and several asphalt producers and pavers did so. Blacktop also facilitated Israeli policy. Yellow license plates granted Israeli automobiles and their drivers access to major roads (often funded by U.S. tax dollars). Green license plates often consigned Palestinian drivers to degraded asphalt or plain dirt roads. In 2019 Israel opened the first road—Route 4370—with segregated lanes separated by a concrete wall topped with fencing rising twenty-six feet above the asphalt. Israel Defense Forces (IDF) would sometimes deploy in battle gear to make arrests of anyone attempting to repair a more modest Palestinian road. The IDF also deployed blacktop as a weapon in a more direct manner. A road from Birzeit to Ramallah connected the two hundred thousand Palestinians who lived in the area's villages to Ramallah's clinics and hospitals. The road had been peaceful until the IDF ripped up asphalt and dug trenches. A *Los Angeles Times* reporter noted the consequences: "Paramedics from Birzeit stopped their ambulance at one of the trenches, loaded a young woman who needed dialysis at a Ramallah hospital onto a stretcher, and then carried her across the quarter-mile stretch to an ambulance waiting on the other side."[5]

While Israel uses asphalt to help contain the so-called Arab demographic danger, other entities use it for their own dubious purposes. In 1913 New York State Highway commissioner John N. Carlisle called asphalt an "unclean thing," given the pervasiveness of paving graft.[6] Corruption remained common a century later. In 2013–14 the U.S. Department of Transportation, through its Office of Inspector General, opened nearly eighty cases of fraud and other criminal activity involving asphalt- and concrete-paving companies, a federal effort that soon took on the (largely mythical) status of the "largest anti-trust probe in U.S. history." (Many of the investigations involved what the department calls DBE—disadvantaged business enterprise—fraud.) One can total the number of prosecutions in these cases, the dollar amount of fines, and the years of the prison sentences. Nonetheless, as the civil engineer and scholar Henry Petroski explained, corruption in the paving business and the larger construction industry defies quantification: "There might be an awful lot of illegal stuff going on that is never detected or perhaps even suspected—or activity that is suspected, detected, but rejected as not being worth getting involved in."[7]

Transparency International, a Berlin-based nonprofit with chapters in more than one hundred nations, compiled a Bribe Payers Index in 2008 that had the construction sector leading all other industries in this category: "propensity to bribe public officials and exert undue influence on government policies and regulations." Risk Advisory Group, a global risk management consultancy, ranked the construction industry, along with "infrastructure, and oil and gas," as the most corrupt.[8] Oxford University researchers explained the core effects of construction-industry corruption, especially for road building and other infrastructure (and involving both contractors and government regulators): If budget decision makers recognize corruption, they "may skew spending away from the sector." If those decision makers are themselves corrupt, they may "skew the budget towards infrastructure spending so as to increase opportunities for corruption. . . . And if there is more opportunity for corruption in road construction than in road maintenance, then roads may be built, allowed to fall apart, and then rebuilt."[9]

Blacktop and concrete corruptions have attracted the World Bank's attention since its founding in 1944. "Our history speaks roads," a bank-research team wrote in a prologue to a report on contemporary corruption. "From earliest times one of the strongest indicators of a society's development has been its road infrastructure, or lack thereof." Between 2000 and 2010 the bank committed nearly $56 billion for road construction and maintenance, with a quarter of those projects drawing "one or more allegations of fraud, corruption, or collusion." The bank's investigative office for such probes, the Integrity Vice Presidency (IVP), surveyed twenty-nine cases of illegal or questionable activity and concluded that the "most common forms of wrongdoing" center on contract bidding and the execution of contracts. The basic problem was circular: "The higher the colluders raise the price, the more they can pay in bribes and kickbacks. The more they pay, the more they have to cheat . . . to make a profit."[10]

If most corruption on the asphalt front is small-bore, exceptions exist at home as well as abroad. Major asphalt-tinged scandals beyond Spiro Agnew's difficulties include those uncovered by the FBI's Operation Silver Shovel investigation in Chicago. Launched in the early 1990s after receiving complaints of broken asphalt dumped illegally in landfills, Silver Shovel expanded to encompass bribery, drug trafficking, and money laundering. Twenty-four Chicago civil servants and current or former aldermen were convicted. The FBI opened a separate investigation of Palumbo Brothers, a Chicagoland asphalt-paving company. In 1996 indictments arrived for three company principals and others on fraud, bribery, and racketeering charges related to schemes that bilked, among others, the City of Chicago and nearly nine hundred Palumbo employees paid for fewer hours than they worked. In 1999 plea deals resulted in prison sentences, fines, restitution, and a ban from state and federal road projects.[11]

A *Chicago Sun-Times* exposé in January 2004 of stolen Chicago asphalt under the Hired Truck Program—where the city hired private trucks and drivers to do city work—scarcely slowed corruption. Over the next few months, city crews deliver 380 tons of stolen asphalt to private construction companies. (These civil servants should not be confused with "Pothole Robin Hoods," who steal small amounts of municipal cold-mix asphalt and use it to repair potholes in their neighborhoods.) U.S. attorney Patrick Fitzgerald zeroed in on the Chicago Transportation Department, known as the "Department of Tony," the *Chicago Tribune* noted, "out of respect" for its former manager. One asphalt company executive hooked into Fitzgerald's prosecution of Illinois governor Rod Blagojevich. The blacktop man in that case—"Individual B" in the Blagojevich criminal complaint— was not charged.[12] Others were charged. One of the most prominent of Fitzgerald's sixteen Operation Board Games indictments, other than the governor and the governor's brother, was asphalt baron William F. Cellini Sr. Known in some circles as the "*consigliere* of Illinois," Cellini was a former transportation secretary for the state of Illinois and executive director of the Illinois Asphalt Pavement Association. In 2011 a jury convicted him of conspiracy to commit extortion and aiding and abetting bribery. He served forty-seven days less than a year in a federal prison.[13]

Organized crime kept a hand in the asphalt business around the world. Random examples: In 1991 Rotterdam police confiscated 1,400 pounds of cocaine hidden in Trinidad asphalt barrels. (Not to be outdone, border agents in Texas, seized 2,445 pounds of marijuana hidden in asphalt buckets.) In the twenty-first century, an assassin murdered a civil servant who exposed corruption in India's Golden Quadri-lateral highway project. After the European Commission concluded that the Calabria-based 'Ndrangheta and other criminal enterprises bled the work, Italy paid back $400 million in grants for maintaining and upgrading A3 Autostrada blacktop. The Islamic Republic of Iran fined an asphalt speculator ("the Sultan of Bitumen!") $100 million for "spreading corruption on earth." Presumably, the man's execution interfered with collection. Russian president Vladimir Putin's power was such, it was said, that "even the asphalt that paves Russia's roads is his." Yet he complained about endemic road corruption—what he called "black holes . . . where the allocated funds disappear." Quebec Superior Court justice France Charbonneau headed a commission that heard testimony from a witness who said he was the target of a car-bomb assassination attempt because he did not always favor "construction contractors of Italian origin." One of those contractors, Nicolo Rizzuto, founder of the Rizzuto crime family (the subject of a Netflix crime drama, *Bad Blood*), controlled Grand Royal Asphalt Paving on his way up. His company's municipal paving contracts included several for Expo 67 (the Montreal World's Fair). In the Charbonneau Commission's wake, Canada's Competition Bureau, an independent law-enforcement agency, raided at least a dozen Quebec-based asphalt companies.[14]

In Brazil the federal police and other entities launched Operation Car Wash (Operación Lavajato) to probe money laundering and bribery allegedly perpetrated by executives of Petrobras, the state-controlled oil and gas company (and a major asphalt producer) as well as executives of various construction and shipping companies.[15] Car Wash expanded into the United States on multiple levels. While the Bill and Melinda Gates Foundation was suing Petrobras and its accountants for fraud, Odebrecht, the largest construction conglom-erate caught up in Car Wash, pleaded guilty in 2016 to violating the U.S. Foreign Corrupt Practices Act. Odebrecht and a petrochemical subsidiary with asphalt interests and assets, Braskem, settled with

U.S., Brazilian, and Swiss prosecutors for as astonishing amount in fines: at least $3.8 billion. At the same time Odebrecht claimed to be a victim of (relatively) minuscule corruption after losing a Dallas drainage-tunnel contract despite submitting a bid $20 million less than Southland Mole's winning bid. A Southland Mole subcontractor, a minority-owned asphalt company named KDAT, compounded the affair, as an earlier FBI sting resulted in a bribery conviction of a company principal. In contrast to KDAT, Odebrecht is an asphalt behemoth with powerful allies. DuPont, for one, helped with the hot-mix chemistry for the paving of an Andean section of the Transoceanic (or Interoceanic) Highway across Brazil and Peru. Odebrecht added a DuPont resin to its blacktop mix so the road surface would hold up to extreme temperature variations.[16]

Some Irish Travelers (or Pavees), an indigenous ethnic minority, ran a criminal enterprise, the Rathkeale Rovers, based in County Limerick, featuring an asphalt driveway con across Europe and "every continent except Antarctica." "They may be illiterate but they are rat cunning and it gets handed down from generation to generation," an Australian police officer said.[17] In Milan, police sent in an undercover officer disguised as a priest to catch a Rathkeale crew attempting to con Roman Catholic nuns. The Rovers (and many others) perpetrate driveway-paving frauds most often by targeting the elderly in suburban and semirural areas. They start work without permission and then strong-arm a homeowner into paying. Or they tell a homeowner that they have leftover asphalt from a nearby job and can offer a steep discount. What underlies the fraud in either case is the use of substandard asphalt or used motor oil masquerading as asphalt. Jackson County, Missouri, where Noah waterproofed his ark, according to Latter Day Saints founder Joseph Smith, and where Harry S. Truman was once a judge and a good-roads booster, witnessed a particularly egregious case. A paver quoted an eighty-four-year-old woman $80 for a job, finished it in an hour, and demanded $10,000. Fearing for her life, the woman wrote the check. Two years later the Jackson County prosecutor filed fraud charges against that paver.[18]

Certain police agencies are prone to their own asphalt abuses under asset-forfeiture laws. In the United States the turning point on civil asset forfeiture came with the Comprehensive Crime Control Act of 1984, a law that allowed state and local police to seize and share cash and other assets with federal law enforcement. The goal was to target major drug dealers. In practice police and prosecutors use asset forfeiture most often in civil cases. Government entities would sue "the item of property, not the person," for example, *U.S. v. $30,000* (an actual case). From 2001 to 2014 deposits to federal forfeiture accounts totaled nearly $29 billion. Even if the owners had not been arrested or convicted, police could seize, keep, or sell, the American Civil Liberties Union noted, any property, including homes and businesses, "they allege is involved in a crime." This incentivized many police departments to make "seizures motivated by profit rather than crime-fighting." Recovering seized property even in the absence of criminal charges, the ACLU added, is notoriously difficult.[19]

Police-seizure programs often rely on Black Asphalt, a for-profit operation under the auspices of Desert Snow. That company's founder, a former California Highway Patrol officer, called it a "family-owned and operated criminal and terrorist interdiction training company." At first, Desert Snow did little more than distribute a training film on stop-and-seizure techniques on highways. After the 9/11 al-Qaeda attacks, the company established ties with Homeland Security, the Drug Enforcement Administration, and Immigration and Customs Enforcement. By 2004 Black Asphalt had an Electronic Networking and Notification System allowing "communication between Road Officers and Narcotics Officers throughout the nation." ICE operates a National Bulk Cash Smuggling Center and two intelligence systems, FALCON and Investigative Case Management, both of which can link to the Black Asphalt database.[20] By 2015 the Black Asphalt network had over twenty-five thousand members, and Desert Snow had trained over fifty thousand police officers ("Knights of the Black Asphalt!"). Computer chips aside, the business model was baby simple: "high volumes of stops for minor traffic infractions and conversations with drivers to look for inconsistencies and obtain permission for warrantless searches."[21] Civil libertarians called it roadside racketeering. In 2019 a unanimous U.S. Supreme Court agreed, ruling that the Eighth Amendment's excessive fines prohibition applied to the states. Police had seized a $42,000 automobile despite a statutory cap of a $10,000 fine for the crime in question (selling less than $300 worth of illegal drugs). It is not clear, however, if the decision in this case, *Timbs v. Indiana*, applied to both property seizures and cash seizures.[22]

Dennis Hastert (R-IL), sworn in as Speaker of the House on the day before Bill Clinton's impeachment trial opened in the Senate, found another legal way to mine gold atop the blacktop. Hastert began his asphalt-to-cash march by buying up land in and around Plano, Illinois, under a blind land trust, Little Rock Trust #225, that he held with two partners. (The name of this trust may have been an inside joke, given where the president's Whitewater troubles started.) Later, in 2005, Hastert increased the value of his investment by earmarking $207 million for the construction of the nearby Prairie Parkway that would connect I-80 and I-88. President George W. Bush helped too, arriving in Hastert's district to celebrate the imminent bulldozing of farmland and burning of fossil fuel by motorists going back and forth from Chicago and its far west and southwest suburbs. Four months after Bush's visit, Hastert sold his land. Representative Rahm Emanuel (D-IL), who would go on to serve as Barack Obama's chief of staff and then mayor of Chicago, noted in amazement, "[Hastert] came in with $300,000 and now has $6 million in real estate, and no one asks a question?" The Federal Highway Administration did have questions and canceled the Prairie Parkway. Others had questions for Hastert on the unrelated subject of pedophilia.[23]

Asset forfeiture and Dennis Hastert's investment suggest that the most striking element of asphalt-tinged scandals often centers on what is legal rather than what is illegal. The adventures of a man often recognized as the late twentieth century's asphalt king further demonstrates that sad proposition. Elmer "Bud" Shuster chaired the House Committee on Transportation and Infrastructure for the last six years of his tenure (1973–2001) as a GOP representative from Pennsylvania's ninth congressional district. His most notable contribution to the committee, prior to assuming the chair, consisted of opposition to automobile airbags. As chair, he pushed for I-99 (the Bud Shuster Highway), a ninety-nine-mile asphalt strip from Bedford to Tyrone (later extended into New York), and delivered pork-barrel projects to construction companies across the nation.

Bud Shuster's political career collapsed gradually, then suddenly (as Hemingway once described the way one goes bankrupt). Things began, as the *Washington Post* chronicled, with an investigation of Shuster's lobbyist ties by the House Committee on Ethics (then the Committee on Standards of Official Conduct).[24] Things ended with the lobbyist in question, Ann Eppard, taking a plea deal. Before entering politics Shuster thrived in the computer business, traveling widely with Eppard, while his wife guarded her privacy on a farm near Everett, a town less than 20 miles from the spot where I-99 would one day cross I-76 and only 130 miles from Washington. Shuster and Eppard were inseparable. Their relationship was complex but not sexual—and, obviously, neither was Richard Nixon's political courtship of Shuster, which included a moonlit cruise aboard the presidential yacht. Shuster was part of the incoming House GOP class in January 1973, and Nixon wanted their support as Plumber bills came due.

Bud Shuster could not help with Watergate. He could help the asphalt industry and his fellow House Republicans by raising campaign funds—having no need for much cash for his own campaigns, as his district was noncompetitive. At his peak Shuster ranked as the sixth-most prolific campaign cash machine in the House. Meanwhile, Ann Eppard formed her own lobby shop and signed such asphalt-centric giants as the American Road and Transportation Builders Association, United Airlines, Federal Express, the Outdoor Advertising Association of America, and . . . the Shuster campaign. The latter paid Eppard $3,000 a month for consulting work. For over a decade she helped Shuster raise money by soliciting contributions from, among others, New Enterprise Stone and Lime, a Pennsylvania construction firm with dozens of ready-mix concrete plants and asphalt plants. While paving I-99, according to the Federal Election Commission, New Enterprise and a subsidiary solicited $80,000 in contributions from their employees and then reimbursed them, a violation of federal election law that resulted in $150,000 in civil penalties. In 1998 Eppard faced charges of embezzling from Shuster's campaign and pocketing $230,000 in illegal payments from at least one blacktop parking-lot owner in connection with Boston's $11 billion highway burial project (the Big Dig).

The Eppard and Shuster experience ended with her misdemeanor plea and his admission of House rules violations (regarding gifts, improper lobbying, and improper use of campaign funds). It took three years for things to settle, given Shuster's negotiations with the Ethics Committee and a discontinuous criminal investigation. Ultimately, the committee granted him limited immunity and the U.S. attorney declined to prosecute. The committee's final report, based on approximately 150 subpoenas and dozens of witness interviews and depositions, included a letter of reproval: "By your actions you have brought discredit to the House of Representatives." On February 3, 2001, Shuster resigned from Congress and abdicated the asphalt throne. "I had reached the pinnacle of my congressional career," he said.[25]

The Big Dig project in Boston that ensnared Ann Eppard was a flash point in the interminable competition between asphalt pavers and concrete pavers. Construction began in 1991 and continued for sixteen years. Bechtel Corporation, the major contractor, had ramps paved with concrete, some of which crumbled under snowplows—leading the state highway administrator to question the original decision for concrete and have the ramps repaved with asphalt.[26] Bechtel might not have used much asphalt for the Big Dig, but the company was in the business. In Saudi Arabia its Jubail project recycled "7,000 tons of demolished asphalt and other granular waste." Qatar's Hamad International Airport, one of dozens of airports Bechtel helped build, had two of the world's longest blacktop runways. During the Second Gulf War, Bechtel was the primary contractor for the reconstruction of

Iraqi roads and other infrastructure. While Bud Shuster became the asphalt king after moving over from the computer business, Bechtel became a construction behemoth after its founder, Warren A. Bechtel, moved over from the track-rail hauling business. Thereafter the company quickly found its true calling: cultivating politicians at Shuster's level and above.[27]

If Shuster never flew as high as Bechtel's best and brightest, his career was dynastic enough to carry his son to the king-of-asphalt throne. In February 2001 William "Bill" Shuster won a special election to fill his father's seat and promptly secured appointment to the House Committee on Transportation and Infrastructure. In 2014, a year after stepping up as chair, he began dating a lobbyist for a major trade association, Airlines for America (A4A), with business before his committee. When that lobbyist first signed on, Bill Shuster told a reporter what he thought: "I think [she] will be a tremendous addition to the A4A team that [CEO] Nick Calio is building."[28] That name suggested asphalt's role in helping dig a deeper hole than any Big Dig hole or those Bud Shuster and Ann Eppard dug for themselves. After 9/11 Nick Calio, as a member of the White House Iraq Group, helped the second President Bush "market" the idea of war with Saddam Hussein's Iraq. Not only did asphalt play a major role in the subsequent invasion of Iraq in 2003 (and the prior invasion of Afghanistan); it played a deep background role in the rise of Osama bin Laden, al-Qaeda, and the 9/11 murders that precipitated what the Bush administration called a never-ending War on Terror.

No Iraqis were among al-Qaeda's hijackers. Fifteen of the nineteen were Saudis. The asphalt story here began in the early 1950s, when the Saudi Binladin Group, founded by Osama bin Laden's father, Mohammed bin Awad bin Laden, received a contract to build the Jeddah-to-Medina road. Initially, as Steve Coll wrote in his bin Laden family chronicle, Thomas Ward, Limited, a British company, was in charge. Construction launched with the British embassy hosting "a dozen princes and ministers" at a roadbed tea party. Thomas Ward promised a "surface of bituminous macadam . . . six meters across." After automobile accidents took the lives of key personnel, the company abandoned the road project, a flight from Saudi rock and sand that coincided with the royal family's "car-buying binge; eight hundred automobiles were handed out as gifts to family members, friends, and government officials in April 1952. The princes were revved up, but they had no place to drive." Bin Laden stepped into the void, taking delivery of twenty-one thousand tons of asphalt from Aramco, Saudi Arabia's state-owned oil and gas company.[29]

In the 1960s, among other road-construction and paving contracts, the Binladen Group built Highway 15, as Coll noted, from "Aseer's tribal heartlands" (and their "jihad-preaching clerics") through the desert to Mecca (Mohammad's birthplace) and beyond to Yemen (bin Laden's ancestral homeland).[30] Some three decades later the builder's son recruited twelve of the fifteen Saudis who were among al-Qaeda's nineteen hijackers from the villages along Highway 15. (One of the son's companies built the Khartoum to Port Sudan Road, but Osama bin Laden did not recruit along that black line.) One of the hijacked planes, American Airlines Flight 77, departed from a concrete runway at Dulles International Airport. The others took off from asphalt runways: American Airlines Flight 11 and United Airlines Flight 175 from Boston Logan International Airport and United Airlines Flight 93 from Newark International Airport. To facilitate cleanup of the rubble from the World Trade Center's Twin Towers, construction crews paved a haul road and staging area. Five years after the towers fell, workers tore up that blacktop to enable a search underneath for bone fragments and other human remains.[31]

Just as bin Laden's father had seized his blacktop opportunities in Saudi Arabia, a U.S. asphalt baron thought he saw War on Terror opportunity in Iraq's deserts. Harry Sargeant III, a former marine and top-gun pilot active in GOP politics in Florida, controlled Sargeant Marine, an asphalt trading, storage, and transportation company founded by his father. Among other innovations the younger Sargeant moved from fifty-five-gallon drums to ISO tank containers with a capacity of over six thousand gallons each. Determined to grow the business abroad, Sargeant bought asphalt tankers, a risky but potentially lucrative business.[32] His purchases included the *Falcon Champion*, rebuilt to carry eight million gallons of liquid asphalt (making it the world's largest asphalt tanker at the time). After registering the tanker as part of the U.S.-flagged fleet under the name *Asphalt Champion*, he complained of trade restrictions and union halls. Hereafter, he would register his tankers abroad.

In 2004 one of Harry Sargeant's start-ups, International Oil Trading Company (IOTC), secured the first of several contracts—eventually totaling $2.7 billion—to supply $3.1 billion worth of fuel to U.S. troops in Iraq.[33] A business partner, Mohammad Anwar Farid Al-Saleh, who happened to be the brother-in-law of Jordan's king, filed suit, claiming Sargeant and another partner owed him a fair share of profits. They were well-earned dollars, Al-Saleh said, because he helped win Jordanian government approval for rights to "off-load fuel from Sargeant's fleet arriving at the Port of Aqaba" and then truck that fuel through Jordan to U.S. bases. Al-Saleh made approximately $27 million through his work with IOTC before Sargeant cut him out, he continued, by creating a second firm and running the paperwork through that firm and not IOTC. Al-Saleh also claimed that IOTC paid bribes to secure rights to ship fuel across Jordan. In 2011 a Florida jury awarded Al-Saleh $28.8 million. Sargeant dodged a bill collector for five years and watched the judgment grow with interest to $38 million. He finally settled with Al-Saleh for a reported $30 million.[34]

Other disputes arose with Venezuela, the Dominican Republic, Dallas Cowboys–owner Jerry Jones, Charles and David Koch, and Sargeant's own family. There was some overlap here. Trigeant, a Sargeant family company that purchased extra-heavy Venezuelan oil, filed for bankruptcy in 2013, listing Petróleos de Venezuela, the state-owned oil company, as its largest creditor. "In court papers," a pithy reporter noted, "Trigeant has said it was mistreated by PDVSA because of rumors the Sargeants disliked late Venezuelan President Hugo Chávez." In 2015 Sargeant settled fourteen lawsuits, walking away, in the words of the *Palm Beach Post*, "with a cool $56 million."

The money came from the $100 million sale of a family-owned asphalt facility in Corpus Christi, Texas. The remaining $44 million went to PDVSA and other creditors. On the downside Sargeant's brother took over Sargeant Marine and the asphalt-tanker fleet, including the *Asphalt Splendor*, a thirty-seven-thousand DWT tanker built on the Yangtze River in China, with sixteen independent floating tanks capable of keeping product liquid at 338 degrees Fahrenheit. Sargeant Marine took delivery in February 2016. A month later the company and the Vitol Group created an asphalt-trading venture, called VALT, that moved "circa 1.3 million metric tons of asphalt per annum." That kept fifteen tankers busy. Vitol now owns 100 percent of VALT.[35]

Nonetheless, embarrassments persisted. In 2017 prosecutors in Brazil accused Sargeant Marine of bribing politicians "in exchange for helping it win asphalt supply contracts [from Petrobras]." Harry Sargeant said he had nothing to do with it: "Sargeant Marine, the entity recently ensnared in the Brazilian Car Wash graft probe, was and is a company owned, controlled, and operated by my father and brothers. I have had no ownership of or involvement in the business and affairs of Sargeant Marine including without limitation any conduct associated with the Brazilian transactions forming part of the 'Lava Jato' probe. . . . I am prepared to cooperate fully with the Brazilian and other authorities in connection with their ongoing investigation and prosecution of corrupt activities by Sargeant Marine."[36]

Harry Sargeant's name also surfaced during the Ukraine scandal investigations that led to Donald Trump's impeachment. Two of the scandal's Florida-based players, Lev Parnas and Igor Fruman, were briefly associates of Sargeant and the president's personal attorney, Rudy Giuliani. "Attending a single, informal dinner in Houston does not place Mr. Sargeant at the center of any . . . Ukrainian business plan," Sargeant's attorney announced. Fiona Hill, the National Security Council's senior director for European and Russian affairs from 2017 to 2019, said Giuliani's back-channel portfolio included "Ukrainian energy interests that had been in the mix in Venezuelan energy sectors as well as the names again of Mr. Parnas and Mr. Fruman, and this gentleman Harry Sargeant. . . . And my colleagues said these guys were notorious in Florida and that they were bad news."[37]

Asphalt's role in the post-9/11 wars ranged far beyond Harry Sargeant's adventures. Two 13,123-foot asphalt runways at Saudi Arabia's Prince Sultan Air Base supported a "logistics, command, and basing hub for U.S. operations in Afghanistan and Iraq." In mid-2003 those functions moved to Qatar's Al Udeid Air Base and its 12,303-foot asphalt runway. Rear Adm. Charles Kubic, the navy construction commander in Iraq before retiring in 2005, took pride in small victories. The dust war along Highway 1's six lanes began with a road oil that a Kuwaiti contractor sold for $5.00 a gallon. Kubic paid that contractor to get a nearby decrepit asphalt plant up and running (a plant supposedly owned by Saddam's oldest son). In short order the plant began producing a dust palliative by cutting asphalt with kerosene and selling it at $1.67 a gallon. Unfortunately (and like the First Gulf War), nothing could keep up. "The sand," one marine said, "was part of the air itself." He described Highway 1 as a dirt road "merely punctuated . . . with intermittent stretches of asphalt." Sewage leaking from broken pipes, a reporter noted, also spread across blacktop destroyed by "the tracks of American tanks." However much pavement crumbled and sand and dust damaged military equipment and human lungs alike, Iraq's tiny natural-asphalt industry hummed along. "Folks jump into the tar pit waist deep," an army captain at Firm Base 1 in Hit said. "[They] roll up the tar [sic] into basketball-like objects of sticky goo, and toss them to their buddies, who stack the tar balls in their carts."[38]

Regardless, Hit's natural asphalt was of no use to U.S. forces. To pave Uranium Road—the "mission-essential 51-kilometer alternate supply route" from Hit to Asad—the Army Corps of Engineers used "extensive asphalt manufacturing modules" on Al Asad Air Base. An Iraqi-owned contractor trucked "about 500 metric tons of asphalt daily . . . to the asphalt pour site." On Labor Day 2007, a few months before Uranium Road construction began, President Bush made a surprise visit to Anbar Province. "Air Force One," he wrote in his memoir, "flew over what looked like a giant sand dune and touched down at Al Asad Air Base, a patch of black asphalt amid miles of brown." Eleven years later President Trump gushed over the base's blacktop: "I couldn't believe the money that was spent on these massive runways."[39]

The bright spot regarding road construction in Afghanistan and Iraq was the relatively modest amount of corruption. Investigative reporters and congressional Democrats did not ignore asphalt scandals, but they focused primarily on the massive reconstruction contracts granted to companies like Bechtel, Halliburton, and KBR. (Halliburton acquired M. W. Kellog in 1998 and merged it with Brown and Root; KBR remained a Halliburton subsidiary until it separated in 2006.)[40] Far down the waste, fraud, and abuse scale, special inspectors general for Afghanistan and Iraq reconstruction (SIGAR and SIGIR) investigated complaints of inferior-grade asphalt on road projects, kickbacks, overbillings, and double billings. Few asphalt projects were in the multimillion dollar range. Most were less than $200,000.[41]

Paving jobs in Iraq and Afghanistan continued as the wars entered their second decade. In 2013 the Army Corps of Engineers awarded a joint venture contract to Anham, a United Arab Emirates company, and ICS Serka, a U.S. company, to repair and pave runways at Afghanistan's Bagram Air Field. This entailed demolishing a decrepit Russian runway, recycling the concrete, and repaving the main runway "with nearly 10,000 cubic meters of asphalt." Air force engineers from a Red Horse unit—Rapid Engineer Deployable Heavy Operational Repair Squadron Engineer—helped by paving Bagram's Ammo Road so munitions could be "delivered to aircraft in a minimal amount of time." Red Horse units, first organized during the Vietnam War, specialized in "runway and ramp construction, maintenance and repair." "I have laid asphalt," one "dirt boy" bragged, "when it was 100 degrees out and 275 degrees underfoot."[42]

While other blacktop projects created jobs for Afghans and Iraqis, things did not always go well. Canadian medical officers in Afghanistan described an asphalt-induced MASCAL (Mass Casualty) event in Kandahar: Afghani workers heated asphalt in fifty-five-gallon drums by pouring in gasoline and igniting the mix with blowtorches. They never got past the first drum, as they quickly closed the lid when the fire became uncontrollable. That created a fuel-air bomb explosion with "casualties . . . walking around looking for help—skin, hair, and clothing dripping off their bodies."[43] Asphalt training of Iraqis was more productive and less likely to end in fiery pain and death. On Joint Base Balad, home to an asphalt plant fortified with concrete barriers and razor wire, the Army Corps of Engineers launched a flagship program in 2007. From the beginning of the reconstruction bonanza, contractors preferred to ship in a labor force of South Asians rather than hire Iraqis because they considered Iraqis to be security risks. The new norm called for hiring Iraqis. Students at Balad, one engineer explained, could learn a skill and improve "area roads at the same time." Many of these "students" were former insurgents attracted by the blacktop pay: $300 a month.[44]

Along with asphalt's minor corruptions and the intrusion of an occasional asphalt baron like Harry Sargeant, the product had an environmental story in theater. The "particulate war" in Iraq, in some areas, bored down to spraying asphalt emulsions on the sand between the tents that housed U.S. troops. A less mundane use for the product occurred after nearly one thousand national guards, reserves, regular army troops, and civilians suffered chemical exposure at the Qarmat Ali Water Treatment Facility, an operation that treated water for industrial use and not human consumption. The most dangerous chemical was sodium dichromate, a hexavalent-chromium compound used to reduce pipe corrosion. U.S. forces provided security for the crew hired by a KBR subsidiary to rebuild the damaged and looted plant, and those forces and others went on to file lawsuits against KBR for knowingly allowing exposure to toxic chemicals. Conceding the risk, Veterans Affairs established a "medical surveillance program" to monitor the health of any soldier exposed. Meanwhile, KBR paved over the Qarmat Ali site with asphalt to contain the sodium-dichromate dust that had not yet blown away.[45]

Hexavalent-chromium exposure was part of a larger problem that blacktop could not contain. In 2012 Congress funded a registry for current and former military personnel exposed to burn pits and sand and dust storms in Iraq, Afghanistan, and other theaters. The military used burn pits to dispose of waste, including hazardous waste. "The toxic metal-, bacteria-, and fungi-laden smoke and fumes from the pits," widely dispersed by storms and even normal breezes, former marine and U.S. Army sergeant Joseph Hickman emphasized, posed a health hazard to the respiratory systems of the people of Iraq, Afghanistan, and many other nations, and of 3.5 million U.S. Americans. One of those was Joe Biden's son, Beau, who served in Iraq as a U.S. Army major, suffered exposure to burn-pit carcinogens, and died, whether related to that exposure or not, from brain cancer at age forty-six in 2015. Data gathered from 28,426 current or former U.S. military personnel exposed to burn pits in Iraq and Afghanistan revealed that one third had respiratory diseases. Of those, many also suffered from insomnia, liver conditions, assorted chronic illnesses, and "decreased physical function, such as walking, running or climbing steps."[46]

Veterans Affairs' tracking of damage to soldiers' lungs and other organs suggests that this might be one of the most widespread and ultimately the most expensive battlefield affliction. More traditional battlefield calamities of death and disfigurement, of course, were ever present. That Joint Base Balad program to train Iraqis to lay asphalt pavement had an unexpected if largely overstated benefit. "We actually had students find IEDs [improvised explosive devices] planted by insurgents," an army engineer said. In the war's forty-seventh month, Secretary of Defense Robert Gates explained the significance of that small fact about IEDs: "These darn things account for about 70 percent of our casualties." IEDs buried in dirt roads and vehicle-borne improvised explosive devices (V-BIEDs, or car bombs) inspired a multibillion dollar "Manhattan Project" to develop "Darth Vader stuff" to protect troops. One contractor, formed after merging with a penny-stock outfit with experience working the low-tech field of dandelion neutralization, received millions to build a gadget intended to neutralize IEDs with "little lightning bolts."[47]

The Pentagon push featured a letterhead campaign that opened with IED-TF (Improvised Explosive Device Task Force) and moved on to several other acronym-heavy bureaucracies before settling on JIEDDT (Joint IED Defeat Team). IED Blitz experimented with a "persistent stare," including "ground-penetrating radar," on twelve miles of Route Tampa asphalt into Baghdad. The project deployed satellites, U-2 spy planes, drones, and helicopters "to assess whether road shoulders had been disturbed by digging." IED Blitz found no IEDs. Nor did "Fido," a "scientific molecular sniffer" mounted on mobile robots. "The Marines admired an Israeli method that used collar-mounted radio receivers to control their [live] dogs," the *Washington Post* noted, "but the animals' linguistic limitations proved problematic: Most understood only Hebrew." The Los Alamos National Laboratory encountered another language barrier when deploying the "proboscis extension reflex" of another species. Concluding that a honeybee's "explosive-detection capabilities have significant reliability issues," the Pentagon terminated the Stealthy Insect Sensor Project and destroyed the $2 million stockpile of tiny harnesses and other bee gear. On occasion the military returned to its roots with a boom-boom approach, clearing ground by dropping bombs on dirt and asphalt roads.[48]

From the labyrinth of Pentagon bureaucracies and profit-seeking contractors, asphalt pavement emerged as a "counter-IED device" on three levels in both Iraq and Afghanistan. First, concrete barriers simply closed some streets and roads to traffic. Lack of maintenance led to grass and weeds "growing out of the cracks in the asphalt," with long stretches of Baghdad blacktop turning into "sundeck[s] for scorpions and lizards." Second, the brass called for asphalt paving wherever streets and roads could not be closed, reasoning, as ever, that insurgents might find it more difficult to bury a roadside bomb in a paved road than a dirt road. Third, road projects created jobs, leading in theory to more forewarning of IEDs in the manner of the asphalt-trained Iraqis at Joint Base Balad. Gen. Karl Eikenberry, the Combined Forces commander in Afghanistan in 2006, made the point with seven words: "Where the roads end, the insurgency begins." In

2007 the Bush administration asked Congress for $370 million for road and bridge paving in Afghanistan, citing blacktop as a counter-IED measure. The House Committee on Appropriations approved the request but demanded that the Pentagon "provide no later than October 1, 2009, a detailed assessment . . . for each section of road funded in this Act, data allowing for a useful comparison of the frequency of IED attacks and the number of casualties before and after the completion of that road section. The report should also include an assessment of how enemy IED tactics in Afghanistan have evolved and adapted."[49]

It is not clear whether asphalt paving decreased the number of roadside bomb attacks. U.S. troops learned what Seabees had learned in Vietnam: "Charlie can booby trap anything from a discarded helmet to an asphalt road." (Only the slur was new; "Charlie" swapped out for "Hadji.") Most often in Iraq (less often in Afghanistan), the better-equipped insurgents used power saws to cut through asphalt, filled the holes with TNT, and then placed asphalt patches over the IEDs to hide them. Before detonation sent deadly baseball-size blacktop chunks flying, the only sign of a bomb was a barely visible wire protruding through the asphalt. A more common response to fresh pavement was more car bombs and other suicide bombings . . . and more Pentagon acronyms: Victim Operated IEDs (VOIEDs), Person-Borne IEDs (PBIEDs), Suicide Vest-Borne IEDs (SVBIEDs), and so on.[50]

When the United States arrived in 2001, Afghanistan had few passable paved roads, given lack of maintenance and damage during the Soviet occupation. By 2016 the U.S. Agency for International Development (USAID) and the Department of Defense had spent nearly $3 billion to construct and repair blacktop roads. Some funds disappeared. DOD, according to an audit, "could not account for spending on 462 of 4,687 road-related projects." Roads disappeared too. Under a $366 million Secondary Roads program, USAID lost track of the "precise locations of roads it constructed."[51] Another problem according to the World Bank and a bevy of analysts: lack of equipment in the provinces meant inadequate maintenance and road decay to the point where "a majority cannot be used by motor vehicles." While asphalt made it more difficult to plant roadside bombs (in theory, at least), all but the most damaged pavement gave the Taliban and other insurgents more opportunities to operate. Control of a single point on a road could facilitate kidnappings, hijackings, ambushes, extortions, and blood lust—and the point of control could move twenty miles in twenty minutes if the asphalt was even halfway decent. Poor security, in turn, not only delayed road projects and maintenance but escalated costs to U.S. taxpayers.[52]

By 2009, according to one study, road projects in Afghanistan "had become the single biggest investment by coalition forces." Mismanagement, however, compounded inadequate maintenance and other problems. "You have colonels in Bagram making decisions about the inches of asphalt, and they have no clue," an Army Corps of Engineers officer complained.[53] Tribal loyalties and favoritism further compounded problems. An analyst offered an example: "Bilal Noori Construction Company signed a $3.1 million contract for asphalt road construction and repair that the company had no capacity to do. Instead of entering into a joint venture with another company, BNCC subcontracted all the construction work. . . . When these [subcontractors] were asked why they did not bid for the project themselves, their reply was that they did not know about it . . . [because] only the politically connected companies" had access to U.S. bases where the bids were posted.[54]

Afghanistan's main asphalt road, the 1,900-mile Ring Road (Highway 1), never fully recovered from the destruction of the Soviet occupation. Extortions, robberies, kidnappings, and beheadings by Taliban and assorted criminal gangs stymied U.S. efforts to rebuild and repave. Zalmay Khalilzad, the U.S. ambassador to Afghanistan, said President Bush "phoned him every other day" about work on the Kabul-Kandahar highway (a 300-mile section of the Ring Road known locally as the "Mr. Bush project"). The president demanded a "black line" of asphalt "before winter snows set in."[55] "Road building brings jobs to young men who might be recruited to the Taliban," the president said. "Roads promote enterprise. Enterprise provides hope.

Hope is what defeats this ideology of darkness. And so we're going to build another 1,000 roads." This faith in asphalt was bipartisan. When visiting Kunar Province a year later, in 2008, then senator Joe Biden (D-DE) answered his own question: "How do you spell hope in Pashto and Dari? A-S-P-H-A-L-T." Unfortunately, that was also the way the Taliban spelled fund-raising. The Commission on Wartime Contracting in Iraq and Afghanistan ranked highway protection payments as the insurgency's second-largest funding source (behind the opium trade): "Afghan contractors hired under the Host Nation Trucking program"—which moved six thousand truckloads each month—"have turned to Afghan private security contractors . . . [who] pay off the insurgents or warlords who control the roads."[56]

Three years after George W. Bush and Joe Biden connected asphalt with hope in Afghanistan, the New Jersey–based Louis Berger Group received an $86 million contract to repair and pave sixty-four miles of the Khost-Gardez road. Earlier the Berger Group served as the principal contractor for the Ring Road's phase one, which it touted in a pamphlet that opened with a chapter titled "From Alexander the Great to the Louis Berger Group." Other equally immodest lines: "A wind swept across the desert terrain under a cloudless blue sky. Mountains loomed in the distance. It was bone-chilling cold. And the blacktop was down . . . a milestone in the 'war on terror' and a civil engineering feat on a scale and at a pace without comparison." For the Khost-Gardez contract, completed on December 31, 2015, there was no boasting. A subcontractor, South Africa–based ISS-Safenet, provided security via a warlord named Arafat, whose ties to a jihadist group were sufficient to land him on the Joint Priorities Effects List (a kill-or-capture list issued to U.S. troops and coalition forces). The man collected $160,000 a month. "If the bad guys have a stake in the project, attacks go way down," an army officer explained (without adding that the cash could fund attacks elsewhere). Regardless, cost overruns attracted reporters, who uncovered the warlord's presence on the payroll. Coincidentally or not, a month after his firing in April 2011, an attack killed thirty-five Khost-Gardez road workers.[57]

Before the Khost-Gardez contract arrived, the Berger Group tried to buy asphalt from Iran. Because the Bush administration refused to waive a ban on Iranian products, the contractors paid a higher price for eight hundred thousand drums of low-grade asphalt from Pakistan. Still, the Berger Group stabilized supply sufficiently to keep seven asphalt plants, including one imported from Italy, "pumping out ATB [asphalt treated base]." That volume was not surprising. The Berger Group's reconstruction contracts inched up to $665 million. Problems beyond violence and asphalt quality arose, with the indictment of the Berger Group's former president and CEO on federal fraud, conspiracy, and overbilling charges. Indictments against other company executives followed, as did guilty pleas, deferred prosecution agreements, and fines. In 2019, moreover, over one hundred Gold Star families sued the Berger Group and several other contractors, alleging that protection money paid to the Taliban and warlords of various stripes helped fund attacks on U.S. troops in violation of the Anti-Terrorism Act.[58]

Meanwhile, death on Iraq's blacktop was ubiquitous enough that U.S. military personnel often called the Second Gulf War a highway war. "Mad Max patrol" meant hunting insurgents by driving up and down asphalt roads while dodging crater-size potholes, wrecked vehicles, and IEDs. Ramadi to Fallujah asphalt was particularly brutal. Roadside checkpoints regardless of location were even more brutal, as force-protection protocols conspired with language barriers to produce hundreds of civilian deaths. Iraqi drivers were too often too confused or scared to stop when directed, and when things went sideways the military usually documented the carnage under a bland header: Escalation of Force Incidents. Nearly every one began with signals (waving arms, flashing lights, firing green lasers and paintball guns), then warning shots, and finally direct fire. The idea was to minimize "all conceivable risk by permitting troops to bypass traditional methods of detecting friend from foe."[59] Checkpoints put everyone on edge. They were a favorite target of suicide bombers, as traffic often backed up, promising heavy casualties.

Approximately seven hundred Iraqi civilians died at U.S. checkpoints. Thousands were injured. A typical escalation-of-force incident report from 2005: soldiers seriously wounded a driver and front-seat passenger while managing to miss the pregnant woman and her sister in the back seat. The report noted the pregnant woman's contractions and time of birth. The blood in that car and on the asphalt below could have been much worse. That same year at a checkpoint near Ramadi, the driver of a maroon Opel did not stop when marines fired warning shots that killed two children and five adults. Four other Iraqis packed into that car survived. A year earlier marines in a Humvee called the Iraqi police after one of their number fired at a tailgating car, and the car went off the blacktop and into a canal. The marine log recorded the bodies the police recovered from the car: "(2) adult females, (3) children ages 5 to 8, and (1) infant . . . all (6) had drowned." Security contractors added to this grim toll. One of the worst incidents occurred on September 16, 2007, on Nisour Square blacktop in Baghdad, when Blackwater guards killed fourteen unarmed Iraqi civilians. In U.S. District Court, juries convicted three of those guards of involuntary manslaughter and a fourth of first-degree murder.[60]

This was horrifying and circular. Blood on asphalt was a constant long before U.S. troops and the security and reconstruction contractors arrived. Saddam Hussein's father used asphalt as a torture tool. His sons, Uday and Qusay, were proponents of the Ba'ath Party practice of forcing hot asphalt into the mouths of their enemies. The Iraqi Olympic Committee was probably the world's only Olympic committee with its own torture center and jail, a facility run by Uday Hussein, who personally beat Iraqi athletes who disappointed him while forcing them to crawl naked across hot asphalt. Given desert sun, even standing on blacktop fully clothed qualified as torture in the minds of U.S. troops. There was only one "building in our area," one soldier said, and it had air-conditioning and satellite television. "The soldiers are all out here baking on the asphalt, dodging these giant dust storms, while the XO observes from his nice cool building. The soldiers call it the plantation house." The sign out front read, "Keep Out."[61]

In July 2003 Uday and Qusay Hussein met their end in Mosul. From the asphalt street in front of the house where they had taken refuge, U.S. forces lay siege for three hours. According to Lt. Gen. Ricardo Sánchez's briefing, the initial assault resulted in four soldiers wounded by AK-47 fire, three on the stairs leading to the second floor and one outside the front door. Next the troops "prep[ped] the target" with fifty-caliber machine guns and helicopters equipped with 2.75-inch rockets. An antitank platoon and a PSYOP team stood by. When a second attempt up the stairs failed, Lt. Gen. Sánchez continued, "we fired 10 TOW missiles into the house." Saddam's sons, his grandson, fourteen, and a bodyguard were in the house. One of the adults survived the TOWs and, until killed by small-arms fire, kept firing his AK-47 during the third attempt up the stairs. Three months later U.S. forces captured Saddam Hussein, who had been hiding in a hole in the ground on the outskirts of ad-Dawr. Three years later, on December 30, 2006, the Iraqi government hanged Saddam at Camp Justice, a joint Iraqi-U.S. military base located in a Baghdad suburb.[62]

Saddam Hussein, the enemy of the United States and al-Qaeda alike, was gone. But a new enemy emerged from the cauldron, al-Dawla al-Islamiya fi al-Iraq wa al-Sham (Daesch)—in English the Islamic State of Iraq and the Levant and commonly known as ISIS (or ISIL). In Iraq and Syria, asphalt was part of the ISIS rampage, as this murder cult occasionally dispatched imagined apostates by throwing them into hot asphalt tanks. More often ISIS targeted asphalt plants. During their rocket attack on a plant north of Mosul, twelve ISIS terrorists died. On the business end ISIS briefly controlled the Qayyara oil field near Mosul, a field "that produces about 8,000 barrels a day of heavier oil that is mostly used locally to make asphalt."[63] Some of the heavy oil that ISIS controlled, laundered, and sold illegally may have ended up as blacktop pavement on U.S. roads and airport runways. An example: Axeon Specialty Products may have unknowingly purchased a shipment of ISIS oil masquerading as "cheap Kurdish crude."[64]

ISIS complicated the civil war in Syria too. In Huma terrorists affiliated with ISIS damaged an asphalt plant and kidnapped the plant director and two others. The United States and Russia also complicated the Syrian civil war. Both nations paved airstrips and runways so warplanes and attack helicopters could help whatever side, whatever faction. On April 4, 2017, in response to the Bashar al-Assad regime's sarin nerve-gas attack on the town of Khan Shaykhun, two U.S. Navy destroyers fired fifty-nine Tomahawk cruise missiles on various structures at Shayrat Air Base. President Trump explained the decision not to target the blacktop that Assad's Russian allies had recently rolled out: "The reason you don't generally hit runways is that they are easy and inexpensive to quickly fix (fill in and top)!"[65]

In 2017 U.S. B-52s and other bombers taking off from the 12,303-foot asphalt runway at Al Udeid Air Base, Qatar, targeted ISIS in Raqqa, a city on the northeast bank of the Euphrates River. There were few civilian casualties, the Pentagon said, as these were surgical strikes. Amnesty International disagreed, counting sixteen thousand civilian deaths in Raqqa attributable to bombing by the United States and its coalition allies. A refugee said the bombing reduced the town to "rubble" and "asphalt." He was one of at least five million Syrian refugees and displaced persons since the civil war began in 2011. Those who fled Syria often walked out along blacktop roads, heading to Hungary with its closed borders or the Slovenia-Austria border, where they slept on blacktop because they feared losing their place in lines waiting for buses that might never arrive. Others made it to Piraeus, the port city in Greece, where luxury liners, in the words of a humanitarian volunteer, "having just plied the Aegean," arrive each day to the sound of *Zorba the Greek*'s theme song and "disgorge sun-sated, archeologically enriched tourists." Near another Piraeus pier, refugees "wait in camps erected on diesel-stained asphalt," suffering "in airless tents broiling under a Mediterranean summer sun, made even hotter by the black asphalt." Refugee camps without asphalt, including those in Syria near Aleppo (the target of air strikes by Syrian and Russian forces), were cooler but otherwise worse. Neither dirt nor gravel could tame the winter mud or the summer dust, snakes, and scorpions.[66]

The asphalt story in Mesopotamia was thousands of years old before Saddam's father beat him with an asphalt-coated stick, and asphalt's use for more formal tortures dates not to Saddam's sons or ISIS butchers but to the ancient Assyrians (if not earlier). Through those many years asphalt remained remarkably consistent in its uses and contradictions. It produced wealth for Cleopatra the Nile queen in the long ago and Diane the Beloit roofer in the here and now. It once attracted imperial monarchs and Nabataean traders and now attracts small-fry con artists and organized criminals on the dark side and small-business dreamers and hedge-fund dealers on the lighter sides of the law. Where Antigonus the One Eyed failed, the Amzi Barbers, Bud Shusters, and Harry Sargeants succeeded, however briefly. They all wore the crown for a few short years: King of Asphalt. Nevertheless, asphalt's real royalty are the contractors, Bechtel and the lot; and the state troopers and sheriff's deputies and other asset-forfeiture trolls who patrol highway blacktop when not resting under highway bridges.

Saudi Arabia had an asphalt king too, and the bin Laden patriarch's son recruited his 9/11 box cutters from the villages along a blacktop highway. When the United States launched its shock-and-awe invasion of Iraq for oil or whatever was in the head of George W. Bush and Dick Cheney, the troops, as ever, brought asphalt with them. In an earlier war a Pentagon functionary walked out of a White House meeting wondering if the administration intended to pave the entirety of South Vietnam with asphalt. In Iraq military strategists seemed hell-bent on paving over every speck and particle of dust and sand while fighting their highway war. The Bush administration's surge policy was more asphalt policy than anything else, as it centered on paying Iraqi insurgents to lay down their arms and lay asphalt. Regardless, neither White House policies nor U.S. Armed Forces and their weapons could stop the insurgency's legacy any more than black goo could conquer dust and sand, let alone the enemy's improvised explosive devices. If blacktop made it easier for marines and others on patrol to spot IEDs, it also made it easier for those who drove car bombs to kill. The spasm of road building in Afghanistan produced the same contradictory result. If pavement set the Taliban back here and there, overall it gave the Taliban more mobility and enabled its extortion enterprise to wring more money out of trucking contractors hired with U.S. cash. If smuggling in the chemical needed to produce heroin from poppies and then smuggling heroin out provided the principal income stream, blacktop extortions and ransoms also helped keep the Taliban in the black.

By the end of the twenty-first century's first decade, we were back once more to Diodorus Siculus and his two-thousand-year-old commentary on how the "odour" of Dead Sea asphalt "renders the bodies of the inhabitants susceptible to disease and makes the people very short-lived."[67] We were back, in other words, to concerns about the threat asphalt might pose to our environment and the fate of humanity, however useful we might otherwise find asphalt for moving ourselves and our cars, our troops and their gear, our planes and their bombs. Notwithstanding the electoral-college math that brought to power the Donald Trump administration and its fossil-fuel manifestos, environmental concerns were now paramount. Those who crusaded against global warming made a compelling case. They argued that humanity faced a choice: either transition from the fossil-fuel age to an age of green and renewable energy or transition to the oil-sand age, the synthetic crude-oil age. Both transitions are ongoing. It is not clear which one will vanquish the other. In either case this much is clear: conversion of natural asphalt to synthetic crude oil has already raised the stakes in what might well be, if the environmentalists are right, the last great game of our human species.

8 Overburden   The Oil-Sand Century

On March 24, 1989, the oil tanker *Exxon Valdez* struck Bligh Reef in Alaska's Prince William Sound, spilling at least eleven million gallons and fouling 11,000 square miles of seawater and 1,300 miles of shoreline. VECO, the primary cleanup contractor, purchased 530 miles of toilet paper ("if unrolled") for the labor force.[1] With such other helpers as one thousand U.S. military personnel, Exxon burned the spilled oil and attacked it with dispersants, high-pressure hoses, and manual labor. Having scrubbed oil from sea otters and rocks, many cleanup workers developed health problems. Other spill-associated damage cascaded through native villages and fisheries.

The *Exxon Valdez* skipper, Joseph Hazelwood, had a backstory of asphalt and alcohol. An excellent sailor when sober, he once saved the *Exxon Chester*, an asphalt tanker caught in a severe storm while heading down the East Coast. When the *Exxon Valdez* met Bligh Reef, Hazelwood was not on the bridge, having turned piloting over to his third mate (who lacked a piloting license). Given a blood-alcohol level of 0.061 percent ten hours after the collision, Hazelwood's lawyers said he began drinking in his cabin because he knew that his career was over. Two days before the spill's first anniversary, an Anchorage jury found Hazelwood not guilty of three felony charges, including operating a vessel while under the influence of alcohol. The jury found him guilty of negligent discharge of oil, a misdemeanor. In 1992 an Alaska court vacated the conviction because the Clean Water Act of 1972 granted immunity to anyone who reported a spill, and Hazelwood had done so. Exxon succeeded in reducing a jury award in a civil lawsuit from $5 billion to $500 million. The company settled a federal lawsuit for $900 million.

The *Exxon Valdez* cleanup recovered no more than 10 percent of the spilled oil. Some of the remaining oil lost its lighter fractions over time, leaving behind a substance as close to asphalt as anything else. The *Exxon Valdez* Oil Spill Trustee Council calculated a ten-acre spread of oil "remain[ing] in surface sediments . . . primarily in the form of highly weathered, asphalt-like or tar deposits." Oil remained in acreage beyond those ten, trapped in "subsurface, intertidal areas . . . not easily exposed to natural weathering processes." In 2014, two years after the *Oriental Nicely* (née *Exxon Valdez*) beached for dismantling in India, the Trustee Council said that "200 tons of oil might still exist" in Prince William Sound. That oil will degrade at a "very slow" rate and someday leave behind no trace beyond asphalt.[2]

Much of the pollution associated with asphalt traces to rail, truck, barge, and tanker accidents; oil refinery and asphalt plant fires; and acts of nature.[3] In 2005 Hurricane Katrina obliterated older or improperly installed asphalt shingles and scoured blacktop off roads in New Orleans and environs. A Beach Enhancement and Asphalt Removal Project at Pensacola Bay's historic Fort Pickens (one of four U.S. forts in the South that did not surrender to the Confederacy) removed enormous amounts of asphalt debris from Katrina and twenty years of storms.[4] The Army Corps of Engineers facilitated levee repair in Katrina's wake by using asphalt debris to construct makeshift roads. Nonetheless, the corps, on occasion, neglected flood-control rule one: do not pave over storm drains (though on rare occasions it might make sense to do so).

Natural disasters and accidents aside, asphalt produced in refineries has a relatively small carbon footprint. Though the Occupational Safety and Health Administration monitors such minutiae as "hazards arising from employees wearing short pants during hot tar and asphalt construction activities," it has no "specific standards for asphalt fumes." In 2002 the Environmental Protection Agency (EPA) "delisted asphalt plants as a major source of air pollution."[5] Asphalt fumes and vapors pose the greatest risk to roofing crews and not paving crews. Though the industry no longer uses two known human carcinogens, coal tar and asbestos, when manufacturing shingles, risk from past use remains. Coal tar roofing was common into the 1980s and these gravel-and-tar roofs last for decades. When they give out, the workers who do the tear down risk exposure.[6]

Just as coal tar poses greater health risks than asphalt for roofing duty, concrete poses greater risks than asphalt for road-paving duty. Kilns at 2,700 degrees Fahrenheit are required to make Portland cement, and they produce more carbon dioxide than asphalt plants. (Because cement production accounts for as much as 8 percent of global carbon dioxide emissions, the industry hopes to develop a cost-competitive geopolymer green cement to replace Portland cement.) Asphalt's other advantages over concrete pavement are initial costs, noise reduction, and speed of construction. Concrete's advantage is that it lasts longer. Both products can be recycled. However, concrete—especially reinforced concrete—is difficult to recycle. Nearly all of the eighteen billion tons of asphalt on U.S. roads is recyclable, with the exception of older pavements that include coal tar. The United States began phasing out coal tar for paving after World War II. European nations began phasing it out in the 1970s. Other asphalt-plant advances on behalf of clean air included the substitution of emulsions for solvents and the addition of surge and storage bins, wet scrubbers, and baghouses to the standard equipment (dryer, tower, screed, and mixer).[7]

Regardless, recycling remains the asphalt industry's principal contribution in the fight for a stable environment. Though a modest effort to recycle asphalt dates to 1915, it became widespread only in the 1970s. It grew so quickly thereafter that blacktop is now the most recycled material in the world. Indeed, recycling boosters have called U.S. roads the world's biggest asphalt mine. Asphalt mixes can also accommodate many other materials in need of recycling beyond the eleven million tons of asphalt shingles that U.S. and Canadian roofers tear down annually. (North America accounts for approximately 80 percent of the global asphalt shingle market.)[8] California recycles forty million scrap tires annually to create a rubberized blacktop (an idea dating to the early twentieth century, when some producers added shredded cork to their mixes). In the 1990s Los Angeles briefly used recycled glass in mixes to make Hollywood Boulevard sparkle. Others produce "asphaltic binders" from sewage effluent, one of many bioasphalt alternatives that show promise but have not proven practical on a large scale.[9]

The asphalt industry's other environmental initiatives include warm mix, perpetual pavement, and permeable pavement (that is, porous pavement).[10] Warm mix reduces energy consumption by producing product at lower temperatures than industry standard hot mix. By perpetual pavement the industry means blacktop that will last at least fifty years before requiring a complete replacement. Progress here under the first U.S. Strategic Highway Research Program, launched in 1987, has been incremental. The Superpave initiative created standards for PG (performance grade) binders, a system that replaced the penetration and viscosity grading systems. To use California standards as an example: superpave-performance grades for unmodified and polymer-modified binders ranged from PG 58-22 to PG 70-10 and PG 58M-34M to PG 76M-22M. The numbers refer to average surface temperatures. Thus, California designated PG 70-10 for desert use, where pavement temperatures range between 70 degrees Celsius (158 degrees Fahrenheit) in the sun and minus 10 degrees Celsius (14 degrees Fahrenheit) at night. That is a temperature variance of 80 degrees Celsius. Polymer modifiers are required if the variance is 92 degrees Celsius or more.

Permeable pavement has the potential to reduce storm-water runoff of chemicals into aquatic ecosystems. Pavement collects particulate matter from the atmosphere and exhaust, debris from brake systems, phosphates from fertilizers, rubber particles from tires (particles that can be microscopic), and dozens of other pollutants, including polynuclear aromatic hydrocarbons. PAHs are a particular problem for asphalt surfaces coated with coal-tar sealants (also called sealcoats). Coal tar is no longer used in paving mixes, as noted, but road crews still apply it by squeegee, brush, or spray, on streets, school playgrounds, and especially parking lots. (Only Washington and Minnesota have adopted statewide coal-tar sealant bans.) Coal-tar sealants have PAH concentrations, according to the U.S. Geological Survey, up to one thousand times higher than asphalt-based sealants. They both increase PAH runoff compared to uncoated surfaces: asphalt sealant by a factor of ten times more and coal-tar sealant by a factor of sixty-five times more, according to a study focused on driveways. Runoff from coal-tar sealant on parking lots ranks as a principal source of pollution for Great Lakes tributaries, a remarkable fact given that the Great Lakes contain an estimated 84 percent of North America's surface freshwater. So far the promise of permeable pavement to reduce storm-water runoff from parking lots and other blacktop surfaces is limited, as permeable pavement can cause storm drains to clog, crumble under heavy loads, and spike cleanup costs after toxic spills.[11]

No one knows how many parking spaces occupy the world. In the United States there could be over two hundred million spaces.[12] Regardless, there is no reason to dispute urban-planning scholar Eran Ben-Joseph's characterization of the parking lot as the "single most salient landscape feature of our built environment." Canadian geographer Edward Relph called it the "simple landscape." Depending on the price of land, the cost to construct a single parking space might be negligible—or it might cost many thousands of dollars. Where land is inexpensive, malls and big-box stores often pave for peak parking days, so space is rarely used to capacity. Acres of empty spaces, in turn, create blacktop deserts constricting municipal tax revenue.[13]

The recession that began in late 2008 combined with the inexorable march of online shopping caused our "over-retailed" nation's shopping malls to shutter at an alarming rate even before the COVID-19 pandemic arrived in 2020. Some abandoned malls—ghost malls— attract gawkers hunting for "retail ruin porn" behind the walls. Other malls that lose their stores and shops rise from the dead, finding such new tenants as schools, churches, health clinics, and such. The same holds true for the parking lots that surround dead malls. Dead-mall lots might sit empty with weeds and even trees poking through the asphalt. Or the lots might be put to new uses, providing space for such things as farmers' markets, flea markets, festivals, RV parking, used car sales, pop-up skate parks, food trucks, drive-in churches, and tent revivals (as tent stakes can pound through asphalt).

Native Americans living in cities ("asphalt reservations") hold pow-wows on mall parking lots (whether dead or vibrant) and many other types of lots. In Indian Country outside the cities, blacktop roads and lots are rare, with callous exceptions. Prior to the Native American Graves Protection and Repatriation Act of 1990, whether knowingly or unknowingly, contractors routinely paved over sacred sites and other historic sites (a practice not confined to the United States).[14] By 1960 the Bureau of Indian Affairs counted a mere eighteen thousand miles of roads across reservation land and scarcely a single lot. (Road mileage grew to twenty-nine thousand by the twenty-first century's second decade.) The BIA ranks roads as proposed, primitive, earth, gravel, chip seal, concrete, and asphalt less than and more than two inches thick. As recently as 1999, those nostalgic for "paved America" at the Oglala Sioux's Pine Ridge Reservation in South Dakota had to drive to Big Bat's Texaco with its neon canopy and quick-back store appendage.[15]

Because nearly all blacktop roads and lots remain impermeable, they pose an environmental risk wherever the population, unlike in Indian Country, is dense. Regardless, asphalt remains a contradictory substance. Its impermeable nature offers reward as well as risk. Since the 1970s fish and wildlife departments in Oregon and Washington have used hydraulic-asphalt concrete pavement to line rearing ponds for fry and fingerlings. To store potable water California relies on over twenty reservoirs with asphalt liners. In Michigan engineers trust that a layer of asphalt and clay will keep the Ludington Pumped Power Storage Plant's twenty-seven billion gallons of water from seeping into the ground. Asphalt caps ("pave overs"), pads, and liners can also reduce environmental hazards at EPA-designated Superfund sites. Asphalt capping is not "true abatement and restoration." It has limitations, as DDT cleanup at Montrose Chemical's plant on the edge of Los Angeles Harbor makes clear. Montrose disassembled the plant in the early 1980s and paved over most of the property. Asphalt capping, however, could not help the fish and seabirds poisoned by DDT in sediment off the coast. How much DDT remains in the Palos Verdes Shelf Superfund site is unknown. Estimates range up to one hundred tons.[16]

Limitations aside, the Nuclear Energy Agency and its member nations consider "asphalt encapsulation of radioactive waste" an effective method to reduce hazards posed by "low- and intermediate-level waste." Radioactive sludge could also "be solidified and permanently fixed in either bitumen (asphalt) or cement." Sometimes called "matrix isolation," this method limits the mobility and "leachability" of waste by mixing it with asphalt (or cement), allowing the mix to cool into a solid, and then burying the solid and covering the area with an asphalt cap. Asphalt's leach rate, according to a Department of Energy assessment of the Niagara Falls Storage Site (constructed to store radioactive materials from the Manhattan Project), "can be 100 to 1,000 times less than for cement-stabilized materials." (Cement, however, is "more radiation resistant.")[17] The department's Waste Isolation Pilot Plant near Carlsbad, New Mexico, also features asphalt to help ensure geologic time storage of transuranic nuclear waste. On its twentieth anniversary in 2019, the site, managed by a contractor, claimed storage of nearly thirteen thousand shipments. (Operations have been in place for seventeen of those twenty years, given a 2014 radiation leak that forced a closure.) Whenever the facility closes for good, asphalt will help plug the 2150-foot shafts leading to fifty-six giant storage rooms carved out of a salt bed.[18]

At the Hanford Nuclear Reservation in Washington, engineers included asphalt in an experimental cap designed to contain buried waste for a millennium. Hanford also paved over a portion of its tank farm with football-field-size caps and buried additional irradiated waste that had arrived by flatbed railcars (which were buried along with their loads). In 2016 remediation at Hunters Point Naval Shipyard in San Francisco included twenty-five thousand tons of asphalt to pave over radionuclides. The Rocky Flats Nuclear Weapons Plant near Denver received an asphalt cap in 1969, after workers removed some five thousand steel drums leaking plutonium-contaminated waste oil and solvents. At the McMurdo Station research facility in

Antarctica, the navy dismantled a reactor (nicknamed "Nukey Poo") in 1972 and delivered twelve thousand tons of dirt contaminated by that reactor to Naval Base Ventura County, California. The blacktop above the dirt is now a parking lot.[19]

The most ambitious attempt to use asphalt capping to contain radioactive material dates to 1986, when the number 4 reactor exploded at the Chernobyl Nuclear Power Plant in the Soviet Union (today Ukraine). Some of the ejected material melted into Kiev's asphalt streets eighty miles away. On-site firefighters faced off against melted asphalt on the ground and blazing asphalt on rooftops. Workers bulldozed the contaminated asphalt, once congealed, and laid fresh pavement. Years later a visitor described the hose-it-down method for keeping radioactive material contained: "Wind blows contaminated dust and sand onto the asphalt, which must be sprayed regularly." That did not suffice. Thirty-one years after those asphalt rooftops blazed, several tons of Belarus mushrooms arrived in France, where customs officials found radiation contamination. Chernobyl, the French nuclear-safety institute stated, was the likely source of the contamination.[20]

Other asphalt-centric approaches to containing environmental dangers or solving safety and maintenance problems are more futuristic than capping. Researchers are trying to develop pavements that de-ice roads and self-heal (beyond the older technique for repairing small areas using infrared heaters that restore product to a workable consistency). France has several hundred miles of Wattway Road (solar panels installed directly on existing roadways). Converting the solar energy that blacktop pavement captures represents the holy grail of green research, as roads and parking lots would function as de facto solar panels. Unfortunately, what makes asphalt a potential source of solar energy also heats up cities. Trees are the best antidote to the urban heat-island phenomena because they absorb carbon dioxide emissions and their canopies provide shade.[21] Cities across the world, however, crowd people into asphalt and concrete areas with little green space. One solution coats pavement with an asphalt-based product certified to increase solar reflectance. Another uses "granule surfaced cap sheets" to make asphalt roofing better "reflect and emit the sun's heat." The green-roof movement emphasizes rooftop vegetation that provides a cooling effect in the summer and thermal insulation in the winter, mitigates air pollution, and reduces storm-water runoff. The National September 11 Memorial roof in New York City provides all those benefits through an "elevated plaza with a canopy of 400 mature swamp white oak trees" covering a subterranean museum. An asphalt waterproofing assembly and asphaltic-urethane membrane protect the roof and foundation.[22]

If asphalt produced in refineries has a mixed environmental record, the vast natural-asphalt deposits in Alberta's oil sands pose a clear threat. This story begins with the coker units and other complex processing units that oil refineries, especially U.S. oil refineries, use to exploit the "crack spread" (the difference in price between light oils and heavy oils). Beyond squeezing more gasoline from crude oil by converting heavy molecules with boiling points of one thousand degrees Fahrenheit or higher, "bottom upgrading technologies" can convert natural asphalt into synthetic crude oil and produce gasoline from that feedstock. At the same time technology to develop hydraulic fracturing flooded the market with light crude.[23] "[This] lead[s] to a paradox," as Canada's oil-sand boosters note:

> The very light end of the barrel, like propane and butane, has a lim-
> ited market in the US and way too much supply. . . . That's why light,
> sweet shale oil [also known as "tight oil"] . . . aren't desirable feedstock
> for U.S. refineries. Although they are technically "higher grades" of
> crude, they don't maximize the production of good stuff (diesel and
> gasoline) and produce too much of the very light stuff, which nobody
> wants. . . . So how have refineries responded? They've added expensive
> secondary upgrading units such as catalytic crackers, hydrocrackers
> and fluid cokers . . . that [drive] up demand for heavy sour crude, just
> like the oil produced in Alberta. The exploding supply of light shale oil
> and declining output of heavy oil from Mexico and Venezuela means
> U.S. refineries are becoming increasingly more reliant on Canadian
> heavy oil.[24]

Nearly all that heavy oil is natural asphalt, though the nomenclature varies. Canada estimates it has at least 2.2 trillion barrels of "oil equivalent" resources, with at least 170 billion barrels of that total deemed recoverable. The industry, as noted, prefers the term *natural bitumen* to characterize those resources to distinguish between the asphalt that exists in nature and the asphalt that oil refineries produce. Others consider the words *natural asphalt* and *natural bitumen* to be synonyms.[25] If the words *extra-heavy oil* and *natural asphalt* are not synonymous, the latter has more in common with the former than conventional crude oil. UN COMTRADE (Commodity Trade Statistics Database), under Commodities Code 2710, defines extra-heavy oil as "petroleum oils and oils obtained from bituminous minerals, other than crude." According to the World Energy Council, natural asphalt and extra-heavy oil are remnants of conventional crude that have degraded. Both are texturally similar to the residuum, destined for use as road asphalt, "generated by refinery distillation of light oil."[26]

The American Petroleum Institute (API) and the U.S. Geological Survey (USGS), in contrast, mark a clear distinction between natural asphalt and extra-heavy oil. The concept of "pour point" illustrates this in simple terms. Conventional light oils flow. That is why the industry has oil wells. Conventional oil can be pumped. Extra-heavy oil and asphalt might not reach their pour points unless heated or diluted. (The substances used to dilute asphalt and extra-heavy oil are called diluents.) In more technical terms API and USGS separate natural asphalt from extra-heavy oil in two ways. First, they compare the weight of a particular hydrocarbon to the weight of water. The measurement is expressed as American Petroleum Institute gravity; that is, API gravity. Thus, anything under ten degrees API, the gravity of water, sinks. Second, API and USGS separate natural asphalt from extra-heavy oil by measuring viscosity in units of centipoise. Natural asphalt generally has a viscosity over ten thousand centipoise, which means it has, for all practical purposes, no mobility within the reservoir. Extra-heavy oil has a viscosity less than ten thousand centipoise, which means it has some mobility within the reservoir. Regardless, this consensus on differences between natural asphalt and extra-heavy oil is a shifting one. Thirty years ago USGS placed "10° API oils in the category of natural asphalt" and objected to the "incorrect terms oil sand and tar sand, which are not always sand and never tar."[27]

Classification cannot rely solely on API gravity or viscosity. Other physical attributes and properties—acidity, molecular structure, impurities, fusibility, hardness, color, sulfur content solubility in organic solvents—are present. Regardless, the primary distinctions between the planet's largest reserves of natural asphalt (in Canada) and extra-heavy oil (in Venezuela) are these: The resource is easier to extract in Venezuela because its deposits are more compact vertically, more saturated with a coarser grained sand, and, most important, closer to the equator. The history of a product called Orimulsion, produced by Bitor (a subsidiary of the state-run oil company PDVSA), suggests how blurry the line can be between extra-heavy oil and natural asphalt. Bitor mixed Orinoco product with water and surfactant to create Orimulsion for use as "liquid coal." The marketing campaign included a push, in the mid-1980s, to rename the Orinoco Heavy Crude Oil Belt as the Orinoco Bituminous Belt. "What Bitor produces, like the upgrading companies," according to Bernard Mommer, who served as Venezuela's governor for OPEC and then chair of OPEC's board of governors, "is extra-heavy crude" indistinguishable from natural asphalt once "above ground." Whatever mobility existed "at reservoir conditions" disappears at the surface if left untreated. Orimulsion feedstock begins to congeal below 86 degrees Fahrenheit.[28]

The average temperature of the reservoirs in the Orinoco Belt is well over 127 degrees Fahrenheit, compared to an average temperature of the reservoirs in the Athabasca oil sands of just over 52 degrees. "It's hot in Venezuela and cold in Canada," Mommer continued for emphasis, "and this affects the state of the natural resource and its classification as extra-heavy crude or natural bitumen." In fact, the great bulk of Venezuela's reserves are not mobile below ground. "The minimum recovery factor" using "cold production" and conventional wells is about 15 percent of the Orinoco's "mean volume of 513 billion barrels of technically recoverable oil," USGS researchers explained. "The median recovery factor" jumps to 45 percent if horizontal drilling and thermal recovery methods are widely used. "The maximum recovery factor" reaches 70 percent if "other processes beyond horizontal drilling and steam-assisted gravity drainage might eventually be applied." In the 1980s Venezuelan officials not only reclassified Orimulsion feedstock as natural bitumen (that is, natural asphalt). They exempted it from their OPEC quota. This fact is also worth repeating: Venezuela did not nationalize Orinoco Belt reserves when nationalizing its oil reserves in 1976.[29]

With Venezuela's oil-industry collapse, nearly all the natural asphalt extracted in the twenty-first century comes from the Athabasca oil sands of Alberta's McMurray Formation and nearby deposits at Peace River and Cold Lake (a "sandbox" of fifty-seven thousand square miles). Fort McMurray, the heart of the oil-sand industry, suffered boomtown headaches. Sex workers called it Fort McMoney. Suicide rates spiked and smugglers shipped in cocaine over Highway 63 blacktop. Those arriving by air landed on a blacktop runway and walked through a terminal featuring two large paintings by Lucas Seaward that symbolized the town's grim reality. Because the artist worked in oil-sand product cut with a varnish, he painted "in a hazmat suit with its own oxygen source."[30]

Peace River and Cold Lake deposits are up to 2,500 feet deep and accessible only through in situ (in-place) extraction. With current technology about 20 percent of the McMurray formation's recoverable resource is accessible through surface mining. The McMurray deposits are at depths ranging from just a few feet to 1,300 feet. It is impractical to mine deeper than 250 feet, given the immense excavation required, and equally impractical to drill in situ at depths shallower than 650 feet, given the risk of blowouts. Once the natural asphalt is extracted by whatever means, sandbox workers upgrade it to synthetic crude oil (syncrude) or create diluted bitumen (dilbit) by adding natural-gas condensate or other diluents imported from the United States. (The industry is trying to develop a diluent-free upgrading technology.) Syncrude and dilbit ship out by pipeline, rail, and truck. Western Canadian Select, a dilbit stream, is Canada's benchmark on the world oil market.

Oil-sand processing has roots dating to ancient world builders, who boiled rock asphalt and cut it with wood pitch. By the late nineteenth century, workers at Santa Barbara County's Carpinteria Tar Pits were cutting asphalt-impregnated sandstone with naphtha (a flammable liquid-hydrocarbon mix) and other solvents; delivering product to a tank; opening the tank valve to feed a pipeline that moved the oil by gravity; pumping back recoverable solvent for reuse; and sending "the sand to the dump." The 1920s witnessed the first true global push to develop synthetic fuels from oil sands, led by, among others, chemists in Mussolini's Italy. The Great Depression dampened the synthetic fuel push. World War II briefly ignited it (especially a massive push in Germany to produce synthetic liquid fuel from coal).[31] In the United States significant funding for the development of oil shale and coal liquids arrived with the Synthetic Fuels Corporation, created by the Energy Security Act of 1980.[32] Given reserves of six trillion barrels of oil shale and five hundred billion short tons of coal, natural asphalt was not a priority.

Under the Combined Hydrocarbon Leasing Act of 1981, the House Resources Committee noted more than twenty years later, the eleven "tar-sand areas in Utah" generated "only one lease sale." Nor did other synthetic fuel projects play out. Exxon abandoned its flagship Colony Project in 1981 after noting that this ambitious oil-shale mine might have required diversion of the Missouri River. By 1985 Big Oil had abandoned every major synthetic fuel project in the United States. Even oil-prices approaching $150 a barrel had little effect on investment decisions. Price spikes did inspire Senators Barack Obama (D-IL), Hillary Clinton (D-NY), and others to co-sponsor a coal-to-liquids fuel bill in 2007. But the bill failed.[33]

The first major push to upgrade Alberta's resource began in 1927, the year an amendment to the Indian Act of 1876 "made it illegal to hire a lawyer to sue the government." In 1929 Karl A. Clark patented a hot-water separation process. A camp called Bitumount followed with mining and refining facilities. Robert Fitzsimmons, a realtor, formed

Tar Sands Paint and Roofing and other companies. In the 1940s new investors struck a deal with Alberta's provincial government but "never sold a drop of oil." In 1962 a Richfield Oil geologist raised eyebrows with a proposal to upgrade the hot-water separation process by dropping a nuclear bomb down a well bore. Under Operation Plowshare (1957–77), the U.S. Atomic Energy Commission invoiced $350,000, via the navy, for a test bomb. After a name change from Project Cauldron to Project Oilsand, the project died for the obvious reason that a nuclear bomb would render the natural asphalt radioactive. The Soviet Union actually tried it on an extra-heavy oil field, and that is exactly what happened, to the surprise of no one.[34]

Suncor arrived in the Alberta oil sands in 1964, with Bechtel taking the engineering and construction lead. Shell and other companies moved in over the next three decades. Boosters included such usual suspects as Alberta politicians and such unusual suspects as the evangelist Billy Graham (who had cultivated Sid Richardson and other Texas oil tycoons for half a century and now planned to take his revivals— what he called crusades—into Canadian cities).[35] Open-pit mining begins with removal of trees for sale to lumber companies. Crews send muskeg (the Canadian term for *bog*) and other vegetation to the dump. Next they dewater and depressurize, building aquifer wells in a race to keep water tables low and safe for mining equipment and remove overburden (sand, shale, silt, clay, and the like with a natural asphalt content less than 7 percent). Initially, the industry mined with bucket-wheel excavators standing sixteen stories tall. Designed for coal, they broke down constantly in the harder oil sands. The industry switched to shovels over thirty feet tall and hauler trucks with nearly thirteen-foot tall-tires that cost upward of $40,000 each. Drivers, sitting in cabs over twenty feet off the ground, said their work was "like trying to steer a house while peering out the window of the upstairs bathroom." By 2018 some drivers were losing their jobs to "Autonomous Haulage Systems" (four-hundred-ton capacity driverless trucks).[36]

The production process begins with crushers to remove oversized material (mostly rocks, ice chunks, and petrified wood) and break up lumps of the prized natural asphalt ore. The water-wet material then travels via a conveyor to a storage facility or directly to a hot-water preparation plant designed to create a slurry. Gravity removes most of the solid material, followed by one or more "froth treatments" that use solvents and gravity to remove as much of the remaining water and fine solids as possible.

At depths too great for the shovels, the industry uses steam-assisted gravity drainage (SAGD), an in situ drilling technique. This requires drilling an upper L-shaped well and a lower L-shaped well parallel to each other, and heating the oil sand by injecting steam, generated by natural gas, into the top well. Because the heat, in effect, melts the natural asphalt, gravity pushes it into the lower well, where it can be pumped out as a slurry (that is, a pumpable emulsion of natural asphalt and condensed steam). Compared to mining, in situ drilling has advantages: smaller footprint, less water usage, no tailing ponds, a more streamlined production process, and lower costs. On the other hand, SAGD requires an immense amount of steam that can super heat and pressurize the ground, causing caprock cracks that leak watery goop for months.

Whether accessed through surface mining or in situ, the oil sands release large amounts of greenhouse gases.[37] (SA-SAGD—solvent-assisted, steam-assisted gravity drainage—reduces emissions, but solvents are expensive and risk liability lawsuits because residual solvents remain in the ground.) The Carnegie Endowment for International Peace ranks Alberta's oil-sand product as the planet's dirtiest oil or oil equivalent (though it is scarcely dirtier than hydrocarbons from Venezuela's Orinoco Belt and California's Midway-Sunset Oil Field). Saudi Arabia's Ghawar field and its "light, sour oil" produces 1,082 pounds of carbon dioxide–equivalent units per barrel of crude compared to 1,622 pounds for Alberta syncrude and 1,470 pounds for Alberta dilbit.[38] Tailing ponds pose another environmental challenge. The oil sands generally contain no more than 12–15 percent natural asphalt. The remainder is clay and mineral (usually 83–85 percent) and water (usually 4–6 percent).[39] Because the "sand" removed during the processing of mined product is not fit for use as hydraulic-fracturing sand, the industry either discards it or uses it to build dams up to 290 feet high. Behind the dams lie the tailings ponds "needed to contain the materials remaining in the water after the bitumen has been separated from the sand. In these ponds the fine particles settle slowly, eventually producing clarified water that is reused in the extraction process." Disposal issues are compounded because those fine particles do not compress to their original mass.[40]

The industry calls the tailing ponds temporary storage facilities. They cover eighty square miles and hold billions of cubic feet of water pulled from the Athabasca River, water needed to service the hot-water separation process for the truck-and-shovel mines. (In situ production requires only 0.3 barrels of water per barrel of product, water mostly sourced from groundwater aquifers.) Though the industry recycles water up to eighteen times, it still takes a net average of 2.6 barrels of water to produce each barrel of mined product. Water use threatens the Peace-Athabasca wetland, North America's largest inland boreal (northern regions) delta, with a "slow motion oil spill" into an ecosystem of rivers, lakes, creeks, marshlands, fens, and groundwater. Tailing ponds also kill wildlife, especially birds. In 2008 over 1,600 ducks died in a single Syncrude Canada pond. In 2015 a contract worker stumbled on an oiled great blue heron (subsequently euthanized) and thirty heron carcasses in an inactive Syncrude sump pond. To limit the carnage these deterrents have had some effect: lasers, propane-fired cannons, robotic birds of prey, and bitu-men (scarecrows in yellow rain jackets attached to empty fifty-five-gallon barrels that bob on pond surfaces).[41]

First Nations people have borne the initial human environmental burden.[42] They have used Alberta's natural asphalt for thousands of years, burning it to ward off mosquitoes and melting it to caulk canoes. At a Hudson's Bay Company outpost in 1715, a Cree offered a sample for trade, perhaps the first colonial transaction for asphalt. In 1787 a Scottish explorer provided the first written description: "Bituminous fountains, into which a pole of 20 feet long may be inserted without the least resistance. In its heated state it emits a smell like that of sea coal." Use of Alberta asphalt to pave roads began in 1915 (and continues today for some sandbox roads). By the twenty-first century, the environmental impact was substantial. South African bishop Desmond Tutu, the keynote speaker at a Fort McMurray conference in 2014, was appalled. Oil-sand "filth," he said, was devastating the climate and "stripping away the rights of First Nations . . . to protect their children, land and water."[43]

By 2019 Canada was exporting over 3 million barrels of oil-sand product a day to the United States. Analysts project production to peak at 5.8 million barrels a day and stay above 5 million barrels a day past midcentury—with dilbit driving nearly all growth. (High-conversion refinery owners prefer dilbit—or, in good times, diluted crude oil from Venezuela—because it is less expensive than syncrude and can be processed more easily into other high-end products besides gasoline.) To date most Alberta product ships through Superior, Wisconsin, the hub for the Great Lakes region's network of pipelines and refineries. Engineers designed long stretches of the existing pipeline system to handle conventional oil. Alberta producers, however, are not legally required to identify the specific diluents used or post notice that they are shipping diluents. Both dilbit and syncrude, furthermore, are "exempt from a U.S. excise tax that pays for oil spill cleanups . . . because the 1980 law that created the tax did not consider bitumen from the 'tar sands' to be crude oil." In response to the *Exxon Valdez* spill, the Oil Pollution Act of 1990 created an Oil Spill Liability Trust Fund and a tax—$0.09 per barrel today—on domestic and imported crude oil. Although the law covers dilbit and syncrude spills, those products remain exempt from the tax, based on an Internal Revenue Service reading of a House Committee on Ways and Means report from 1980: "the term crude oil does not include synthetic petroleum, e.g., shale oil, liquids from coal, tar sands."[44]

Enbridge, a Canadian company based in Calgary, handles most of the dilbit and syncrude flowing through the Midwest. Its two key networks, Enbridge System (Canadian mainland) and Lakehead System (U.S. mainland), stretch across 3,000 miles. The Hardisty terminal 350 miles south of Fort McMurray can store 16 million barrels underground. The Superior terminal can store 10 million barrels aboveground. Enbridge Line 67, the main dilbit pipeline in Canada ("Alberta Clipper"), runs from Hardisty to Superior and originally carried 450,000 barrels a day. In 2017 the U.S. Department of State and the EPA approved an expansion, through the border segment at Superior, to 890,000 barrels per day.[45] From Superior, heading south through Wisconsin and deep into Illinois, Line 61, the main dilbit pipeline in the United States, carries 996,000 barrels a day. A planned upgrade will boost that number to 1.2 million barrels. (Several environmental groups claim the company plans to build a Line 61 "twin"—a new Line 66—with a capacity of 800,000 barrels per day.) A fourth pipeline, Line 13A, runs north from Manhattan, Illinois, to Fort Saskatchewan, Alberta, carrying 180,000 barrels of flammable diluent per day. In the event of a leak, one Wisconsinite said, Enbridge delivered safety instructions ("they basically tell you to run. . . . Upwind") and a glow stick (because flipping a light switch might cause an explosion). Line 13A and the other Wisconsin pipelines cross over one thousand private properties and go under hundreds of streams and wetlands and eight rivers (the Namekagon, Thornapple, Black, Fox, Jump, Rock, Saint Croix, and Wisconsin).[46]

The Marathon Refinery in Detroit and British Petroleum's Whiting Refinery south of Chicago are the principal processors of Alberta dilbit. In 2012–13 BP invested $4 billion to modernize the refinery to run on an 85 percent dilbit diet. Barrel-bottom products include road asphalt, with BP touting Whiting as one of the world's "largest asphalt producing refineries"; and petroleum coke ("petcoke"), dubbed "the coal hiding in the tar sands" because it competes with coal as power-plant and cement-kiln fuel mostly in nations with lax air-quality standards. "Like Mordor," one Illinois resident said of petcoke dust near Chicago's Calumet River. "Like living inside a refinery," a Detroit resident said of her neighborhood near the Marathon Refinery. Uncovered petcoke piles along the Detroit River reached three stories high and three blocks long before the owners, Koch Carbon (a subsidiary of Koch Industries), removed them.[47]

Enbridge's 645-mile Line 5 pipeline—built by Bechtel and in service since 1953—begins at Superior and ends in Sarnia, Ontario, sixty-five miles northeast of Detroit. It carries 540,000 barrels a day of Alberta syncrude and fracked oil and natural-gas liquids from North Dakota's Bakken shale play. The load is destined for Canadian gasoline markets and Michigan propane markets. Because Line 5 runs underground in northern Wisconsin near a point in the Bad River suffering erosion, the Bad River Ojibwe sued to force removal of the pipeline from reservation land. Farther north Line 5 splits into twin pipelines for the 20 miles under the Mackinac Straits, which connect Lake Michigan to Lake Huron. A worst-case scenario for a Line 5 underwater rupture: contamination of 3,500 square miles of Lake Michigan and 13,500 square miles of Lake Huron. Enbridge's plan for a new Line 5 in a tunnel a hundred feet below the lake bottom faces opposition from Michigan governor Gretchen Whitmer and others. Meanwhile, the company promises to prevent a repeat of such hazards as the April 1, 2018, vessel anchor strike that damaged Line 5.[48]

Enbridge does not ship dilbit through Line 5 (though it might do so if the company replaces the old Line 5). Dilbit ships through Michigan in Lines 6B, 17, and 79. Over three hundred miles southwest of the Mackinac Straits in 2010, one million gallons of Line 6B dilbit spilled into a Kalamazoo River tributary at flood stage. Although the EPA has monitored thousands of oil spills, dilbit spills pose unique problems, given higher levels of acidity, sulfur, and abrasive sediments than conventional oil.[49] Its higher viscosity means pipelines must operate at temperatures up to 158 degrees Fahrenheit and pressures up to 1,440 pounds per square inch (compared to ambient temperatures and 600 PSI for conventional oil). This means higher pipeline tolls and slower transit time. The proprietary nature of diluents further complicates things. Manual labor preformed some of the Kalamazoo floodplain cleanup and wildlife rehabilitation because natural asphalt congeals as the diluents evaporate. Asphalt, however, is difficult to remove if it sinks. Enbridge spent $1.2 billion trying, and failing, to recover all of that sunk product.[50]

Built in 1961 and stretching from Alberta across Minnesota and on to Superior, Enbridge's Line 3 suffered fifteen spills of two thousand or more gallons before the big one. In 1991 the Grand Rapids, Minnesota, area witnessed the largest inland oil spill in U.S. history, when Line 3 dumped 1.7 million gallons, with nearly a third of that seeping into the Prairie River via a storm sewer. As part of the Kalamazoo settlement, Enbridge agreed to replace the U.S. portion of Line 3, assuming permits were forthcoming. The old Line 3 remains in service today, with Enbridge planning to leave it in the ground while building a $9.3 billion replacement that would avoid Ojibwa watershed and treaty territories by running around rather than through the Leech Lake Reservation and the Fond du Lac Reservation. "The largest project in Enbridge history," the company says; 1,031 miles of "advanced pipeline technology" that will carry 760,000 barrels of dilbit, syncrude, and other product per day. Construction has finished for the new Line 3 in Wisconsin and North Dakota. Construction for the Minnesota segment is expected to finish in 2021.[51]

Enbridge claims an excellent pipeline safety record. Others say that 1,276 spills from 1996 to 2014 totaling over nine million gallons is a horrid record.[52] Pipelines spills, in turn, have sparked a resistance. In Canada protestors focused on three oil-sand projects: Houston-based Kinder Morgan's proposed expansion of its Trans Mountain Pipeline; Calgary-based TransCanada's proposed Energy East Pipeline; and Enbridge's proposed Northern Gateway Pipeline (a dual pipeline, as it would carry natural-gas condensate into Alberta and dilbit back out). In the United States the resistance focused on TC Energy (formerly TransCanada) and its proposed Keystone XL Pipeline, which oil-sand producers support for a simple reason: both the number of barrels and the price per barrel would increase if the oil-sand industry had greater access to U.S. Gulf Coast refineries. In 2018, while waiting for Keystone XL to come online, Alberta premier Rachel Notley announced a province-wide production cut of 8.7 percent, hoping to relieve a storage glut of thirty-five million barrels. An antipipeline resistance helped create this bottleneck by organizing hundreds of protests. One featured a Cowboy-Indian Alliance of ranchers and farmers who lived along the proposed Keystone XL route. In Washington DC they rode down Pennsylvania Avenue blacktop on horseback.[53]

The resistance won a few battles. Lack of reliable pipeline capacity helped convince Vancouver-based Teck Resources to withdraw its application to build the mammoth Frontier oil sands mine north of Fort McMurray. TC Energy canceled its Energy East Pipeline (which would have carried 1.1 million barrels of dilbit per day 2,800 miles to the Bay of Fundy in New Brunswick). Another victory came when Prime Minister Justin Trudeau "shelved" Enbridge's Northern Gateway line and imposed a partial ban on oil tankers on the northwest Pacific Coast, where dilbit from Kinder Morgan's Trans Mountain Pipeline loads for transport to Asian refineries (and to a lesser extent U.S. refineries). Trudeau's decision dismayed oil-sand boosters who hoped to develop Asian markets: "You've got one shot to use that hydrocarbon molecule well," one booster said, "and we're giving it away to Donald Trump and his friends for a huge discount."[54] The prime minister's Liberal government, however, supported other oil-sand projects, most notably by purchasing Kinder Morgan's Trans Mountain assets for US$3.4 billion.[55]

Unlike Justin Trudeau, Donald Trump did not send mixed signals. In 2017 the Trump administration approved TC Energy's resubmission of its Keystone XL permit application, which the Department of State promptly approved. "They failed," President Trump said of Keystone XL lobbyists. "I got it approved."[56] The resistance to Keystone XL centered on the line's river crossings and proximity to the Ogallala Aquifer (which covers over 170,000 square miles underneath portions of eight Great Plains states and provides water, as noted, for one-fifth of the United States' agricultural harvest.)[57] The Alberta government's support for Keystone XL included $1.2 billion outright plus $4.2 billion in credit guarantees—largesse announced in the midst of the COVID-19 pandemic and the global collapse of oil prices (including oil-sand prices). With much of Canada and the United States under stay-at-home orders to blunt the virus impact, the timing virtually guaranteed that protesters would not be on-site to stop Keystone xl construction. Pipeline workers received an exemption from stay-at-home orders. And the prospect of their work camps heightened fears of the virus spread in those camps and nearby towns. tc Energy's announcement that construction would begin immediately was hollow as President Joe Biden revoked the border-crossing permit.[58]

That was only the latest setback. On July 6, 2020, six months into the pandemic, the U.S. Supreme Court upheld a federal judge's order halting Keystone xl construction because water-crossing permits violated the Endangered Species Act. If ever built, Keystone xl will carry 830,000 barrels of dilbit and 100,000 barrels of Bakken oil a day across six states before merging in Steele City, Nebraska, with the existing Keystone system (which has suffered at least ten spills since it came online in 2010, including a 2019 spill of nearly four hundred thousand gallons into North Dakota wetlands).

Pipeline-resistance victories usually boil down to delaying construction long enough to convince investors to move on. Keystonization of megaprojects creates infrastructure bottlenecks that burn through corporate and investor cash and keep carbon in the ground. (A pipeline delayed or not built, however, means diversion of more oil-sand product to rail.) American Indian tribes in the United States, First Nations communities in Canada, municipalities in both countries, and multinational environmental groups like Stop the Money Pipeline are among the principal kill-or-delay litigants. And generational class-action lawsuits filed by and on behalf of children are common. *Time* magazine named Swedish teenager Greta Thunberg Person of the Year in December 2019, just two months after she toured Alberta's oil-sand region. She also helped inspire the Global Climate Strike that took place that same month.

The logic of direct actions and lawsuits by whatever group in whatever age bracket is clear: Big Oil has understood the science of climate change for half a century but pushed ahead regardless. In 1988, a quarter century after the Lyndon B. Johnson administration raised the specter of global warming, a secret Royal Dutch Shell report noted the prevailing scientific consensus that greenhouse gases had enlisted humanity in a "global 'experiment'" that would not end in time for "countermeasures to reduce the effects or even to stabilize the situation."[59] While Exxon's public posturing emphasized "intractable uncertainty," its business model, as resistance organizer Bill McKibben noted, recognized the certainty of climate change. The company raised "drilling platforms to compensate for rising seas" and otherwise tried to "climate-proof its facilities."[60]

Donald Trump, who once called global warming a Chinese hoax, promised to deliver "American energy dominance . . . all over the world."[61] So the administration not only approved Keystone xl but the 1,168-mile Dakota Access Pipeline, which has carried Bakken fracked oil since it became operational in mid-2017. The asphalt connection here was symbolic and best captured in a photograph of Native American protestors with yellow-and-black paint streaks across their faces, moving down a blacktop road on horseback near Cannon Ball, North Dakota. They were protesting the last stages of Dakota Access construction, especially sensitive stages because the pipeline would pass beneath the Missouri River and threaten the water supply for the Standing Rock Sioux. Energy Transfer Partners, the Dallas-based Dakota Access owners, said pipeline transport is safer than rail transport. In 2013, for example, seventy-seven tank cars carrying Bakken oil derailed in Lac-Mégantic, Quebec, spilling 1.3 million gallons. The resulting explosion and fire killed forty-seven people. A year later seventeen Bakken tank cars derailed in Lynchburg, Virginia, spilling thirty thousand gallons. Some of it burned off. Some went into the James River.[62]

For the Sioux, access to water has been problematic since the mid-nineteenth century. Oahe Dam construction (1948–62) under Army Corps of Engineers supervision demonstrated the persistence of that fact, leading to Standing Rock Reservation displacement and loss of land (even more so at the Cheyenne River Reservation). That history, combined with the threat of pipeline leaks in the present, was too much to bear. "We have to be here," explained Standing Rock tribal chair David Archambault II, from the Sacred Stone Camp, the base for Dakota Access protests. The Oahe Dam also provided the opportunity to file a federal lawsuit because the pipeline section under Lake Oahe, a Missouri River reservoir behind the dam, required a federal permit. Energy Transfer Partners countered with a RICO (Racketeer Influenced and Corrupt Organization) Act lawsuit against Earth First!, Greenpeace, and others, claiming "criminal activity" by "rogue eco-terrorist groups." The company asked for $900 million. Billy Roy Wilson, the federal judge who dismissed the federal claims in this lawsuit with prejudice, said "donating to people whose cause you support does not create a RICO enterprise."[63]

Energy Transfer Partners said Dakota Access would carry Bakken oil and not Alberta dilbit. The company's lawsuit, however, condemned protestors for claiming the oil sands posed an existential threat to the physical and human environment; engaging in "eco-terrorism" by shutting valves at oil-sand pumping stations and thereby risking ruptures and explosions; and crusading "to cut off Plaintiffs' access to the capital markets" with (allegedly threatening) appeals to investors. Indeed, a dozen cities divested at least $2 billion from the pipeline.[64] This stopped neither the protestors nor the bulldozers. To protect their workers and equipment, Energy Transfer Partners sent in private security (and their attack dogs) who arrived in SUVs and pickups barreling down an asphalt road. To stop protestors and their "jihadist insurgency model," one security firm recommended "intelligence preparation of the battlefield."[65] A typical "jihadist" action was blocking traffic on Highway 1806, a blacktop strip named to mark the year that Meriwether Lewis and William Clark moved through the area.

The state of North Dakota ordered a medical trailer and potable-water tanks removed from the Sacred Stone Camp. Local and state police arrived with such equipment as fourteen-ton military vehicles used during the Second Gulf War. Now they lined up against Native Americans in a camp large enough to have a day-care center. Others on site included drone operators, social-media techs, undercover FBI agents, and North Dakota Army National Guard crews for two unarmed AN/TWQ-1 Avenger Air Defense Missile Systems mounted on modified Humvees.

On December 4, 2016, the Army Corps of Engineers denied a pipeline easement under the Missouri River, a victory the resistance enjoyed for a mere two months. President Trump reversed that decision within weeks of taking his oath of office. By then over five hundred arrests and winter—made even more unbearable by police use of water cannons—had taken its toll. The protestors drifted away, leaving behind a mess requiring an expensive and taxpayer-funded cleanup. Regardless of any environmental irony in that fact, the protestors were correct in their central contention. Well before June 1, when Dakota Access became operational, it experienced "the first rule of pipelines": they leak: two spills of over one hundred gallons in March and an eighty-four-gallon spill in April.[66] Even after their retreat from the Sacred Stone Camp, the Standing Rock Sioux won a victory when a federal judge ruled, in 2020, that the Army Corps of Engineers, when approving federal permits for the pipeline, had violated the National Environmental Policy Act of 1970. The judge did so after the Trump administration narrowed that law's scope with new rules that exempted pipelines and other infrastructure projects from environmental review of their impacts on local communities and, more generally, global warming. Nevertheless, the judge ordered the Army Corps of Engineers to complete a full environmental-impact study.[67]

Before, during, and after these pipeline wars, the United States' preeminent asphalt barons, Charles Koch and David Koch, were lightning rods for what many consider the twin evils of fossil fuels: environmental and political pollution. The brothers claimed "no financial stake in the Keystone pipeline." Nonetheless, ALEC (the American Legislative Exchange Council), supported by the Koch brothers, stepped up with a "model bill" for other states to adopt, the Critical Infrastructure Protection Act, intended to criminalize pipeline protests.[68] And the Koch brothers bought Alberta product—which they called "garbage crudes"—for their Pine Bend refinery in Rosemount, Minnesota. Keystone XL troubles have not slowed the expansion of Flint Hills Resources, the Koch brothers' principal asphalt earner and the operator of Pine Bend. In 2016, as part of a $750 million investment in the refinery, Flint Hills replaced equipment dating from the 1960s with new technology allowing conversion of "asphalt, or 'bottoms', into higher-value fuels." By June 2020 the lawsuits against Big Oil for allegedly peddling false information about fossil fuels and climate change included a filing by Minnesota attorney general Keith Ellison against Koch Industries, Flint Hills Resources, and Flint Hills Resources' Pine Bend Refinery.[69]

For half a century Charles and David Koch have ranked high among "Canada's largest crude oil purchasers, shippers and exporters." And they were among the largest dilbit refiners as well, with Enbridge's Line 3 feeding a Koch pipeline near Clearbrook, Minnesota, that ends at Rosemount.[70] The Koch asphalt empire's roots trace to 1927, when their father, Fred Koch, developed a thermal-cracking process for converting heavy oil into gasoline. Frustrated by patent-infringement lawsuits, he decamped to the Soviet Union, where he helped build oil refineries under Stalin's Five Year Plan. Consulting work abroad also included several trips to Germany, as the Reich needed help with an oil refinery on the Elbe River that provided fuel for the Luftwaffe until B-17s destroyed it. At home Fred Koch compared FDR's New Deal unfavorably with Hitler's National Socialism on the matter of instilling a work ethic among the masses; attended the John Birch Society's founding meeting; and offered his thought on the "colored man." In 1969, two years after their father's death, Charles and David Koch took over the Pine Bend Refinery.[71]

According to one of their many trackers, in 2002 the Koch brothers "sold 47 asphalt terminals in the U.S. and 13 in Mexico, plus other related assets, to SemGroup, a [Tulsa-based energy] company [since merged with Energy Transfer, the Dakota Access Pipeline owner]. The following year, Koch sold asphalt interests . . . in China to Royal Dutch Shell." The Koch brothers' asphalt terminal holdings in the United States shrank again in 2005, when they sold over fifty terminals.[72] Regardless, Koch Industries remained an oil-sands player until 2019, three years into an oil-sands selloff sparked by global-warming concerns and crusades—a remarkable development given dramatic progress in cutting costs. (Mining and upgrading costs dropped from the forty dollars a barrel range in 2013 to the twenty-five dollars a barrel range in 2019.)[73] Eight major oil companies divested "significant Canadian assets." "[Collapsing] societal acceptance of the energy system as we have it," a Shell executive said when explaining his company's flight. Rachel Notley was more upbeat. The Alberta premier called "asset sales a 'reorganization' of the Canadian energy sector and not a withdrawal of capital." She also noted that Canadian Natural Resources, having purchased Shell assets, was now the largest oil sands mine operator.[74]

Charles and David Koch (Charles alone after David retired in mid-2018 and died in 2019) have used their wealth, built up from those initial asphalt dollars (garbage-crude billions), to wield enormous political power. The giddy reaction to their largesse is such that Wisconsin governor Scott Walker, in 2011, fell for a prank call from a blogger pretending to be David Koch. The brothers funded (and Charles continues to fund) political campaigns, lobby shops, media, universities, think tanks, and even a kochfacts.com website devoted to countering the "new McCarthyites" (that is, environmentalists who raise climate-change alarm). Based on data from 2014 that ranked the hundred worst corporate polluters in the United States, Koch Industries was the only corporation to rank among the top dozen for both air pollution (eighth) and water pollution (eleventh). The Koch brothers buttressed their economic interests with a level of political engagement that resembled a "privatized political party" on the same page as the GOP.[75]

Charles and David Koch's relationship with Donald Trump, however, ran hot and cold. Beyond his support for Keystone XL, asphalt figured in Donald Trump's rise to the Oval Office beginning with a reference in his announcement speech on June 16, 2015: "You come into LaGuardia Airport, it's like we're in a third world country. You look at the patches and the 40-year-old floor. They throw down asphalt, and they throw."[76] He could be equally dismissive of bike-path blacktop, even if pristine. Since 2010 Pennsylvania Avenue has included a median bicycle way littered with bike-share stations. There was even a bike-share station on White House grounds until Trump had it removed. On the other hand, the president could praise any blacktop that he owned, describing a golf-cart path at one of his clubs as the "most beautiful asphalt you've ever seen." The LaGuardia reference was to a never fulfilled campaign promise of a $1 trillion infrastructure investment (later bumped to $1.5 trillion). Federal funding would be limited to $200 billion and sourced by cuts to "highway, transit, Amtrak, and water infrastructure funding over the next 10 years." Peter DeFazio (D-OR), the ranking member of the House Committee on Transportation and Infrastructure, called the Trump administration proposal a "scam."[77]

Given Donald Trump's background in development and real estate, it is hardly surprising that he crossed paths with other rich and powerful business people, both at home and abroad, who dabbled in the asphalt business. Trump met the Azerbaijani-Russian developer Aras Agalarov, for one, in 2013, when he helped bring the Miss Universe Pageant, co-owned by Trump, to Moscow's Crocus City. "We purchased three asphalt facilities and asphalt spreaders," Agalarov said of one infrastructure project under his Crocus Group: "one in Russia and two in China."[78] Agalarov also helped Trump pursue a hotel project (never built) in Moscow and then the presidency in the United States. With his son, Agalarov helped arrange the controversial June 9, 2016, meeting at Trump Tower in New York, attended by a self-described Russian "government lawyer," a Georgia immigrant on the Crocus payroll, a lobbyist formerly with a Soviet military office, and Trump's son-in-law (Jared Kushner) and campaign manager (Paul Manafort).[79] For his part Manafort reportedly owed another Russian, Oleg Deripaska, as much as $18.9 million. Though Deripaska made his billions primarily in the aluminum industry, he had major stakes in Strabag, the Vienna-based construction company that owned Deutsche Asphalt Group; and GAZ Group, Russia's largest producer of asphalt pavers. Another Deripaska entity owned Transstroy, a blacktop contractor for Moscow's Ring Road and the Third Ring Road.[80]

The Trump Organization pursued another hotel project in Baku, Azerbaijan, just a few miles from the Binagadi Asphalt Lake, with the help of Ziya Mammadov. This asphalt baron moved from transportation minister to billionaire status, a difficult move for a civil servant without facilitating things like this (according to Adam Davidson's reporting in the *New Yorker*): In 2007 the U.S. ambassador noted that a Bechtel executive had met with Mammadov regarding a road project and estimated a cost of $6 million per kilometer. Mammadov assigned the work, at $18 million per kilometer, to an Iranian construction firm with ties to Iran's Revolutionary Guard Corps. The Trump Organization said "Trump . . . was 'merely a licensor' who allowed his famous name to be used by a company headed by Ziya Mammadov's son." But Trump's daughter included this boast on her website before scrubbing it: "Ivanka has overseen the development of Trump International Hotel and Tower Baku since its inception." The Mammadov family's reputation as "the Corleones of the Caspian," moreover, was no secret.[81]

Closer to home the Trump International Golf Club in Puerto Rico, which held a license to use the Trump brand, filed for bankruptcy in 2015, under the name Coco Beach Golf and Country Club. The course was the lifelong dream of Arturo Díaz Jr., who died in 2012. His family-run construction conglomerate, Díaz Companies, grew out of Betteroads Asphalt. "We've been all over the Caribbean," Díaz's son said. "We did two asphalt projects in Guantanamo Bay (Cuba), [and] we were in Granada after the (U.S.) invasion." In 2017, shortly before Hurricane Maria severely damaged Puerto Rico's blacktop, Betteroads Asphalt filed for bankruptcy and shuttered its fifteen asphalt plants.[82]

At home Martin Whitmer served as "team lead" for President-elect Trump's transition group for transportation policy. His lobby shop, Whitmer and Worrall, represented the National Asphalt Pavement Association and the American Road and Transportation Builders Association. The transition team for energy featured Mike McKenna, whose MWR Strategies represented Koch Industries and the National Petrochemical and Refiners Association (now American Fuel and Petrochemical Manufacturers); and Michael Catanzaro, whose CGCN Group also represented Koch brother interests along with Halliburton. Later Trump selected Catanzaro as head of domestic energy issues for the White House National Economic Council. Rex Tillerson, former CEO of ExxonMobil, an oil company that also ranked among the world's leading asphalt producers, served as the administration's first secretary of state. Elaine Chao, the U.S. Senate majority leader's wife, resigned from the Vulcan Materials board of directors to serve as transportation secretary. She held her stock in Vulcan, the nation's largest aggregate producer and a major asphalt producer and paver, for more than two years while serving in the cabinet. Walter Shaub, former chief of the Office of Government Ethics, an independent federal agency, considered it unethical "for the head of the DOT to have a financial interest in an asphalt company."[83]

Asphalt also surfaced as a sideshow to candidate and then president Trump's signature issue: construction of a wall on the Mexican border that Mexico would pay for. Barrier construction along the United States–Mexico border began long before the 2016 U.S. presidential campaign. Tijuana–San Diego fence construction dates to 1910, with barbed-wire strands designed to stop cows from wandering and spreading bovine diseases. A bit of chain-link fencing arrived in the 1950s. In the 1990s the Clinton administration built fence with surplus metal airstrip mats from the Vietnam War. Construction of an assortment of barriers along portions of the 1,954-mile border accelerated after the Secure Fence Act of 2006 (which a majority of both parties supported). For remote areas the Department of Homeland Security spent $1 billion on a "virtual fence" with electronic-sensor alarms, the comedians said, set off by border-crossing insects. Under the Trump administration, so far, a principal feature of the nonvirtual barriers is not a concrete wall big enough, as promised, to be visible from the earth's orbit. Rather, the original feature from 1910: "barbed wire used properly," the president said in 2019, "can be a beautiful sight."[84]

It was really razor wire, "barbed tape concertina wire," marketed as "military tactical barrier" for "battlefield."[85] In Nogales, Arizona, to cite an example of its use, soldiers stacked up to six rows, making sure the bottom row rested on or hovered near the dirt, concrete, or asphalt below and that all six rows above clung to the two-story bollard fencing. It was difficult to remember when, in developed areas, the most common barrier separating the United States and Mexico was yellow paint on blacktop roads.

Existing border barriers have been sufficient to disrupt ecosystems for decades. One Homeland Security contractor with a long blacktop history, the Kiewit Corporation, finished the Smuggler's Gulch project in San Diego County in 2009, having moved 1.3 million cubic yards of dirt and rock to fill part of a canyon a few miles inland from the Pacific Ocean and adjacent to the Tijuana River National Estuarine Research Reserve. An asphalt road atop that fill allows efficient Border Patrol coverage. The blacktop provides an additional advantage, according to the Border Patrol: "changes in the area will actually help the environment, because fewer people will be trampling on sensitive habitat, and the asphalt roads have reduced the amount of dust in the air." Others disagreed. In 1996 the project received a waiver from state and federal environmental laws. Its completion thirteen years later after protracted legal battles threatened one of the nation's largest wetlands restoration projects. Erosion from the project's blacktop segments posed the greatest risk of sending sediment into the estuary.[86]

Residents of a Tijuana neighborhood also claim the culprit was not the border barrier per se, in this case a fence, but the blacktop pavement supporting the fence on the U.S. side. Before construction of that road, even makeshift homes generally withstood storm water, with the exception of five major floods between 1891 and 1937. Asphalt changed the dynamic. Routine storms now wash away those makeshift homes or saturate them with mud. Things were worse in Nogales and its sister city, Nogales, in the Mexican state of Sonora. Ten years before immigrants and their children from Mexico and other Latin American nations began arriving at the processing center in the Arizona city, a mere two inches of rain in two hours unleashed flooding because a concrete barrier, built by the United States, not only prevented traffickers from using drainage tunnels but also blocked storm runoff channels. And landing-mat fencing acted as a dam because it clogged with storm debris on the Mexican side. Two people died in that flood. In 2014, two years after bollard fencing was installed at Nogales on the U.S. side, another flood pushed enough debris to topple a portion of the new fence.[87]

Long ago Nabataean Arabs brought Dead Sea asphalt to market, while Aristotle and Diodorus noted the "deadly fumes" that made the area's people "very short-lived." Today we build barrier walls on our southern border to keep people out, and Alberta Clipper and Keystone XL pipelines across our northern border to bring in what Bishop Desmond Tutu called natural asphalt "filth" from the oil sands.[88] This speaks to what so many consider the central problem in twenty-first-century U.S. democracy. One side sees the other as a gaggle of nativist politicians warning of immigrants "taking our jobs" and committing grisly crimes. The other side warns of greed that minimizes carbon bombs and global-warming calamities. Whether buried black and deep in oil sands or in its pavement form, asphalt once and always rests in the context of utility and profit, just as the ancient world's One Eyed King and his enemies saw it. Chop it out of the Dead Sea. Pack it on camels. Trek the desert. Sell it to the Egyptian embalmers. Get rich. The environmentalists say that tack is not much different than today's scratching in Alberta. Mine and melt the stuff. Convert it to dilbit or syncrude. Build pipelines. Send it across the prairie. Get rich. Regardless, the environmental angle is as old as the search for profits. Nearly everyone from the writers of the Bible and the Koran and down through Dante and Milton saw asphalt most often not as something useful and profitable. They saw it as an allegorical substance that bled from the earth or floated up from the depths. They saw it as something that defiles, something that keeps the fires of hell always burning.

Allegory aside, the release of hydrogen sulfide gas certainly damaged human lungs around the Dead Sea in the BCE centuries of Aristotle and Diodorus. But that release was an act of nature. For almost the entirety of its history as a natural substance and a product produced in refineries, asphalt, as we have seen, was rarely purposefully burned (beyond its use by indigenous peoples as mosquito repellant or likely inclusion by others in that mysterious weapon of war, Greek Fire, and then other weapons of war on into our own century). This means that asphalt served as a carbon sink whether it stayed where it lay in nature, or refineries produced it for blacktop duty. Asphalt-related threats to the environment for most of the blacktop age were limited, mostly confined to hurricanes, earthquakes, and accidents. Hydrogen sulfide leaks and refinery and asphalt-plant explosions were relatively rare, however spectacular in the individual case.[89] Hot asphalt spills from trucks, rail cars, and river barges, unfortunately, were relatively common. Nonetheless, asphalt products were not destined for any human or divine kiln of the sort Dante imagined or even the sort needed to make cement. This was true when Amzi Barber paved roads with asphalt chopped from Pitch Lake. It remained true when refinery asphalt overtook natural asphalt as a construction material for roads and roofs.

One rather large problem aside (high-velocity storm-water runoff of pollutants that collect on blacktop and especially blacktop parking lots), asphalt today is well positioned for the green revolution, given the ease of recycling and dreams of permeable pavements everywhere and every road, lot, and roof serving one day as a de facto solar panel. But the oil sands make a mockery of that promise, from their primary incarnations (dilbit and syncrude) to such refinery waste as petcoke (which can always fetch a buyer willing to burn it and poison however many lungs). When a derailment or other accident causes a railcar filled with Alberta dilbit to ignite (as did Canadian Pacific cars in Saskatchewan in late 2019 and early 2020), the fireballs should remind us that the cargo will burn even if it arrives safe and sound. After all, that is the point.

Conclusion   The Other Black Hole

"Violence is a part of America's culture. It is as American as cherry pie." H. Rap Brown, one of the most visible Black militants of the turbulent 1960s, spoke those words on July 27, 1967, the day before the Detroit uprising ended, with forty-three deaths and nearly two thousand injuries.[1] Brown could have added a coda: asphalt is part of the United States' violent culture for the simple reason that so much violence and death occurs on streets and roads. One can argue whether Brown's characterization is true or not. It is harder to argue against this plain fact: a great deal of blood spills on blacktop.

U.S. violence on blacktop disproportionately visits African Americans. Rodney King certainly understood that fact. On March 3, 1991, a car chase ended on Foothill Boulevard blacktop with Los Angeles police beating King to the point of their own exhaustion. A bystander's videotape aside, it was as if the beating never happened in the telling. King, an officer said, "laid with his . . . right ear on the asphalt. So he was looking at me. So under the protection of myself . . . I told him to turn his head away so I could make my approach." After a jury in suburban Simi Valley acquitted the four officers prosecuted for whaling on King, rioting left sixty people dead. King sued and settled with the city of Los Angeles for $3.8 million. A quarter century and half a continent away, Michael Brown, eighteen—and, like King, unarmed—did not survive his encounter with a Missouri police officer. For four hours, journalism professor Jelani Cobb wrote, Brown's body stayed where it lay, "a dismal stream of blood winding its way across the asphalt." "The other option would have been just to, you know," explained the Ferguson police chief, "scoop up Michael Brown, take some photographs and get the hell out of there."[2] Nine months after the killing, on August 9, 2014, municipal workers tore up the blood-stained blacktop. "A lot of it was real crumbly," Brown's stepfather said. "We got most of the big pieces." In 2016 the city paid the family a reported $1.5 million. At nearly the same time, a jury in Maryland awarded nearly as much, $1.26 million, to the white family who owned Vern, a dog shot by a police officer.[3]

While continuing to assure taxpayers that "not one dime of city money was used" to remove that bloodstained blacktop, Ferguson and surrounding municipalities spent an additional $5.7 million responding to those who protested a Saint Louis County grand jury's failure to indict the officer who killed Michael Brown. Peaceful demonstrators and looters and arsonists alike faced off against long-gun police snipers perched atop military vehicles and SWAT teams massed on the blacktop with body armor, gas masks, tear gas, rubber bullets, assault rifles, and flash bangs (stun grenades). Afterward a U.S. Department of Justice investigation found that racial bias, in part, drove Ferguson police practices, while city officials encouraged revenue-driven policing that targeted Blacks for any offense that could generate fines and help balance budgets.[4]

"Instead of calling 911," the novelist and social critic Darryl Pinckney said, "black America now pulls out its smartphones, in order to document the actions of the death squads that dialing 911 can summon."[5] Two months after city workers ripped up Ferguson asphalt, another Black teen's death suggested that Pinckney's words rang true too often for too many. On October 20, 2014, a Chicago police officer shot Laquan McDonald sixteen times, a number one less than his age. Though McDonald had slashed a police cruiser's tire, he was walking away when shot, and eight other officers at the scene did not shoot. A police dashboard camera recorded all sixteen shots, with many of them tearing up the asphalt as McDonald lay dying. The City of Chicago paid the McDonald family $5 million. A Cook County jury convicted the police officer who did the killing of second-degree murder and sixteen counts of aggravated battery with a firearm.

The Department of Justice investigated the Chicago Police Department and released a report noting questionable arrests, harassments, and shootings. Even if the word *asphalt* is not in the report, Chicago's streets, like those in every other U.S. city, are mostly asphalt. The word *street* accompanies this example of a shooting and nearly every other one: "A man had been walking down a residential street with a friend when officers drove up, shined a light on him, and ordered him to freeze, because he had been fidgeting with his waistband. The man ran. Three officers gave chase." They fired forty-five shots. "The officers claimed the man fired at them during the pursuit," the report continued. "Officers found no gun on the man . . . and forensic testing determined there was no gunshot residue on the man's hands."[6]

On May 25, 2020, a video camera recorded the slow-motion blacktop death in Minneapolis of George Floyd. He was not beaten like Rodney King or shot sixteen times like Laquan McDonald. But while lying handcuffed and prone, he managed to say "I can't breathe" at least sixteen times. He died because a police officer kneeled on his neck for eight minutes and forty-six seconds. Minneapolis and other urban areas suffered looting, vandalism, and arson in the aftermath of this killing. Several dozen police officers suffered injuries from chucked rocks, bottles, and asphalt chunks. Regardless, the Black Lives Matter protests that swept across approximately 2,500 cities and towns in the United States and sixty other nations were overwhelmingly peaceful and lawful. For the Donald Trump administration, in contrast, everything played out in "battlespace." That is what Secretary of Defense Mark Esper called the black and white, the asphalt pavement and concrete sidewalks, where the democratic bedlam took place, and what the pundit Charles Pierce called a "roiling combination of the March on Washington and the burning of Watts."[7]

The Greeks called it Thalassa Asphaltites (Asphaltite Sea) and so did the Romans: Palus Asphaltites. But the latter also called it Mare Mortuum (Dead Sea). They are appropriate names either way. Asphalt and death have rarely been more than a breath apart. Nowadays ecologists complain of "death by incremental asphalt," where one bit of green is paved, then another, and soon all is blacktop and nothing greenway. Most blacktop death is more direct, as the Brown, McDonald, Floyd, and so many other families well know. While the asphalt connection is coincidental for most deaths that occur on asphalt, where we die matters, whether or not there is causation involving place. The sheer volume of blood shed on asphalt demands our attention no matter the cause.

Nor are we alone. Many creatures die in, on, or under asphalt. It has been that way long before La Brea began trapping prehistoric mammals. Today invertebrates are most likely to die above asphalt. Trillions of insects splatter each year on vehicle windshields (though the numbers are plummeting, given recent and alarming declines in insect populations). They also die crawling across pavement that fragmentizes habitat. Horizontally polarized light, a "cue for creatures to locate water," reflects from asphalt to create "ecological traps." Invertebrates become "confused," for lack of a better word, searching on roads and lots for food and places to breed and lay eggs. Predators follow prey onto the blacktop, and they die there too—so do far too many mammal and bird species.[8] They might be looking for pickles and fries tossed out car windows, or they might simply be crossing roads and lots. In round numbers vehicle collisions kill over five hundred thousand small animals, four thousand large animals, and three hundred thousand birds each day on U.S. roads alone. The large animal collisions also kill about two hundred drivers and passengers each year. Obviously, most collisions do not cause accidents of any kind, let alone human fatalities. Road kill is usually too small to notice. Size and geography dictates what we notice. U.S. Americans notice dead deer. Finns notice dead reindeer. Brazilians notice dead giant anteaters on BR-262, one of the world's deadliest blacktop roads for wildlife.[9]

Vehicle-animal collisions account for only a tiny fraction of the forty thousand U.S. Americans who die each year on our streets, roads, and highways. (The color line is present here as well, as vehicle crashes are more likely to take the lives of racial and ethnic minorities "compared with the much larger non-Hispanic White population.")[10] Road deaths, whether on unpaved roads or concrete pavement or blacktop, are down from over fifty thousand a year from 1966 to 1973 and again from 1978 to 1980. In the current century road deaths first dipped under forty thousand in 2008 and stayed under that number for eight years before creeping up. Global traffic deaths top one million a year. Motor-vehicle accidents also injure and kill pedestrians and cyclists, whether pedaling in Spandex or gunning "donorcycles" in leathers. Even bicycle-motorcycle encounters kill. In 1935 in Dorset, England, T. E. Lawrence and his Brough Superior ss100 swerved to miss two boys on bicycles. Lawrence survived Arabia but not Dorset blacktop. He died of head injuries six days later.

Yet we need to remember that the history of asphalt is contradictory. While so many die in traffic accidents, pavement or its absence might be the difference between a decent road and an impassable track, the difference between getting to a hospital or not, the difference between living or not. That could hold true on a grand scale. In 2014 the Army Corps of Engineers evaluated and supervised the repair of the runway at Roberts International Airport in Liberia. An Ebola outbreak in West Africa would have killed more than it did had the engineers not gotten Roberts asphalt in shape, a task that allowed the Barack Obama administration's Operation United Assistance and other humanitarian aid to arrive by air. "The tarmac work," Obama said, helped save a million lives.[11] Unfortunately, asphalt could also help spread Ebola or whatever other disease under other circumstances. In 2017 a virologist made the point from a rainforest camp in the Congo near a five-hundred-mile-long road running to Brazzaville: during the 2014 outbreak the road to the city's 1.8 million inhabitants was dirt. Now if Ebola roars out of the forest near that road, the new blacktop could help put the virus in Brazzaville in one day and in Boston in two.[12]

Sun and asphalt can also kill via accident or negligence. In summer 2016 twelve k-9 dogs died of heat exhaustion in Texas and other states when left unattended in police cars. An unknown number of pets across the world die this way each year in cars and trucks owned by private citizens. We have no idea how many climate refugees die each year on blacktop, but we do have an idea of how many Latino immigrants die each year while packed into trucks parked on U.S. asphalt. One case in 2017: when unlocking a tractor trailer on a Walmart lot, San Antonio police found eight corpses and dozens suffering heat exhaustion. We have a better idea of how many infants and children die each year from juvenile vehicular hyperthermia when left on sunny days in cars parked on asphalt: forty to fifty in the United States alone. After the National Highway Traffic Safety Administration launched a campaign against hyperthermia in 2019, electronic signs along major highways began carrying the message: "Where's Baby? Look Before You Lock."

There is a link between homicide and asphalt too, with street-gang activity producing such horrors as blood-splattered Tinker Bell backpacks "sitting on the asphalt." On a blacktop lot outside a restaurant in Waco, Texas, shots exchanged between rival biker gangs and a SWAT team left nine bikers dead.[13] Hundreds of drivers and passengers are injured and a few killed each year by asphalt chunks dropped from overpasses by "pranksters." Others have wielded asphalt chunks as murder weapons. In 1994, to cite the most highly publicized case, a Mexican citizen raped, strangled, and bludgeoned a San Antonio girl, sixteen, with a forty-pound piece of asphalt. The assailant's appeal of a Texas court's death sentence rested on a simple fact: state authorities never informed him of his right to inform the Mexican consulate of his arrest. The Obama administration petitioned the U.S. Supreme Court to stay the execution, arguing that it would damage foreign policy interests. The petition failed.[14]

Asphalt plays a role even in apocalyptic scenarios, including a modern-day Noah's Ark, a Global Seed Vault intended to preserve biodiversity in the event a cataclysm threatens to eradicate the human race. Even if only a few people survived, the thinking goes, the vault's seeds would allow humanity to start over. Lemminkäinen, a Scandinavian construction firm, shipped an asphalt paver north of the Arctic Circle after winning a contract to pave access roads, a tunnel entrance, and storage areas for the Svalbard Global Seed Vault on

Spitsbergen, the largest island on Norway's Svalbard Archipelago. The work needed 210 tons of asphalt. (Lemminkäinen also rehabilitated and repaved the 8,146-foot asphalt runway at Svalbard Airport, the world's northernmost public airport that dates to a Luftwaffe airstrip built during World War II.) Funded by Norway, several other nations, and the United Nations–affiliated Global Crop Diversity Trust, the seed vault opened in 2008 as a backup for the nearly two thousand seed banks around the world. Lying beneath Platåberget Mountain permafrost, sandstone, siltstone, and claystone a mere five hundred miles from the North Pole, the Svalbard vault's plastic boxes can store 4.5 million seeds.

The assumption was both simple and arrogant: the seeds in this Global Seed Vault would be safe from anything, even (however unlikely) nuclear attack. "If someone fired a rocket straight down the entrance, or a nuclear blast came along the corridor," the Global Crop Diversity Trust's executive director explained, it would hit a bowled area in the rock face. "After that there is only one place it can go—back out where it came from." A stainless-steel sculpture symbolizing the "mother of all rice" marks the blast deflector's dead center. Still, even the seed vault's engineers did not appreciate a more likely threat: global warming. They designed the vault to survive for centuries. In less than a decade, melting permafrost flooded the vault's entry-tunnel blacktop.[15]

Whatever careful tending Svalbard asphalt received, blacktop has suffered in the twenty-first century. In the United States asphalt pavement gained dominance over concrete during World War II, lost some of its dominance with Interstate Highway System construction, and pushed forward again with the rise of such tax-cutting frenzies as Reaganomics in the 1980s and austerity politics thereafter. This was so because asphalt pavement's initial costs were lower, and it was less expensive to resurface or patch worn-out concrete with asphalt. In some cases after the Great Recession, which began in late 2008, this cost advantage did not matter. A Rand Corporation analyst explained why: "A lot of states and especially those with rural areas have been challenged, from a budget perspective." The most cash-strapped counties allowed blacktop to deteriorate. Once the potholes got too bad—duck landings is one sign—a county might send in a "rotary mixer to grind the road up, making it look more like the old homesteader trail it once was." "You got three choices," reasoned Rick Perry, former Texas governor and energy secretary in the Trump cabinet. "You got tax roads. You got toll roads. Or you believe in the asphalt fairy."[16]

Partisanship and demographics also drove this gravel renaissance. President Obama's stimulus package, the American Recovery and Reinvestment Act of 2009, included over $100 billion in direct infrastructure spending. It received three Republican votes in the Senate and none in the House. Even in the face of austerity, new road construction and the extension and widening of existing roads still managed to outstrip population growth over the past forty years. Fewer taxpayers per road mile means even more tax resentment and even less maintenance.[17] Less road maintenance, in turn, means more wear and tear on vehicles and thus more vehicle maintenance. Underutilization of carpooling and public transportation extracts another hidden tax in the form of excess carbon dioxide released by vehicles idling or limping along in traffic jams. Each year U.S. drivers spend over four billion hours stuck in traffic.

The road lobby demands more maintenance and new construction dollars, dreaming of a national infrastructure bank ("Bank of Asphalt") and promoting roads as a matter of national security. T. Peter Ruane, arguably the nation's principal road lobbyist from 1988 to 2018, had all the right credentials to lead the crusade. He served on the Bush-Cheney transportation transition team in 2000 in the midst of his long career as president of the American Road and Transportation Builders Association (ARTBA). However, he did not lead with that experience; rather, he led with his combat experience in Vietnam: "We're not sitting here in the rear with the gear. We lead from the front. . . . Some say we may be too aggressive, but you can never be too aggressive, especially when you're right." The asphalt and concrete cadres embraced the interstates as a Cold War imperative decades before Ruane spoke those words. After 9/11 they embraced increased infrastructure spending as a War on Terror imperative. They are "trying to make political hay out of terrorism jitters," the *Wall Street Journal* stated, by building roads "big enough to accommodate mass evacuations in the event of another terrorist attack." "It's just common sense," said the former marine astride ARTBA. Others said tax subsidies for suburban sprawl provided financial security for the pavers and anxiety relief for those suffering racial and nativist phobias. Asphalt, as ever, marked and helped enforce segregation.[18]

The road lobby is equally relentless on the state and local levels, with asphalt lobbyists enjoying a particular success landing positions as state transportation directors. In Ohio Jerry Wray earned a blunt nickname: the Asphalt Sheriff. In the 1990s he served as state transportation director before moving to the private sector as vice president of Flexible Pavements of Ohio. Beginning in 2011 he served a second stint as state transportation director under Republican governor John Kasich. "His people that he will bring on will understand," Kasich explained when announcing Wray's appointment: "no games, no politics, no train." The train reference made the governor's preference for blacktop clear enough. "That train is dead," he reiterated when turning down $400 million in federal stimulus money to build a high-speed rail linking Cleveland, Columbus, and Cincinnati.[19]

In Oklahoma Gary Ridley was the asphalt sheriff. He was hired in the Department of Transportation in the 1960s and worked his way up from equipment operator. He left to run the Oklahoma Asphalt Paving Association in 1997, returned to state employ in 2001, and rose to a state cabinet post (secretary of transportation). One of his predecessors as director of the Department of Transportation, Neal McCaleb, dubbed Ridley the "best transportation director in the state's history." Oklahoma senator (and global-warming denier) Jim Inhofe trumped that, calling Ridley the "best secretary of transportation in the country."[20] Ridley's most dramatic service, managing the response in 2002 to the I-40 bridge disaster near Webbers Falls, involved no lobbying. After its captain fainted and a towboat pushed two empty asphalt tank barges, each 297 feet long, into a pier, the allision collapsed a 503-foot section of a concrete bridge onto the barges below. Eight cars and three trucks traveling on I-40 went into the void, and fourteen people died.[21]

Antiroad movements are active in every industrialized nation. In the mid-1990s, at the so-called Third Battle of Newbury (after civil war battles nearby in 1643–44), British police arrested over eight hundred people, including some camped in a tunnel network dug by hand. They were among some seven thousand people protesting the construction of the Newbury bypass, which is now part of the A34 road, sixty miles west of London. A demolished asphalt runway at RAF Greenham Common, an airbase used by the RAF and USAF during the Cold War, provided most of the aggregate. The protests failed. After bulldozers took ten thousand mature trees, the contractors and their paving machines laid down nine miles of blacktop.[22]

In the United States the North American Free Trade Agreement of 1994 underlay protests against proposed extensions to I-69. Free traders and protectionists alike dubbed I-69 the "NAFTA Superhighway" because it begins on the Canadian border at Port Huron, Michigan, and would end, if the extensions go through in their entirety, on the Mexican border at three separate cities in Texas. I-69 protestors targeted the Gohmann Asphalt Company of Clarksville, Indiana, stopping a company truck and chaining themselves to the undercarriage. Indiana governor Mitch Daniels was sufficiently alarmed to move the groundbreaking ceremony for an I-69 extension indoors. After a Gohmann executive drove a front-end loader and dumped dirt on a tarp, the governor and assorted dignitaries lined up for the cameras, golden-blade shovels in hand, to scoop dirt. In 2007, a year before that "make-believe digging," Gohmann's make-believe billing on paving contracts resulted in an $8.2 million settlement with Indiana, Kentucky, and the Federal Highway Administration. The company also returned a $5.3 million bonus it received for early completion of reconstruction work on I-64 (which crosses I-69 just north of Evansville, Indiana).[23]

I-69's story included a public-private partnership (P3) adventure for infrastructure construction and operation of the sort trumpeted by Donald Trump during the 2016 presidential campaign. Indiana governor Mike Pence (Daniels's successor) signed a P3 deal in 2014 with Isolux Corsán, a Spanish company, to extend and maintain I-69 from Bloomington to Martinsville. On June 18, 2017, Vice President Pence suffered the indignity of an *Indianapolis Star* report titled "Mike Pence's Infrastructure Mess: What Went Wrong with I-69?" President Trump was no doubt familiar with one problem plaguing Isolux Corsán: subcontractors claiming they were not paid and walking off the job in protest. That was not what Pence promised. When first announcing the project, he said the private sector would "harness a different character of innovation."[24]

The NAFTA Superhighway remains unfinished, as does asphalt's role in humanity's larger stories of empire and war, progress and poverty. People died fighting over asphalt as a natural resource that could bring riches in the time of one-eyed kings and Nabataean traders, Egyptian queens and Roman generals. They died in a less direct manner too, as Aristotle and Diodorus noted when commenting on hydrogen sulfide gas and Dead Sea asphalt. People are still dying over asphalt. No one is likely to go to war over this lowly hydrocarbon nowadays. Nonetheless, adversaries in modern wars are relentless in their efforts to build or destroy asphalt roads and runways (that U.S. cruise-missile attack on Syria's Shayrat Air Base aside). It has been this way, for roads, since the Spanish-American War of 1898. For runways it has been this way since Japan attacked Pearl Harbor. For carnage quantified, traffic fatalities on blacktop roads outrace martial deaths, as if determined to offer a blood-soaked take on number 226 in the Perry Index (Aesop's fable of tortoise and hare).

People will continue to die because of asphalt in a less direct manner if Alberta oil-sand extraction and attendant environmental damage continues unabated. For nearly all of human history, as we have seen, elites and common people alike used asphalt to solve practical problems. They used it to create Nebuchadnezzar's bricks, Amzi Barber's sheets, a Rock County billionaire's shingles, the bottoms that refineries little and big sell as binder for the blacktop covering over 90 percent of the United States' paved roads and nearly the same percentage covering the world's paved roads. In final form from the blacktop age back to however many thousands of years ago, nearly every product created with asphalt has served as a carbon sink. Now the search for profits has transformed the planet's largest source of natural asphalt from carbon sink to carbon bomb through conversion into dilbit and syncrude and such final forms as gasoline and other things that burn all the way down to petcoke ("the coal hiding in the tar sands").[25] A head start of however many millennia aside, it is not given that the tortoise (asphalt as carbon sink) will beat the hare (asphalt as carbon bomb). Even the last best hope for defusing this carbon bomb—low conventional oil prices, which would render the oil sands unprofitable—has a downside. Low oil prices might slow the march away from hydrocarbons of whatever sort and push the march toward clean and green renewable energy sources a few more decades down the road.

Black Death has always been part of asphalt's story. If the oil sands are ever fully unleashed, that might well accelerate global warming and threaten carnage, if not extinction, regardless of the 4.5 million seeds that might (or might not) remain high and dry beyond the blacktop tunnel leading to the Platåberget Mountain vault. Yet asphalt has also helped our species survive and thrive. Asphalt pavement and the bicycle entered their heydays together, with the former, as ever, presupposed and thus largely ignored, and the latter often given credit for its startling effect on such immodest subjects as human evolution. Because bicycles enabled more people to travel greater distances than they could by foot, they helped create what geneticists call a "breeding population" large enough to "ensure that chance alone does not disrupt genetic equilibrium." In simple terms bicycles increased the gene pool by enabling their owners to "access" more potential mates. The bicycle demolished distance as a breeding barrier and obliterated genetic drift, which was common when communities were confined, leading to some lines dying out entirely and others continuing via inbreeding. The latter—once a "powerful and rapid" evolutionary force—was reduced to the point of genetic irrelevance. "Without doubt," British geneticist Steve Jones said (perhaps with some exaggeration), "the most important event in human evolution was the invention of the bicycle."[26]

That invention certainly allowed greater mobility, though not to the degree allowed by the forgotten hydrocarbon that led to the sheet asphalt and then the full-depth blacktop pavement under so many of those bicycle wheels and automobile wheels that would follow. That is this hydrocarbon's final incongruity. Not only utility and profit but life and death lie in the same black hole.

ACKNOWLEDGMENTS

It does not take a village to write a nonfiction book. Nonetheless, an author rarely produces one solo. So thanks are due. At the University of Alaska Anchorage, where I taught for over two decades, Steve Haycox has provided sound advice since the day he (and Will Jacobs) hired me out of graduate school. At Milwaukee Area Technical College, Michael Rosen cleared a number of hurdles; Enrique Ferreira helped with fact checking; Lisa Stanolis, Jhoua Vang, and Nicole Lee helped with research; Herb Flaig helped with the German translation; and Jennifer Medved and Kathy Blume helped with interlibrary loans. James G. Speight, a chemist, geologist, petroleum engineer, and grand authority on asphalt, patiently answered my questions, and on the engineering end so did Hussain Bahia, director of the Modified Asphalt Research Center at the University of Wisconsin–Madison. Dawn Turner helped me find a decent title for the conclusion. Tara O'Reilly and Maureen O'Reilly helped with various tasks. I am also in debt to Spencer Howard at the Herbert Hoover Presidential Library; Kendra Lightner at the Franklin D. Roosevelt Presidential Library; David Clarke at the Harry S. Truman Presidential Library; Kevin M. Bailey and Chalsea Millner at the Dwight D. Eisenhower Presidential Library; Brittany Parris and Keith Shuler at the Jimmy Carter Presidential Library; Laura Schieb at Dartmouth College's Rauner Special Collections Library; and Megan Ó Connell and Kate Collins of the David M. Rubenstein Rare Book and Manuscript Library at Duke University. Martha Silver of the National Asphalt Pavement Association solved a vexing mystery for me. Paul Bogard answered my questions about what lies beneath asphalt pavement. Janet McDonnell, a fellow graduate student back in the day, pointed me in fruitful directions regarding asphalt use by the U.S. Army. And Karen J. Hall did the same regarding asphalt in Appalachia.

Bridget Barry, my editor at the University of Nebraska Press, was wonderful. I am thankful for her patience and hard eye in helping to get this book in reasonable shape. Bridget also did a superb job in selecting Sterling Evans and the anonymous manuscript reviewers who were thorough and thoughtful, analytic on the sweeping questions, and precise on the details. I am in their debt too. And thanks are due to the other members of the UNP team who made this book possible.

NOTES

PREFACE

1. The pipeline company's original preferred route crossed the Ogallala.
2. James Hansen, "Game Over for the Climate," *New York Times*, May 9, 2012.
3. Milton, *Paradise Lost*, bk. 12, lines 40–42.

INTRODUCTION

1. Most B-52s took off from blacktop runways in Thailand and on Guam and Okinawa.
2. McNaughton, qtd. in Wittner, *Cold War America*, 279.
3. Prados, *Blood Road*. Nowadays as many as one million French and U.S. tourists arrive in Vietnam annually (with such exceptions as pandemic years). Some bike the Ho Chi Minh Highway, a blacktop ribbon that includes bits and pieces of the wartime blood road.
4. Asphalt was present at the end as well. Roosevelt Avenue and other Arlington National Cemetery roads are blacktop. So are nearly all the roads at the United States' 136 national cemeteries.
5. Hitchcock, "Velocity and Viscosity," 58.
6. Gordon, *Rise and Fall*, 5–23.
7. Schnapp, "Three Pieces of Asphalt."
8. Meyer and De Witt, *Definition and World Resources*, 1. For nomenclature, see Speight, *Asphalt*, 3–43.
9. Johnson, "World's Slowest Moving Drop."
10. "Annual Homeless Assessment Report," 34–50; Shaner, "Asylums, Asphalt, and Ethics." See also UNICEF, *World's Children*.
11. Stilgoe, *Borderland*, 152; Lenzner, "Always the Last Crop."
12. Howells, *Literature and Life*, 89; Benjamin, *Arcades Project*, 372.
13. Ehrenburg, qtd. in Edwards, *William F. Buckley Jr.*, 116.
14. "Emissions of Greenhouse Gases," tables 13, 14, pp. 29–30. See also the EIA data on carbon dioxide emissions: "Frequently Asked Questions."
15. On sunny days at another notable house, the College Settlement on Rivington Street in New York's Lower East Side, Eleanor Roosevelt, at age eighteen, taught immigrant children how to dance and do calisthenics out on the blacktop.

16. Moses, qtd. in Michael T. Kaufman, "Moses Rips into 'Venomous' Biography," *New York Times*, August 27, 1974.

17. Bélanger, "Synthetic Surfaces," 241, 248, 260. See also Bélanger, *Landscape as Infrastructure*.

18. Wells, *Car Country*, xxxi.

19. "Outline of Operation Overlord."

1. NATURE

1. "History of Alvin."

2. Marcon et al., "Slow Volcanoes," 195, 202; Sahling et al., "Seafloor Observations," 101.

3. Lippsett, "Asphalt Volcanoes," 39; Alden, "NOAA Expedition." See also Valentine et al., "Asphalt Volcanoes"; Jones et al., "Asphalt Mounds"; and Lipuma, "Asphalt Volcanos."

4. In more recent times blowouts from offshore oil-drilling platforms are more likely to create hypoxic dead zones. The Santa Barbara Basin spill in 1969 and two Gulf of Mexico spills—the Bay of Campeche spill in 1979 and the Deepwater Horizon Spill in 2010—were three of the worst. The Santa Barbara spill was among the environmental disasters that led to the first annual Earth Day demonstration in 1970; creation of the Environmental Protection Agency in 1970 and the California Coastal Commission in 1972; and passage of the California Environmental Quality Act of 1970, the National Environmental Policy Act of 1970, and the Clean Water Act of 1972. Easton, *Black Tide*; Sabol Spezio, *Slick Policy*.

5. Asphalt entered outer space in 1997 in a payload canister aboard the U.S. space shuttle *Columbia*. The purpose was to expose asphalt to exosphere conditions. *Columbia* landed on concrete, not asphalt. But NASA has designated asphalt runways at Moron Air Base in Spain and Istres-Le Tubé Air Base in France as space shuttle transoceanic abort landing (TAL) sites.

6. Pliny the Elder, *Natural History*, 35:15.

7. Meyer, Attanasi, and Freeman, "Heavy Oil"; Meyer and De Witt, *Definition and World Resources*, 11; "Survey of Energy Resources," 125.

8. Speight, *Chemistry and Technology*, 17.

9. See "Athabasca Oil Sands."

10. Jassim and Al-Gailani, "Hydrocarbons," 240.

11. The major asphalt seeps are Los Angeles's La Brea Tar Pits (literally "the Tar Tar Pits" and thus a tautology); Kern County's McKittrick Tar Pits; and Santa Barbara County's Carpinteria Tar Pits.

12. The major South American asphalt seeps and lakes are Peru's Talara Pits; Ecuador's La Carolina Pits; Venezuela's Mene de Inciarte and Lake Bermudez (or Lake Guanoco); and Trinidad and Tobago's Pitch Lake on the island of Trinidad.

13. Meckenstock et al., "Water Droplets in Oil"; Crosby, "Native Bitumens," 239. For Robert J. Hill, the USGS researcher, see Hill, *Cuba and Porto Rico*, 369.

14. Speight, *Asphalt*, 57–58; Lindsey and Seymour, "Western Neotropics," 111.

15. Sánchez-Villagra, Aguilera, and Carlini, *Urumaco and Venezuelan Pleontology*.

16. Lindsey and Seymour, "Western Neotropics"; J. Harris, *La Brea and Beyond*, 112, 114.

17. Merriam, "Death Trap."

18. "Pit 91."

19. The practice could be dangerous. Hamilton and Meehan, "Ross Store Explosion."

2. USE

1. Marchand, *Down from Olympus*, 350n31. See also Arnold, "*Arierdämmerung*."

2. Koldewey, *Excavations at Babylon*, v.

3. Masó, "Babylon's Ishtar Gate."

4. Boëda et al., "New Evidence."

5. Gaines, Eglinton, and Rullkotter, *Echoes of Life*, 260–62; "Akkadian Cuneiform Tablet."

6. Nissenbaum, "Dead Sea Asphalts." (The *AAPG Bulletin* is the journal of the American Association of Petroleum Geologists.)

7. Aristotle, qtd. in Forbes, *Bitumen and Petroleum*, 29; Diodorus, *Universal History*, bk. 2, line 48. Stink aside, the Greek philosopher Plutarch (ca. 46–120 CE) had budding entrepreneurs using Dead Sea asphalt in cyphi, a perfume that doubled as an antidepressant that could reduce "the distress and strain of our daily carking cares." Plutarch, *Moralia*, 5:80.

8. Oxilia et al., "Dawn of Dentistry"; for Pliny, see Nissenbaum, "Dead Sea," 127–42.

9. Nissenbaum, "Dead Sea," 131; Lloyd, "Building in Brick," 1:466, 469–70.

10. Zivie, *Lost Tombs of Saqqara*, 44.

11. Clark, Ikram, and Evershed, "Significance of Petroleum Bitumen"; Peters and Walters, *Biomarker Guide*, 1:323–25.

12. H. Pringle, *Mummy Congress*, 46; Herodotus, *Histories*, 2.89.

13. Pliny the Elder, *Natural History*, 2.335; Thucydides, *Peloponnesian War*, 4, 100.4; Forbes, *Bitumen and Petroleum*, 95–100. See also Mayor, *Greek Fire*.

14. Connan, "Use and Trade"; Forbes, *Bitumen and Petroleum*, 56, 87.

15. Herodotus, *Histories*, 1:179.1–4.

16. Lloyd, "Building in Brick," 1:466–70.

17. Diodorus, *Universal History*, bk. 2, line 10; Forbes, "Cosmetic Arts," 1:252 and *Bitumen and Petroleum*, 49. Near the end of his reign, Nebuchadnezzar began mixing asphalt with a lime mortar. Thereafter, Babylon's rulers, the Persians and Seleucids, abandoned asphalt "and confined themselves generally to the use of loam mortar, a decidedly retrograde step." Forbes, *Bitumen and Petroleum*, 60.

18. Koldewey, *Excavations at Babylon*, 12.

19. Haupt, "Xenophon's Account," 103–4.

20. Garcia, "Ishtar Gate."

21. Stokl, "Nebuchadnezzar," 257–69. See also Sass, *Substance of Civilization*, 124–33.

22. Herodotus, *Persian Wars*, 8.98. The Farley post office building in New York City bears a version of the quotation.

23. Koldewey, *Excavations at Babylon*, 54. The index lists twenty-nine pages under *asphalt* and seven under *bitumen*. It is not clear which civilization—neo-Babylonians? Indus Valley?—can lay claim to the first use of asphalt as a mortar or binder for road construction.

24. Forbes, *Bitumen and Petroleum*, 74.

25. Spring, *Great Walls*, 40–41. In prehistoric Mesopotamia, Ubaid and Uruk cultures used asphalt and bricks for barrages—"artificial obstructions in a watercourse"—to facilitate irrigation. Mithen with Mithen, *Thirst*, 59.

26. Hornblower, *Hieronymous of Cardia*, 145. For life in the desert, see Evenari, Shanan, and Tadmor, *Negev*; and Mithen with Mithen, *Thirst*, 104–24.

27. Diodorus, *Universal History*, bk. 19, lines 99–100; Hammond, "Nabataean Bitumen Industry"; Waterfield, *Dividing the Spoils*; Mithen with Mithen, *Thirst*, 107–8. The price asphalt could fetch, according to several economists who accounted for variables over the centuries as best they could, was in the range of modern-day asphalt produced in oil refineries. Forbes, "Cosmetic Arts," 1:253.

28. Diodorus, *Universal History*, bk. 19, lines 95–97.

29. Diodorus, *Universal History*, bk. 19, line 97.

30. Diodorus, *Universal History*, bk. 19, line 100.

31. Waterfield, *Dividing the Spoils*, 123–26.

32. Josephus, *War of the Jews*, bk. 1, line 36; Schiff, *Cleopatra*, 210–11, 267.

33. Shakespeare, *Antony and Cleopatra*, act 5, scene 2, line 16.

34. Cassius Dio, qtd. in Forbes, *Bitumen and Petroleum*, 61. For "Roman ladies," see Danby, *Natural Rock Asphalts*, 42–43.

35. Strabo, *Geography*, 16:4.23, 26.

36. Strabo, *Geography*, 7:5.8.

3. FAITH

1. Exod. 1:22, 2:3 (NAB); Gen. 6:13–16, 11:62–65 (NIV); *Epic of Gilgamesh*, 99.

2. Trollinger and Trollinger, *Righting America*.

3. Eighth-century Viking shipbuilders were likely the first to mass produce tar from resin-rich wood.

4. Coffee, "Pitching Noah's Ark."

5. Gen. 2:7 (AV).

6. Clark, Ikram, and Evershed, "Significance of Petroleum Bitumen."

7. Sass, *Substance of Civilization*, 126; G. Harris, *Destruction of Sodom*, 75; Forbes, "Cosmetic Arts," 1:251.

8. Forbes, *Bitumen and Petroleum*, 91.

9. Pliny the Elder, *Natural History*, 7.15. See also 28.23.

10. Churchill and Churchill, *Collection of Voyages*, 2:752.

11. Forbes, *Bitumen and Petroleum*, 91.

12. Josh. 6:20 (AV); Gen. 14:1–12, 11:3 (AV).

13. *Book of Jubilees*, 10:20–21; *Testament of Solomon*, 69.

14. Agricola, *De re metallica*, 582n. Agricola, considered the founder of geology as a discipline, referred to Dead Sea asphalt as "bituminous juice."

15. Milton, *Paradise Lost*, bk. 11, lines 728–31; bk. 1, lines 411–14, 271–80, 701–30; bk. 10, lines 297–305; bk. 12, lines 38–42.

16. D. Pringle, *Pilgrimage to Jerusalem*, 117, 284; Voltaire, *Philosophical Dictionary*, 1:144.

17. H. Pringle, *Mummy Congress*, 196–97; Dunand and Lichtenberg, *Mummies and Death*, 134; Aldersey-Williams, *Sir Thomas Browne*, 53–54; Fagan, *Rape of the Nile*, 35. See also Browne, *Hydriotaphia*.

18. Fagan, *Rape of the Nile*, 33–36, 41; Steegmuller, *Flaubert in Egypt*, 204–7. Sanderson's account is in Purchas, *Purchas His Pilgrimes*, 9:418–19.

19. Dannenfeldt, "Egyptian Mumia," 167; "Dead Man's Corner." See also Noble, *Medicinal Cannibalism*; and Sugg, *Mummies, Cannibals and Vampires*. Raw mummy had a few other uses, though documentation is thin. The artist Edward Burne-Jones (1833–98) held a burial ceremony in his yard for a tube of a pigment sold as "mummy brown" that supposedly contained pulverized mummy. Rudyard Kipling (1865–1936), then in his teens and a nephew of the artist's wife, attended, and for the remainder of his days claimed he "could drive a spade within a foot of where that tube lies." Pinney, *Rudyard Kipling*, 9–10; McCouat, "Life and Death."

20. Agricola, *De re metallica*, 584.

21. The Warao, of course, had long used Pitch Lake asphalt for hydraulic purposes. In pre-Columbian South America, moreover, the Inca may have used Talara Tar Pit asphalt for construction of bits and pieces of their twenty-five-thousand-mile road system. "It was built of heavy flags of freestone," wrote a visitor in 1847, "and in some parts at least covered with a bituminous cement." In other parts a "fine bituminous glue" filled in narrow gaps between the stones. Prescott, *History of the Conquest*, 1:65–66, 159–60.

22. Raleigh, *Discovery of Guiana*, 13; Burger et al., "Identification."

23. Forbes, "Petroleum," 5:103. In the early eighteenth century, a Greek entrepreneur tried to market rock asphalt from Val-de-Travers, Switzerland, for such tasks as eradication of field mice. Forbes, *Early Petroleum History*, 13–27.

24. Lord Cornwallis, qtd. in Stead, *Centenary of 1798*, 76. Asphalt left a mark on photography too. Joseph Nicéphore Niépce smeared asphalt on pewter plates and made the first exposure in a camera: *View from the Window at Le Gras* (1826). In the 1880s the photochrom process produced colorized prints with the help of asphalt diluted in benzene.

4. TRIUMPH

1. Marko, "Negro Morality," 80.
2. McAdam, *Remarks*, 46.
3. For this section, I relied on Tilson, *Street Pavements*; Holley, "Blacktop"; and Holley, *Highway Revolution*.
4. Twain, *Innocents Abroad*, 158.
5. Cochrane and Bourne, *Life*, 2:320–23. See also Cordingly, *Cochrane*.
6. Murray, "Abraham Gesner"; Rhodes, *Energy*, 140–45.
7. Cochrane and Bourne, *Life*, 2:319.
8. U.S. Department of State, *Reports from the Consuls*, 38; bill of sale for over one hundred acres of the Mon Plaisir Estate, Legal and Financial Documents, box 9, CF. For "considerable litigation," see "Birth of Trinidad."
9. Dando-Collins, *Tycoon's War*, 29–30.
10. For Grant, see Senate Committee, *Message from the President*. Edward de Smedt had supervised additional trials in New York City, using the asphaltite grahamite from West Virginia's Ritchie County mines. These mines closed in 1873 after a deadly explosion, reopened in 1885, and closed for good in 1909.
11. Nichols, "Sam Gilson." From the late 1950s to 1973, a Colorado refinery upgraded Gilsonite and patented the most profitable end product, gasoline, as Gilsoline.
12. Severance, "Amzi Lorenzo Barber"; "Amzi Lorenzo Barber," obituary, *Washington Post*, April 21, 1909; McNichol, *Paving the Way*, 56–69.
13. Lewis, *Washington*, 215–18.
14. Massey and Denton, *American Apartheid*, 9, 16, 19, 26.
15. Mencken, *Happy Days*, 234.
16. Eli Ransome Sutton, "In the Land of Revolution," ca. 1901, Scrapbooks, 1898–1934, ERS.
17. "Limit," 3.
18. "History and Argument Which Can Be Sustained by Written and Oral Evidence in the Case of Averell, Agt. Barber et al.," ca. 1879, box 20, WWA.
19. Veblen, *Theory*, 68–101.
20. In his pageant play, *The Rock* (1934), T. S. Eliot's choruses noted such lands "of lobelias and tennis flannels." Later John F. Kennedy borrowed from Eliot for a presidential campaign speech: "Here were decent godless people: / Their

only monument the asphalt road / And a thousand lost golf balls." Kennedy, "Remarks."

21. Baehr, "City Streets." For Wilder, see Reid, *Roads Were Not Built*, 119. For "gathering places," see Petroski, *Road Taken*, 38. For the decline of streets as public places, see McShane, *Down the Asphalt Path*.

22. Holley, "Blacktop," 712, 709–10, 724. See also Gillespie, *Century of Progress*, 82; J. J. Staley, "Building for the Road Builder," *Better Roads and Streets*, January 1914, 7–8, 54. The first portable asphalt plants hauled by trucks and trailers arrived in 1913.

23. Lay, *Ways of the World*, 221, 233, 239. For Richardson's book, see *Asphalt Pavement*.

24. Senate Committee, *Itemized Statement*, 208; Glaeser, *Triumph of the City*, 102–3. For Roosevelt, see Zacks, *Island of Vice*.

25. "New Immigration Depot," *New York Daily Tribune*, December 27, 1891; "Again at Ellis Island," *New York Daily Tribune*, December 17, 1900.

26. Plowden, *Motor Car and Politics*, 24–25. Another British cyclist, King Edward VII, inspired the song "Daisy Bell (a Bicycle Built for Two)" (1892).

27. Louise Dawson, "How the Bicycle Became a Symbol of Women's Emancipation," *Guardian*, November 4, 2011; M. Hall, *Muscle on Wheels*.

28. Schnapp, "Three Pieces of Asphalt," 7; H. Earle, *Autobiography*, 62.

29. Weingroff, "Portrait of a General"; Stone, *New Roads*.

30. Chapot, "Great Bicycle Protest," 179.

31. George, "Modern Methods," 251.

32. "A Family of Road Builders," *National Magazine*, October 1921, 251–55.

33. Lavis and Griest, *New Rapid Transit System*, 27–29; Brennan, "Abandoned Stations"; Walker, *Fifty Years*.

34. George, "Modern Methods," 265.

35. Careless, "Seven Lesser-Known Uses for Asphalt."

36. McBeth, *Gunboats, Corruption, and Claims*, 105–30; Maurer, *Empire Trap*, 80–85.

37. Coates, *Legalist Empire*, 115.

38. The American Bitumastic Enamels Company coated not only all submerged valves and gates but all "fixed irons and steel work at Pedro Miguel lock" (and, presumably, the canal's eleven other locks as well). U.S. Governor, *Annual Report*, 55. Asphalt-industry interest in Panama eventually expanded to include security for West Coast oil shipments to Gulf Coast refineries. A National Asphalt Pavement Association delegation discussed these shipments with David Rubenstein, domestic policy adviser in the Jimmy Carter White House and later co-founder of the Carlyle Group. Richard Reiman to Rubenstein, June 12, 1979, Office of Anne Wexler, Richard Reiman's Chron file, box 334, JC.

39. For "dripping with asphalt," see "Week," 511; for "Dagos" and other pejoratives used by Roosevelt and other U.S. officials, see Mann, *Sources of Social Power*, 95–96.

40. Bowen et al., *Matter of the Charges*, 3–9 (for Roosevelt), 9–23 (for Taft). For asphaltic slime, see Milton, *Paradise Lost*, bk. 10, line 298.

41. Roosevelt, qtd. in Mann, *Sources of Social Power*, 96.

42. U.S. Department of State, *Correspondence Relating to Wrongs*; Coates, "Securing Hegemony"; Maurer, *Empire Trap*, 85.

43. For the nationalization story, see Rabe, *Road to OPEC*.

44. U.S. Department of Agriculture, *Report of the Office*, 331–33.

45. Other Office of Road Inquiry successors include the Bureau of Public Roads (1918–39) and the Public Roads Administration (1939–49) in the Department of Agriculture and then the Federal Works Agency; a new Bureau of Public Roads (1949–66) in the Department of Commerce; and the Federal Highway Administration in the Department of Transportation (1967–present). The annual budget grew from $10,000 to nearly $50 billion.

46. "Federal Highway Administrators"; U.S. Department of Agriculture, *Report of the Director*, 430–31, 433. Common asphalt laborers faced racial and nativist barriers when attempting to organize. In Milwaukee Local 88 was all Black. In California one local might be all Latinos; another might ban Latinos. Employers had their own biases. "'Cholos' are better workers than Japanese, Chinese, or Negroes," a Los Angeles contractor proclaimed. An organizer explained prejudice against an all-Mexican union refused admission to the AFL: "They said . . . [we] were going to take their jobs." Monroy, *Rebirth*, 102, 241; Trotter, *Black Milwaukee*, 63.

47. For the decline of asphalt imports from 1903 to 1907, see U.S. Geological Survey, *Mineral Resources*, 729–30. A rough estimate for refinery asphalt production at the turn of the century is ten to eleven barrels of asphalt for every hundred barrels of crude oil refined. Tilson, *Street Pavements*, 65.

48. McFerrin, "Kentucky Rock Asphalt Company."

49. U.S. Department of the Interior, *Report of the United States*, 71, 79; Kidwell, "Resurgence of the Choctaws."

50. Belle and Finegold, *Ellis Island*, 1:152–74. See also Cannato, *American Passage*. Asphalt tile fell out of favor in the twentieth century's last third, as the tiles often contained asbestos adhesives and mastics.

51. "Network of Roads Will Release Locked-Up Riches of the Nation," *American Motorist*, November 1916, 12–13, 54; Goddard, *Getting There*, 2–4.

52. States' rights advocates objected not to post roads per se but rather the threat to state sovereignty posed by the physical presence of "a post office—a federal outpost—in every town and village." Gallagher, *Post Office*, 32.

53. Hendricks, *Combat and Construction*, 8.

54. Holley, "Blacktop," 732. For an overview of funding, see Federal Highway Administration, *America's Highways*. For MacDonald, see Goddard, *Getting There*, 45–

198. Chain-gang labor persisted. "Beaten, he says, into confessing to a burglary," a reporter wrote about one escapee in 1964, "he was sentenced to 21 years in prison and sent to a chain gang to dig ditches and lay asphalt on Alabama's muddy back roads." Sarah Lyall, "1964 Chain-Gang Escape Follows Man North to L. I.," *New York Times*, June 24, 1991.

55. U.S. Department of Commerce, *Elimination of Waste.*

56. William Randolph Hearst Jr., speech, January 12, 1955, New Orleans, Subject File: Press (1), box 4, NHP; P. J. Croghan to Harold Phelps Stokes, June 18, 1926, Roads and Highways 1921–26, Commerce Series, box 521, HH; Sam S. Porter to Warren Harding, October 5, 1921, Arthur Woods to John Tomme, January 28, 1922, Woods to R. E. Maxwell, January 23, 1922, all in Unemployment Public Works, Roads and Highways Correspondence, Commerce Series, box 655, HH.

57. Hugh R. Pomeroy, secretary for the Los Angeles County Regional Planning Commission, to Dwight F. Davis, secretary of war, July 6, 1926, Roads and Highways, 1921–26, Commerce Series, box 521, HH.

58. J. M. Mackall, Maryland State Roads Commission, to Albert C. Ritchie, August 3, 1921, Highway Construction, Letters to/from Governors, Commerce Series, box 256, HH.

59. Evans, "Klan's Fight," 38–39; Rangel, "Ambiguously Articulating 'Americanism'"; *Hiram W. Evans*, U.S. Tax Court, 5 TCM 336; *Georgia*, 316 U.S. 159.

60. For the Mississippi, see Morris, *Big Muddy.*

61. Hoover, qtd. in Kelman, *River and Its City*, 192.

62. U.S. Department of War, *Report of the Chief*, 1643, 1701–2; U.S. Army Corps of Engineers, "District's First Decade." Asphalt "mattressing" remains common. The *Jan Heijmans*, a Dutch ship commissioned in 1968, could lay 250 tons of asphalt per hour at a depth of eighty feet.

63. U.S. Department of Agriculture, *Report of the Chief* (1931), 2–7.

64. Dickson and Allen, *Bonus Army*, 216.

5. DUTY

1. Teer, oral history, 1–14.

2. Teer, Teer, and Daugrid, *Courage Ever*, 28. See also K. Hall, *Blue Ridge Parkway.*

3. Will O'Neil, "America's WPA Army," *Chicago Tribune*, September 2, 1938; Teer, Teer, and Daugrid, *Courage Ever*, 19; Teer, oral history, 13.

4. Teer, oral history, 11.

5. N. Taylor, *American Made*, 418, 447–520; McNichol, *Paving the Way*, 204.

6. See John Ihlder to C. E. McGuire, August 10, 1936, and the other documents in Protest re Paving of P Street, 1937, box 21, JI.

7. O'Neil, "America's WPA Army."

8. Maher, *Nature's New Deal*, 71.

9. The right to build roads on public lands dates to Revised Statute 2477 (1886). When repealing RS 2477 in 1976, Congress preserved "valid existing rights." Today Bureau of Land Management approval for paving on any of the 250 million acres that it administers occasionally provokes lawsuits by environmental groups hoping, like those P Street residents, to halt the blacktop march.

10. Caro, *Power Broker*, 836; "Triborough." For "power to lay down asphalt," see Richard Murdocco, "Give Robert Moses His Due," *New York Daily News*, July 29, 2019; for "ghetto folks," see Michael T. Kaufman, "Moses Rips into 'Venomous' Biography," *New York Times*, August 27, 1974. Though Moses used asphalt to reshape New York, he objected to the "hideous" aesthetics of the city's modernist asphalt plant, built during World War II and closed in 1968.

11. F. Wright, *Frank Lloyd Wright*, 492; U.S. National Recovery Administration, *Code of Fair Competition*.

12. Comey, remarks.

13. Steinbeck, *Grapes of Wrath*, 118; McNichol, *Paving the Way*, 168–71.

14. Steinbeck, *Wayward Bus*, 140; Jackson, *Crabgrass Frontier*, 167.

15. "Hitler at Autobahn Ceremony."

16. Franklin D. Roosevelt to Lewis W. Douglas, director of the Bureau of the Budget, June 6, 1934, OF 1054, International Roads Congress, FDR. Allied bombers were more likely to target asphalt plants and truck factories than the Autobahn. See U.S. Strategic Bombing Survey, *Ebano Asphalt Werke*.

17. For Organisation Todt, see Lepage, *Hitler's Armed Forces Auxiliaries*, 5–57.

18. Trotsky, *Revolution Betrayed*, 44. See also Harold Denny, "Soviet to Rebuild Moscow in 10 Years: Modern City Thrice as Big as the Present One to House 5,000,000 Is Planned," *New York Times*, July 11, 1935.

19. Dulias, "Surviving the Soviet Gulag."

20. Applebaum, *Gulag*, 89–90.

21. Drew Pearson, "Washington-Merry-Go-Round," *Washington Post*, November 1, 1947, October 19, 1948. See also Vogel, *Pentagon*.

22. Lane, *Ships for Victory*.

23. Cindy Chang, "For Japanese Americans: A Backtrack to a Sad Past at Santa Anita," *Los Angeles Times*, March 29, 2014.

24. The navy used damaged Liberty and Victory ships as "'guinea pig' vessels" in "special [mine] sweep squadrons," ballasting them with asphalt drums to absorb underwater blasts. Hornfischer, *Fleet at Flood Tide*, 470.

25. Adams, *Kaiser Goes to Washington*, 17, 19; Foster, *Henry J. Kaiser*, 197–98.

26. Bernard Baruch to Roosevelt, June 18, 1943, PPF 88, Baruch, Bernard, 1941–45, FDR. For Kaiser and other industrial titans, see Herman, *Freedom's Forge*. Warren Brothers

bailed out Kaiser when he lost money on his initial paving contracts. Kaiser owned 50.5 percent of Bechtel-Kaiser-Warren Company stock. Warren A. Bechtel owned the rest. See the documents in folder 53 (Bechtel-Kaiser-Warren Company), series 1, box 1; and folder 7 (Warren Brothers Company, 1932–36), series 1, box 2, HJK.

27. Ward, *Closest Companion*, 302.

28. Lubin to Roosevelt, March 23, 1945, and Roosevelt to Lubin, March 26, 1945, PPF 2924, Kaiser, Henry J., FDR; Wilson, "Making 'Goop.'" For the FBI investigation, see the documents in the Henry J. Kaiser FBI File (62-76095), J. Edgar Hoover FBI Building, Washington DC.

29. Bunker, *Liberty Ships*, 12, 16, 202. See also W. Carter, *Black Oil*.

30. Schubert, "Persian Gulf Command," 305–15.

31. "Northway Staging Field"; Billberg, *Shadow of Eagles*, 122–23; Van Tuyll, *Feeding the Bear*, 52, 56.

32. Raisman, "Alaska-Siberia Friendship Route," 341–43; Lebedev, *Aviation Lend-Lease*, 120–22, 191; Van Tuyll, *Feeding the Bear*, 52, 167.

33. Virtue, *Black Soldiers*.

34. House Committee on Military Affairs, *Hearings*, 113–21.

35. Garfield, *Thousand-Mile War*.

36. Bowman, "Toxic Cleanup"; Lauren Rosenthal, "Officials Plan Ambitious Cleanup Effort," *Anchorage Daily News*, October 19, 2015.

37. "Cold Bay Fort Randall"; "Removal Action." See also Denfeld, *Defense of Dutch Harbor*.

38. Sorensen, "Civilian Conservation Corps," 235–40; Dod, *Corps of Engineers*, 19, 295–96. See also "Alaska Defensive Posts."

39. From 1942 to 1945, 33 Seabees received Silver Stars and approximately 2,000 received Purple Hearts. Over 500 Seabees died in accidents, and 290 died in combat.

40. Beck et al., *Corps of Engineers*, 431–32.

41. Racism was such that U.S. Army Air Forces officers even monitored use of "colored race" muscle labor for any "sacrifice of efficiency." Hartzer, "Black Aviation Engineer Units."

42. For the EABS, see Pearson, "Engineer Aviation Units." For an overview of Seabee work, see Bureau of Yards and Docks, *Building the Navy's Bases*; and "Seabee History: Formation."

43. Urwin, *Victory in Defeat*, 179; Cogan, *Captured*, 196.

44. "Oil from Asphalt Lake Is Not Waste," *Curaçao Chronicle*, November 15, 2018, https://curacaochronicle.com/local/oil-from-asphalt-lake-curacao-is-not-waste/. In 2012 Antwerp Oilchart International and a subcontractor, Asphalt Lake Recovery, began remediation, which ceased in 2016, given environmental concerns.

45. Bokel and Clark, "Acquisition," 134. Mexico also supported the war through the Bracero Program, guaranteeing migrant workers a minimum wage of thirty cents an hour, and nearly fifteen thousand Mexican nationals served in U.S. Armed Forces. Zamora, "Mexican Nationals," 97–105.

46. Henry Byroade, oral history, September 19, 21, 1988, HST, 20–24.

47. Davis, *North Carolina*, 53; "Cloth-Paper Runway."

48. When the Douglas XB-19, the prototype long-range bomber, rolled out of its Clover Field hanger in Santa Monica in June 1941, it broke "through the apron to a depth of about one foot." For help in developing sturdy surfaces, the army relied on the Asphalt Institute and the Portland Cement Association. Command overturned its decision for concrete after the engineers argued that "ground conditions at each site ought to determine the type of construction." Coll, Keith, and Rosenthal, *Corps of Engineers*, 56–57; Fine and Remington, *Corps of Engineers*, 614–49; Turhollow, "Airfields for Heavy Bombers," 207–14.

49. Bureau of Yards and Docks, *Building the Navy's Bases*, 2:201, 228–31, 350.

50. Craven and Cate, *Army Air Forces*, 2:403, 405–6, 5:596; Reybold, "General MacArthur Told Me," 90.

51. Jack Cornwell, "A Seabee on Iwo Jima: The Men Who Drove Cranes and Cats Also Served," *Navy Times*, February 22, 2019, www.navytimes.com/news/your -navy/2019/02/22/a-seabee-on-iwo-jima-the-men-who-drove-cranes-and-cats -also-served/.

52. Reybold, "General MacArthur Told Me," 90.

53. Bureau of Yards and Docks, *Building the Navy's Bases*, 2:358; Larson, *Road to Tinian*. The marine assault include MRLS—multiple rocket launchers—that the Japanese called "automatic artillery." Though unrelated to MRLS, asphalt has a rocket story dating to 1942, when John "Jack" Whiteside Parsons, a California Institute of Technology chemist, used asphalt in the first castable composite solid propellant.

54. Bureau of Yards and Docks, *Building the Navy's Bases*, 2:358–69. For molasses, see Conway and Toth, "Building Victory's Foundation," 254.

55. Larson, *Seabee's Story*, 205–6.

56. Wilson, "Making 'Goop,'" 10–11; Kent, "Fighting with Fire." Until the 1980s manufacturers routinely used roof asphalt as a liner for aerial bombs. Even today the armed forces use asphalt as a fill cover for M1123 infrared artillery rounds.

57. Howes and Herzenberg, *Day in the Sun*, 162–63.

58. Kelly, *Manhattan Project*, 176. For Morrison, see Rhodes, *Atomic Bomb*, 681.

59. Reybold, "General MacArthur Told Me," 90.

60. U.S. National Park Service, "Special Study." Pollution continued to plague Tinian. For half a century a defunct asphalt plant and asphalt-barrel dumpsite

were well within eyesight of Tinian International Airport's terminal and blacktop runway.

61. Ramsey, *Invasion Airfields*; Beck et al., *Corps of Engineers*, 140–41, 226, 394. For the asphalt landing at Normandy, see "Outline of Operation Overlord." For the mountain of maps, see Reybold, "General MacArthur Told Me," 90. Teller mines had a sheet-metal casing. Soviet TMB and TMSB mines frustrated metal detectors with casings constructed from wood and asphalt-impregnated cardboard.

62. Middlebrook, *Battle of Hamburg*, 266–67.

63. Megargee, *Encyclopedia of Camps*, 929. See also Roseman, *Wannsee Conference*.

64. Frischauer, *Himmler*, 67.

65. Thibault, *Trapped in a Nightmare*, 48, 55.

66. Pressac with Van Pelt, "Machinery of Mass Murder," 221–22, 234. In 1958 a memorial-design committee proposed the construction of an "asphalt road diagonally across the main Auschwitz camp and letting the rest of the ruins crumble, forcing visitors to 'confront oblivion.'" Curry, "Can Auschwitz Be Saved?" Seven years later, in 1965, the United States sold its shares of GAF Materials Corporation, having seized the company in 1941, as it was an asset of I. G. Farben (the German conglomerate that produced Zyklon-B, the hydrogen-cyanide pesticide used to gas Jews and others at Auschwitz). Today GAF is the largest asphalt roofing-materials manufacturer in North America.

67. For these and other examples of the word *asphalt* being used as a pejorative, see Thacker, *Joseph Goebbels*, 75, 82, 96, 127; Kahmann, "Antisemitism and Anti-urbanism," 486–87; Klemperer and Martin, *Third Reich*, 225. See also Keegan, *Waffen SS*. Use of the word as a pejorative continues; for example, mujahideen in Afghanistan use the term "asphalt Fedayeen."

68. That made it shocking forty years later, when Ronald Reagan attended a wreath-laying ceremony at a cemetery in Bitburg, the final resting place for forty-nine Waffen-SS soldiers.

69. Anne Frank was also marched to Bergen-Belsen, but not from Ahlem. The Nazis relocated her from Auschwitz. Her friend Eva Schloss, like Anne fifteen years old in 1945, remained at Auschwitz and survived. Anne did not survive Bergen-Belsen. Schloss published the last of her books about the camps and her friendship with Anne Frank in 2020 at age eighty-five: *Amsterdam, 11. Mai 1944*. The photograph of Auschwitz on the book's cover is courtesy of *Asphalt Magazine*.

70. N. Ferguson, *Kissinger*, 1:163–68; Wüstenberg, *Civil Society and Memory*, 178–79; Megargee, *Encyclopedia of Camps*, 1133.

71. Buggein, *Slave Labor*, 81–82, 110, 245; Megargee, *Encyclopedia of Camps*, 1172. In cooperation with the SS, Deutsche Asphalt formed Steinöl to construct a shale-oil facility. That enterprise used slave labor from the Schandelah subcamp.

The ss again stepped up after contractors ignored complaints about the lack of medicine and coal. The concern was not humanitarian. Rather, mistreatment interfered with productivity. Højgaard and Schultz a/s was another company in the asphalt business that used "forced and slave labor in Estonia, Poland, and Serbia." Lund, "Building Hitler's Europe," 479–80.

72. Megargee, *Encyclopedia of Camps*, 929.

73. A rock-asphalt discovery near Holzen in 1860 led to a boom, with Deutsche Asphalt and other companies formed. By 1914 the area had eight asphalt plants. The principal product was a powder used to make asphalt tiles and paving blocks. Danby, *Natural Rock Asphalts*, 122–23.

74. Mommsen, *Volkswagenwerk*, 830; Waltzer, "Moving Together," 99.

75. Mommsen, "Place of Remembrance"; Mommsen, *Volkswagenwerk*, 830–52.

76. "Rules and Regulations"; Stauffer, *Quartermaster Corps*, 184.

77. Reitan, "Nazi Camps," 62.

78. Hecking, "Voice for the Dead."

79. Hecking, "Voice for the Dead." See also Svoboda, "Unearthing the Atrocities"; Arad, *Belzec, Sobibór, Treblinka*; and Matt Lebovic, "Is Sobibór to Be the New 'Disneyland' of Nazi Death Camps?," *Times of Israel*, December, 4, 2014.

80. Beschloss, *Conquerors*, 238n1. It was not surprising that Hitler's remains remained under blacktop for decades. The remains of several Romanovs murdered by the Bolsheviks ended up under asphalt as well. In 1977, moreover, the Politburo had the Ipatiev House in Yekaterinburg, where the Bolsheviks murdered Nicholas and Alexandria and their children, demolished. Communist Party functionary Boris Yeltsin, who later served as Russia's first president (1991–99), supervised the blacktop crew who paved over the site.

6. CRUSADES

1. Mercher, *Chavez Ravine*.

2. *Wilkinson*, 365 U.S. 399; Sherrill, *First Amendment Felon*, 228.

3. Zirin, *People's History of Sports*, 125.

4. Llamoca, "Remembering the Lost Communities." See also "Map."

5. Grathwol and Moorhus, *Bricks, Sand, and Marble*, 15.

6. Madden, *Istanbul*, 349; Steil, *Marshall Plan*, 374. For "dollar aid" and "road program," see Machado, *Usable Past*, 92.

7. Robinson Newcomb, oral history, August 6, 1977, HST, 38–42. After firing MacDonald, Commerce Secretary Sinclair Weeks planned a retirement dinner with President Eisenhower to present a citation. MacDonald declined the invitation, saying he did not know when he would "have any free time." See the correspondence in folder 57: Mac, 1953–58, Series 7: Department of Commerce, box 34, sw.

8. "Henry W. Mack."

9. Fowle and Lonnquest, *Forgotten War*, 351, 386, 390.

10. Neufeld and Watson, *Coalition Air Warfare*, 269; Floyd Whaley, "Shadows of an Old Military Base," *New York Times*, April 26, 2013.

11. Asphalt played a more modest role in the North American Aerospace Defense Command. NORAD's Cheyenne Mountain Complex in Colorado Springs has a blacktop access-tunnel road.

12. Naske, *Paving Alaska's Trails*, 240, 247. In Valdez the March 27, 1964, earthquake damaged the port's asphalt tank and killed over thirty people who were waiting on the dock to greet the ss *Chena*. A *Chena* crewmember died onboard when asphalt barrels broke free and crushed him. Committee, *Great Alaska Earthquake*, 523, 528–29. Later, asphalt pushed across the Arctic Circle to support the Trans-Alaska Pipeline System. The asphalt-and-gravel Dalton Highway ends at Deadhorse Airport and its 6,500-foot blacktop runway.

13. Robert Landry, oral history, February 28, 1974, HST, 80. See also the documents in Asphalt versus Concrete Runways, Landry Files, box 1, HST.

14. Subcommittee for Special Investigations, *Asphalt Paving Materials*.

15. American Society of Newspaper Editors, "The Chance for Peace," April 16, 1953, Speech Series, box 3, DDE. See also Ledbetter, *Unwarranted Influence*.

16. Moynihan, "Policy vs. Program," 90, 93–94.

17. Eisenhower, qtd. in McNichol, *Roads That Built America*, 100.

18. "Rubble to Runway." Tegel was in the French occupation sector.

19. The road lobby's "card carrying members," broadly defined, included all licensed drivers. Kelley, *Pavers and the Paved*, 4, 43.

20. Lucius Clay to Dwight Eisenhower, August 30, 1954, Subject File: Dwight D. Eisenhower, box 1, NHP. See also Joseph P. Walsh, statement, October 8, 1954, Hearings: American Petroleum Institute, box 5, NHP; President's Commission on a National Highway Program, meeting, December 9–10, 1954, Subject File: Committee Business (2), box 1, NHP; and U.S. President's Advisory Committee, *National Highway Program*.

21. As chief counsel to the Senate Rackets Committee (the Select Committee on Improper Activities in Labor and Management), Robert F. Kennedy grilled Beck about Teamster funds. Beck took the Fifth Amendment 117 times. After serving thirty months in prison on income-tax and other charges, Beck received pardons from Washington's governor and President Gerald Ford. He made a fortune thereafter by investing in real estate, especially parking lots, in his hometown of Seattle.

22. Gillespie, *Century of Progress*, 120; McNichol, *Paving the Way*, 216–17; "History."

23. Buchanan's letter and documentation are in Asphalt Institute, Staff Files, box 5, Bragdon Records, DDE.

24. John S. Bragdon to A. K. Branham, November 24, 1959; "Excessive Costs in the Federal-Aid Highway Program," memo, October 21, 1959; Bragdon to Study Group II and IV, October 3, 1959; Branham to Bragdon, September 23, 1959, all in Asphalt Institute, Staff Files, box 5, Bragdon Records, DDE.

25. Bragdon to Dwight Eisenhower, June 17, 1959, Highway Review Program, Directive of the President, Staff Files, box 41, Bragdon Records, DDE; memo for the record, April 8, 1960 Staff Notes, April 1960, Diary Series, box 49, DDE.

26. DiMento, "Stent (or Dagger?)"; Semuels, "Role of Highways." See also DiMento and Ellis, *Changing Lanes.*

27. Rose and Mohl, *Interstate Highway Politics,* 104, 108; Mohl, "Race and Space," 100–158.

28. Qtd. in Rose and Mohl, *Interstate Highway Politics,* 104.

29. For Booker, see his oral history, July 24, 1970, HU. For socioeconomic aspects of transportation policy, see Bullard, Johnson, and Torres, *Highway Robbery.* For a broader perspective, see Zimring, *Clean and White.* Halting interstate projects was difficult but not impossible. See Crockett, *People before Highways.*

30. See Weingroff, "Greatest Decade," for all quotations in this paragraph. The federal gas tax began in 1933 at 1.0 cent a gallon. Today it is 18.4 cents a gallon. State gas taxes range from 14.7 to 58.7 cents a gallon.

31. Weingroff, "Greatest Decade."

32. Committee of the Whole House, *Defense Highway Needs,* 51; "Highway Funds Authorized." See also Records of the Special Subcommittees on the Federal-Aid Highway Program, 86th–90th Cong. (1961–68), NA. Another missile and asphalt plan that was never implemented: the Pentagon hoped to build a Multiple Protective Structure with three hundred missiles and thousands of decoys moving around dozens of hardened "'racetracks,' each about 45 km in circumference." Construction would have required at least 250 million gallons of liquid asphalt. Miller, *Cold War,* 106.

33. Russell Baker, "One of Our States Is Missing," *New York Times,* May 11, 1988.

34. Even numbered two-digit interstates run east and west; odd numbered two-digit interstates run north and south.

35. J. M. Forbes, director, Bureau of Mines, to Frank C. Turner, October 28, 1954, Subject File: Committee Business (2), box 1, NHP.

36. U.S. Senate Committee, *Hearings on Effects.* See also Merlin and Gonzalez, "Environmental Impacts," 167–202; "Loss-of-Use Damages."

37. Later Kwajalein Island, the largest island in the atoll, hosted the Ronald Reagan Test Site for the Strategic Defense Initiative (SDI), a research project to develop, among other things, kinetic-energy weapons launched from orbiting platforms with a mission to destroy incoming Soviet ICBMs. The asphalt plant kept running

while s d i scientists and mathematicians burned through $30 billion but failed to produce a missile defense. Today Kwajalein Island remains a base for other high-tech and expensive defense projects. The island's airport, with a blacktop runway only nine feet above sea level, faces the threat of rising seas. Regardless of location, the Department of Defense has concluded that climate change threatens blacktop roads, lots, and runways at more than 3,500 military installations. "Climate Related Risk."

38. Maclellan, *Grappling with the Bomb*, 275.
39. Danielsson, "Poisoned Pacific." When the Algerian war began in 1954, the French lay blacktop to counter the nationalist habit of digging up paving stones and constructing barricades with them. A century earlier, as noted, the French had done the same in Paris to prevent barricade construction.
40. Layden, "Artificial Turf"; Michael Brick, "Football's Turf Wars," *Houston Chronicle*, January 6, 2016.
41. "Game On." When S. T. Bunn entered the asphalt business in the 1930s, Alabama certainly needed paved roads. Valerian Osinskii, a Soviet good-roads booster, described them as "Russian squared, worse than in remote parts of Tambov Province." Siegelbaum, *Cars for Comrades*, 131. By the 1980s the Bunn family was active in the booster club for the University of Alabama football team (which played on AstroTurf from 1968 to 1991). A tragic death darkened 2017, when a university student hanged herself after accusing a Bunn family member of rape (see Stephanie Taylor, "Files Detail Investigation into Megan Rondini Case," *USA Today*, updated July 2, 2019, https://stories.usatodaynetwork.com /investigativefiles/).
42. Mallozzi, *Asphalt Gods*; Wheelock and Hartmann, "Midnight Basketball"; "Game Over," *Chicago Reporter*, September 18, 2007, www.chicagoreporter.com/game -over-hoops-disappear-school-playgrounds/.
43. Mick Dumke and Kevin Warwick, "Basketball Controversies," *Chicago Reader*, April 15, 2016; Michael Gill, "Where Hoop Dreams Die," *Cleveland Scene*, June 30, 2010, www.clevescene.com/cleveland/where-hoop-dreams-die/Content?oid =1939861.
44. The blacktop story extends beyond football and basketball to baseball, as city kids played hardball on asphalt playgrounds and stickball in the streets (more so in the mid-twentieth century than today). None of this is strictly Americana. Pelé began his soccer run as a child kicking rag-stuffed socks on São Paulo's dirt roads and pitted blacktop streets.
45. "Augusta National Accepts First Black," *Los Angeles Times*, September 11, 1990; Jonker, "Reconciliation with the Dead," 103–4.
46. Honey, *Black Workers Remember*, 57, 81; *City of Parma*, 494 F. Supp. 1049.

47. Parker, *Covert Ops*, 229; Leary, "CIA Air Operations"; Pfeiffer, *Official History*, vol. 1, pt. 1, p. 156; vol. 2, pt. 1, pp. 10–11; McCoy *Politics of Heroin*, 290.

48. Leeker, "Air America."

49. Traas, *Engineers at War*, 398–99; Tregaskis, *Southeast Asia*, 21, 66; Bob Cutts, "Cut the Stem and the Flower Dies," *Stars and Stripes*, December 7, 1968. As part of the Da Nang Airport Remediation Project in 2012, a Pasadena-based contractor, Tetra Tech, treated over one hundred thousand cubic yards of soil, contaminated by the dioxin in Agent Orange, and then used the soil as fill for airport projects. Today blacktop covers much of that fill.

50. Traas, *Engineers at War*, 123, 211.

51. Blazich, "April to July."

52. B. Grant, "51st Asphalt Platoon."

53. Traas, *Engineers at War*, esp. 27, 72, 123, 132, 154, 211, 256, 420, 488, 419, 441; Tregaskis, *Southeast Asia*, 421. See also Lt. Gen. Carroll H. Dunn's *Base Development*. Dunn served as the first director of construction and logistics for the Military Assistance Command in Vietnam.

54. Ploger, *U.S. Army Engineers*, 117, 119; Tregaskis, *Southeast Asia*, 409, 412–14.

55. Shellenbarger, *9th Engineer Battalion*, 120; Traas, *Engineers at War*, 333, 461; J. Carter, *Inventing Vietnam*, 202; Appy, *American Reckoning*, 107; Tregaskis, *Southeast Asia*, 42; "Ronald Reagan Interview," *Fresno Bee*, October 10, 1965.

56. "Bert Perkins Bosses $1-Billion Job in Vietnam," *Engineering News-Record*, April 20, 1967, 58–62.

57. Caro, *Years of Lyndon Johnson*, 371–73.

58. J. Carter, *Inventing Vietnam*, 181, 200–203. Later, when serving as secretary of defense during the Second Gulf War, Rumsfeld showed no concern with Vice President Dick Cheney's recent stint as Halliburton CEO or the bloated reconstruction contracts granted Haliburton in Iraq.

59. *Public Papers*, 2:1017.

60. White House tapes, April 25, 1973, RN; Maddow, "Turn It Off." See also Whitcover, *Very Strange Bedfellows*.

61. Virginia Ellis, "Tax Board Says No to Agnew's Bid for Refund," *Los Angeles Times*, April 7, 1989. For "bad stuff," see Whitcover, *Very Strange Bedfellows*, 295–96. For Agnew's take, see his *Go Quietly*. The FBI's Agnew file is available at the bureau's electronic reading room; see "Spiro Agnew."

62. New York State, *Final Report*, 26, 144–45; Feldman and Benjamin, *Sausage Factory*, 116; Feldman and Eichenthal, *Art of the Watchdog*, 128–31.

63. Kennett Love, "Royalists Oust Mossadegh; Army Seizes Helm," *New York Times*, August 20, 1953.

64. *Iran-Contra Matters*, 159–72.

65. Jesus Sanchez, "Castellucci Set to Take Over Edgington Oil Co," *Los Angeles Times* September 1, 1988; Donald Woutat, "Khashoggi's Pet Cash Cow Happy Milking Is Over," *Los Angeles Times*, October 3, 1988. See also Kessler, *Richest Man*.

66. Hoffman, *Billion Dollar Spy*, 43–48; Peterson, *Widow Spy*. A photograph of the CIA "equipment"—the hollowed-out asphalt chunk—is at Goldmanis, "TRIGON Numbers Station."

67. Taubman, *Khrushchev*, 213; Nemtsova, "Ukraine Tears Down."

68. Stoddard and Thomas, *Richmond Cemeteries*, 9–10; Maria Glod, "Slaves' History Buried in Asphalt," *Washington Post*, October 27, 2008; Rachel Solnit, "Across America, Racist and Sexist Monuments Give Way to a New Future," *Guardian*, January 2, 2019; Kevin Waite, "The Largest Confederate Monument in America Can't Be Taken Down," *Washington Post*, August 22, 2017. Asphalt also lies unseen under the copper roofing and green patina of more wholesome structures, including dozens of government buildings in the District of Columbia. Shingles and other asphalt products help waterproof the White House's underground tunnel network and the roofs of the Jefferson Memorial and the Lincoln Memorial. The contractor who did the original waterproofing for the Lincoln Memorial Reflecting Pool used a "bituminous membrane" and "asphalt mastic." Concklin, *Lincoln Memorial*, 52.

69. "1991 Kuwait Oil Fires."

70. McDonnell, *Army Corps of Engineers*, 101–2.

71. McDonnell, *Army Corps of Engineers*, 129.

72. "Seabee History: Operations." Regarding drone facilities abroad: The Seabees brought their own asphalt-batching plant with them for work at Camp Simba in Manda Bay, Kenya. A drone base in Agadez, Niger, budgeted $10 million for asphalt. John Vandiver, "Building a Base from Nothing," *Stars and Stripes*, April 24, 2018; John Reed, "Seabees to Build New Runway in Kenya," *Stars and Stripes*, December 28, 2011.

73. Joseph Giordono, "U.S. Troops Revisit Scene of Deadly Gulf War Barrage," *Stars and Stripes*, February 23, 2003; McDonnell, *After Desert Storm*, 133–35. Another asphalt road leading out of Kuwait City, Highway 8, emerged as a second Highway of Death, with more military vehicles than civilian vehicles spread out over more miles of blacktop.

74. This was neither the first nor the last time. Tanks moved down Pennsylvania Avenue blacktop to celebrate English royals (1939); presidential inaugurations of Harry Truman (1949), Dwight Eisenhower (1953 and 1957), and John Kennedy (1961); and the Fourth of July (2019).

75. Mark Fineman, "Surprises Greet Southland Marines in Mogadishu," *Los Angeles Times*, December 12, 1992.

76. "Maintaining Camps."

77. *U.S. Army's Role.*

78. "Testimony."

79. U.S. Department of Defense, *Base Structure Report*. The report does not mention several hundred additional bases considered secret. Presumably, nearly all of those have asphalt roads, lots, or other linear structures beyond the ones listed in the official *Base Structure Report*.

80. Bloom, *Kerouac's "On the Road,"* 174.

7. ANGLES

1. Diane Hendricks, "Government Needs to Get Out of the Way of Business," *USA Today*, November 3, 2010; Choma, "Four Years Ago." This last article includes a link to a video of the Walker-Hendricks conversation.

2. Cary Spivak, "Beloit Billionaire Posts String of Zeros on State Returns," *Milwaukee Journal Sentinel*, June 9, 2016; Murphy, "Mistakes Made."

3. Brian Lavery, "Building Materials Company Ireland Loves to Hate," *New York Times*, September 5, 2002; "Upset over Ansbacher Links," *Irish Times*, March 1, 2000; Tribunal of Inquiry, *Report*.

4. Rappaport, "Israel's Separation Fence"; for Trump's quotation, see "Cable Exclusive."

5. Davan Maharaj, "Israel's Blockade in West Bank Tightens Vise on Palestinians," *Los Angeles Times*, March 12, 2001.

6. "The Investigation of the New York State Highway Work," *Engineering News*, December 4, 1913, 1142.

7. Petroski, *Road Taken*, 215.

8. "Global Construction Sector"; "Corruption Challenges Index." See "Bribe Payers Index" for the years 1999, 2002, 2006, 2008, and 2011.

9. Collier and Hoeffer, "Economic Costs," 12–13.

10. "Curbing Fraud," vii–x, 8–9, 17.

11. *Palumbo Brothers*, 742 F. 2d 656; Matt O'Connor, "'Silver Shovel' Investigation Goes Out with a Wimper," *Chicago Tribune*, January 27, 2001.

12. *Blagojevich*, 662 F. Supp. 2d 998; Tim Novak and Steve Warmbir, "Hired Trucks Thrive in Daley's Ward," *Chicago Sun-Times*, January 26, 2004; John Kass, "Hired Truck's Bridgeport Ties Start to Add Up," *Chicago Tribune*, October 10, 2004; Matt O'Connor, "Former Hired Truck Boss Gets 2-Year Term for Bribes," *Chicago Tribune*, August 3, 2005.

13. Bernard Schoenburg, "Asphalt Pavement Group to Discuss Cellini's Status," *Springfield State Journal-Register*, November 3, 2011; *Cellini*, 596 F. Supp. 2d 1194; Natasha Korecki, "Timeline: 'Operation Board Games,'" *Chicago Sun-Times*,

October 15, 2008. Cellini visited the Oval Office at least once. "President's Daily Diary," 1974–77, March 5, 1976, box 80, GF.

14. "Iran Executes Trader Dubbed 'Sultan of Bitumen' in Anti-corruption Drive," *Times of Israel*, December 22, 2018; Adam Taylor, "Is Vladimir Putin Hiding a $20 Billion Fortune?," *Washington Post*, February 20, 2015; Raspopova, "Putin Made a Road." For Charbonneau, see Quebec Commission, *Final Report*.

15. In effect, Operation Car Wash was a circular scandal, as it also ensnared several federal prosecutors.

16. Tristan Hallman, "A $209 Million Contract, a Felon, and a Mess at Dallas City Hall," *Dallas News*, May 2016, www.dallasnews.com/news/dallas-city-hall/2016 /05/25/a-209-million-contract-a-felon-and-a-mess-at-dallas-city-hall. For the fine, see the press release (with links to the plea agreements): "Odebrecht and Braskem." The Transoceanic Highway is not to be confused with Brazil's Trans-Amazonian Highway, a 2,500-mile mix of blacktop and dirt track. Nearly all deforestation in the region occurs within four miles of a road. Fraser, "Carving Up the Amazon."

17. Mark Morri, "Gypsy Clans in NSW," *Sydney Daily Telegraph*, August 29, 2011.

18. Wagar, "Two Men Investigated." England's largest Traveler encampment, Dale Farm in Essex, sparked a protracted (2001–11) eviction battle that the Travelers lost. In 2017, however, Traveler bands spread six hundred tons of asphalt on other green-belt lands in Essex creating what the British press called Dale Farm II.

19. Rothschild and Block, "Don't Steal," 45–56. For data on seizures, see "Asset Forfeiture Management Staff" and the ACLU's reports: "Asset Forfeiture Abuse." For the law, see Edgeworth, *Asset Forfeiture*.

20. Palantir Technologies, a data-mining firm, built both systems.

21. For Black Asphalt, see Michael Sallah et al., "Stop and Seize," *Washington Post*, September 6, 2014; and Radley Balko, "New Frontiers in Asset Forfeiture," *Washington Post*, June 8, 2016.

22. *Timbs*, 139 S. Ct. 682.

23. "It's the End of the Road [. . .]," *Chicago Tribune*, August 23, 2012. In 2015 Hastert pleaded to lesser charges as the statute of limitations had run out. The judge called him a serial child molester. See "Hastert's Sentencing Memorandum."

24. For Shuster's story, see Pianin and Babcock, "Easy Street." See also these *Washington Post* articles: Roberto Suro and Eric Pianin, "Federal Probe Targets Shuster," September 10, 1997; Eric Pianin, "Shuster Calls Probe 'Baloney,'" September 11, 1997; Pianin, "A Mover on the Hill," September 16, 1997; John E. Yang, "House Begins Investigating Rep. Shuster," November 15, 1997; Charles R. Babcock, "Lobbyist Tied to Shuster Is Indicted," March 7, 1998; Charles R. Babcock and Eric Pianin, "Ex-Aide to Shuster Indicted," April 10, 1998; Juliet Eilperin, "Eppard Left

Tracks in Highway Bill," April 11, 1998; Anik Jesdanun, "Shuster Not Targeted in Probe, Lawyer Says," June 10, 1998; and Lorraine Adams, "Lobbyist Prospers as Charges Loom," April 10, 1999.

25. Committee on Standards, *Matter of Representative*, 3D–3J.

26. "New Round."

27. Examples include George P. Shultz (secretary of labor, OMB director, and secretary of the treasury under Nixon and secretary of state under Reagan); Caspar W. Weinberger (FTC chair, OMB director, and HEW secretary under Nixon and secretary of defense under Reagan until ensnared in Iran-Contra); and Richard Helms (CIA director under Lyndon Johnson and Nixon until dismissed and then ambassador to Iran under Nixon and Gerald Ford before pleading no contest to a charge of lying to Congress).

28. Ackley, "K Street Files." Bill Shuster retired from Congress in January 2018 and joined the law firm of Squire Patton Boggs, the nation's third-largest lobby shop.

29. Coll, *Bin Ladens*, 54–57; L. Wright, *Looming Tower*, 66.

30. Steeds, "Highway 15"; Charles M. Sennott, "Why bin Laden Plot Relied on Saudi Hijackers," *Boston Globe*, March 3, 2002. Another example of asphalt's duality: blacktop helped bin Laden recruit in Saudi Arabia, but its absence elsewhere might have meant a fertile ground for recruiting terrorists. Koseli, "Terrorism Relationship," 115–17.

31. David W. Dunlap, "Search for Remains Will Go On beneath an Asphalt Lot," *New York Times*, February 1, 2007.

32. Asphalt tankers are risky for reasons such as this: pirates can mistake them for oil tankers. In 2010 Somalian pirates captured the *Asphalt Venture* and held its crew captive for nearly four years.

33. "Competition Issues."

34. Margot Patrick, "Jet-Set Debt Collectors Join a Lucrative Game," *Wall Street Journal*, November 7, 2017; *Hall*, 18-80748-Civ.

35. Jeff Ostrowski, "Billionaire's Boca-Raton Based Asphalt Company Files for Chapter 11 Bankruptcy," *Palm Beach Post*, December 3, 2013; Jane Musgrave, "Web of 14 Lawsuits Settled Stemming from Sargeant Family Fight," *Palm Beach Post*, May 2, 2015.

36. Izzy Kapnick, "Mogul Accuses Brother of Snatching Business Docs, 'Intimate Videos,'" *Courthouse News*, June 26, 2018, www.courthousenews.com/mogul-accuses-brother-of-snatching-business-docs-intimate-videos/; "Statement by Harry Sargeant III." In 2020 Sargeant Marine paid a $16.6 million fine.

37. "Inaccurate Media Reports"; House Intelligence Committee et al., "Deposition," 40, 59, 205–6.

38. Kubic, *Bridges to Baghdad*, 274–76; Folsom, *Highway War*, 123, 146; Badkhen, "War Zone"; Badkhen, "Life in Iraq."

39. "Transcript"; Bush, *Decision Points*, 383; K. Smith, "Longest Road Project."

40. Halliburton dabbles in the asphalt business with such products as BDF-662 shale stabilizer, a synthetic Gilsonite for use in hydraulic fracturing.

41. "Afghanistan's Road Infrastructure." The Iraq inspector general raised similar concerns.

42. Amber Grimm, "Dirty Jobs: Getting Dusty with the Dirt Boyz," *Osan Air Base News*, July 10, 2015, www.osan.af.mil/News/Article-Display/Article/640161/dirty-jobs-getting-dusty-with-the-dirt-boyz/.

43. Pigott, *Canada in Afghanistan*, 127.

44. "Paving the Road."

45. "Qarmat Ali."

46. "Report on Data"; Hickman, *Burn Pits*.

47. For the little-lightning-bolt saga, see Weinberger, "Lightning Gun Company"; and Miles, "Gates, Pace."

48. Rick Atkinson, "There Was a Learning Curve . . . and a Lot of People Died," *Washington Post*, October 1, 2007. See also Atkinson, *Left of Boom*. IED survivors often suffered brain injuries. The father, a marine, twenty, of "two-year-old Krisiauna Calaira Lewis," *New York Times* reporters wrote, "slammed her against a wall when he was recuperating in Texas from a bombing near Fallujah that blew off his foot and shook up his brain." Krisiauna's body went into the ground in Longview, 458 miles of I-20 blacktop from the Bush family home in Midland. Deborah Sontag and Lizette Alvarez, "Across America, Deadly Echoes of Foreign Battles," *New York Times*, January 13, 2008.

49. House Committee on Appropriations, *Making Emergency Supplemental Appropriations*, 188. See also "Afghan Reconstruction." For sundecks, see Zand, "Contract Carnage." In the 1960s the United States and the USSR began paving Afghanistan's dirt and rock roads (or spraying them "with a double bituminous surface treatment"). Grathwol and Moorhus, *Bricks, Sand, and Marble*, 206–17.

50. *Annual Report FY 2008.*

51. "Afghanistan's Road Infrastructure."

52. "Quarterly Report."

53. Hodge, *Armed Humanitarians*, 276, 281.

54. Pan, "Silent Kingmaker," 40.

55. Scott Peterson, "Kansas in Middle East? How U.S. Has—and Hasn't—Changed Afghanistan," *Christian Science Monitor*, December 19, 2019; Kevin Sieff, "After Billions in U.S. Investment, Afghan Roads Are Falling Apart," *Washington Post*, January 30, 2014.

56. "Final Report," 73–75. For Bush, see *Public Papers*, 1:152. For Biden, see Goodhand, "Boundary Wars," 138n39.

57. Alissa J. Rubin and James Risen, "Costly Afghanistan Road Project Is Marred by Unsavory Alliances," *New York Times*, May 1, 2011; Cronin, *Asphalt Ribbon*, iii.

58. Andrew Higgins, "U.S. Ambitions Run into Reality on an Afghan Road," *Wall Street Journal*, February 6, 2004; Troilo and Tyson, "Dark Cloud." For the CEO's guilty plea, see "Former Louis Berger Group." For the Gold Star complaint, see *Cabrera et al.* The Berger Group is now part of WSP, a Canadian company.

59. Jonathan Steele, "Iraq War Logs: Civilians Gunned Down at Checkpoints," *Guardian*, October 22, 2010.

60. Eileen Sullivan, "Found Guilty, Again, in Deadly 2007 Iraq Shooting," *New York Times*, December 19, 2018 (later pardoned by President Trump); Steele, "Iraq War Logs." Wikileaks has posted "The Iraq War Logs"—391,832 reports in all.

61. Brown, *Battleground Iraq*, 56.

62. Sánchez, qtd. in Rhem, "Military Commander."

63. Ted Thornhill, "ISIS Executes Six People by Boiling Them in Tar after Iraqi Sharia Court Accuses the Men of Being Spies," *Daily Mail*, August 15, 2016; Erika Solomon, Robin Kwong, and Steven Bernard, "Syria Oil Map: The Journey of a Barrel of ISIS Oil," *Financial Times*, February 29, 2016, http://ig.ft.com/sites/2015/isis-oil/.

64. Erin Banco, "How ISIS Oil Ended Up on US Streets," *International Business Times*, March 31, 2016, www.ibtimes.com/how-isis-oil-ended-us-streets-2344465. In 2017 Axeon considered closing its Paulsboro, New Jersey, refinery, the nation's largest producer of liquid asphalt.

65. For the president's tweet of April 8, 2017, see Dooley, "Trump Defends Decision."

66. Elliott, "What I Learned Volunteering"; "Rhetoric versus Reality."

67. Diodorus, *Universal History*, bk. 2, line 48.

8. OVERBURDEN

1. "*Exxon Valdez* Oil Spill," 6.

2. For lingering oil updates from the state of Alaska, see "*Exxon Valdez* Oil Spill."

3. As unlikely as it sounds, spontaneous combustion of asphalt roofing mops has caused fires.

4. "Asphalt Removal Project Completed."

5. "National Emission Standards," 6522. A major reason for asphalt's delisting: the industry no longer uses coal tar in paving mixes.

6. "Coal Tar Pitch Volatiles."

7. Gillespie, *Century of Progress*, 16.

8. "Trends of Asphalt." The industry manufacturers the three-tab shingles that dominate residential roofing in North America by impregnating fiberglass mats or organic felt mats with an asphalt-limestone filler and then adding granules.

Mica or a similar substance applied to the underside prevents shingles from sticking to one another before installation, as they are stacked and sold in bundles. Asphalt impregnates another common roofing product, underlay paper, or underlayment, which sells in rolls.

9. New York City, the nation's recycling dynamo, produces over one million tons of new and recycled asphalt annually at its Hamilton Avenue facility in Brooklyn and its Harper Street Yard in Queens. See Sadik-Khan, *Streetfight*.

10. Research is relentless. The Army Corps of Engineers research center is in Vicksburg, Mississippi. Auburn University hosts the National Center for Asphalt Technology. The University of Wisconsin–Madison has a Modified Asphalt Research Center. Dozens of other universities conduct asphalt research, and so does the Federal Highway Administration and oil-industry chemists around the world.

11. "Coal-Tar-Based Pavement"; Brabec, Schulte, and Richards, "Impervious Surfaces"; Frazer, "Paving Paradise." For the Great Lakes, see Baldwin et al., "Primary Sources." In 2017 Hurricane Harvey provided both an extreme example of pollution from storm-water runoff in the greater Houston area and cause for reflection on Houston's pre-blacktop landscape: a "green scum lake, studded with giant sweet gum trees, and water from one to two and a half feet deep." Allen, *City of Houston*. Pavement erodes habitat health from below as well. We do not know how much methane—a more potent greenhouse gas than carbon dioxide—escapes from buried natural-gas pipelines through manhole covers and concrete and blacktop cracks.

12. The car-culture competition between asphalt and concrete spilled over in the twentieth century's last third to parking. Asphalt dominates "horizontal parking." Concrete dominates "vertical parking" in underground and above-grade, open-deck structures.

13. Ben-Joseph, *Rethinking a Lot*, 43; Relph, *Place and Placelessness*, 136. See also Shoup, *High Cost*; and Jakle and Sculle, *Lots of Parking*.

14. In 2013 the University of Leicester discovered, under a parking lot, the remains of a royal immortalized by Shakespeare. Richard III's skeleton showed idiopathic scoliosis and nearly a dozen wounds, as he died in 1485 during the Battle of Bosworth Field. In New York City half a millennium later, the Bard is not under asphalt but on asphalt, not Shakespeare in the Park but Shakespeare in the Parking Lot, "complete with graffiti and cracked asphalt." Having lost use of one Lower East Side lot, the Drilling Company, which puts on the parking-lot plays, moved to a parking lot on Suffolk Street and then moved again to a lot at Ludlow and Broome. Vergano, "DNA Confirms"; Ken Jaworowski, "Review: An 'As You Like It' on Asphalt, from Shakespeare in the Parking Lot," *New York Times*, July 13, 2015.

15. Frazier, *On the Rez*, 40, 51; "Audit Report: Bureau of Public Roads . . . 1955 and 1956," WHCF, OF 2-L, Bureau of Public Roads July 1953–June 1957 (2), box 19, DDE, 52.

16. Kinkela, *American Century*. DDT was dumped via sewage pipe and barge.

17. U.S. Department of Energy, *Environmental Impact Statement*, C-8.

18. "Shaft Sealing Construction Procedures," app. B.

19. "Final Operating Report"; Wilkes and Mann, "Story of Nukey Poo."

20. Hannah Lawrence, "France Finds Traces of Radioactive Material on Imported Mushrooms," *Independent*, December 1, 2017; Myclo, *Wormwood Forest*, 219.

21. Hoffman, Shandas, and Pendleton, "Effects of Historical Housing." The EPA publishes a *Heat Island Reduction Newsletter*. The Lawrence Berkeley National Laboratory has a Heat Island Group.

22. "National September 11 Memorial."

23. Beyond increasing seismic activity and polluting groundwater and the atmosphere, fracking's environmental damage extends to blacktop, given the heavy trucks needed to haul fracking fluid and waste.

24. "Heavy Oil."

25. See, for example, Inter-organization Programme, *Chemical Assessment Document*, 7; and Haug and Pauls, "Non-traditional Dry Covers," 13.

26. "Survey of Energy Resources," 123.

27. Meyer and De Witt, *Definition and World Resources*, 9–10. Federal Energy Administration ruling FE-76-4, upheld by U.S. courts and the IRS since 1976, defines oils sands as hydrocarbon-bearing rocks from which an "extremely viscous hydrocarbon . . . is not recoverable in its natural state by conventional oil well production methods." Speight, *Asphalt*, 26.

28. Mommer, "Extra-Heavy Crude Oil," D1–11.

29. Mommer, "Extra-Heavy Crude Oil," D4; "Form F-20"; Schenk et al., "Recoverable Heavy Oil Resources"; Meyer and De Witt, *Definition and World Resources*, 11; "2010 Survey," 9.

30. Johns, "Love the Way." For the boom town's rise and the first of its several falls, see Turner, *Patch*.

31. "Alcatraz Asphalt"; Ellis, *Bituminous Sands*, 123–24; Gooch, *Mussolini and His Generals*, 80.

32. Shale oil is oil trapped in shale in a liquid state. Oil shale is a fine-grade sedimentary rock containing kerogen. The industry can upgrade kerogen to a synthetic crude oil.

33. For Utah's oil sands, see House Committee on Natural Resources, *Combined Hydrocarbon Leasing*, 1. For health concerns, see Federal Interagency Committee on the Health and Environmental Effects of Energy Technologies, "Health and

Environmental Effects of Synthetic Fuels," 1979, Domestic Policy Staff, Tom Lambrix Subject Files, Synthetic Fuels Corporation, box 79, JC. For resource estimates, see Subcommittee on Energy and Mineral Resources, *Vast North American Resource*, pts. 1–2.

34. Marsden, *Last Drop*, 2–5, 14–24; Chastko, *Developing Alberta's Oil Sands*, 97. For Clark, see also Sheppard, *Oil Sands Scientist*.

35. Dochuk, *Anointed with Oil*, 419–20.

36. Kolbert, "Unconventional Crude," 46–51; Vincent McDermott, "Pending Review, Suncor Could See More Automated Trucks," *Fort McMurray Today*, July 18, 2017.

37. Problems transcend the physical environment. See Clarke et al., *Bitumen Cliff*; Takach, *Tar Wars*; Sweeny, *Black Bonanza*; Black et al., *Line in the Tar*; Taft, *Oil's Deep State*; Nikiforuk, *Tar Sands*; Avery, *Pipeline and the Paradigm*; Pratt, *Tar Sands*; Stahl and Cameron, "Politico-Economic Problems"; and Kellogg, "Political Economy," 139–70 (the original title for this essay was "Boiling Mud: Towards a Comparative Political Economy of Venezuela and Alberta"). The oil sands are only the most recent addition to Canadian mining. See Bélanger, *Extraction Empire*.

38. For the rankings (disputed by the Canadian Association of Petroleum Producers), see "Assessing Global Oils." See also Lattanzio, "Canadian Oil Sands."

39. Orinoco hydrocarbons, in contrast, are "oil wet." The hot-water separation process will not work, as solvents are required to separate the natural asphalt from the solids.

40. Marsh, "Bitumen Extraction," 255; "Composition for Recovering Bitumen." The industry removes some of the residual asphalt, titanium minerals, and zircon sand from the tailings.

41. Wells et al., "Danger in the Nursery." An investigation conducted for the North American Agreement on Environmental Cooperation (between the United States, Mexico, and Canada) concluded that Canada had not adequately enforced laws regarding "discharges of deleterious substances to fish-bearing waters from oil sands tailings ponds." "Alberta Tailings Ponds II."

42. McLachlan, "Living Thing"; Slowey and Stefanick, "Development at What Cost?," 195–224. Not all First Nation communities oppose oil-sands development.

43. Jason Franson, "Desmond Tutu Calls Oil Sands 'Filth' Created by Greed in Fort McMurray Speech," *National Post*, May 31, 2014, https://nationalpost.com/news /canada/desmond-tutu-calls-oilsands-filth-created-by-greed-in-fort-mcmurray -speech.

44. Ramseur, "Oil Sands." The IRS confirmed the exception. See "National Office Technical Advice."

45. The EPA approval of Enbridge's Line 67 expansion came while EPA administrator Scott Pruitt was renting a room for fifty dollars a night in a Capitol Hill condo-

minium owned by the wife of an Enbridge lobbyist. Because he was embroiled in a host of other controversies, Pruitt launched a legal defense fund. Donors included Diane Hendricks, the billionaire Beloit roofer. Pruitt resigned on July 5, 2018.

46. Dan Egan, "Greasing Oil's Path," *Milwaukee Journal Sentinel*, November 9, 2017.

47. Black and Grant, "On the Front Lines"; Stockman, "Petroleum Coke"; Fishman, "Mountains of Trouble"; Ian Austen, "A Black Mound of Canadian Oil Waste Is Rising over Detroit," *New York Times*, May 17, 2013.

48. Keith Matheny, "Line 5 Oil Pipeline in Straits of Mackinac Dented by Ship," *Detroit Free Press*, April 11, 2018; Matheny, "Enbridge Pipes Political Money to Chamber's Effort to Fight Ballot Initiatives," *Detroit Free Press*, May 7, 2018; Matheny, "Tunnel Could Replace Straits of Mackinac Underwater Pipelines," *Detroit Free Press*, June 15, 2018; Schwab, "Statistical Analysis"; "State's Statement"; Dan Egan, "Opening a Wisconsin Spigot?," *Milwaukee Journal Sentinel*, November 9, 2017. Fusion-bonded epoxy dominates the pipeline-coating industry. From the 1940s through the 1960s, however, asphalt and coal-tar enamel dominated.

49. The industry counters with a U.S. Transportation Research Board finding that dilbit is not particularly corrosive. TRB *Special Rept. 311.*

50. National Academies, *Spills of Diluted Bitumen*; Royal Society of Canada, *Behavior and Environmental Impacts*, 321–26. For the EPA on the Kalamazoo spill, see "EPA Response." Another major dilbit spill occurred in 2013, when a seam on ExxonMobil's Pegasus pipeline broke and spread 210,000 gallons on residential streets in Mayflower, Arkansas.

51. Egan, "Greasing Oil's Path"; Egan, "Opening a Wisconsin Spigot?"; Winona LaDuke, "The Largest Inland Oil Spill in U.S. History Happened Today in Minnesota," *Indian Country Today*, March 3, 2017.

52. For the spill data, compiled by 350.org from Enbridge postings, see "Enbridge Major Spills," 5.

53. Klein, *This Changes Everything*, 312; Bellefontaine, "Alberta Premier Announces." Additional demonstrations took place in Europe, beginning in 2014, with the arrival of the first six hundred thousand barrels of dilbit at the port of Bilbao, Spain.

54. Murphy, "Trans Mountain."

55. John Ivison, "Trudeau Said He'd Solve Pipeline Stalemate Problem: It's Become a Political Disaster," *National Post*, August 30, 2018, https://nationalpost.com /opinion/john-ivison-on-justin-trudeaus-trans-mountain-pipeline-stalemate.

56. Regardless, the Koch-funded Seminar Network and other groups claimed a role in securing the presidential permit. The assault on California's greenhouse-gas and fuel-economy standards began in the oil sands and not in Trump's Oval Office. A $22 million contract, awarded in 2014 by Natural Resources Canada, pitched Keystone XL with a "direct message to the American public." In 2017 Exxon character-

ized a lawsuit brought by three California counties and four cities as an attempt to impose a "uniform perspective on climate change"—part of a broader plot "hatched . . . at a conference of special interests in La Jolla, California." For that conference, see "Establishing Accountability." For the filing, see "Exxon Mobile Corporation." Exxon makes repeated reference to "the La Jolla playbook."

57. Farmers are withdrawing water faster than nature can replace it. Opie, Miller, and Archer, *Ogallala*.

58. McKibben, "Coronavirus Pandemic"; Executive Order 13990, January 20, 2021.

59. Climate Files has posted the Shell report; see "Greenhouse Effect." See also the documents at "Shell Document Index." Climate Files has also posted this Johnson administration document: "Restoring the Quality."

60. McKibben, "What Exxon Did." See also Rich, *Losing Earth*.

61. "Remarks by President Trump." The administration's formal policy document included a section titled "Embrace Energy Dominance." Various Trump-era Department of Energy officials use words like "molecules of U.S. freedom" when referring to fossil fuels. Regardless, even with Trump in the Oval Office, the Department of Defense considered global warming to be a serious threat to blacktop runways, roads, parking lots, and other infrastructure. Office of the Under Secretary, "Climate-Related Risk."

62. Heated tank cars reduce the amount of diluent and thus reduce the risk of explosion—so do tank-car standards mandated after the Lac-Mégantic tragedy. But leaks remain a problem. Fourteen of the thirty-two new DOT-117R tank cars that derailed in 2018 near Doon, Iowa, leaked 230,000 gallons of dilbit into Rock River floodwaters. Thomas, "Bitumen Isn't Necessarily Safer." In 2017 the Trump administration rescinded an Obama-era regulation requiring, by 2021, electronically controlled pneumatic braking systems on trains carrying Bakken crude and Alberta dilbit.

63. *Energy Transfer Equity et al.*, order, February 14, 2019, 8.

64. *Energy Transfer Equity et al.*, complaint, August 22, 2017, 1, 9. The Climate Change Litigation Database has posted all the filings and motions in this lawsuit. The database is a joint project of the law firm Arnold and Porter and the Sabin Center for Climate Change Law, Columbia University.

65. Brown, Parish, and Speri, "Leaked Documents."

66. Jack Healy, "Occupying the Prairie," *New York Times*, August 23, 2016. See also Michels, "These Stunning Photos"; and Estes, *History Is the Future*.

67. Bloomberg Law has posted this ruling; see *Standing Rock Sioux*. On July 6, 2020—the same day TC Energy and Keystone XL suffered a setback—a federal judge ordered the Dakota Access Pipeline shut down pending further environmental review. However, the U.S. Court of Appeals for the District of Columbia quickly overturned that order.

68. On June 3, 2019, the Trump administration submitted a legislative proposal calling for a penalty of up to twenty years in prison for pipeline protestors who block or otherwise disrupt the construction of interstate pipelines. The International Center for Not-for-Profit Law has a "US Protest Law Tracker."

69. Dickinson, "Koch Brothers' Toxic Empire"; Richard Mial, "Refinery Takes Canadian Oil and Turns It into Gasoline," *La Crosse Tribune*, March 8, 2010; David Shaffer, "Flint Hills Resources Plant Plans $750 Million in Capital Investment at Its Minnesota Refinery," *Minneapolis Star Tribune*, February 4, 2016. For "garbage crudes," see *William Koch et al.*, 969 Fed. Supp. 1460 at 41.

70. Sassoon, "Koch Brothers' Political Activism."

71. Mayer, *Dark Money*, 27–31.

72. Sassoon, "Koch Brothers' Political Activism."

73. Geoffrey Morgan, "'Unloved': Despite the Oil Sands' Relentless Cost Cutting, Investors Are Still Warry of Jumping Back In," *Financial Post*, August 6, 2019, https://business.financialpost.com/commodities/energy/unloved-despite-oilsands-relentless-cost-cutting-investors-still-wary-of-jumping-back-in.

74. "CNRL Catapults." The big investment banks were also moving away from oil-sand investments, though the move slowed with Trump's 2016 election.

75. "Toxic 100 Air Polluters"; "Toxic 100 Water Polluters." Koch Industries numbers improved, comparatively, for 2017: ranking as the seventeenth worst greenhouse-gas polluter and the thirteenth worst water polluter. For the brothers' political activism, see Mayer, *Dark Money*; Leonard, *Kochland*.

76. Munzenrieder, "Jetsetter Donald Trump."

77. "DeFazio." Before proposing that additional $500 billion, President Trump disbanded the National Infrastructure Advisory Council.

78. "Maths of Construction."

79. See Mueller, *Report on the Investigation*, 1:110–20; Senate Select Committee, *Russian Active Measures Campaigns*, 5:259–463. The Trump campaign wanted derogatory information on Hillary Clinton. The Russians wanted relief from U.S. sanctions imposed by the Magnitsky Act of 2012, a law named after a Moscow law-firm auditor who exposed a tax-fraud scheme and was subsequently jailed, tortured, and murdered.

80. Mueller, *Report on the Investigation*, 1:131–43. For Deripaska's response, see "It's All a Lie."

81. Davidson, "Donald Trump's Worst Deal"; Weiss, "Corleones of the Caspian."

82. Jacqueline Palank, "Trump Golf Club in Puerto Rico Files for Bankruptcy," *Wall Street Journal*, July 13, 2015; "Empresas Díaz Inc."; Weider and Hall, "Ex–Puerto Rico Partner."

83. Ted Mann and Brody Mullins, "Transportation Secretary Still Owns Stock She Pledged to Divest," *Wall Street Journal*, May 28, 2019.

84. Molly Hennessy-Fiske, "Trump Says Barbed Wire 'Can Be a Beautiful Sight,'" *Los Angeles Times*, March 24, 2019.

85. "BTC Barbed Tape Concertina."

86. Thomas Watkins, "San Diego Officials Mark Completion of Border Berm," *San Diego Union-Tribune*, July 6, 2009; Reese, "Border Fence."

87. Barbara Zaragoza, "Border Construction May Cause Flooding in Poor Tijuana Neighborhoods," *San Diego Free Press*, January 13, 2016; Bosque, "Trump's Border Wall"; Sadasivam, "Texas-Mexico Border Wall." Manned floodgates in populated areas are now common, and they prevent damage. But in remote areas the floodgates are episodically monitored and left open in summer (because opening and closing the gates requires work crews and forklifts). These floodgates are wide enough for undocumented immigrants and smugglers to pass through along with water and debris.

88. Aristotle, qtd. in Forbes, *Bitumen and Petroleum*, 29; Diodorus, *Universal History*, bk. 2, line 48; Franson, "Desmond Tutu."

89. An example: On April 26, 2018, a fluid catalytic-cracking–unit explosion at the Husky Superior Refinery in Superior, Wisconsin, sent a single piece of debris through the side of an asphalt storage tank some two hundred feet away, releasing fifteen thousand barrels of asphalt into the refinery. After two hours the fire from the explosion heated the asphalt to the point where it ignited. That fire, in the understated words of the U.S. Chemical Safety and Hazard Investigation Board, a federal agency, was "large." See "Factual Investigative Update."

CONCLUSION

1. While serving a sentence for armed robbery at Attica Correctional Facility in upstate New York in the 1970s, Brown changed his name to Jamil Abdullah Al-Amin. A quarter century later he received a life sentence for shooting two sheriff's deputies in Fulton County, Georgia. One of the deputies died. This has led some commentators to characterize the violence-and-cherry-pie words as a self-fulfilling prophecy.

2. Cobb, "Anger in Ferguson"; David Hunn and Kim Bell, "Why Was Michael Brown's Body Left There for Hours?," *St. Louis Post-Dispatch*, September 14, 2014. Stacey Koon, the Los Angeles Police Department sergeant on the scene of the Rodney King beating, said King's injuries were "due to contact with asphalt." Richard A. Serrano, "Police Documents Disclose Beating Was Downplayed," *Los Angeles Times*, March 20, 1991.

3. Rachel Pacella, "Jury Awards $1.26 Million," *Capital Gazette*, May 10, 2017; Jessica Lussenhop, "Michael Brown's Family Had the Section of the Road Where He Died Removed," *River Front Times*, May 22, 2015.

4. "Investigation of the Ferguson Police Department," 54–61. For a broader survey, see U.S. Commission on Civil Rights, *Targeted Fines*.

5. Pinckney, "Black Lives," 68.

6. "Investigation of the Chicago Police Department," 25–26.

7. Giovannini, "Owning the Asphalt"; Pierce, "Republicans." Joseph Giovannini, an architect and critic, concluded that "asphalt matter[ed] more than [President Trump's fiery] Twitter [account] . . . [because] the public used the wall-less open streets as a fortress of democracy, and . . . a sound stage that bumped Trump off the air. . . . Taking the streets was a way to take back the country. Asphalt has proved the soil of democracy." Those police who disagreed welcomed the presence of self-professed militia who promised to help restore order and protect property. In Kenosha, Wisconsin, three months after the George Floyd killing, a police officer left Jacob Blake paralyzed from the waist down after shooting him seven times in the back, as he tried to enter his car, with his children in the car. Peaceful BLM demonstrations by day again gave way to looting and arson by night that damaged or destroyed dozens of Kenosha businesses. Police not only treated blacktop vigilantes on scene as allies. They allowed one of them, seventeen and not yet old enough to own or carry a firearm legally, to walk around with a long gun and walk away after killing two demonstrators and wounding a third. He was arrested the next day in Antioch, Illinois, where he lived with his mother and worked as a YMCA lifeguard.

8. Horváth et al., "Polarized Light Pollution"; Sánchez-Bayo and Wyckhuys, "Worldwide Decline." Because pollination is necessary for our food supply, the Fish and Wildlife Service has created corridors for migrating butterflies (most notably, one along I-35's 1,500 miles of asphalt and concrete).

9. Seiler and Helldin, "Mortality in Wildlife," 166–68; Knutson, *Flattened Fauna*; Loss, Will, and Marra, "Bird-Vehicle Collision Mortality." Bridges, underpasses, and other wildlife crossings in dozens of nations have scarcely slowed the carnage.

10. "Race and Ethnicity," 1.

11. Greg Hinz, "Invoking the Specter of Nazi Germany, Obama Warns against Complacency," *Chicago Business*, December 6, 2017; Holland, "Liberia's Fight."

12. Kupferschmidt, "Hunting for Ebola."

13. Penn, "Untold Story." For the backpack, see Leovy, *Ghettoside*, 30, 219.

14. *Humberto Leal Garcia*, 564 U.S. 940.

15. M. Hodges, "Earth's Backup."

16. Lauren Etter, "Roads to Ruin," *Wall Street Journal*, July 17, 2010.

17. The American Society of Civil Engineers issues an annual infrastructure report card.

18. Laing, "Ex-marine Turned Street Warrior"; Jeffrey Ball, "Highway Lobby Cites Threat of Terror in Push for Asphalt," *Wall Street Journal*, March 27, 2003.

19. Schmitt, "Meet Jerry Wray."

20. Schmitt, "Oklahoma's Gary Ridley."

21. "U.S. Towboat."

22. Hindle, *Nine Miles*.

23. Dellinger, *Interstate 69*, 289–93. For the Gohmann fines and restitution, see U.S. Attorney, press release.

24. Governor Daniels, formerly Office of Management and Budget director in the George W. Bush administration, had a P3 adventure too. In 2006 he presided over the seventy-five-year leasing of the Indiana Toll Road's 156 miles to a foreign consortium. In 2014 Mike Pence approved yet another foreign firm as the operator.

25. Stockman, "Petroleum Coke."

26. Jones, *Language of the Genes*, 248.

BIBLIOGRAPHY

ARCHIVES AND MANUSCRIPT MATERIALS

CF. Cochrane Family Papers, David M. Rubenstein Rare Book and Manuscript Library, Duke University, Durham NC.

DDE. Dwight D. Eisenhower Papers, Dwight D. Eisenhower Presidential Library, Abilene KS.

ERS. Eli Ransome Sutton Papers, Bentley Historical Library, University of Michigan, Ann Arbor.

FDR. Franklin D. Roosevelt Papers, Franklin D. Roosevelt Presidential Library, Hyde Park NY.

GF. Gerald Ford Papers, Gerald Ford Presidential Library, Ann Arbor MI.

HH. Herbert Hoover Papers, Herbert Hoover Presidential Library, West Branch IA.

HJK. Henry J. Kaiser Papers, Bancroft Library, University of California, Berkeley.

HST. Harry S. Truman Papers, Harry S. Truman Presidential Library, Independence MO.

HU. Moorland-Spingarn Research Center, Howard University, Washington DC.

JC. Jimmy Carter Papers, Jimmy Carter Presidential Library, Atlanta.

JI. John Ihlder Papers, Franklin D. Roosevelt Presidential Library, Hyde Park NY.

NA. Center for Legislative Archives, National Archives, Washington DC.

NHP. President's Advisory Committee on a National Highway Program Records, Dwight D. Eisenhower Presidential Library, Abilene KS.

RN. Richard Nixon Presidential Library, Yorba Linda CA.

SW. Sinclair Weeks Papers, Rauner Special Collections Library, Dartmouth University, Hanover NH.

WWA. William Woods Averell Papers, Manuscripts and Special Collections, New York State Library, Albany.

PUBLISHED WORKS

"1991 Kuwait Oil Fires." Goddard Space Flight Center, NASA. March 21, 2003. www .nasa.gov/centers/goddard/news/topstory/2003/0321kuwaitfire.html.

"2010 Survey of Energy Resources." World Energy Council. 2012. www.worldenergy .org/assets/downloads/ser_2010_report_1.pdf.

"The 2018 Annual Homeless Assessment Report (AHAR) to Congress." Pt. 1. U.S. Department of Housing and Urban Development. December 2018. https://files .hudexchange.info/resources/documents/2018-AHAR-Part-1.pdf.

Abraham, Herbert. *Asphalts and Allied Substances.* 4th ed. New York: Van Nostrand, 1938.

Ackley, Kate. "K Street Files: Rubino Lands at Airline Lobby." *Roll Call.* March 1, 2012. www.rollcall.com/news/k_street_files_rubino_lands_at_airline_lobby-212787-1.html.

Adams, Stephen B. *Mr. Kaiser Goes to Washington.* Chapel Hill: University of North Carolina Press, 1997.

"Afghanistan's Road Infrastructure." Special Inspector General for Afghanistan Reconstruction. October 2016. www.sigar.mil/pdf/audits/sigar-17-11-ar.pdf.

"Afghan Reconstruction: Progress Made in Constructing Roads, but Assessments for Determining Impact and a Sustainable Maintenance Program Are Needed." U.S. Government Accountability Office. 2008. www.gao.gov/products/gao-08-689.

Agnew, Spiro T. *Go Quietly . . . or Else.* New York: Morrow, 1980.

Agricola, Georgius. *De re metallica.* Translated by Herbert Hoover and Lou Henry Hoover. 1556. Reprint, New York: Dover, 1950.

"Akkadian Cuneiform Tablet." New York Metropolitan Museum of Art. ca. 2350–2150 BCE. www.metmuseum.org/art/collection/search/321721.

"Alberta Tailings Ponds II: Article 15(1)." Natural Resources Defense Council and Environmental Defence. April 19, 2018. www.cec.org/sites/default/files /submissions/2016_2020/17-1-adv_en.pdf.

"Alcatraz Asphalt." *Engineering Record,* March 23, 1901, 273–74.

Alden, Andrew. "NOAA Expedition Finds Asphalt 'Tar Lillies' in Gulf of Mexico." KQED, Northern California PBS. May 2, 2014. www.kqed.org/science/17114/noaa -expedition-finds-ashphalt-volcanic-tar-lilies-in-gulf-of-mexico#.

Aldersey-Williams, Hugh. *In Search of Sir Thomas Browne.* New York: Norton, 2015.

Allen, O. F. *The City of Houston from Wilderness to Wonder.* Temple TX: Printed by the author, 1936. https://texashistory.unt.edu/ark:/67531/metapth46823/m1/13/.

Anderson, Jack. "The Great Highway Robbery." *Parade,* February 4, 1962, 18–20.

Annual Report FY 2008. Washington DC: Joint Improvised Explosive Device Defeat Organization, U.S. Department of Defense, 2009.

Applebaum, Anne. *Gulag: A History.* New York: Anchor Books, 2004.

Appy, Christian G. *American Reckoning: The Vietnam War and Our National Identity.* New York: Viking, 2015.

Arad, Yitzhak. *Belzec, Sobibór, Treblinka: The Operation Reinhard Death Camps.* Bloomington: Indiana University Press, 1999.

Arnold, Bettina. "'*Arierdämmerung*': Race and Archeology in Nazi Germany." *World Archeology* 38, no. 1 (2006): 8–31.

"Asphalt Removal Project Completed at Fort Pickens Area." National Park Service. March 18, 2017. www.nps.gov/guis/learn/news/asphaltremoval17.htm.

"Assessing Global Oils." Oil-Climate Index. Accessed May 11, 2019. http://oci .carnegieendowment.org/.

"Asset Forfeiture Abuse." American Civil Liberties Union. Accessed July 25, 2019. www.aclu.org/issues/criminal-law-reform/reforming-police/asset-forfeiture -abuse.

"Asset Forfeiture Management Staff." U.S. Department of Justice. Accessed July 25, 2020. www.justice.gov/afp.

Atkinson, Rick. *Left of Boom: The Struggle to Defeat Roadside Bombs*. Washington DC: Washington Post, 2007.

Avery, Samuel. *The Pipeline and the Paradigm: Keystone XL, Tar Sands, and the Battle to Defuse the Carbon Bomb*. Washington DC: Ruka, 2013.

Badkhen, Anna. "Has Life in Iraq Improved?" *Salon*. May 21, 2008. www.salon.com /2008/05/21/services/.

———. "Life in a War Zone: Philly Steaks and Tar Pits." *Salon*. May 3, 2007. http:// blog.sfgate.com/foreigndesk/2007/05/03/life-in-a-war-zone-philly-steaks-and -tar-pits/.

Baehr, Carl. "City Streets: Jefferson Street Became Asphalt Showcase." *Urban Milwaukee*. March 4, 2016. http://urbanmilwaukee.com/2016/03/04/city-streets-jefferson -street-became-asphalt-showcase/.

Baldwin, Austin K., Stephen R. Corsi, Samantha K. Oliver, Peter L. Lenaker, Michelle A. Nott, Marc A. Mills, Gary A. Norris, and Pentti Paatero. "Primary Sources of Polycyclic Aromatic Hydrocarbons to Streambed Sediment in Great Lakes Tributaries Using Multiple Lines of Evidence." *Environmental Toxicology and Chemistry* 39 no. 7 (2020): 1392–408.

Barber, Amzi L. *The Best Roads and the Right Way to Make Them*. New York: Barber Asphalt, 1909.

Barth, Edwin J. *Asphalt: Science and Technology*. New York: Gordon and Breach, 1962.

Beck, Alfred M., Abe Bortz, Charles W. Lynch, Lida Mayo, and Ralph F. Weld. *The Corps of Engineers: The War against Germany*. Washington DC: Army Center of Military History, 1985.

Bélanger, Pierre, ed. *Extraction Empire: Undermining the Systems, States and Scales of the Largest Resource Mining Nation on the Planet*. Cambridge MA: MIT Press, 2018.

———. *Landscape as Infrastructure*. New York: Routledge, 2017.

———. "Synthetic Surfaces." In *The Landscape Urbanism Reader*, edited by Charles Waldheim, 239–66. New York: Princeton Architectural Press, 2006.

Belle, Beyer B., and Anderson N. Finegold. *Ellis Island, Statue of Liberty National Monument: Existing Condition Survey*. Vol. 1, *Historic Structure Report: The Main*

Building. 4 vols. Washington DC: National Park Service, U.S. Department of the Interior, 1988.

Bellefontaine, Michelle. "Alberta Premier Announces 8.7% Oil Production Cut to Increase Prices." CBC. December 2, 2018. www.cbc.ca/news/canada/edmonton /alberta-premier-oil-differential-announcement-1.4929610.

Benjamin, Walter. *The Arcades Project.* Translated by Howard Eiland and Kevin McLaughlin. Cambridge MA: Belknap, 2002.

Ben-Joseph, Eran. *Rethinking a Lot: The Design and Culture of Parking.* Cambridge MA: MIT Press, 2012.

Beschloss, Michael R. *The Conquerors: Roosevelt, Truman and the Destruction of Hitler's Germany, 1941–1945.* New York: Simon and Schuster, 2002.

Billberg, Rudy. *In the Shadow of Eagles.* Portland OR: Alaska Northwest Books, 2009.

"The Birth of Trinidad Asphalt Holdings, and a Product Known as Tah." Neuchatel Co. Accessed April 16, 2019. www.neuchatel.co.nz/2017/11/.

Black, Toban, and Sonia Grant. "On the Front Lines of the Great Lakes." *Briar Patch Magazine.* January 2, 2015. https://briarpatchmagazine.com/articles/view/on-the -front-lines.

Black, Toban, Stephen D'Arcy, Tony Weis, and Joshua K. Russell. *A Line in the Tar Sands.* Oakland CA: PM, 2014.

Blazich, Frank A., Jr. "April to July of 1965: NMCB 10 and the Sands of Chu Lai." *Seabee Magazine.* May 8, 2015. https://seabeemagazine.navylive.dodlive.mil/2015/05/08/surmounting -the-sands-of-chu-lai-nmcb-10-and-the-marine-expeditionary-airfield-of-1965/.

Bloom, Harold, ed. *Jack Kerouac's "On the Road."* Philadelphia: Chelsea House, 2004.

Boëda, Eric, Stéphanie Bonilauri, Jacques Connan, Dan Jarvie, Norbert Mercier, Mark Tobey, Hélène Valladas, and Heba al Sakhel. "New Evidence of Significant Use of Bitumen in Middle Paleolithic Technical Systems at Umm el Tlel (Syria) around 70,000 BP." *Paléorient* 34, no. 2 (2008): 67–83.

Bokel, John E., and Rolf Clark. "Acquisition in World War II." In Gropman, *Big L,* 97–144.

The Book of Jubilees. Translated by Robert H. Charles. Sacred Texts. 1917. www.sacred -texts.com/bib/jub/index.htm.

Bosque, Melissa del. "Trump's Border Wall Could Cause Deadly Flooding in Texas." *Texas Monthly.* December 2018. www.texasmonthly.com/news/trumps-border -wall-cause-deadly-flooding-texas-federal-officials-planning-build-anyway/.

Bowen, Herbert W., Francis Butler Loomis, Theodore Roosevelt, and William H. Taft. *In the Matter of the Charges of Mr. Herbert W. Bowen, United States Minister to Venezuela, against Mr. Francis B. Loomis, First Assistant Secretary of State, and the Counter Charges of Mr. Loomis against Mr. Bowen.* Washington DC: Government Printing Office, 1905.

Bowman, Bonney. "On Attu, Toxic Cleanup Decades in the Making." KTVA, Anchorage. July 19, 2016. www.ktva.com/on-attu-toxic-cleanup-decades-in-the-making/.

Brabec, Elizabeth, Stacey Schulte, and Paul L. Richards. "Impervious Surfaces and Water Quality." *Journal of Planning Literature* 16, no. 4 (2002): 499–514.

Brennan, Joseph. "Abandoned Stations." Columbia University. 2002. www.columbia .edu/~brennan/abandoned/worth.html.

"Bribe Payers Index." Transparency International. Accessed July 25, 2020. www .transparency.org/research/bpi/overview.

Brown, Alleen, Will Parish, and Alice Speri. "Leaked Documents Reveal Counterterrorism Tactics at Standing Rock to 'Defeat Pipeline Insurgencies.'" *Intercept.* May 27, 2017. https://theintercept.com/2017/05/27/leaked-documents-reveal -security-firms-counterterrorism-tactics-at-standing-rock-to-defeat-pipeline -insurgencies/.

Brown, Todd S. *Battleground Iraq: Journal of a Company Commander.* Washington DC: Department of the Army, 2008.

Browne, Thomas. *Hydriotaphia, or Urne-Buriall.* Edited by Stephen Greenblatt and Ramie Targoff. Classics ed. 1658. Reprint, New York: New York Review of Books, 2012.

"BTC Barbed Tape Concertina." Atkore Razor Ribbon. Accessed August 13, 2020. www.razorribbon.com/military-border-security/btc-barbed-tape-concertina/.

Buggein, Marc. *Slave Labor in Nazi Concentration Camps.* Translated by Paul Cohen. New York: Oxford University Press, 2014.

"Building the Alaska Defensive Posts." Army Corps of Engineers. Accessed February 24, 2019. www.poa.usace.army.mil/Portals/34/docs/akdistrict/green_book_ii.pdf.

Bullard, Robert A., Glenn S. Johnson, and Angel Torres, eds. *Highway Robbery: Transportation Racism and New Routes to Equality.* Boston: South End, 2004.

Bunker, John G. *Liberty Ships: The Ugly Ducklings of World War II.* Annapolis MD: Naval Institute Press, 1972.

Bureau of Yards and Docks. *Building the Navy's Bases in World War II: History of the Bureau of Yards and Docks and the Civil Engineer Corps, 1940–1946.* 2 vols. Washington DC: Government Printing Office, 1947.

Burger, Pauline, Rebecca J. Stacey, Stephen A. Bowden, Marei Hacke, and John Parnell. "Identification, Geochemical Characterization and Significance of Bitumen among the Grave Goods of the 7th Century Mound 1 Ship-Burial at Sutton Hoo (Suffolk, UK)." *Plos One.* December 1, 2016. https://journals.plos.org/plosone /article?id=10.1371/journal.pone.0166276.

Bush, George W. *Decision Points.* Rev. ed. New York: Crown, 2010.

"Cable Exclusive: President Trump Sits Down with Sean Hannity at White House." Fox News transcript. January 26, 2017. www.foxnews.com/transcript/cable -exclusive-president-trump-sits-down-with-sean-hannity-at-white-house.

Cabrera et al. v. Black and Veatch et al. U.S. District Court for the District of Columbia. December 27, 2019. https://afghanistan.terrorismcase.com/wp-content /uploads/2019/12/2019-12-27-001-complaint.pdf.

Cannato, Vincent J. *American Passage: The History of Ellis Island*. New York: Harper Perennial, 2010.

Careless, James. "Seven Lesser-Known Uses for Asphalt." *Asphalt Magazine*. Accessed February 14, 2019. http://asphaltmagazine.com/seven-lesser-known-uses-for-asphalt/.

Caro, Robert. *The Power Broker: Robert Moses and the Fall of New York*. New York: Knopf, 1974.

——. *The Years of Lyndon Johnson*. Vol. 1, *The Path to Power*. New York: Knopf, 1982.

Carter, James M. *Inventing Vietnam: The United States and State Building, 1954–1968*. New York: Cambridge University Press, 2008.

Carter, Worrall Reed. *Beans, Bullets, and Black Oil: The Story of Fleet Logistics Afloat in the Pacific during World War II*. Washington DC: U.S. Department of the Navy, 1953.

Chandonnet, Fern, ed. *Alaska at War, 1941–1945*. Fairbanks: University of Alaska Press, 2008.

Chapot, Hank. "The Great Bicycle Protest of 1896." In *Critical Mass: Bicycling's Defiant Celebration*, edited by Chris Carlsson, 175–82. Oakland CA: AK, 2001.

Chastko, Paul. *Developing Alberta's Oil Sands: From Karl Clark to Kyoto*. Calgary: University of Calgary Press, 2004.

Choma, Russ. "Four Years Ago Scott Walker Promised This Woman He'd Bust Wisconsin's Unions." *Mother Jones*. July 31, 2015. www.motherjones.com/politics/2015 /07/scott-walker-diane-hendricks-unitimidated-pac/.

Churchill, Awnsham, and John A. Churchill. *A Collection of Voyages and Travels* [. . .]. 4 vols. London: Osborne, 1745. https://archive.org/details/collectionofvoya02osbo /page/n5.

Clark, K. A., Salima Ikram, and Richard P. Evershed. "The Significance of Petroleum Bitumen in Ancient Egyptian Mummies." *Philosophical Transactions of the Royal Society A* 374 (October 28, 2016). http://rsta.royalsocietypublishing.org/content /374/2079/20160229.

Clarke, Tony, Jim Stanford, Diana Gibson, and Brendan Haley. *The Bitumen Cliff*. Ottawa: Canadian Centre for Policy Alternatives, 2013.

"Climate Related Risk to DOD Infrastructure: Initial Vulnerability Assessment Survey." U.S. Department of Defense. January 2018. https://climateandsecurity.files .wordpress.com/2018/01/tab-b-slvas-report-1-24-2018.pdf.

"Cloth-Paper Runway Is Rolled Out on Airfield." *Popular Mechanics*, February 1945, 88.

"CNRL Catapults from Fourth Largest Player in the Sandbox to #1 Spot." *Oil Sands Magazine*. June 1, 2017. www.oilsandsmagazine.com/news/2017/6/1/cnrl-catapults -from-fourth-largest-player-in-the-sandbox-to-top-spot.

"Coal-Tar-Based Pavement Sealcoat, PAHs, and Environmental Health." U.S. Geological Survey. Accessed August 12, 2020. www.usgs.gov/mission-areas/water-resources/science/coal-tar-based-pavement-sealcoat-pahs-and-environmental-health?qt-science_center_objects=0#qt-science_center_objects.

"Coal Tar Pitch Volatiles." Occupational Safety and Health Administration. Accessed April 24, 2019. www.osha.gov/sltc/coaltarpitchvolatiles/hazards.html.

Coates, Benjamin A. *Legalist Empire: International Law and American Foreign Relations in the Early Twentieth Century*. New York: Oxford University Press, 2016.

——. "Securing Hegemony through Law: Venezuela, the U.S. Asphalt Trust, and the Uses of International Law, 1904–1909." *Journal of American History* 102, no. 2 (2015): 380–405.

Cobb, Jelani. "The Anger in Ferguson." *New Yorker*. August 13, 2014. www.newyorker.com/news/daily-comment/anger-ferguson.

Cochrane, Thomas B., and Henry R. F. Bourne. *The Life of Thomas, Lord Cochrane, Tenth Earl of Dundonald*. 2 vols. London: Bentley, 1869.

Coffee, Lane. "Pitching Noah's Ark: And Its Implications." *Reasons to Believe*. February 9, 2009. https://reasons.org/explore/publications/rtb-101/read/rtb-101/2008/02/05/pitching-noahs-ark--and-its-implications.

Cogan, Frances. *Captured: The Japanese Internment of American Civilians in the Philippines*. Athens: University of Georgia Press, 2000.

"Cold Bay Fort Randall." Alaska Division of Spill Prevention and Response. October 6, 2005. https://dec.alaska.gov/spar/csp/sites/coldbayftr.htm.

Coll, Blanche D., Jean E. Keith, and Herbert H. Rosenthal. *The Corps of Engineers: Troops and Equipment*. Washington DC: Army Center of Military History, 1988.

Coll, Steve. *The Bin Ladens: An Arabian Family in the American Century*. New York: Penguin, 2008.

Collier, Paul, and Anke Hoeffer. "The Economic Costs of Corruption in Infrastructure." In *Global Corruption Report, 2005: Special Focus; Corruption in Construction and Post-conflict Reconstruction*, edited by Diana Rodriguez, Gerard Waite, and Sarah Blair, 12–18. London: Pluto, 2005.

Comey, James B. Remarks. International Conference on Cyber Security, New York, January 7, 2015.

Committee of the Whole House on the State of the Union. *Defense Highway Needs*. H. Rept. 363, 87th Cong., 1st Sess. (1961).

Committee on Standards of Official Conduct. *In the Matter of Representative E. G. "Bud" Shuster*. 106th Cong., 2nd Sess. (2000).

Committee on the Alaska Earthquake, National Research Council. *The Great Alaska Earthquake of 1964*. Vol. 6, *Engineering*. 8 vols. Washington DC: National Academies Press, 1968.

"Companies Sustaining the Israeli Occupation." American Friends Service Committee. Accessed April 11, 2018. www.afsc.org/.

"Competition Issues and Inherently Governmental Functions Performed by Contractor Employees on Contracts to Supply Fuel to U.S. Troops in Iraq." Report D-2011-049. U.S. Department of Defense. March 15, 2011. https://media.defense.gov/2011/Mar/15/2001711989/-1/-1/1/d-2011-049.pdf.

"Composition for Recovering Bitumen from Oil Sands." Free Patents Online. September 26, 2013. www.freepatentsonline.com/y2015/0083645.html.

Concklin, Edward F. *The Lincoln Memorial in Washington*. Washington DC: Government Printing Office, 1927.

Connan, Jacques. "Use and Trade of Bitumen in Antiquity and Prehistory: Molecular Archeology Reveals Secrets of Past Civilizations." *Philosophical Transactions of the Royal Society B* 354, no. 1379 (1999): 33–50.

Conway, Hugh, and James E. Toth. "Building Victory's Foundation." In Gropman, *Big L*, 193–264.

Cordingly, David. *Cochrane: The Real Master and Commander*. New York: Bloomsbury USA, 2010.

"Corruption Challenges Index." Risk Advisory Group. 2019. www.riskadvisory.com/campaigns/corruption-challenges-index-2019-reveal/#panel-2.

Craven, Wesley Frank, and James Lea Cate. *The Army Air Forces in World War II*. 7 vols. Chicago: University of Chicago Press, 1948–58.

Crockett, Karilyn. *People before Highways: Boston Activists, Urban Planners, and a New Movement for City Making*. Amherst: University of Massachusetts Press, 2018.

Cronin, Xavier A. *The Asphalt Ribbon of Afghanistan: Rebuilding the Kabul-to-Khandahar Highway*. Washington DC: Berger Group, 2010.

Crosby, William O. "Native Bitumens and the Pitch Lake of Trinidad." *American Naturalist* 13, no. 4 (1879): 229–46.

"Curbing Fraud, Corruption and Collusion in the Roads Sector." World Bank. 2011. http://documents.worldbank.org/curated/en/975181468151765134/Curbing-fraud-corruption-and-collusion-in-the-roads-sector.

Curry, Andrew. "Can Auschwitz Be Saved?" *Smithsonian Magazine*. February 2010. www.smithsonianmag.com/history/can-auschwitz-be-saved-4650863/.

Danby, Arthur. *Natural Rock Asphalts and Bitumens: Their Geology, History, Properties, and Industrial Application*. London: Constable, 1913.

Dando-Collins, Stephen. *Tycoon's War: How Cornelius Vanderbilt Invaded a Country to Overthrow America's Most Famous Military Adventurer*. New York: Da Capo, 2008.

Danielsson, Bengt. "Poisoned Pacific: The Legacy of French Nuclear Testing." *Bulletin of the Atomic Scientists* 46, no. 2 (1990): 22–31.

Dannenfeldt, Karl H. "Egyptian Mumia: The Sixteenth Century Experience and Debate." *Sixteenth Century Journal* 16, no. 2 (1985): 163–80.

Dante. *Divine Comedy.* Translated by Henry F. Cary. Project Gutenberg. 1814. www .gutenberg.org/files/8800/8800-h/8800-h.htm.

Davidson, Adam. "Donald Trump's Worst Deal." *New Yorker,* March 13, 2017, 48–57.

Davis, Anita Price. *North Carolina and World War II.* Jefferson NC: McFarland, 2015.

"Dead Man's Corner." *Harper's,* November 1858, 799–805.

"DeFazio: Trump Infrastructure Proposal a Scam [. . .]." Press release. February 12, 2018. https://defazio.house.gov/media-center/press-releases/defazio-trump -infrastructure-proposal-a-scam-fails-to-address-critical.

"Defendant John Dennis Hastert's Sentencing Memorandum." U.S. District Court. Northern District of Illinois. Eastern Division. April 16, 2016. https://assets .documentcloud.org/documents/2791325/Hastert-sentencing-memo.pdf.

Dellinger, Matt. *Interstate 69: The Unfinished History of the Last Great American Highway.* New York: Scribner, 2010.

Denfeld, Colt D. *The Defense of Dutch Harbor, Alaska from Military Construction to Base Cleanup.* Anchorage: Army Corps of Engineers, 1987.

Dickinson, Tim. "Inside the Koch Brothers' Toxic Empire." *Rolling Stone.* September 24, 2014. www.rollingstone.com/politics/politics-news/inside-the-koch-brothers -toxic-empire-164403/.

Dickson, Paul, and Thomas B. Allen. *The Bonus Army.* New York: Walker, 2004.

Diderot, Denis. "Pentateuch." In *The Encyclopedia of Diderot and d'Alembert Collaborative Translation Project.* Translated by Susan Emanuel. Ann Arbor: University of Michigan Library, 2013. http://hdl.handle.net/2027/spo.did2222 .0001.233.

DiMento, Joseph F. C., and Cliff Ellis. *Changing Lanes: Visions and Histories of Urban Freeways.* Cambridge MA: MIT Press, 2013.

———. "Stent (or Dagger?) in the Heart of Town: Urban Freeways in Syracuse, 1944–1967." *Journal of Planning History* 8, no. 2 (2009): 133–61.

Diodorus. *Universal History.* Translated by Charles H. Oldfather. Perseus Digital Library. 1933. www.loebclassics.com/view/lcl279/1933/volume.xml.

Dochuk, Darren. *Anointed with Oil: How Christianity and Crude Made Modern America.* New York: Basic Books, 2019.

Dod, Karl C. *The Corps of Engineers: The War against Japan.* Washington DC: Army Center of Military History, 1966.

Dooley, Erin. "Trump Defends Decision Not to Hit Runway on Syrian Air Base." ABC News. April 8, 2017. https://abcnews.go.com/Politics/trump-defends-decision -hit-runway-syrian-airbase/story?id=46677805.

Dulias, Gottfried P. "Surviving the Soviet Gulag." Warfare History Network. January 17, 2016. http://warfarehistorynetwork.com/daily/wwii/gottfried-p-dulias-surviving-the-soviet-gulag/.

Dunand, Françoise, and Roger Lichtenberg. *Mummies and Death in Egypt*. Ithaca NY: Cornell University Press, 2006.

Dunn, Carroll H. *Base Development in South Vietnam, 1965–1970*. Washington DC: Government Printing Office, 1972.

Earle, Horatio. *The Autobiography of "By Gum" Earle*. Lansing MI: State Review, 1929.

Easton, Robert. *Black Tide: The Santa Barbara Oil Spill and Its Consequences*. New York: Delacorte, 1972.

Edgeworth, Dee R. *Asset Forfeiture: Practice and Procedure in State and Federal Courts*. 3rd ed. 2004. Reprint, Chicago: American Bar Association, 2015.

Edwards, Lee. *William F. Buckley Jr.: The Maker of a Movement*. Wilmington DE: Intercollegiate Studies Institute, 2010.

Eliot, T. S. *The Rock*. London: Faber and Faber, 1934.

Elliott, Roberta. "What I Learned Volunteering with Refugees in Greece." *Forward*. July 5, 2015. http://forward.com/scribe/344275/what-i-learned-volunteering-with-refugees-in-greece/.

Ellis, S. C. *Bituminous Sands of Northern Alberta*. Ottawa: Acland, 1926.

"Embrace Energy Dominance." *National Security Strategy of the United States of America*. White House. December 2017. https://trumpwhitehouse.archives.gov/wp-content/uploads/2017/12/NSS-Final-12-18-2017-0905.pdf.

"Emissions of Greenhouse Gases in the United States, 2009." U.S. Energy Information Administration. March 2011. www.eia.gov/environment/emissions/ghg_report/pdf/0573(2009).pdf.

"Empresas Díaz Inc.: BetteRoads Asphalt Corp." *Construction Today*. December 12, 2011. www.construction-today.com/sections/civil/609-empresas-diaz-inc-betteroads-asphalt-corp.

"Enbridge Major Spills, 2000–2014." 350.org. Accessed April 11, 2019. http://world.350.org/kishwaukee/files/2017/02/EnbridgeMajorSpills_1996-2014.pdf.

Energy Transfer Equity et al. v. Greenpeace et al. U.S. District Court. District of North Dakota. 2017. http://climatecasechart.com/case/energy-transfer-equity-lp-v-greenpeace-international/.

"EPA Response to Enbridge Spill in Michigan." Environmental Protection Agency. Updated May 4, 2020. www.epa.gov/enbridge-spill-michigan.

Epic of Gilgamesh. Translated by Maureen Gallery Kovacs. Stanford CA: Stanford University Press, 1989.

"Establishing Accountability for Climate Change Damages: Lessons from Tobacco Control." Climate Accountability. 2012. www.climateaccountability.org/pdf/Climate%20Accountability%20Rpt%20Oct12.pdf.

Estes, Nick. *Our History Is the Future: Standing Rock versus the Dakota Access Pipeline, and the Long Tradition of Indigenous Resistance.* New York: Verso, 2019.

Evans, Hiram W. "The Klan's Fight for Americanism." *North American Review*, March–May 1926, 33–63.

Evenari, Michael, Leslie Shanan, and Naphtali Tadmor. *The Negev.* Cambridge MA: Harvard University Press, 1971.

"Exxon Mobile Corporation Verified Petition for Pre-Suit Depositions [. . .]." District Court. Tarrant County, Texas. January 8, 2018. www.documentcloud.org /documents/4345487-Exxon-Texas-Petition-Jan-2018.html.

"*Exxon Valdez* Oil Spill: FAQs, Links, and Unique Resources at ARLIS." Alaska Resources Library and Information Services. Updated March 22, 2019. www.arlis .org/docs/vol2/a/EVOS_FAQs.pdf.

"Factual Investigative Update: April 26, 2018; Husky Superior Refinery Explosion and Fire." U.S. Chemical Safety and Hazard Investigation Board. August 2, 2018. www.csb.gov/assets/1/6/husky_factual_update.pdf.

Fagan, Brian. *The Rape of the Nile: Tomb Robbers, Tourists, and Archeologists in Egypt.* Boulder CO: Westview, 2004.

"Features of the Athabasca Oil Sands." Regional Aquatics Monitoring Program. Accessed March 10, 2019. www.ramp-alberta.org/river/geography/geological +prehistory/mesozoic.aspx.

Federal Highway Administration. *America's Highways: A History of the Federal Aid Program.* Washington DC: Government Printing Office, 1976.

"Federal Highway Administrators: Logan Waller Page, 1905–1918." Federal Highway Administration. Updated August 24, 2015. www.fhwa.dot.gov/administrators /lpage.cfm.

Feldman, Daniel L, and David R. Eichenthal. *The Art of the Watchdog: Fighting Fraud, Waste, Abuse, and Corruption in Government.* Albany: State University of New York Press, 2014.

Feldman, Daniel L, and Gerald Benjamin. *Tales from the Sausage Factory: Making Laws in New York State.* Albany: State University of New York Press, 2010.

Ferguson, Bruce K. *Porous Pavements.* Boca Raton FL: CRC, 2005.

Ferguson, Niall. *Kissinger.* Vol. 1, *1923–1968: The Idealist.* 2 vols. New York: Penguin, 2015.

"Final Operating Report for the PM-3A Nuclear Power Plant McMurdo Station, Antarctica." Report 69, 1964–73. Naval Nuclear Power Unit. September 30, 1973. www.vbdr.org/meetings/2012/Presentations/McMurdo_Station_Nuc_Reactor _Final_Report-Sec6-ocred.pdf.

Final Report of the Independent Counsel for Iran-Contra Matters. Vol. 1, *Investigations and Prosecutions.* 3 vols. U.S. Court of Appeals. District of Columbia Circuit. 1993. https://fas.org/irp/offdocs/walsh/index.html.

"Final Report: Transforming Wartime Contracting." Commission on Wartime Contracting in Iraq and Afghanistan. 2011. https://cybercemetery.unt.edu/archive/cwc/20110929213815/http://www.wartimecontracting.gov/.

Fine, Lenore, and Jesse A. Remington. *The Corps of Engineers: Construction in the United States*. Washington DC: Army Center of Military History, 1972.

Fishman, Elly. "Mountains of Trouble." *Chicago Magazine*. July 27, 2015. www.chicagomag.com/Chicago-Magazine/August-2015/kcbx-pet-coke/.

Folsom, Seth W. B. *The Highway War: A Marine Company Commander in Iraq*. Washington DC: Potomac Books, 2007.

Forbes, Robert J. *Bitumen and Petroleum in Antiquity*. Leiden, Netherlands: Brill, 1936.

———. "Chemical, Culinary, and Cosmetic Arts." In Singer et al., *History of Technology*, 1:238–98.

———. "Petroleum." In Singer et al., *History of Technology*, 5:102–23.

———. *Studies in Early Petroleum History*. Leiden, Netherlands: Brill, 1958.

"Former Louis Berger Group Inc. Chairman, CEO, and President Admits 20-Year Conspiracy to Defraud Federal Government." Press release. U.S. Attorney's Office. District of New Jersey. Updated August 20, 2015. www.justice.gov/usao-nj/pr/former-louis-berger-group-inc-chairman-ceo-and-president-admits-20-year-conspiracy.

"Form F-20." U.S. Securities and Exchange Commission. Filed by PDVSA. November 17, 2006. www.sec.gov/Archives/edgar/data/906424/000114036106016747/form20-f.htm#i19.

Foster, Mark S. *Henry J. Kaiser: Builder in the Modern American West*. Austin: University of Texas Press, 1989.

Fowle, Barry W., ed. *Builders and Fighters: U.S. Army Engineers in World War II*. Fort Belvoir VA: Army Corps of Engineers, 1992.

Fowle, Barry W., and John C. Lonnquest. *Remembering the "Forgotten War": U.S. Army Engineer Officers in Korea*. Alexandria VA: Office of History, Army Corps of Engineers, 2004.

Fraser, Barbara. "Carving Up the Amazon." *Nature*, May 22, 2014, 418–19.

Frazer, Lance. "Paving Paradise: The Peril of Impervious Surfaces." *Environmental Health Perspectives* 113, no. 7 (2005): A456–62.

Frazier, Ian. *On the Rez*. New York: Picador, 2000.

"Frequently Asked Questions." U.S. Energy Information Administration. Updated May 15, 2019. www.eia.gov/tools/faqs/faq.cfm?id=307andt=11.

Frischauer, Willi. *Himmler*. 1953. Reprint, London: Unmaterial Books, 2013.

Gaines, Susan M., Geoffrey Eglinton, and Jurgen Rullkotter. *Echoes of Life: What Fossil Molecules Reveal about Earth History*. New York: Oxford University Press, 2009.

Gallagher, Winifred. *How the Post Office Created America*. New York: Penguin, 2016.

"Game On: Koch Asphalt Takes the Field." *Koch News*. February 2, 2018. https://news.kochind.com/news/2018/big-game.

Garcia, Brittany. "Ishtar Gate." *Ancient History Encyclopedia*. August 23, 2013. www.ancient.eu/Ishtar_Gate/.

Garfield, Brian. *The Thousand-Mile War: World War II in Alaska*. Fairbanks: University of Alaska Press, 1995.

George, Henry. "Modern Methods of 'Finance': The Asphalt Trust Catastrophe." *Pearson's Magazine*, March 1904, 251–65.

———. *Progress and Poverty*. New York: Appleton, 1879.

Georgia v. Evans. 316 U.S. 159 (1942).

Gillespie, Hugh M. *A Century of Progress: The History of Hot Mix Asphalt*. Lanham MD: National Asphalt Pavement Association, 1992.

Giovannini, Joseph. "Owning the Asphalt." *Los Angeles Review of Books*. June 18, 2020. https://lareviewofbooks.org/article/owning-the-asphalt/.

Glaeser, Edward. *Triumph of the City*. New York: Penguin, 2011.

"Global Construction Sector Most Corrupt." Transparency International. December 9, 2008. www.transparency.org.uk/press-releases/global-construction-sector-most-corrupt/.

Goddard, Stephen B. *Colonel Albert Pope and His American Dream Machines: The Life and Times of a Bicycle Tycoon Turned Automotive Pioneer*. Jefferson NC: McFarland, 2000.

———. *Getting There: The Epic Struggle between Road and Rail in the American Century*. Chicago: University of Chicago Press, 1996.

Goldmanis, Māris. "TRIGON Numbers Station: The Case of Alexandr Ogorodnik." Numbers Stations. Accessed July 25, 2020. www.numbers-stations.com/articles/trigon-numbers-station-the-case-of-alexandr-ogorodnik/.

Gooch, John. *Mussolini and His Generals*. New York: Cambridge University Press, 2007.

Goodhand, Jonathan. "Boundary Wars: NGOs and Civil-Military Relations in Afghanistan." In *Reconstructing Afghanistan*, edited by William Malley and Susanne Schmeidl. New York: Routledge, 2015.

Gordon, Robert. *The Rise and Fall of American Growth*. Princeton NJ: Princeton University Press, 2016.

Grant, Bob. "History of the 51st Asphalt Platoon." Arizona Construction Equipment. Accessed February 2, 2018. www.azce.com/concrete/51stAsphaltPlatoon.html (site discontinued).

Grathwol, Robert P., and Donita M. Moorhus. *Bricks, Sand, and Marble: U.S. Army Corps of Engineers Construction in the Mediterranean and Middle East, 1947–1991*. Washington DC: Army Center of Military History, Army Corps of Engineers, 2009.

"The Greenhouse Effect." Climate Files. 1988. www.climatefiles.com/shell/1988-shell -report-greenhouse/.

Gropman, Alan, ed. *The Big L: American Logistics in World War II*. Washington DC: National Defense University Press, 1997.

Hall, Karen J. *Building the Blue Ridge Parkway*. Charleston SC: Arcadia, 2007.

Hall, M. Ann. *Muscle on Wheels: Louise Armaindo and the High-Wheel Racers of Nineteenth-Century America*. Montreal: McGill-Queens University Press, 2018.

Hall v. Sargeant. 18-80748-Civ (S.D. Fla. Mar. 30, 2020).

Hamilton, Douglas H., and Richard L. Meehan. "Cause of the 1985 Ross Store Explosion and Other Gas Ventings, Fairfax District, Los Angeles." Special issue, *Engineering Geology Practice in Southern California* 4 (1992): 145–57.

Hammond, Philip C. "The Nabataean Bitumen Industry at the Dead Sea." *Biblical Archaeologist* 22, no. 2 (1959): 40–48.

Harris, Graham. *The Destruction of Sodom: A Scientific Commentary*. Cambridge: Lutterworth, 2015.

Harris, John M., ed. *La Brea and Beyond: The Paleontology of Asphalt-Preserved Biotas*. Science Series 42. Los Angeles: Natural History Museum of Los Angeles County, 2015.

Hartzer, Ronald B. "A Look Back at Black Aviation Engineer Units of World War II." *Air Force News*. February 27, 2013. www.af.mil/News/Article-Display/Article /109658/a-look-back-at-black-aviation-engineer-units-of-world-war-ii/.

Haug, Moir D., and Gordon Pauls. "A Review of Non-traditional Dry Covers." Mine Environment Neutral Drainage Report 2.21.3b. 2002. http://mend-nedem.org/wp -content/uploads/2013/01/2.21.3b.pdf.

Haupt, Paul. "Xenophon's Account of the Fall of Nineveh." *Journal of the American Oriental Society* 28 (1907): 99–107.

Hecking, Claus. "A Voice for the Dead: Recovering the Lost History of Sobibór." *Der Spiegel*. September 26, 2014. www.spiegel.de/international/zeitgeist/the -archeological-excavations-that-led-to-the-gas-chambers-of-sobibor-a-993733.html.

Hendricks, Charles. *Combat and Construction: U.S. Army Engineers in World War I*. Fort Belvoir VA: Army Corps of Engineers, 1993.

"Henry W. Mack, Ph.D.: Profile of a Korean War Veteran." Korean War Memorial Foundation. June 21, 2016. www.kwmf.org/henry-w-mack-profile-korean-war -veteran/.

Herman, Arthur. *Freedom's Forge: How American Business Produced Victory in World War II*. New York: Random House, 2012.

Herodotus. *The Histories*. Translated by Alfred D. Godley. Perseus Digital Library. 1920–25. www.perseus.tufts.edu/hopper/text?doc=Perseus%3atext%3a1999.01 .0126%3abook%3d2andforce=y.

————. *The Persian Wars*. Translated by George Rawlinson. Modern Library. 1942. http://mcadams.posc.mu.edu/txt/ah/Herodotus/Herodotus8.html.

Hickman, Joseph. *The Burn Pits: The Poisoning of America's Soldiers*. New York: Hot Books, 2016.

"Highway Funds Authorized; Probe Starts." *CQ Almanac*. 1960. https://library.cqpress.com/cqalmanac/document.php?id=cqal60-1330619.

Hill, Robert J. *Cuba and Porto Rico with the Other Islands of the West Indies*. New York: Century, 1898.

Hindle, Jim. *Nine Miles: Two Winters of Anti-road Protest*. Isle of Arran, Scotland: Underhill Books, 2007.

Hiram W. Evans v. Commissioner. U.S. Tax Court. 5 TCM 336 (1946).

"History." Maine Turnpike Authority. Accessed June 9, 2019. www.maineturnpike.com/About-mta/History.aspx.

"History of Alvin." Woods Hole Oceanographic Institute. December 1, 2005. www.whoi.edu/what-we-do/explore/underwater-vehicles/hov-alvin/history-of-alvin/.

Hitchcock, Peter. "Velocity and Viscosity." In *Subterranean Estates: Life Worlds of Oil and Gas*, edited by Hannah Appel, Arthur Mason, and Michael Watts, 45–60. Ithaca NY: Cornell University Press, 2015.

"Hitler at Autobahn Ceremony; Goebbels Speaks." Newsreel. U.S. Holocaust Memorial Museum. July 3, 1935. https://collections.ushmm.org/search/catalog/irn1001237.

Hodge, Nathan. *Armed Humanitarians: The Rise of the Nation Builders*. New York: Bloomsbury, 2011.

Hodges, Michael. "Earth's Backup: Inside Svalbard's Indestructible 'Doomsday' Seed Vault." *Wired*. February 24, 2017. www.wired.co.uk/article/natures-backup.

Hoffman, David. *The Billion Dollar Spy*. New York: Doubleday, 2015.

Hoffman, Jeremy S., Vivek Shandas, and Nicholas Pendleton. "The Effects of Historical Housing Policies on Resident Exposure to Intra-Urban Heat: A Study of 108 US Urban Areas." *Climate* 8, no. 1 (2020). www.mdpi.com/2225-1154/8/1/12.

Holland, Megan. "Assessment to Aid Liberia's Fight against the Ebola Virus." Army Corps of Engineers. March 9, 2015. www.erdc.usace.army.mil/Media/News-Stories/Article/572287/assessment-to-aid-liberias-fight-against-the-ebola-virus/.

Holley, Irving B. "Blacktop: How Asphalt Paving Came to the Urban United States." *Technology and Culture* 44, no. 4 (2003): 703–33.

————. *The Highway Revolution: How the United States Got Out of the Mud*. Durham NC: Carolina Academic Press, 2008.

Honey, Michael K. *Black Workers Remember*. Berkeley: University of California Press, 2000.

Hornblower, Jane. *Hieronymous of Cardia*. New York: Oxford University Press, 1981.

Hornfischer, James D. *The Fleet at Flood Tide: America at Total War in the Pacific, 1944–1945*. New York: Bantam, 2016.

Horváth, Gábor, György Kriska, Péter Malik, and Bruce Robertson. "Polarized Light Pollution: A New Kind of Ecological Photopollution." *Frontiers in Ecology and the Environment* 7, no. 6 (2009): 317–25.

House Committee on Appropriations. *Making Emergency Supplemental Appropriations for the Fiscal Year Ending September 30, 2007, and for Other Purposes*. 110th Cong., 1st Sess. (2007).

House Committee on Military Affairs. *Hearings*. 74th Cong., 1st Sess. (1935).

House Committee on Natural Resources. *Combined Hydrocarbon Leasing*. 108th Cong., 1st Sess. (2003).

House Intelligence Committee et al. "Deposition of: Fiona Hill." October 14, 2019. https://docs.house.gov/meetings/ig/ig00/cprt-116-ig00-d010.pdf.

Howells, William Dean. *Literature and Life*. New York: Harper and Brothers, 1902.

Howes, Ruth H., and Caroline L. Herzenberg. *Their Day in the Sun: Women of the Manhattan Project*. Philadelphia: Temple University Press, 1999.

"How Much for that Heavy Oil?" *Oil Sands Magazine*. December 26, 2016. www.oilsandsmagazine.com/news/2015/12/26/how-much-for-that-heavy-oil.

Humberto Leal Garcia v. Texas. 564 U.S. 940 (2011).

Hutchinson, L. L. *Rock Asphalt, Asphaltite, Petroleum, and Natural Gas in Oklahoma*. Bulletin 2. Norman: Oklahoma Geological Survey, 1911.

"Indiana Contractor Agrees to Pay $8.2 Million to Settle Federal and State Fraud Claims." Press release. U.S. Attorney. Western District of Kentucky. December 10, 2007. www.oig.dot.gov/sites/default/files/GohmannSettlementMedia_Release _FINAL.pdf.

Inter-organization Programme for the Sound Management of Chemicals. *Concise International Chemical Assessment Document 59: Asphalt (Bitumen)*. Geneva: World Health Organization, 2004.

"Investigation of the Chicago Police Department." U.S. Department of Justice. January 13, 2007. www.justice.gov/opa/file/925846/download.

"Investigation of the Ferguson Police Department." U.S. Department of Justice. March 4, 2015. www.justice.gov/sites/default/files/opa/press-releases/attachments/2015 /03/04/ferguson_police_department_report.pdf.

"The Iraq War Logs." Wikileaks. Accessed September 11, 2020. https://wikileaks .org/irq/.

"'It's All a Lie,' Russian Billionaire Deripaska Says [. . .]." *PBS NewsHour*. April 16, 2019.

Jackson, Kenneth T. *The Crabgrass Frontier: The Suburbanization of the United States*. New York: Oxford University Press, 1985.

Jakle, John A., and Keith A. Sculle. *Lots of Parking: Land Use in a Car Culture.* Charlottesville: University of Virginia Press, 2005.

Jaremko, Gordon. *Steward: 75 Years of Alberta Energy Regulation.* Edmonton: Energy Resources Conservation Board, 2013.

Jassim, Saad Z., and Mohammad Al-Gailani. "Hydrocarbons." In *Geology of Iraq*, edited by Saad Z. Jassim and Jeremy C. Goff, 232–50. Prague: Dolin, 2006.

Johns, Stephanie. "Love the Way We Bitumen." *Coast*. December 22, 2014. www .thecoast.ca/halifax/love-the-way-we-bitumen/Content?oid=4479130.

Johnson, Richard. "World's Slowest Moving Drop." *Nature*. July 18, 2013. www.nature .com/news/world-s-slowest-moving-drop-caught-on-camera-at-last-1.13418.

Jones, Daniel O. B., Anne Walls, Michael Clare, Mike S. Fiske, Richard J. Weiland, Robert O'Brien, and Daniel F. Touzel. "Asphalt Mounds and Associated Biota on the Angolan Margin." *Deep Sea Research, Part I: Oceanographic Research Papers* 94 (December 2014): 124–36.

Jones, Steve. *The Language of the Genes: Biology, History, and the Evolutionary Future.* New York: Doubleday, 1994.

Jonker, Julian. "Reconciliation with the Dead, and Other Unfamiliar Pathways." In *Pathways to Reconciliation: Between Theory and Practice*, edited by Philipa Rothfield, Cleo Fleming, and Paul A. Komesaroff, 103–14. Burlington VT: Ashgate, 2008.

Josephus, Flavius. *War of the Jews.* Translated by William Whiston. Perseus Digital Library. 1737. www.perseus.tufts.edu/hopper/text?doc=Perseus%3Atext%3A1999 .01.0148.

Kahmann, Bodo. "Antisemitism and Antiurbanism: Past and Present." In *Deciphering the New Antisemitism*, edited by Alvin H. Rosenfeld, 482–507. Bloomington: Indiana University Press, 2016.

Kanter, Rosabeth Moss. *Move: Putting America's Infrastructure Back in the Lead.* New York: Norton, 2015.

Kay, Jane Holtz. *Asphalt Nation: How the Automobile Took Over America and How We Can Take It Back.* New York: Crown, 1997.

Keegan, John. *Waffen ss: The Asphalt Soldiers.* New York: Ballantine, 1970.

Kelley, Ben. *The Pavers and the Paved.* New York: Scribner's Sons, 1971.

Kellogg, Paul. "The Political Economy of Oil and Democracy in Venezuela and Alberta." In Shrivastava and Stefanick, *Alberta Oil*, 139–70.

Kelly, Cynthia C., ed. *Manhattan Project: The Birth of the Atomic Bomb in the Words of Its Creators, Eyewitnesses, and Historians.* New York: Black Dog and Leventhal, 2007.

Kelman, Ari. *A River and Its City: The Nature of Landscape in New Orleans.* 2nd ed. Berkeley: University of California Press, 2006.

Kennedy, John F. "Remarks of Senator John F. Kennedy [. . .] Silver Spring, Maryland." October 16, 1960. www.jfklibrary.org/archives/other-resources/john-f-kennedy-speeches/silver-spring-md-19601016.

Kent, John L. "Fighting with Fire." *Popular Mechanics*, November 1945, 28–33.

Kerouac, Jack. *On the Road*. New York: Viking, 1957.

Kessler, Ronald. *The Richest Man in the World: The Story of Adnan Khashoggi*. New York: Warner Books, 1986.

Kidwell, Clara Sue. "The Resurgence of the Choctaws in the Twentieth Century." *Indigenous Nations Study Journal* 3, no. 1 (2002): 3–18.

Kinkela, David. *DDT and the American Century: Global Health, Environmental Politics, and the Pesticide That Changed the World*. Chapel Hill: University of North Carolina Press, 2011.

Klein, Naomi. *On Fire: The (Burning) Case for a Green New Deal*. New York: Simon and Schuster, 2019.

———. *This Changes Everything: Capitalism vs. the Climate*. New York: Simon and Schuster, 2014.

Klemperer, Victor, and Brady Martin. *Language of the Third Reich*. 2000. Reprint, New York: Bloomsbury Academic, 2006.

Knutson, Roger M. *Flattened Fauna*. Rev. ed. 1987. Reprint, New York: Ten Speed, 2006.

Kolbert, Elizabeth. "Unconventional Crude: Canada's Synthetic-Fuels Boom." *New Yorker*, November 12, 2007, 46–51.

Koldewey, Robert. *The Excavations at Babylon*. Translated by Agnes S. Johns. London: Macmillan, 1914.

Koseli, Mutlu. "The Poverty, Inequality and Terrorism Relationship." In *Understanding Terrorism*, edited by Suleyman Ozeren, Ismail D. Gunes, and Diab M. Al-Badayneh, 109–19. Amsterdam: IOS, 2007.

Kubic, Charles R. *Bridges to Baghdad: The U.S. Navy Seabees in the Iraq War*. Gettysburg PA: Thomas, 2009.

Kupferschmidt, Kari. "Hunting for Ebola among the Bats of the Congo." *Science Magazine*. June 1, 2017. www.sciencemag.org/news/2017/06/hunting-ebola-among-bats-congo.

Laing, Keith. "Ex-marine Turned Street Warrior." *Hill*. May 14, 2013. http://thehill.com/business-a-lobbying/lobbyist-profiles/299471-ex-marine-turned-street-warrior.

Lane, Frederic Chapin. *Ships for Victory: A History of Shipbuilding under the U.S. Maritime Commission in World War II*. 1951. Reprint, Baltimore: Johns Hopkins University Press, 2001.

Larson, George A. *The Road to Tinian: The Story of the 135th USNCB*. N.p.: Printed by the author, 1988.

———. *A Seabee's Story*. N.p.: Printed by the author, 2012.

Lattanzio, Richard K. "Canadian Oil Sands: Life-Cycle Assessments of Greenhouse Gas Emissions." Congressional Research Service. March 10, 2014. https://fas.org /sgp/crs/misc/r42537.pdf.

Lavis, Fred, and Maurice E. Griest. *Building the New Rapid Transit System of New York City*. New York: Hill, 1915.

Lay, Maxwell G. *Ways of the World: A History of the World's Roads and the Vehicles That Used Them*. New Brunswick NJ: Rutgers University Press, 1999.

Layden, Tim. "Artificial Turf: Change from the Ground Up." *Sports Illustrated*. May 21, 2014. http://mmqb.si.com.

Leary, William M. "CIA Air Operations in Laos, 1955–1974." Central Intelligence Agency. Updated June 27, 2008. www.cia.gov/library.

Lebedev, Igor. *Aviation Lend-Lease to Russia*. Commack NY: Nova, 1997.

Ledbetter, James. *Unwarranted Influence: Dwight D. Eisenhower and the Military Industrial Complex*. New Haven CT: Yale University Press, 2011.

Leeker, Joe F. "Air America in Laos II: Military Aid." McDermott Library, University of Texas at Dallas. August 24, 2015. www.utdallas.edu/library/specialcollections /hac/cataam/Leeker/history/Laos2part2.pdf.

Lenzner, Robert. "Asphalt Is Always the Last Crop." *Forbes*. June 15, 1998. www.forbes .com/forbes/1998/0615/6112186a.html#75f3301c267e.

Leonard, Christopher. *Kochland: The Secret History of Koch Industries and Corporate Power in America*. New York: Simon and Schuster, 2019.

Leovy, Jill. *Ghettoside: A True Story of Murder in America*. New York: Spiegel and Grau, 2015.

Lepage, Jean-Denis G. G. *Hitler's Armed Forces Auxiliaries*. Jefferson NC: McFarland, 2015.

Lewis, Tom. *Washington: A History of Our National City*. New York: Basic Books, 2015.

"The Limit." *Harper's*, August 30, 1913, 3–4.

Lindsey, Emily L., and Kevin L. Seymour. "'Tar Pits' of the Western Neotropics: Paleontology, Taphonomy, and Mammalian Biogeography." In Harris, *La Brea and Beyond*, 111–24.

Lippsett, Lonny. "Asphalt Volcanoes on the Ocean Floor." *Oceanus Magazine*, Fall 2011, 35–39.

Lipuma, Lauren. "Asphalt Volcanos Erupt in Slow Motion." *Eos*. March 15, 2016. https://eos.org/articles/asphalt-volcanoes-erupt-in-slow-motion.

Llamoca, Janice. "Remembering the Lost Communities Buried under Center Field." National Public Radio. October 31, 2017. www.npr.org/sections/codeswitch/2017 /10/31/561246946/remembering-the-communities-buried-under-center-field.

Lloyd, Seton. "Building in Brick and Stone." In Singer et al., *History of Technology*, 1:456–94.

Loss, Scott R., Todd Will, and Peter P. Marra. "Estimation of Bird-Vehicle Collision Mortality on U.S. Roads." *Journal of Wildlife Management* 78, no. 5 (2014): 763–71.

"Loss-of-Use Damages from U.S. Nuclear Testing in the Marshall Islands." Congressional Research Service. 2005. https://fas.org/sgp/crs/nuke/rl33029.pdf.

Lund, Joachim. "Building Hitler's Europe: Forced Labor in the Danish Construction Business during World War II." *Business History Review* 84, no. 3 (2010): 479–99.

Machado, Barry. *In Search of a Usable Past: The Marshall Plan and Postwar Reconstruction Today.* Lexington VA: Marshall Foundation, 2007.

Maclellan, Nic. *Grappling with the Bomb: Britain's Pacific H-Bomb Tests.* Acton: Australian National University Press, 2017.

Madden, Thomas F. *Istanbul.* New York: Viking, 2016.

Maddow, Rachel. "Turn It Off." Episode 4 of *Bag Man*, podcast. November 12, 2018. www.nbcnews.com/msnbc/maddow-bag-man-podcast/transcript-episode-4 -turn-it-n935286.

Maher, Neil M. *Nature's New Deal: The Civilian Conservation Corps and the Roots of the American Environmental Movement.* New York: Oxford University Press, 2008.

"Maintaining Camps for Those Who Safeguard Freedom and Security." DynCorp. January 20, 2017. www.dyn-intl.com/what-we-do/case-studies/operations /maintaining-camps-for-those-who-safeguard-freedom-and-security/.

Mallozzi, Vincent M. *Asphalt Gods: An Oral History of the Rucker Tournament.* New York: Doubleday, 2003.

Mann, Michael. *The Sources of Social Power.* Vol. 3, *Global Empires and Revolution, 1890–1945.* 4 vols. New York: Cambridge University Press, 2012.

"Map: Diagram of Proposed Dodger Stadium in Chavez Ravine." *Los Angeles Examiner* Photographs Collection, University of Southern California. 1957. http:// digitallibrary.usc.edu/cdm/ref/collection/p15799coll44/id/91758.

Marchand, Suzanne. *Down from Olympus: Archaeology and Philhellenism in Germany, 1750–1970.* Princeton NJ: Princeton University Press, 1996.

Marcon, Yann, Heiko Sahling, Ian R. MacDonald, Paul Wintersteller, Christian dos Santos Ferreira, and Gerhard Bohrmann. "Slow Volcanoes: The Intriguing Similarities between Marine Asphalt and Basalt Lavas." *Oceanography* 31, no. 2 (2018): 194–205.

Marko, W. M. "Negro Morality and a Colored Clergy." *America*, November 12, 1921, 80–81.

Marsden, William. *Stupid to the Last Drop: How Alberta Is Bringing Environmental Armageddon to Canada (and Doesn't Seem to Care).* Toronto: Vintage, 2008.

Marsh, James H., ed. "Bitumen Extraction." In *The Canadian Encyclopedia.* Toronto: McClelland and Stewart, 2000. www.thecanadianencyclopedia.ca/en/article/bitumen.

Masó, Felip. "Inside the 30-Year Quest for Babylon's Ishtar Gate." *National Geographic.* January 5, 2018. www.nationalgeographic.com/archaeology-and-history/magazine /2017/11-12/history-babylon-ishtar-gate-quest/.

Massey, Douglas S., and Nancy A. Denton. *American Apartheid: Segregation and the Making of the Underclass.* Cambridge MA: Harvard University Press, 1993.

"Maths of Construction." Crocus Group. September 25, 2012. http://crocusgroup .com/press-center/news/776/.

Maurer, Noel. *The Empire Trap: The Rise and Fall of U.S. Intervention to Protect American Property Overseas, 1893–2013.* Princeton NJ: Princeton University Press, 2013.

Mayer, Jane. *Dark Money: The Hidden History of the Billionaires behind the Rise of the Radical Right.* New York: Doubleday, 2016.

Mayor, Adrienne. *Greek Fire, Poison Arrows, and Scorpion Bombs: Biological and Chemical Warfare in the Ancient World.* New York: Overlook Duckworth, 2017.

McAdam, John Loudon. *Remarks on the Present System of Road Making.* 7th ed. 1820. Reprint, London: Longman, Hurst, Rees, Orme, and Brown, 1823.

McBeth, Brian S. *Gunboats, Corruption, and Claims: Foreign Intervention in Venezuela.* Westport CT: Praeger, 2001.

McCouat, Philip. "The Life and Death of Mummy Brown." *Journal of Art in Society.* Updated 2019. www.artinsociety.com/the-life-and-death-of-mummy-brown.html.

McCoy, Alfred W. *The Politics of Heroin: CIA Complicity in the Global Drug Trade.* Rev. ed. Chicago: Hill Books, 2003.

McCullough, David. *Truman.* New York: Simon and Schuster, 1992.

McDonnell, Janet A. *After Desert Storm: The U.S. Army and the Reconstruction of Kuwait.* Washington DC: U.S. Department of the Army, 1999.

———. *The U.S. Army Corps of Engineers in the Persian Gulf War.* Alexandria VA: Office of History, Army Corps of Engineers, 1996.

McFerrin, John B. "The Kentucky Rock Asphalt Company." *Southern Economic Journal* 4, no. 4 (1938): 455–65.

McKibben, Bill. *Falter: Has the Human Game Begun to Play Itself Out?* New York: Holt, 2019.

———. "In the Midst of the Coronavirus Pandemic, Construction Is Set to Resume on the Keystone Pipeline." *New Yorker.* April 2, 2020. www.newyorker.com/news /daily-comment/in-the-midst-of-the-coronavirus-pandemic-construction-is-set -to-resume-on-the-keystone-pipeline.

———. "It's Not Just What Exxon Did—It's What the Company Is Still Doing." *Grist.* February 19, 2016. https://grist.org/business-technology/its-not-just-what-exxon -did-its-what-the-oil-company-is-still-doing/.

McLachlan, Stéphane M. "'Water Is a Living Thing': Environmental and Human Health Implications of the Athabasca Oil Sands for the Mikisew Cree First

Nation and Athabasca Chipewyan First Nation in Northern Alberta." Environmental Conservation Laboratory. 2014. https://landuse.alberta.ca/Forms%20and%20Applications/RFR_ACFN%20Reply%20to%20Crown%20Submission%206%20-%20TabD11%20Report_2014-08_PUBLIC.pdf.

McNichol, Dan. *Paving the War: Asphalt in America*. Lanham MD: National Asphalt Pavement Association, 2006.

———. *The Roads That Built America: The Incredible Story of the U.S. Interstate System*. New York: Sterling, 2006.

McShane, Clay. *Down the Asphalt Path: The Automobile and the American City*. New York: Columbia University Press, 1994.

Meckenstock, Rainer U., Frederick von Netzer, Christine Stumpp, Tillmann Lueders, Anne M. Himmelberg, Norbert Hertkorn, Philipp Schmitt-Kopplin, et al. "Water Droplets in Oil Are Microhabitats for Microbial Life." *Science* 345, no. 6197 (2014): 673–76.

Megargee, Geoffrey P., ed. *Encyclopedia of Camps and Ghettos, 1933–1945*. Vol. 1, *Early Camps, Youth Camps, and Concentration Camps and Subcamps under the SS-Business Administration Main Office (WVHA)*. 3 vols. Bloomington: Indiana University Press; Washington DC: Holocaust Memorial Museum, 2009.

Mencken, H. L. *Happy Days: Mencken's Autobiography, 1880–1892*. 1940. Reprint, Baltimore: Johns Hopkins University Press, 1996.

Mercher, Jordan, dir. *Chavez Ravine: A Los Angeles Story*. San Francisco: ITVS (Independent Television Service), 2003.

Merlin, Mark D., and Ricardo M. Gonzalez. "Environmental Impacts of Nuclear Testing in Remote Oceania, 1946–1996." In *Environmental Histories of the Cold War*, edited by John R. McNeill and Corinna R. Unger, 167–202. New York: German Historical Institute/Cambridge University Press, 2010.

Merriam, John C. "Death Trap of the Ages." *Sunset*, October 1908, 465–75.

Meyer, Richard F., and Wallace de Witt Jr. *Definition and World Resources of Natural Bitumens*. U.S. Geological Survey Bulletin 1944. Washington DC: Government Printing Office, 1990.

Meyer, Richard F., Emil D. Attanasi, and Philip A. Freeman. "Heavy Oil and Natural Bitumen Resources in Geological Basins of the World." Open-File Report 2007-1084. U.S. Geological Survey. 2007. https://pubs.usgs.gov/of/2007/1084/OF2007-1084v1.pdf.

Michels, Patrick. "These Stunning Photos Show the Real Cost of a Pipeline." *Mother Jones*. May 27, 2017. www.motherjones.com/environment/2017/05/first-nations-indigenous-pipeline-canada/.

Middlebrook, Martin. *The Battle of Hamburg: Allied Bomber Forces against a German City in 1943*. New York: Scribner's Sons, 1981.

Miles, Donna. "Gates, Pace: No Plans for War, but U.S. Won't Tolerate Iran's Interference." DOD News. February 2, 2007. https://archive.defense.gov/news/newsarticle.aspx?id=2909.

Miller, David. *The Cold War: A Military History.* New York: St. Martin's Press, 1999.

Milton, John. *Paradise Lost.* Edited by Thomas H. Luxon. John Milton Reading Room. Accessed August 5, 2020. www.dartmouth.edu/~milton.

Mithen, Steven, with Sue Mithen. *Thirst: Water and Power in the Ancient World.* Cambridge MA: Harvard University Press, 2012.

Mohl, Raymond A. "Race and Space in the Modern City: Interstate-95 and the Black Community in Miami." In *Urban Policy in Twentieth-Century America,* edited by Arnold R. Hirsch and Raymond A. Mohl, 100–158. New Brunswick NJ: Rutgers University Press, 2013.

Mommer, Bernard. "The Value of Extra-Heavy Crude Oil from the Orinoco Belt." *Middle East Economic Survey.* March 15, 2004. www-personal.umich.edu/~twod/venezuela/nwaeg_mar07/doktor_mommer_orimulsion.pdf.

Mommsen, Hans. *Das Volkswagenwerk und seine Arbeiter im Dritten Reich.* Dusseldorf: Econ, 1996.

———. "Place of Remembrance of Forced Labor in the Volkswagen Factory." Volkswagen. Accessed January 15, 2017. www.volkswagenag.com/presence/konzern/documents/history/englisch/Katalog_Erinnerungsst%c3%a4tte_en.pdf.

Monroy, Douglas. *Rebirth: Mexican Los Angeles from the Great Migration to the Great Depression.* Berkeley: University of California Press, 1999.

Morris, Christopher. *The Big Muddy: An Environmental History of the Mississippi and Its Peoples from Hernando de Soto to Hurricane Katrina.* New York: Oxford University Press, 2012.

Moynihan, Daniel Patrick. "Policy vs. Program in the '70's." *Public Interest* 20 (Summer 1970): 90–100.

Mueller, Robert S., III. *Report on the Investigation into Russian Interference in the 2016 Presidential Election.* Washington DC: U.S. Department of Justice, 2019. www.justice.gov/sco.

Munzenrieder, Kyle. "Jetsetter Donald Trump Is Obsessed with America's 'Third World' Airports." *W Magazine.* September 27, 2016. www.wmagazine.com/story/donald-trump-is-obsessed-with-americas-third-world-airports.

Murphy, Bruce. "Mistakes Made on Hendricks Home." *Urban Milwaukee.* May 22, 2017. http://urbanmilwaukee.com/2017/05/22/mistakes-made-on-hendricks-assessment/.

Murphy, Jessica. "Trans Mountain: The Billion-Dollar Oil Pipeline Canadians Own and Can't Build." BBC. November 26, 2018. www.bbc.com/news/world-us-canada-45972346.

Murray, T. J. "Dr. Abraham Gesner: Father of the Petroleum Industry." *Journal of the Royal Society of Medicine* 86, no. 1 (1993): 43–44.

Myclo, Mary. *Wormwood Forest: A Natural History of Chernobyl.* Washington DC: Henry, 2005.

Naske, Claus-M. *Paving Alaska's Trails: The Work of the Alaska Road Commission.* New York: University Press of America, 1986.

National Academies of Sciences, Engineering, and Medicine. *Spills of Diluted Bitumen from Pipelines: A Comparative Study of Environmental Fate, Effects, and Response.* Washington DC: National Academies Press, 2016.

"National Office Technical Advice Memorandum." Internal Revenue Service. January 12, 2011. www.documentcloud.org/documents/405311-oil-spill-liability-trust -fund-irs-2011-memo.html.

"National September 11 Memorial." Wiss, Janney, Elstner Associates. 2011. www.wje .com/assets/pdfs/projects/National_September_11_Memorial.pdf.

Nemtsova, Anna. "Ukraine Tears Down Soviet Symbols, Winks at Nazi Ones." *Daily Beast.* May 29, 2015. www.thedailybeast.com/ukraine-tears-down-soviet-symbols -winks-at-nazi-ones.

Neufeld, Jacob, and George M. Watson Jr. *Coalition Air Warfare in the Korean War, 1950–1953.* Washington DC: Air Force History and Museums Program, 2005.

"New Round of Big Dig Repairs Could Cost State." CBS News Boston. June 7, 2012. http://boston.cbslocal.com/2012/06/07/new-round-of-big-dig-repairs-could-cost -state-1-million/.

New York State Organized Crime Task Force. *Final Report: Corruption and Racketeering in the New York City Construction Industry.* New York: New York University Press, 1991.

Nichols, Jeffrey D. "Sam Gilson Did Much More Than Promote Gilsonite." *History to Go.* May 1995. https://historytogo.utah.gov/.

Nikiforuk, Andrew. *Tar Sands: Dirty Oil and the Future of a Continent.* Rev. ed. Vancouver: Greystone Books, 2010.

Nissenbaum, Arie. "The Dead Sea: An Economic Resource for 10,000 Years." In *Saline Lakes V: Proceedings of the Vth International Symposium on Inland Saline Lakes,* edited by Stuart H. Hurlbert, 127–42. Berlin: Springer Science+Business Media, 1993.

———. "Dead Sea Asphalts: Historical Aspects." *AAPG Bulletin* 62, no. 5 (1978): 837–44.

Noble, Louise. *Medicinal Cannibalism in Early Modern English Literature and Culture.* New York: Palgrave Macmillan, 2011.

"Northway Staging Field." Alaska Environmental Conservation Department. September 2008. https://dec.alaska.gov/spar/csp/sites/northway.htm.

"Odebrecht and Braskem Plead Guilty and Agree to Pay at Least $3.5 Billion in Global Penalties to Resolve Largest Foreign Bribery Case in History." Press release. U.S. Department of Justice. December 21, 2016. www.justice.gov/opa/pr/odebrecht-and -braskem-plead-guilty-and-agree-pay-least-35-billion-global-penalties-resolve.

Office of the Under Secretary of Defense for Acquisition, Technology, and Logistics. "Climate-Related Risk to DOD Infrastructure: Initial Vulnerability Assessment Survey." U.S. Department of Defense. January 2018. https://climateandsecurity .files.wordpress.com/2018/01/tab-b-slvas-report-1-24-2018.pdf.

Opie, John, Char Miller, and Kenna Lang Archer. *Ogallala: Water for a Dry Land*. 3rd ed. Lincoln: University of Nebraska Press, 2018.

"Outline of Operation Overlord." 8-3.4 AA Vol. 7. U.S. Army. 1944. https://history .army.mil/documents/WWII/g4-OL/g4-ol.htm.

Oxilia, Gregorio, Flavia Fiorillo, Francesco Boschin, Elisabetta Boaretto, Salvatore A. Apicella, Chiara Matteucci, Daniele Panetta, et al. "The Dawn of Dentistry in the Late Upper Paleolithic." *American Journal of Physical Anthropology* 163, no. 3 (2017): 446–61.

Pan, Jonathan. "Silent Kingmaker: The Need for a Unified Wartime Contracting Strategy." *JFQ* 60 (2011): 38–41. www.dtic.mil/dtic/tr/fulltext/u2/a536619.pdf.

Parker, James E. *Covert Ops: The CIA's Secret War in Laos*. New York: St. Martin's Press, 1997.

"Paving the Road to Reconstruction." Army News Service. June 6, 2009. www.army .mil/article/22288/paving_the_road_to_reconstruction.

Pearson, Natalie M. "Engineer Aviation Units in the Southwest Pacific Theater during World War II." Master's thesis, Army Command and General Staff College, Fort Leavenworth KS, 2005.

Penn, Nathaniel. "The Untold Story of the Texas Biker Gang Shoot Out." *GQ*. May 17, 2015. www.gq.com/story/untold-story-texas-biker-gang-shoot-out.

Peters, Kenneth E., and Clifford C. Walters. *The Biomarker Guide*. Vol. 1, *Biomarkers and Isotopes in the Environment and Human History*. 2nd ed. 2 vols. New York: Cambridge University Press, 2005.

Peterson, Martha. *The Widow Spy: My CIA Journey from the Jungles of Laos to Prison in Moscow*. Wilmington NC: Red Canary, 2012.

Petroski, Henry. *The Road Taken: The History and Future of America's Infrastructure*. New York: Bloomsbury, 2016.

Pfeiffer, Jack. *Official History of the Bay of Pigs Operation*. 5 vols. Washington DC: National Security Archive, 1979–84.

Pianin, Eric, and Charles R. Babcock. "Easy Street: The Bud Shuster Interchange." *Washington Post Magazine*. April 5, 1998. www.washingtonpost.com/wp-srv /politics/special/highway/stories/hwy040598a.htm.

Pierce, Charles. "Republicans Have Set Up Shop at the Crossroads [. . .]." *Esquire*. June 26, 2020. www.esquire.com/news-politics/politics/a32979177/trump -administration-aca-supreme-court-brief/.

Pigott, Peter. *Canada in Afghanistan: The War So Far*. Toronto: Dundurn Group, 2007.

Pinckney, Darryl. "Black Lives and the Police." *New York Review of Books*, August 18, 2016, 68–72.

Pinney, Thomas, ed. *Rudyard Kipling: Something of Myself and Other Autobiographical Writings*. New York: Cambridge University Press, 1990.

"Pit 91." La Brea Tar Pits and Museum. Accessed July 21, 2018. https://tarpits.org /experience-tar-pits/pit-91.

Pliny the Elder. *The Natural History*. Translated by John Bostock and Henry T. Riley. Perseus Digital Library. 1855. www.perseus.tufts.edu/hopper/text?doc= Plin.+Nat.+toc.

Ploger, Robert R. *U.S. Army Engineers, 1965–1970*. Washington DC: Government Printing Office, 1974.

Plowden, William. *The Motor Car and Politics, 1896–1900*. London: Bodley Head, 1971.

Plutarch. *Moralia*. Vol. 5, *Isis and Osiris*. Translated by Frank Cole Babbitt. Loeb Classic Library ed. 15 vols. Cambridge MA: Harvard University Press, 1935.

Prados, John. *The Blood Road: The Ho Chi Minh Trail and the Vietnam War*. New York: Wiley, 1999.

Pratt, Larry. *The Tar Sands: Syncrude and the Politics of Oil*. Edmonton: Hurtig, 1976.

Prescott, William H. *History of the Conquest of Peru*. 3rd ed. 2 vols. 1847. Reprint, Philadelphia: Lippincott, 1902.

Pressac, Jean-Claude, with Robert-Jan Van Pelt. "The Machinery of Mass Murder at Auschwitz." In *Anatomy of the Auschwitz Death Camp*, edited by Yisrael Gutman and Michael Berenbaum, 183–235. Bloomington: Indiana University Press, 1998.

Pringle, Denys, trans. *Pilgrimage to Jerusalem and the Holy Land, 1187–1291*. New York: Routledge, 2012.

Pringle, Heather Anne. *The Mummy Congress: Science, Obsession, and the Everlasting Dead*. New York: Hyperion, 2001.

Public Papers of the Presidents of the United States: George W. Bush 2007. 2 bks. Washington DC: Government Printing Office, 2009.

Purchas, Samuel. *Purchas His Pilgrimes*. 20 vols. London: Stansby, 1615.

"Qarmat Ali Water Treatment Facility." U.S. Department of Veteran Affairs. Accessed August 30, 2019. www.publichealth.va.gov/exposures/qarmat-ali/.

"Quarterly Report to the United States Congress." Special Inspector General for Afghanistan Reconstruction. January 30, 2016. www.sigar.mil/pdf/quarterlyreports /2016-01-30qr.pdf.

Quebec Commission on the Award and Management of Public Contracts in the Construction Industry. *Final Report*. 4 vols. National Archives of Quebec. 2015. www.ceic.gouv.qc.ca/.

Rabe, Stephen G. *The Road to OPEC: United States Relations with Venezuela, 1919–1976*. Austin: University of Texas Press, 1982.

"Race and Ethnicity in Fatal Motor Vehicle Traffic Crashes, 1999–2004." U.S. Department of Transportation. 2006. https://crashstats.nhtsa.dot.gov/Api/Public/ViewPublication/809956.

Raisman, David S. "The Alaska-Siberia Friendship Route." In Chandonnet, *Alaska at War*, 341–44.

Raleigh, Sir Walter. *Discovery of Guiana*. 1596. Reprint, London: Cassell, 1901.

Ramseur, Jonathan L. "Oil Sands and the Oil Spill Liability Trust Fund: The Definition of 'Oil' and Related Issues for Congress." Congressional Research Service. 2017. https://fas.org/sgp/crs/misc/R43128.pdf.

Ramsey, Winston. *Invasion Airfields Then and Now*. Old Harlow, Essex: After the Battle, 2017.

Rangel, Nicolas Jr. "Ambiguously Articulating 'Americanism': The Rhetoric of Hiram Wesley Evans and the Klan of the 1920s." *American Communication Journal* 11, no. 2 (2009). http://ac-journal.org/journal/2009/Summer/8ambiguouslyArticulating.pdf.

Rappaport, Meron. "Israel's Separation Fence (part 1)." *Electronic Intifada*. May 31, 2003. https://electronicintifada.net/content/israels-separation-fence-part-1/4604.

Raspopova, Alina. "Putin Made a Road Disassembly." *Gazeta.ru*. August 10, 2014. www.gazeta.ru/auto/2014/10/08_a_6254481.shtml.

Read, Alexander. *Chirurgorum Comes, or The Whole Practice of Chirurgery*. London: Jones, for Wilkinson, 1687.

Reese, April. "Border Fence: Smuggler's Gulch Project a 'Disaster' for Estuary, Critics Say." E&E News. January 15, 2009. www.eenews.net/stories/73133.

Reid, Carlton. *Roads Were Not Built for Cars*. Washington DC: Island, 2015.

Reitan, Jon. "The Nazi Camps in the Norwegian Historical Culture." In *Historicizing the Uses of the Past*, edited by Helle Bjerg, Claudia Lenz, and Erik Thorstensen, 57–76. Bielefeld, Germany: Transcript, 2011.

Relph, Edward. *Place and Placelessness*. London: Pion, 1965.

"Remarks by President Trump at the Unleashing American Energy Event." White House. June 29, 2017. https://factba.se/topic/latest/whitehouse/remarks-president-trump-unleashing-american-energy-event-20170629.

"Removal Action: Containerized Waste and Petroleum-Contaminated Soil." Army Corps of Engineers. October 29, 2013. www.poa.usace.army.mil/Portals/34/docs/civilworks/publicreview/ColdBayfudseafonsioct2013.pdf.

"Report on Data from the Airborne Hazards and Open Burn Pit (AH&OBP) Registry." VA Office of Public Health. 2015. www.publichealth.va.gov/docs/exposures/va-ahobp-registry-data-report-june2015.pdf.

"Restoring the Quality of Our Environment." U.S. President's Science Advisory Committee, Environmental Pollution Panel. 1965. www.climatefiles.com/climate-change-evidence/presidents-report-atmospher-carbon-dioxide/.

Reybold, Eugene. "General MacArthur Told Me: 'This Is Distinctly an Engineers' War.'" *Popular Science*, May 1945, 90–99.

Rhem, Kathleen T. "Military Commander Details Mission That Killed Hussein's Sons." DOD News. July 23, 2003. https://archive.defense.gov/news/newsarticle.aspx?id=28686.

"Rhetoric versus Reality in the War in Raqqa." Amnesty International. 2019. https://raqqa.amnesty.org/.

Rhodes, Richard. *Energy: A Human History*. New York: Simon and Schuster, 2018.

———. *The Making of the Atomic Bomb*. New York: Simon and Schuster, 1986.

Rich, Nathaniel. *Losing Earth: A Recent History*. New York: MCD/Farrar, Strauss and Giroux, 2019.

Richardson, Clifford. *The Asphalt Pavement*. New York: Wiley and Sons, 1905.

Rose, Mark H., and Raymond A. Mohl. *Interstate Highway Politics and Policy since 1939*. Knoxville: University of Tennessee Press, 2012.

Roseman, Mark. *The Wannsee Conference and the Final Solution*. New York: Picador, 2002.

Rothschild, Daniel, and Walter E. Block. "Don't Steal; the Government Hates Competition: The Problem with Civil Asset Forfeiture." *Journal of Private Enterprise* 31, no. 1 (2016): 45–56.

Royal Society of Canada. *The Behavior and Environmental Impacts of Crude Oil Released into Aqueous Environments*. Ottawa: Royal Society of Canada, 2015.

"Rubble to Runway: The Triumph of Tegel." National Museum of the U.S. Air Force. June 1, 2015. www.nationalmuseum.af.mil/Visit/Museum-Exhibits/Fact-Sheets/Display/Article/197657/rubble-to-runway-the-triumph-of-tegel/.

"Rules and Regulations for the Operations of German Prisoner of War Camps." Office of the Commanding General Army Services Forces. Ca. 1941. http://lawofwar.org/German%20pow%20rules.htm.

Sabol Spezio, Teresa. *Slick Policy: Environmental and Science Policy in the Aftermath of the Santa Barbara Oil Spill*. Pittsburgh: University of Pittsburgh Press, 2018.

Sadasivam, Naveena. "The Texas-Mexico Border Wall Comes with a Dangerous, Costly Side Effect: Flooding." *Texas Observer*. August 17, 2018. www.texasobserver.org/the-texas-mexico-border-wall-comes-with-a-dangerous-costly-side-effect-flooding/.

Sadik-Khan, Janette. *Streetfight: Handbook for an Urban Revolution*. New York: Viking, 2016.

Sahling, Heiko, Maxim Rubin Bloom, Christian Borowski, and Gerhard Bohrmann. "Seafloor Observations at Campeche Knolls, Southern Gulf of Mexico: Coexistence of Asphalt Deposits, Oil Seepage, and Gas Venting." *Biogeosciences Discussions*, March 2016, 101–3.

Sánchez-Bayo, Francisco, and Kris A .G. Wyckhuys. "Worldwide Decline of the Entomofauna: A Review of Its Drivers." *Biological Conservation* 232 (April 2019): 8–27.

Sánchez-Villagra, Marcello R., Orangel A. Aguilera, and Alfredo A. Carlini, eds. *Urumaco and Venezuelan Pleontology*. Bloomington: Indiana University Press, 2010.

Sass, Stephen L. *The Substance of Civilization: Materials and Human History from the Stone Age to the Age of Silicon*. New York: Arcade, 2011.

Sassoon, David. "Koch Brothers' Political Activism Protects Their 50-Year Stake in Canadian Heavy Oils." Inside Climate News. May 10, 2012. https://insideclimatenews.org/news/20120510/koch-industries-brothers-tar-sands-bitumen-heavy-oil-flint-pipelines-refinery-alberta-canada.

Schenk, Christopher J., Troy A. Cook, Ronald R. Carpentier, Richard M. Pollastro, Timothy R. Klett, Marilyn E. Tennyson, Mark A. Kirschbaum, Michael E. Brownfield, and Janet K. Pitman. "An Estimate of Recoverable Heavy Oil Resources of the Orinoco Oil Belt, Venezuela." Fact Sheet 2009-3028. U.S. Geological Survey. 2010. https://pubs.usgs.gov/fs/2009/3028/.

Schiff, Stacy. *Cleopatra: A Life*. Boston: Little, Brown, 2010.

Schloss, Eva. *Amsterdam, 11. Mai 1944: Das Ende meiner Kindheit* [Amsterdam, May 11, 1944: The end of my childhood]. *Weimar:* Eckhaus, 2015.

Schmitt, Angie. "Meet Jerry Wray, Ohio's 'Asphalt Sheriff.'" Streetsblog USA. January 30, 2013. http://usa.streetsblog.org/2013/01/29/the-state-dot-revolving-door-meet-jerry-wray-ohios-asphalt-sheriff/.

———. "Oklahoma's Gary Ridley: Asphalt Lobbyist, DOT Chief." Streetsblog USA. January 30, 2013. http://usa.streetsblog.org/2013/01/30/the-revolving-door-oklahomas-gary-ridley-asphalt-lobbyist-dot-chief/.

Schnapp, Jeffrey T. "Three Pieces of Asphalt." *Grey Room* 11 (Spring 2003): 5–21.

Schubert, Frank N. "The Persian Gulf Command: Lifeline to the Soviet Union." In Fowle, *Builders and Fighters*, 305–16.

Schwab, David J. "Statistical Analysis of Straits of Mackinac Line 5: Worst Case Spill Scenarios." University of Michigan Water Center. 2016. http://graham.umich.edu/media/pubs/Mackinac-Line-5-Worst-Case-Spill-Scenarios.pdf.

Schwartz, Gary T. "Urban Freeways and the Interstate System." *Southern California Law Review* 49 (March 1976): 406–513.

"Seabee History: Formation of the Seabees and World War II." Naval History and Heritage Command. 2015. www.history.navy.mil/research/library/online-reading -room/title-list-alphabetically/s/seabee-history0/world-war-ii.html.

"Seabee History: Operations Desert Shield/Desert Storm." Naval History and Heritage Command. 2015. www.history.navy.mil/research/library/online-reading -room/.

Seely, Bruce E. *Building the American Highway System: Engineers as Policy Makers.* Philadelphia: Temple University Press, 1987.

Seiler, Andreas, and J-O Helldin. "Mortality in Wildlife Due to Transportation." In *The Ecology of Transportation*, edited by John Davenport and Julia Davenport, 165–90. New York: Springer, 2006.

Semuels, Alana. "The Role of Highways in American Poverty." *Atlantic.* March 18, 2016. www.theatlantic.com/business/archive/2016/03/role-of-highways-in -american-poverty/474282/.

Senate Committee on Relations with Cuba. *Itemized Statement of Expenditures Made under the Heading of Sanitation in the Island of Cuba.* Washington DC: Government Printing Office, 1900.

Senate Committee on the District of Columbia. *Message from the President of the United States Communicating the Report of the Commissioners Created by the Act Authorizing the Repavement of Pennsylvania Avenue.* 44th Cong., 2nd Sess. (1876).

Senate Select Committee on Intelligence. *Report on Russian Active Measures Campaigns and Interference in the 2016 U.S. Election.* Vol. 5, *Counterintelligence Threats and Vulnerabilities.* 5 vols. 116th Cong, 1st Sess. (2020).

Severance, James R. "Amzi Lorenzo Barber." *Oberlin Alumni Magazine,* June 1909, 341–46.

"Shaft Sealing Construction Procedures." Waste Isolation Pilot Plant. 2010. www .env.nm.gov/.

Shakespeare, William. *Antony and Cleopatra.* Ca. 1607, 1623. Folger Shakespeare Library. Accessed November 11, 2019. www.folger.edu/antony-and-cleopatra.

Shaner, Andrew. "Asylums, Asphalt, and Ethics." *Hospital and Community Psychiatry* 40, no. 8 (1989): 785–86.

"Shell Document Index." Climate Investigations Center. Accessed February 11, 2019. http://climateinvestigations.org/shell-oil-climate-documents/document-index/.

Shellenbarger, Jean, ed. *The 9th Engineer Battalion, First Marine Division, in Vietnam.* Jefferson NC: McFarland, 2007.

Sheppard, Mary Clark, ed. *Oil Sands Scientist: The Letters of Karl A. Clark, 1920–1949.* Edmonton: University of Alberta Press, 1989.

Sherrill, Robert. *First Amendment Felon: The Story of Frank Wilkinson.* New York: Nation Books, 2009.

Shoup, Donald C. *The High Cost of Free Parking*. Chicago: Planners/American Planning Association, 2005.

Shrivastava, Meenal, and Lorna Stefanick, eds. *Alberta Oil and the Decline of Democracy in Canada*. Edmonton: Athabasca University Press, 2015.

Siegelbaum, Lewis H. *Cars for Comrades*. Ithaca NY: Cornell University Press, 2008.

Simple Sabotage Field Manual. Office of Strategic Services. January 17, 1944. www.cia.gov/news-information/featured-story-archive/2012-featured-story-archive/CleaneduosssimpleSabotage_sm.pdf.

Singer, Charles J., Eric J. Holmyard, Alfred R. Hall, and Trevor I. Williams, eds. *A History of Technology*. 5 vols. Oxford: Clarendon, 1954–84.

Slowey, Gabrielle, and Lorna Stefanick. "Development at What Cost? First Nations, Ecological Integrity, and Democracy." In Shrivastava and Stefanick, *Alberta Oil*, 195–224.

Smith, Jason Scott. *Building New Deal Liberalism: The Political Economy of Public Works, 1933–1956*. New York: Cambridge University Press, 2006.

Smith, Kendal. "Longest Road Project in Iraq Marks Security Success." American Forces Press Service. February 19, 2008. http://archive.defense.gov/news/newsarticle.aspx?id=49001.

Sorensen, W. Connor. "The Civilian Conservation Corps in Alaska (1933–1942) and Military Preparedness." In Chandonnet, *Alaska at War*, 235–40.

Sorin, Gretchen. *Driving While Black: African American Travel and the Road to Civil Rights*. New York: Liveright, 2020.

Speight, James G. *Asphalt: Materials Science and Technology*. Waldham MA: Elsevier/Butterworth-Heinemann, 2016.

———. *The Chemistry and Technology of Petroleum*. Boca Raton FL: CRC, 1999.

"Spiro Agnew." Federal Bureau of Investigation. Accessed September 10, 2020. https://vault.fbi.gov/Spiro%20Agnew.

Spring, Peter. *Great Walls and Linear Barriers*. Barnsley, England: Pen and Sword, 2015.

Stahl, Alexander G., and David R. Cameron. "The Politico-Economic Problems of Developing the Alberta Oil Sands." Climate Files. 1981. www.climatefiles.com/exxonmobil/1981-imperial-oil-problems-of-developing-tar-sands/.

Standing Rock Sioux v. Army Corps of Engineers. Bloomberg Law. March 25, 2020. www.bloomberglaw.com/public/desktop/document/standingrocksiouxtribevunitedstatesarmycorpsofengineersdocketNo11/1?1585165801.

"Statement by Harry Sargeant III on Sargeant Marine and Brazilian Car Wash Probe." PR Newswire. August 19, 2017. www.prnewswire.com/news-releases/statement-by-harry-sargeant-iii-on-sargeant-marine-and-brazilian-car-wash-probe-300506835.html.

"Statement on Inaccurate Media Reports Involving Harry Sargeant III and Ukraine."
PR Newswire. October 7, 2019. www.prnewswire.com/news-releases/statement-on
-inaccurate-media-reports-involving-harry-sargeant-iii-and-ukraine-300933333.html.

"State's Statement Regarding Draft of Alternatives Analysis." Michigan Petroleum
Pipelines. June 29, 2017. https://mipetroleumpipelines.com/document/alternatives
-analysis-straits-pipeline.

Stauffer, Alvin P. *The Quartermaster Corps: Operations in the War against Japan.*
1956. Reprint, Washington DC: U.S. Department of the Army, 1956.

Stead, William Thomas. *The Centenary of 1798.* London: Review of Reviews Office,
1898.

Steeds, Oliver. "Highway 15: Kingdom at the Crossroads." 2003. http://oliversteeds
.com/docs/Highway_15_Kingdom_at_the_Crossroads.pdf.

Steegmuller, Francis, trans. *Flaubert in Egypt.* 1972. Reprint, New York: Penguin, 1996.

Steil, Benn. *The Marshall Plan.* New York: Simon and Schuster, 2018.

Steinbeck, John. *The Grapes of Wrath.* 1939. Reprint, New York: Penguin, 2006.

———. *The Wayward Bus.* New York: Viking, 1947.

Stilgoe, John. *Borderland: Origins of the American Suburb.* New Haven CT: Yale
University Press, 1988.

Stockman, Lorne. "Petroleum Coke: The Coal Hiding in the Tar Sands." *Oil Change
International.* January 2013. http://priceofoil.org/content/uploads/2013/01/OCI
.Petcoke.FINALSCREEN.pdf.

Stoddard, Christine, and Misty Thomas. *Richmond Cemeteries.* Charleston SC:
Arcadia, 2014.

Stokl, Jonathan. "Nebuchadnezzar: History, Memory, and Myth-Making in the
Persian Period." In *Remembering Biblical Figures in the Late Persian and Early
Hellenistic Periods,* edited by Diana V. Edelman and Ehud Ben Zvi, 257–69. New
York: Oxford University Press, 2013.

Stone, Roy. *New Roads and Road Laws in the United States.* New York: Van Nostrand, 1904.

Strabo. *Geography.* Translated by H. C. Hamilton and William Falconer. Perseus
Digital Library. 1854–57. www.perseus.tufts.edu/hopper/text?doc=Perseus%3atext
%3a1999.01.0239.

Subcommittee for Special Investigations, House Armed Services Committee. *Hearings on Asphalt Paving Materials.* 85th Cong. (1957–58).

Subcommittee on Energy and Mineral Resources, House Committee on Natural
Resources. *The Vast North American Resource Potential of Oil Shale, Oil Sands,
and Heavy Oils.* 109th Cong., 1st Sess. (2005).

Sugg, Richard. *Mummies, Cannibals and Vampires: The History of Corpse Medicine
from the Renaissance to the Victorians.* New York: Routledge, 2011.

Svoboda, Elizabeth. "Unearthing the Atrocities of Nazi Death Camps." *Scientific American*. April 30, 2016. www.scientificamerican.com/article/unearthing-the -atrocities-of-nazi-death-camps/.

Sweeny, Alastair. *Black Bonanza*. Mississauga ON: Wiley and Sons Canada, 2010.

Swift, Robert. *The Big Roads: The Untold Story of the Engineers, Visionaries, and Trailblazers Who Created the American Superhighways*. Boston: Houghton Mifflin Harcourt, 2011.

Taft, Kevin. *Oil's Deep State: How the Petroleum Industry Undermines Democracy and Stops Action on Global Warming—in Alberta, and in Ottawa*. Toronto: Lorimer, 2017.

Takach, George F. *Tar Wars*. Edmonton: University of Alberta Press, 2017.

Taubman, William. *Khrushchev: The Man and His Era*. New York: Norton, 2003.

Taylor, Candacy. *Overground Railroad: The Green Book and the Roots of Black Travel in America*. New York: Abrams, 2000.

Taylor, Nick. *American Made: The Enduring Legacy of the wpa; When FDR Put America to Work*. New York: Bantam, 2008.

Teer, Dillard. Oral history. *Documenting the American South*. University of North Carolina– Chapel Hill. January 20, 1997. https://cdn.lib.unc.edu/blue-ridge -parkway/media/Teer/19970120_Teer.pdf.

Teer, Dillard, Robert D. Teer, and Anna Daugrid. *Courage Ever: An American Success Story; Nello L. Teer, Sr., and His Company*. Durham NC: Teer Associates, 2001.

Testament of Solomon. Translated by Frederick C. Conybeare. Early Jewish Writings. 1898. www.earlyjewishwritings.com/testsolomon.html.

"Testimony of Oklahoma State Trooper Charles J. Hanger concerning His Arrest of Timothy McVeight." School of Law, University of Missouri–Kansas City. April 19, 1995. http://law2.umkc.edu/faculty/projects/ftrials/mcveigh/mcveigharrest.html.

Thacker, Toby. *Joseph Goebbels: Life and Death*. New York: Palgrave Macmillan, 2009.

Thibault, Cecilia Ziobro. *Trapped in a Nightmare*. Bloomington IN: iUniverse, 2011.

Thomas, David. "Why Bitumen Isn't Necessarily Safer Than Bakken." *Railway Age*. February 23, 2015. www.railwayage.com/index.php/safety/why-bitumen-isnt -necessarily-safer-than-bakken.html.

Thucydides. *Peloponnesian War*. Translated by Alfred D. Godley. Perseus Digital Library. 1920. www.perseus.tufts.edu/hopper/text?doc=Perseus%3atext%3a1999 .01.0126%3abook%3d2%3achapter%3d89%3asection%3d1.

Tilson, George William. *Street Pavements and Paving Materials*. New York: Wiley and Sons, 1912.

Timbs v. Indiana. 139 S. Ct. 682 (2019).

"Toxic 100 Air Polluters Index." Political Economy Research Institute. University of Massachusetts Amherst. Accessed September 22, 2019. www.peri.umass.edu /toxic-100-air-polluters-index-2016-report-based-on-2014-data.

"Toxic 100 Water Polluters Index." Political Economy Research Institute. University of Massachusetts Amherst. Accessed September 22, 2019. www.peri.umass.edu /water-100-polluters-index.

"Transcript: President Trump on 'Face the Nation.'" Interview by Margaret Brennan. CBS News. February 3, 2019. www.cbsnews.com/news/transcript-president-trump -on-face-the-nation-february-3-2019/.

Trass, Adrian G. *Engineers at War*. Washington DC: Army Center of Military History, 2010.

Tregaskis, Richard. *Southeast Asia: Building the Bases, the History of Construction in Southeast Asia*. Washington DC: Government Printing Office, 1975.

"Trends of Asphalt Shingle Market Share Reviewed for 2019 with Industry Size, Outlook to 2025." *Market Watch*. September 11, 2019. www.marketwatch.com /press-release/trends-of-asphalt-shingles-market-share-reviewed-for-2019-with -industry-size-outlook-to-2025-2019-09-11.

"Triborough (Robert F. Kennedy) Bridge: Historic Overview." New York City Roads. Accessed December 11, 2017. www.nycroads.com/crossings/triborough/.

Tribunal of Inquiry into Payments to Politicians and Related Matters. *Report*. 2 pts. Dublin: Stationary Office, 2011. https://moriarty-tribunal.ie/.

Troilo, Pete, and Jeff Tyson. "Dark Cloud of Legal Trouble Begins to Lift Away from Louis Berger." Devex. August 31, 2015. www.devex.com/news/dark-cloud-of-legal -trouble-begins-to-lift-away-from-louis-berger-86671.

Trollinger, Susan L., and William V. Trollinger Jr. *Righting America at the Creation Museum*. Baltimore: Johns Hopkins University Press, 2016.

Trotsky, Leon. *The Revolution Betrayed*. Translated by Max Eastman. Garden City NY: Doubleday, Doran, 1937.

Trotter, Joe William. *Black Milwaukee: The Making of an Industrial Proletariat, 1915–1945*. 2nd ed. Urbana: University of Illinois Press, 2007.

Turhollow, Anthony F. "Airfields for Heavy Bombers." In Fowle, *Builders and Fighters*, 207–14.

Turner, Chris. *The Patch: The People, Pipelines, and Politics of the Oil Sands*. New York: Simon and Schuster, 2017.

Twain, Mark. *The Innocents Abroad*. Hartford CT: American, 1869.

UNICEF. *The State of the World's Children*. www.unicef.org/sowc/.

United States v. Blagojevich. 662 F. Supp. 2d 998 (N.D. IL 2009).

United States v. Cellini. 596 F. Supp. 2d 1194 (N.D. IL 2009).

United States v. City of Parma, Ohio. 494 F. Supp. 1049 (1979).

United States v. Palumbo Brothers. 742 F. 2d 656 (7th Cir. 1998).

Urwin, Gregory J. W. *Victory in Defeat: The Wake Island Defenders in Captivity*. Annapolis MD: Naval Institute Press, 2010.

U.S. Army Corps of Engineers, Omaha District. "The District's First Decade." Accessed July 5, 2018. www.nwo.usace.army.mil.

The U.S. Army's Role in Peace Enforcement Operations, 1995–2004: Bosnia-Herzegovina. Army Center of Military History. 2005. www.history.army.mil/html/books/070 /70-97-1/cmhPub_70-97-1.pdf.

U.S. Commission on Civil Rights. *Targeted Fines and Fees against Communities of Color: Civil Rights and Constitutional Implications.* Washington DC: Commission on Civil Rights, 2017.

U.S. Department of Agriculture. *Report of the Chief of the Bureau of Public Roads for 1923.* Washington DC: Government Printing Office, 1923.

———. *Report of the Chief of the Bureau of Public Roads for 1930.* Washington DC: Government Printing Office, 1930.

———. *Report of the Chief of the Bureau of Public Roads for 1931.* Washington DC: Government Printing Office, 1931.

———. *Report of the Director of the Office of Public Roads for 1905.* Washington DC: Government Printing Office, 1905.

———. *Report of the Office of Public Road Inquiries for 1903.* Washington DC: Government Printing Office, 1903.

U.S. Department of Commerce. *Elimination of Waste: Simplified Practice; Asphalt.* Washington DC: Government Printing Office, 1923.

U.S. Department of Defense. *Base Structure Report: Fiscal Year 2017 Baseline; A Summary of the Real Property Inventory.* Washington DC: U.S. Department of Defense, 2018.

U.S. Department of Energy. *Environmental Impact Statement: Long-Term Management of the Existing Radioactive Wastes and Residues at the Niagara Falls Storage Site.* Washington DC: U.S. Department of Energy, 1986.

U.S. Department of State. *Correspondence Relating to Wrongs Done to American Citizens by the Government of Venezuela.* S. Doc. 412, 60th Cong., 1st Sess. (1908).

———. *Reports from the Consuls of the United States.* No. 120. Washington DC: Government Printing Office, 1890.

U.S. Department of the Interior. *Report of the United States Indian Inspector for the Indian Territory for the Year Ended June 30, 1906.* Washington DC: Government Printing Office, 1906.

U.S. Department of War. *Report of the Chief of Engineers, U.S. Army, 1936.* Washington DC: Government Printing Office, 1936.

U.S. Environmental Protection Agency. "National Emission Standards for Hazardous Air Pollutants: Revision of Source Category List under Section 112 of the Clean Air Act." *Federal Register,* February 12, 2002, 6522.

"U.S. Funded Capital Assets in Afghanistan [. . .]." 2021. https://www.sigar.mil/pdf/ inspections/SIGAR-21-20-IP.pdf.

U.S. Geological Survey. *Mineral Resources of the United States.* Pt. 2, *Non-Metallic Products.* Washington DC: Government Printing Office, 1908.

U.S. Governor of the Canal Zone. *Annual Report for the Fiscal Year Ended June 30, 1917.* Washington DC: Government Printing Office, 1917.

U.S. National Park Service. "Special Study North Field Historic District." September 2001. www.botany.hawaii.edu/basch/uhnpscesu/htms/Tinian/index.htm.

U.S. National Recovery Administration. *Code of Fair Competition for the Asphalt Single and Roofing Industry.* Registry 1003-1-01. Washington DC: Government Printing Office, 1933. http://ufdc.ufl.edu/AA00007877/00001.

U.S. President's Advisory Committee on a National Highway Program. *A 10-Year National Highway Program.* H. Doc. 93, 84th Cong., 1st Sess. (1955).

"US Protest Law Tracker." International Center for Not-for-Profit Law. Accessed September 10, 2020. www.icnl.org/usprotestlawtracker/.

U.S. Senate Committee on Energy and Natural Resources. *Hearings on Effects of U.S. Nuclear Testing Program in the Marshall Islands.* 109th Cong., 1st Sess. (2005).

U.S. Strategic Bombing Survey. *Ebano Asphalt Werke AG Harburg Refinery Hamburg, Germany.* Washington DC: Strategic Bombing Survey/Oil Division, 1947.

"U.S. Towboat *Robert Y. Love* Allision with Interstate 40 Highway Bridge Near Webbers Falls, Oklahoma." Highway/Marine Accident Report NTSB/HAR-04/05. National Transportation Safety Board. May 26, 2002. www.ntsb.gov/investigations /AccidentReports/Reports/har0405.pdf.

U.S. Transportation Research Board. *Superpave Performance by Design: Final Report of the TRB Superpave Committee.* Washington DC: TRB of the National Academies, 2005.

——. *TRB Special Rept. 311: Effects of Diluted Bitumen on Crude Oil Transmission Pipelines.* Washington DC: TRB of the National Academies, 2013.

Valentine, David, Christopher M. Reddy, Christopher Farwell, Tessa M. Hill, Oxcar Pizarro, Dan R. Yoerger, Richard Camilli, et al. "Asphalt Volcanoes as a Potential Source of Methane to Late Pleistocene Coastal Waters." *Nature Geoscience* 3 (May 2010): 345–48.

Van Tuyll, Hubert P. *Feeding the Bear: American Aid to the Soviet Union, 1941–1945.* New York: Greenwood, 1989.

Veblen, Thorstein. *The Theory of the Leisure Class.* 1899. Reprint, New York: Macmillan, 1912.

Vergano, Dan. "DNA Confirms: Here Lieth Richard III, under Yon Parking Lot." *National Geographic.* December 1, 2014. http://news.nationalgeographic.com/news /2014/12/141202-richard-iii-genes-shakespeare-science/.

Virtue, John. *The Black Soldiers Who Built the Alaska Highway.* Jefferson NC: McFarland, 2012.

Vogel, Steve. *The Pentagon: A History; The Untold Story of the Wartime Race to Build the Pentagon and to Restore It Sixty Years Later*. New York: Random House, 2007.

Voltaire. *A Philosophical Dictionary*. 2 vols. 1764. Reprint, London: Dugdale, 1843.

Wagar, Linda. "Two Men Investigated by Problem Solvers in 2015 Are Finally Facing Charges." Fox4KC, Kansas City MO. January 23, 2018. https://fox4kc.com /2018/01/23/two-men-investigated-by-problem-solvers-in-2015-are-finally-facing -charges/.

Walker, James Blaine. *Fifty Years of Rapid Transit*. New York: Law, 1918.

Walsh, Lawrence. *Final Report of the Independent Counsel for Iran/Contra Matters*. Vol. 1, *Investigations and Prosecutions*. 3 vols. Washington DC: U.S. Court of Appeals, District of Columbia Circuit, 1993.

Waltzer, Kennedy. "Moving Together, Moving Alone." In *Jewish Families in Europe, 1939–Present*, edited by Joanna B. Michlic, 85–109. Waltham MA: Brandeis University Press, 2017.

Ward, Geoffrey C., ed. *Closest Companion: The Unknown Story of the Intimate Friendship between Franklin Roosevelt and Margaret Suckley*. New York: Simon and Schuster, 1995.

Waterfield, Robin. *Dividing the Spoils: The War for Alexander the Great's Empire*. New York: Oxford University Press, 2011.

"The Week." *Nation*, December 29, 1904, 511–13.

Weider, Ben, and Kevin G. Hall. "Trump's Ex–Puerto Rico Partner Hits a Bumpy Road—Even before Maria." McClatchy. October 1, 2017. www.mcclatchydc.com /news/nation-world/national/article176234111.html.

Weinberger, Sharon. "Lightning Gun Company: New Name, Old Game." *Wired*. February 18, 2008. www.wired.com/2008/02/ionatron-new-na/.

Weingroff, Richard F. "The Greatest Decade, 1956–1966." Pt. 2, "The Battle of Its Life." Federal Highway Administration. Updated June 27, 2017. www.fhwa.dot .gov/infrastructure/50interstate2.cfm.

———. "Portrait of a General: General Roy Stone." Federal Highway Administration. Accessed September 15, 2019. www.fhwa.dot.gov/infrastructure/stone.pdf.

Weiss, Michael. "The Corleones of the Caspian." *Foreign Policy*. June 10, 2014. https:// foreignpolicy.com/2014/06/10/the-corleones-of-the-caspian/.

Wells, Christopher W. *Car Country: An Environmental History*. Seattle: University of Washington Press, 2012.

Wells, Jeff, Susan Casey-Lefkowitz, Gabriela Chavarria, and Simon Dyer. "Danger in the Nursery: Impact on Birds of Tar Sands Oil Development in Canada's Boreal Forest." Natural Resources Defense Council. December 2008. www.borealbirds .org/sites/default/files/publications/backgrounder-report-birdstarsands.pdf.

Wheelock, Darren, and Douglas Hartmann. "Midnight Basketball and the 1994 Crime Bill Debates: The Operation of a Racial Code." *Sociological Quarterly* 48, no. 2 (2007): 315–42.

Whitcover, Jules. *Very Strange Bedfellows: The Short and Unhappy Marriage of Richard Nixon and Spiro Agnew.* New York: Public Affairs, 2007.

Wilder, Laura Ingalls. *On the Way Home: The Diary of a Trip from South Dakota to Mansfield, Missouri, in 1894.* Edited by Rose Wilder Lane. New York: Harper, 1962.

Wilkes, Owen, and Robert Mann. "The Story of Nukey Poo." *Bulletin of the Atomic Scientists*, October 1978, 32–36.

Wilkinson v. United States. 365 U.S. 399 (1961).

William Koch et al. v. Koch Industries et al. 969 Fed. Supp. 1460 (1997).

Wilson, Mark R. "Making 'Goop' Out of Lemons: The Permanente Metals Corporation, Magnesium Incendiary Bombs, and the Struggle for Profits during World War II." *Enterprise and Society* 12, no. 1 (2011): 10–45.

Wittner, Lawrence S. *Cold War America.* New York: Holt, Rinehart and Winston, 1978.

World Health Organization. Inter-organization Programme for the Sound Management of Chemicals. *Concise International Chemical Assessment Document 59: Asphalt (Bitumen).* Geneva: WHO, 2004.

Wright, Frank Lloyd. *Frank Lloyd Wright: An Autobiography.* 1943. Reprint, San Francisco: Pomegranate, 2005.

Wright, Lawrence. *The Looming Tower: Al-Qaeda and the Road to 9/11.* New York: Knopf, 2006.

Wüstenberg, Jenny. *Civil Society and Memory in Postwar Germany.* New York: Cambridge University Press, 2017.

Yergin, Daniel. *The Prize: The Epic Quest for Oil, Money and Power.* New York: Simon and Schuster, 1991.

———. *The Quest: Energy, Security and the Remaking of the Modern World.* New York: Penguin, 2011.

Zacks, Richard. *Island of Vice: Theodore Roosevelt's Doomed Quest to Clean Up Sin-Loving New York.* New York: Doubleday, 2012.

Zamora, Emilio. "Mexican Nationals in the U.S. Military: Diplomacy and Battlefield Sacrifice." In *Beyond the Latino World War II Hero: The Social and Political Legacy of a Generation*, edited by Maggi Rivas-Rodriguez and Emilio Zamora. Austin: University of Texas Press, 2009.

Zand, Bernhard. "Contract Carnage: Blackwater's Hail of Gunfire." *Spiegel International.* September 24, 2007. www.spiegel.de/international/world/contract-carnage-blackwater-s-hail-of-gunfire-a-507513.html.

Zimring, Carl A. *Clean and White: A History of Environmental Racism in the United States*. New York: New York University Press, 2017.

Zirin, David. *A People's History of Sports in the United States*. New York: New Press, 2008.

Zivie, Alain-Pierre. *The Lost Tombs of Saqqara*. Translated by David Lorton. Cairo: American University of Cairo Press, 2008.

INDEX

rights movement, 132; and the Cold War, 119–42; colonial transactions for, 195; color of, 38–39; as a commodity, 25, 35–36, 42–44; and concrete, 121, 123–25, 129; and corruption, 153–62, 166, 174; and CRH Americas Materials, 151; and crime, 87, 155–57; and cultural change, 9–10, 234n24; and the Dead Sea, 25–26, 27, 31–35; and death, 174–76, 213–18; in dentistry, 26; and diseases, 217; disinterment and reburial uses of, 112–13; and disposal areas, 96; duality of, 7–8, 23, 40, 56, 60, 131, 148, 217, 250n30; and emulsions, 168; and the environment, 182–87, and environmental story in theater, 168–69; European empire's use for, in the Americas, 46; exported from Trinidad's Pitch Lake, 53; and the First Gulf War, 143–46; first uses of, 25, 232n23; as form of underworld evil, 39–42; funerary uses of, 26–27, 38–39; and government buildings in the District of Columbia, 247n68; and gradual spread in the United States, 54–55; and the Great Mississippi Flood, 77–78; and heat exhaustion, 217–18; and heliports, 134; and highway construction, 87–89; hydraulic properties of, 46; impact of, 3; in imperial construction, 28–29; in internment camps, 90–91; and the Iran-Contra affair, 140–41; and ISIS, 176; and Israeli policy, 152–53; and Kandahar MASCAL event, 167–68; and the Koch brothers, 205–6; and lakes, 95–96; leach rate of, 186; and Long Tieng, 133; and martial culture, 10–11; and mastics, 28–29, 64; mattresses, 78,

237n62; medicinal value of, 26, 39–40, 231n7; in medieval and early modern Europe, 44–46; and melting, 107; and merchant fleet construction, 90, 91; and military purposes, 27–28; mined in Indian Territory, 72–73; and mines, 110–12; mixed with sulfur, 27–28; and mummification, 26–27, 38–39; and murder, 218, 242n80; and Navy Seabees, 98–104; and Nazi Germany, 107–14; and Nebuchadnezzar, 28–31; and 9/11, 163; and NORAD, 243n11; and the Northern Mariana Islands, 103; and oil spills, 180–81; and the Oklahoma City bombing, 147–48; and Operation Reinhard, 113; in outer space, 230n5; and paving in the United States, 53–54; and Pennsylvania Avenue, 74; and photography, 234n24; plants, 64, 107, 111, 118, 130, 140, 144, 166, 168, 174, 176–77, 182, 244n37; and pollution, 181–84; and portable plants, 59; in post-9/11 wars, 166; and poverty, 5; in POW camps, 90; produced in a refinery, 5, 23, 70, 72–73, 181, 188–89, 197, 236n47; and the public-health lobby, 59–60; quality of, 70–71; and racial justice, 132; and radioactive waste, 186–87; recycling of, 96, 152, 182–83, 253n9; and reservations, 185; and revetments, 78–79; and road construction, 74–75, 107; and Robert Moses, 85–86; and rockets, 240n53; Romans' use of, 34–35; and sanitation, 60; and Sargeant Marine, 163–65; and Saudi Arabia, 162–63; and scientific research, 70–71, 74–75, 79, 253n10; and the Second Gulf War, 145–46; and segregation 55–56, 132, 221;

asphalt (*cont.*)
and the settlement-house movement,
229n15; and shingles, 6, 86, 90, 129,
150–51, 181–82, 252n8; and ship construction, 93; and shortages, 99–100,
102; as socioeconomic marker, 131;
and solar energy, 187; and sports and
recreation, 130–32, 245n44; and spy
games, 141–42; and the Strategic Air
Command, 120–21; in subways, 64; as
a symbolic material, 38–42, 46, 79–80,
148–49, 202; tankers, 164–65, 250n32;
and testing methods of asphalt
properties, 70–71; tile, 73, 236n50;
and tool-making, 26; as a torture tool,
45–46, 175; and training of Iraqis,
168; and the Trans-Atlantic Pipeline
System, 243n12; and transuranic
nuclear waste, 186; trusts, 62–66, 68–
69; ubiquity of, in the United States,
5–7; and Vietnam, 1–3, 134–38; and
violence, 213–15; volcanoes, 15–17; as a
war material, 93–94; and the War on
Terror, 162–76, 221; warranties, 71; in
Washington DC, 56; and World War I,
74; and World War II, 84, 89–91, 96
Asphalt Americana, 6–7
Asphalt and Roofing, 111
Asphalt Association. *See* Asphalt
Institute
asphalt cement. *See* liquid asphalt
Asphalt Champion, 164
Asphalt Institute, 74–75, 240n48
asphaltite minerals, 17–18, 54–55,
234n10
Asphalt Lake, Curaçao, 99
Asphalt Lake Recovery, 239n44
Asphalt Mining and Kerosene Gas
Company, 53

asphaltoids, 18
asphalt pavement: and airports, 6, 84,
146, 148, 151–52, 161–63, 219; and the
Alaska-Canada Military Highway,
95; and barrier construction, 152;
and the Big Dig project (Boston),
161; and border construction, 210;
and carbon dioxide emissions, 8;
and concrete pavement, 3, 72, 74–76,
182, 253n12; and cost, 219–20; and
environmental initiatives, 183–84;
and IEDs, 169–72; and imperme-
ability, 50, 185–86; and interstate
highway construction, 123–27, 129;
and New Deal–era projects, 84–86;
and nuclear testing, 129–30; and
pollution, 253n11; produced by Amzi
Barber's companies, 64; and road
construction in Siberia, 89; as self-
healing, 187; and social mobility, 56;
used in national parks, 85
Asphalt Ridge, 18
Asphalt Splendor, 165
Asphalt Trust, 58
Asphalt Venture, 250n32
asset forfeiture, 158–59
Assyrians, 28, 39, 45
AstroTurf, 130–31
Atchafalaya Basin, 78
Athabasca oil sands, xi–xii, 18, 188–206,
212, 223–24, 256n56. *See also* oil sands
Athabasca River, 18, 195
Athenaeus, 32
Atlantic Refining, 74
Atlantic theater (World War II), 97,
106–7
atmospheric distillation, 5
Attu Island, 95–96
Auburn University, 253n10

black mummy trade, 42–44, 233n19

Black Tom pier, 73

Black Warrior basin, 18

Blagojevich, Rod, 155

Blake, Jacob, 260n7

Blatnik, John A., 128

Bloom, Harold, 149

Blue Ridge Parkway, 83

Bockscar, 106

boiling asphalt, 107

bollard fencing, 209–11

bombs, 104–6, 107, 147–48, 177. *See also*
    IEDs (improvised explosive devices)

bone beds. *See* tar pits

Bonneville dam, 91

Bonus Expeditionary Forces (BEF),
    79–80

Booker, Reginald H., 127

border barriers, 209–11

Border Patrol, 210

Bosnian War, 146–47

bottom upgrading technologies, 188

Bowen, Herbert W., 68

Boyle, Robert, 43

Braden, Carl, 117

Bragdon, John S., 123–25

Braskem, 156–57

Brazzaville, Congo, 217

Bribe Payers Index, 153–54

bridge-clearance minimums, 128

Britain's Corps of Royal Engineers, 100

British Petroleum's Whiting Refinery, 197

broken-stone system of paving, 50–51

Brown, Herman, 137

Brown, H. Rap, 213, 259n1

Brown, Michael, 213–14

Brown and Root, 136–38

Browne, Thomas, 43

Buchanan, J. E. "Jess," 124–25

bucket-wheel excavators, 193

Buffalo-Springfield Roller Company, 74

Bureau of Chemistry, 70

Bureau of Indian Affairs (BIA), 185

Bureau of Land Management, 238n9

Bureau of Navy Yards and Docks, 97

Bureau of Public Roads (BPR), 74–76,
    79, 119, 126, 128, 236n45

Bureau of Standards, 75–76

Burial Ground for Negroes, 143

Burne-Jones, Edward, 233n19

burn pits, 169

Busca Bay, 99

Bush, George H. W., 131, 141, 143, 146

Bush, George W., 159, 166–67, 171–72, 174

Byrd, Harry F., 83, 90

Byroade, Henry, 100

Cairo IL, 78

California: and asphalt worker segrega-
    tion, 236n46; and internment camps,
    90–91; and Keystone XL messaging,
    256n56; and McCarthyism, 116–18;
    and Midway-Sunset oil field, 194;
    and natural asphalt, 15, 20–22, 54,
    72; and Pasadena Expressway, 87;
    and recycling, 182–83; and Santa
    Barbara oil spill, 230n4; and Spanish
    missions, 46; and Spiro Agnew, 139;
    and Superpave, 183

California Coastal Commission, 230n4

California Environmental Quality Act
    (1970), 230n4

California Senate Fact-Finding
    Subcommittee on Un-American
    Activities, 116–17

Calio, Nick, 162

Camden NJ, 126

Campeche Knolls, 15–16

McKittrick Tar Pits, 54, 230n11

McMurdo Station research facility, 186–87

McMurray Formation, 18, 191

McNaughton, John, 1–2

McVeigh, Timothy, 147–48

medicinal mummy, 42–44, 233n19

medicinal value of asphalt, 26, 39–40, 231n7

Mena Intermountain Municipal Airport, 148

Mencken, H. L., 56

Mene de Inciarte, 230n12

menstrual blood, 39–40

Merchant Marine Act (1936), 90

Mesopotamia, 25, 232n25

Messerschmitt, 111

methane, 253n11

Mexican American removal. *See* Chávez Ravine

Mexico, 209, 240n45

Michigan, 185, 198

microfossils, 22

Middle East and Africa Projects Office, 145

Midnight Basketball, 131

Midway-Sunset oil field, 54

migrant workers, 240n45

Milan, Italy, 157

military spending, 121–22

Milton, John, 41–42

minimum wages for workers, 86, 240n45

Minneapolis MN, 94, 215

Minoans, 30

Minsk-Mogilev highway, 111

Mississippi River, 77–79

Mississippi River Commission, 77–78

Mitchell, Dana P., 105

Mitchell, William "Billy," 95

Modified Asphalt Research Center, 253n10

Mohl, Raymond A., 126

Mommer, Bernard, 190

Mommsen, Hans, 112

Monkey Mountain, 136

Montrose Chemical, 185–86

Monument Avenue, 143

monument purges, 142–43

Morrison, Philip, 105–6

Morrison-Knudsen, 93, 96, 136–37

Morurora atoll, 130

Moscow, Russia, 207

Moses, 37

Moses, Robert, 9–10, 85–86, 123, 238n10

Moses Brown School, 130

motor-vehicle accidents, 217

Mounds Landing MS, 78

Mount Hope Asphalt, 139–40

Moynihan, Daniel Patrick, 122

Mullinix Field, 101

multiple rocket launchers (MRLs), 240n53

mūmiyah, 42–44

mummification, 26–27, 38–39

Munich, Germany, 88

municipal paving contracts, 62–63, 70–71

MWR Strategies, 208

Nabataeans, 31–36

napalm, 104

naphtha, 192

National Asphalt Company, 65

National Asphalt Pavement Association, 208, 235n38

National Bulk Cash Smuggling Center, 158

318   Index

World War II, 1, 10–11, 84, 89–91, 95–96, 98–114, 192. *See also* Atlantic theater (World War II); Pacific theater (World War II)
Wray, Jerry, 221
Wright, Frank Lloyd, 86
wurtzilite, 18

Xenophon, 29

Yasser Arafat International Airport, 151–52
Yeltsin, Boris, 242n80
Yosemite, 85

Ziobro, Cecylia, 108